Judgment Calls

Polemics Series

Series Editors

Michael Calvin McGee and Barbara Biesecker, *University of Iowa*

John M. Sloop, *Vanderbilt University*

Judgment Calls: Rhetoric, Politics, and Indeterminacy,
edited by John M. Sloop and James P. McDaniel

*The Rise of Rhetoric and Its Intersections with
Contemporary Critical Thought,*
Omar Swartz

Without Apology: Andrea Dworkin's Art and Politics,
Cindy Jenefsky

Judgment Calls

Rhetoric, Politics, and Indeterminacy

John M. Sloop
James P. McDaniel

Westview Press
A Member of Perseus Books, L.L.C.

Polemics Series

Copyright © 1998 by Westview Press, A Member of Perseus Books, L.L.C.

Published in 1998 in the United States of America by Westview Press, 5500 Central Avenue, Boulder, Colorado 80301-2877, and in the United Kingdom by Westview Press, 12 Hid's Copse Road, Cumnor Hill, Oxford OX2 9JJ

Library of Congress Cataloging-in-Publication Data
Judgment calls : rhetoric, politics, and indeterminacy / edited by
  John M. Sloop and James P. McDaniel
    p.   cm. — (Polemics series)
  Includes bibliographical references and index.
  ISBN 0-8133-9097-4
  1. Judgment (Ethics)   2. Judgment.   3. Rhetoric.
4. Postmodernism.   5. Judgment (Aesthetics)   6. Judgment in
literature.   I. Sloop, John M., 1963-   .   II. McDaniel, James P.
III. Series.
BJ1408.5.J83   1998
128'.3—dc21   98-13960
                                                                          CIP

The paper used in this publication meets the requirements of the American National Standard for Permanence of Paper for Printed Library Materials Z39.48-1984.

10   9   8   7   6   5   4   3   2   1

Contents

Acknowledgments   vii

   Hope's Finitude: An Introduction,
   James P. McDaniel and John M. Sloop   1

Part 1   Judgment and the Theoretical Quagmire

  1 *Phronesis* in the Gadamer Versus Habermas Debates,
     Michael Calvin McGee   13

  2 Judgment and the Problem of Agency/Accountability:
     A Postcolonial Critique of Poststructuralist Theory,
     K. E. Supriya   42

  3 Decentering Judgment: Toward a Postmodern
     Communication Ethic, *Martha Cooper*   63

  4 Judgment and Jouissance: Eliot, Freud, and Lacan
     Read *Hamlet*, *Susan Schwartz*   84

  5 More than Meets the Eye: An Exposé on Patriotic Libido
     and Judgment at the Level of the Image in American
     War Culture, *James P. McDaniel*   102

Part 2   Case Studies in Judgment Calls

  6 "Had Judas Been a Black Man . . . ": Politics, Race,
     and Gender in African America, *Karen L. Dace*   163

  7 The Fictions of Racialized Identities,
     Marouf A. Hasian, Jr. and Thomas K. Nakayama   182

  8 Judging Parents, *Ronald Walter Greene and Darrin Hicks*   196

9 Property and Propriety: Rhetoric, Justice, and
    Lyotard's *Différend, Maurice Charland*   220

    Afterword: Justifying, Positioning, Persuading
    in the Intermediate World, *Robert Hariman*   237

About the Editors and Contributors   251
Index   253

Acknowledgments

As always, this project could not have come to fruition without the help and support of numerous of our colleagues and friends. In particular, we would like to thank Cathy Pusateri at Westview for her patience and guidance, John Murphy, the University Research Council of Vanderbilt University, the Department of Communication Studies at Vanderbilt University, Kent Ono, Karen Shimakawa, Robert Hariman, Allen Scult, and Barbara Hodgdon.

John M. Sloop
James P. McDaniel

Hope's Finitude:
An Introduction

James P. McDaniel and John M. Sloop

At the outset of one of modernism's best-known fictional works, *The Great Gatsby*, Nick reflects on advice his father had given him in his "younger and more vulnerable years" (Fitzgerald, 1925, 11). It is this advice that sets the narrative in motion—an overlay of memory and desire persisting in the consciousness of a mature man. The advice concerns reserving judgment, and the prospects of everlasting hope.

> "Whenever you feel like criticizing any one," he told me, "just remember that all the people in this world haven't had the advantages you've had."
>
> He didn't say any more, but we've always been unusually communicative in a reserved way, and I understood that he meant a great deal more than that. In consequence, I'm inclined to reserve all judgments, a habit that has opened up many curious natures to me and also made me the victim of not a few veteran bores. The abnormal mind is quick to detect and attach itself to this quality when it appears in a normal person, and so it came about that in college I was unjustly accused of being a politician, because I was privy to the secret griefs of wild, unknown men. Most of the confidences were unsought—frequently I have feigned sleep, preoccupation, or a hostile levity when I realized by some unmistakable sign that an intimate revelation was quivering on the horizon; for the intimate revelations of young men, or at least the terms in which they express them, are usually plagiaristic and marred by obvious suppressions. Reserving judgments is a matter of infinite hope. I am still a little afraid of missing something if I forget that, as my father snobbishly suggested, and I snobbishly repeat, a sense of the fundamental decencies is parceled out unequally at birth. (Fitzgerald, 1925, 1)

Nick, it would seem, does a poor job at following his father's advice even while praising it as noble and full of hope. He is quick to separate the "normal" from the "abnormal," the "plagiaristic" from the "original," the "suppressed" from the "full," the "political" from the "ethical"—and to organize these polarities into a hierarchy of order which is self-admittedly "snobbish." Yet Nick has a warrant for violating his own (father's) advice: namely, experience, one of modernity's great tropes of authority. While speaking of reserving judgment out one side of his mouth, from the other side Nick judges; while retaining a sense of youthful innocence, Nick assumes the voice of a mature and even worldly man. This is an exemplary habit of knowledge-action which today has fallen on hard times: to preach one thing, and practice another. Theorize here, practice there.

Often, this hypocrisy has been practiced by those asserting a postmodern allegiance of theory and practice, or preaching and practice, in contradistinction to the modernist habit of knowledge-action. It's obviously not possible to clearly distinguish between "modernism" and "postmodernism," but we feel comfortable noting that hypocrisy of some sort is amenable to either. However, the fact that this hypocrisy now has become a conspicuous topic of intellectual/academic conversations of inquiry perhaps is a sign of hope. The disease has become so blatant, that we are frantically in search of "the cure." This is the constitutive contradiction of *Judgment Calls*: hope from malaise, malaise from hope.

This malaise is found inscribed with force in the works of the most influential European social theorists. Baudrillard, Derrida, Heidegger, Foucault, Lacan, Lyotard, Nietzsche: each of these names drags behind or casts in front of them a shadow of the undecidable, a radical threat to judgment. Or perhaps each, in a different way, makes visible that which has been present but concealed all along. With Baudrillard, we are reminded time and again that the basis of social life is imaginary and, to take a perilous step further, that no "original" or "real" grounds judgment. We live, suffer, enjoy, and die in a cartoon cool world, where the "toons" are more real than us. With Derrida, we encounter the always already deconstructed organization of hierarchies, a deconstructedness which is (for convenience and comfort's sake) repressed. We act "as if" hierarchies were natural, for without this metaphorical illusion-become-reality, we would see the mark of the undecidable in all things. Judgment, says Derrida, is madness in the garb of "good reasons." Heidegger waits for Being to tell him what judgments to make, though he listens to the "call of conscience" with a Nazi ear. He makes us wonder: is the call of conscience, an urge toward judgment, always and only political in a very narrow sense of the term? Foucault revels in the undecidable, the "unjudgable," because it (temporarily) eludes the grips of power-knowledge. You can "style" your way out of judgment, slip through the cracks. But the panopticon is looking for you, judging you even from within—a super-ego function that surveys your every move, producing guilt or enjoyment according a structure not of your choosing. Judgment "belongs" to the Other. So too with Lacan, who insists that our reasoning capacity merely occludes or holds at bay the libidinal forces that outstrip judgment as a normative activity. Yet the resources of libido, as Marcuse argued in *Eros and Civilization*, may fuel the generation of refigured principles of judgment and social interaction. And Lyotard finds in the gaps between judgment and justice a revolutionary force—in the unspeakable (*differénd*) a clue to a higher ethic of communication and community. Finally, Nietzsche rounds out our short list: with him, the rhetoricity that abides between subject and object, self and world, renders all judgments contingent, partial, and consequently shaky. The way by which judgments are made to "seem" or "appear" stable is itself rhetorical. From malaise to hope, hope to malaise.

A round of clichés: The status of judgment in "postmodern" thought is highly problematic, and leans rather heavily toward the negative. It has become an academic commonplace to say that one can't develop a positive politics or ethics out of deconstruction, though many have and continue to try. Frankfurt School attempts to recuperate the judgmental schema of "scientific" psychoanalysis into theories that work toward a "just society" have hardly been convincing. Lyotard's politics of difference offers a critique of stable society, yet supplies no discernible pattern for vital social change. Baudrillard is a gloomy genius, or a guy who knows one trick very well and can make it look novel. Foucault died just when his work was getting interesting, emancipatory. Nietzsche fuels Aryanism. And so it goes.

Perhaps it is the case that these authors and works ask readers to be slow to judge, assuming in a sense the paternal voice of Nick's father. Sitting near a hot tub one hot summer day in Alta, Utah, we mused aloud about the advice that seemed to emanate from the "posties." Sloop, who had already published on the vital importance of judgment and commitment in critical praxis, expressed the opinion that grounds for judgment get vexed, complicated, and perhaps even radically toppled in the wake of postmodern thought and culture. McDaniel, who was preparing to deliver a paper on similar issues in Habermas and Nietzsche, agreed. We further mused that work in the field of rhetoric and communication had yet to shoulder the burden of the postmodern critique of judgment, and less still, to shoulder that burden and move productively forward. "Productively forward": on these words our conversation stalled. How were we to think of "productive" and "forward," knowing full well the critiques of progress and social goods we had just been discussing under the aegis of postmodernism?

This is not a dead-end question, nor should it be construed as a conversation-stopper, as many use it today in intellectual discussions. Instead, this is a question that should be most intimate to any and all critical projects in the theory and practice of rhetoric and communication. It is a question that requires critics and theorists to practice what they preach, to locate and reflect on the profound instability which gives rise to their questioning, and to propose better ways of life in light of such reflections. Responses to this question are bound to be problematic, in fact it is likely that each will encounter the aporia of judgment so well surveyed by the postmodern avant garde. Like other obligations, the obligation to respond to a troubling question may be neglected. *Judgment Calls* is a volume in which theorists of rhetoric and communication take this obligation as their ethic, a circuitous commitment to *telos* in which negation and affirmation constitute the field of critical play.

Unlike Nick, who finds in living through the vehicle of his father's advice "infinite hope," we encounter in *Judgment Calls* hope's radical finitude. We do not luxuriate here in reserving judgment, though the reader will mark several hesitations in many of the chapters where critical choices must be made between one act and another, one concept and another—which is to say: one way of life and another. Nick recounts his enjoyment of others in terms of a certain distance between him and them— a distance which is characteristic of modernist approaches to criticism. He needn't hesitate, for he is merely collecting data, novelties, a gallery of personalities for chilly circumspection. Perhaps, Nick cares more than he lets on, particularly about Gatsby. Too, he enjoys feigning sleep, boredom, and other forms of neglect which let him off the hook. Hope for him is infinite, perhaps, not because he reserves judgment but because he does not (oblige himself to) feel the bite of the other's pain. It remains part of a fantasy he is in control of. For the authors in this volume, hope appears as something historically and textually situated, bounded by a field of human concern that still may reach toward a transcendence of situation and boundary. Hope is irruptive, dis/appearing in a flash and not exactly within one's control. The yearning to extend hope from one situation to another, to rupture boundaries of despair and disaffection, is itself a mark of our finitude, our always-failing struggle with death and limit. Judgment is the passion of our human enterprise: an activity rhetorically carried out in the face of contingency, with countless uncertainties, and incredible consequences.

The first section of essays in the book investigates theoretical discussions of judgment from a rhetorical perspective. In the first chapter of this volume, Michael Calvin McGee performs a rhetorical study of the debate between Hans-Georg Gadamer and Jürgen Habermas, in which *phronesis* or practical wisdom is at issue, and in which judgment's passion is submitted finally to reason for political purposes. The uneasy relationship between rhetoric and ethics is a primary tension explored by McGee through Habermas and Gadamer's competing views on *phronesis*. Additionally, and refiguring this relationship at the level of *praxis*, at least two models of the *phronimos* or "judge" are found to be in contest: that in which judgment is in service of existing authority or tradition to rearticulate and nourish structures of validity (Gadamer), and that in which judgment is in service of emancipatory decentering of authority and tradition to embrace a community's diversity (Habermas). Here, the classic structure of Frankfurt School sociology—the emancipation-domination complex—is explored by McGee in an interesting way, for he asks if the resources of domination might not also be the resources of emancipation. We are left with an implicit gradualism which hinges on making "reasonable" judgments—appeals to dominant structures of reason from emancipatory perspectives. McGee seems to be arguing that cries for social change, however radical, must endure a sort of "waiting period" or must conform to certain communicative protocols before being heard. The idea that we can transparently "communicate" desire for social change is displaced by McGee to suggest that we have recourse only to rhetoric, which attends to strictures in audience, situation, power, and voice more carefully. The implication of McGee's argument is that the voice of the Other is judged by the voice of the Same, that emancipation must be channeled through the decorum of domination. This is a central problem in social theory, and McGee's articulation of it through the Gadamer-Habermas debates is provocative. It leans heavily on a model of legal controversy, where litigants must obey codes of discourse in order to be "heard." Thus it may be placed as a sort of grid or reading machine on numerous sorts of social conflict, leading rhetorical critics and theorists to discover or create for interest groups means of emancipatory persuasion that must speak "reasonably" to the forces of domination.

K. E. Supriya's chapter on agency and accountability in poststructural discourse theory emerges from a passionate and interested engagement with the problems of postcolonialism. Supriya boldly argues for a return of sorts to humanism as a resource for transcultural judgment, which poststructural theory has evacuated in its brutal critiques of hegemony, totality, ethical foundationalism, and universalism—the baby has been thrown out with the bath water. In contrast to what she terms the Eurocentrism of poststructural critiques, Supriya strives to develop a critical ethical humanism out of postcolonial theory. Besides her synoptic take on poststructuralism and its quirks with respect to humanism, which will be useful to many late-comers to this ongoing conversation, her critical return to humanism through postcolonial theory attempts to show how accountability (from individual to national levels of signification) gets articulated around the varying conceptions of the subject, subjecthood, agency, victim, oppressor, and so forth in contemporary global capitalism. The West, claims Supriya, has managed somehow to reify itself at once as subject, non-agent, and non-subject: it is the best of both/all worlds, responsible for ever expanding 'goods' (e.g., democratic capitalism) yet negligent of accepting responsibility for the subjugation of sub-altern peoples. Supriya links this strategy of deferral/disavowal to habits of poststructuralism that radically decenter agency, and, consequently, judgment. She finds in this habit not only disavowal, but also perversity. Humanism offers a normative-judgmental field through which a more ethically comprehensive and politically effective way of establishing ac-countability—a thesis that will put Supriya against many of the figures she cites, particularly Spivak. Where Supriya, Spivak, and rhetoricians may meet is on the ground that holds humanism to be a strategic dis-course practice rather than a strictly essential one. But strategy implies some obedience to circumstance, begging the ethical question: when hu-manism, when not? Supriya's response is passionate, even if it too is problematic: when there is perversity, depravity, and cruelty, we should act as humanists of sorts. These terms each erect the rhetoric of liberal pathos, a normative structure of political challenge and response whose normativity has been purchased at considerable expense.

Martha Cooper's chapter on decentering judgment argues that the "postmodern condition" requires a reconceptualization of the traditional *telos* of rhetoric as judgment. After reviewing the various theoretical problematics of "judgment" and contemporary rhetorical theory's reac-tions to these problematics, Cooper constructs a model of "postmodern communication ethics." Drawing upon cases from her life story and in-teractions with theory, Cooper suggests that there are three ethics and ac-companying communicative practices involved in contemporary ethics: a discourse ethic that encourages questioning, an ethics of care that en-courages various forms of response and an ethic of resistance that en-courages affirmation. Cooper's essay emphasizes the ethical complexity of various situations but offers hope by allowing that complexity to call forth a variety of responses. It is not that one picks and chooses between the ethics Cooper provides, it is that one uses each to work toward both tolerance and empowerment.

Susan Schwartz's psychoanalytic reflections on judgment and *jouis-sance* find their transferential playground in T.S. Eliot, Freud, and Lacan's literary assessments of Hamlet. To some extent, Schwartz's is a meta-crit-ical study in aesthetic or literary judgment located in the play between text and virtuoso readers (Eliot, Freud, Lacan). Each of these readers, she argues, establishes a structured defense against the unruliness of the play by imposing "law and order in the place of the traumatic jouissance of the mother." Eliot erects a formula—his well-known "objective correla-tive"—in response to Hamlet's threat to literary judgment, to Shake-speare's alleged lack of formal control over the fantasy which rifles through the play. To summarize Schwartz's complex and critical synop-sis, her reading of readings of Hamlet: Freud reads the play formulaically against Oedipus Rex, confirming in a sense what he already knows rather than accepting the full force of a traumatic irruption in what Schwartz provocatively calls Hamlet's textual unconscious. Lacan reads the play in terms of a compulsion to repeat the scene of mourning, which marks the radical loss of an object: first, Hamlet loses his father, then he loses Ophelia. Both father and Ophelia (O phallos, puns Lacan) are read as phallic, but it is Hamlet's relation to Gertrude, the (M)Other which Lacan attempts to zero in on but misses or overshoots when he attempts to define the essence of feminine desire. Schwartz's point here is that (literary) judgment, in these cases and perhaps in all, requires the taming of the unruly. The basic habit of such judgment, she argues, is modernist, formulaic. Her reading of readings of the play advances an argument: that the structuring trauma of Hamlet, defended against by the readers she studies, is the (M)Other's desire, which, according to the ears of patriarchal cultures and reading machines, does not signify, makes no sense. This lack/surplus of signification, no-sense, and irruptivity of jouissance mark the limit of judgment—that which calls judgment forth, and which marks its nether boundary. Thus, Schwartz's essay extends well beyond the realm of literary or aesthetic judgment and into the broader domain of praxis, suggesting that critics and theorists may locate the rhetorical strategies which defend against feminine jouissance. Can this jouissance be rhetorically exploited, or put to work, or does it remain unspeakable—an unintelligible irruption of the Real of the (M)Other's desire which vexes decision making? This is the provocative question Schwartz's chapter leaves us with.

Also a psychoanalytic study, James McDaniel's chapter draws an analogy between Second World War photojournalism and pornography, suggesting that war coverage and its traces in popular film and even in advertisements for silverware may function to excite the patriotic imagination the way pornographic films cause erotic reaction formations in their viewers. Working in early sections through intersections of sex, death, love, perversity, war, guilt, image-making, rhetoric, democracy, and ideology in classical and contemporary contexts, McDaniel takes aim at the production of patriotic desire and judgment at the level of the image. Through a series of illustrations drawn from *Life* magazine of 1943, he argues that patriotic libido rhetoric functioned like an "open secret." McDaniel presents this war discourse for judgment, holding American patriotic culture and citizens responsible for their enjoyment of war pornography in which the enemy-other is situated as erotic prop and a threat to be destroyed. He seeks to reveal the "heinous enjoyment" and the idiocy of American patriotism by employing a Lacanian cartography of jouissance. Rather than viewing jouissance as the limit of judgment, McDaniel locates it as judgment's idiotic core in America's war culture. After reflecting on the ethics of investigations into rhetorics of perversity of times past, and a quick reading of American public address surrounding the Persian Gulf conflict that reaffirms the critique of patriotism-as-perversity, McDaniel inverts his argument to admit the radical utility (perhaps even the necessity) of patriotic perversity in times of war. While intent on recklessly demolishing patriotism for most of the essay, he hesitates when push comes to shove, marking the moment of radical undecidability that attends the complexity of human affairs in which life, death, love, and freedom are at stake. Is patriotism a necessary, or at least felicitous evil? Though recommending a fickle affirmative here, he leaves an open question for us, along with entailments, regarding the critique of patriotism, and ideology more generally. He argues for a shift in ideology critique to include the intersection of affectivity and choice and the ways in which subjects may be held accountable for their own desire and enjoyment.

The second half of the collection, which concentrates more directly on case studies, begins quite ably with Karen Dace's "Had Judas Been a Black Man . . ." In the essay, Dace investigates a grounded and contemporary pattern of judgment within a broadly conceived African American community. By drawing upon the cases of Lani Gunier, Jocelyn Elders, Clarence Thomas and Mike Tyson, among others, Dace reveals a pattern in which the men of the African American community have been consistently judged as worthy of support (or at least of a lack of condemnation) while women, quite often the "other side" of the same public cases, have been condemned or their cases dismissed. While Dace provides an historic account for this pattern and offers explanations for its pattern, the essay attempts to push toward complicating public understandings of the actions of African American men and women in public discussed cases.

In "The Fictions of Racialized Identities," Marouf Hasian and Thomas Nakayama take on the case of Susie Phipps in order to investigate judgments about racial identity. In this case, Susie Phipps, a self-identified "white" Louisiana woman went to court to attempt to change her racial designation to Caucasian after being denied a passport on the grounds that her self-designation did not match her birth certificate racial designation as "colored." Hasian and Nakayama work through the legal and public arguments that were made during the case to point out the variety of ways in which whiteness operates as a political category. Tying their discussion of this case and other contemporary examples such as the conversations concerning Tiger Woods' racial designation, the authors note that, rather than pointing to the groundlessness of racial categories, critics must continue to work to publicly problematize arguments over racial designation and contest the histories and powers that give rise to racial categories to begin with.

Ronald Greene and Darrin Hicks want to advance a "new empiricism" for the study of rhetorical judgment in their essay, "Judging Parents."

While in general agreement with the constitutive turn of rhetorical judgment, they fear that an overemphasis on theorizing rhetorical judgment displaces the actual existing public debates over public judgments. Greene and Hicks investigate the history of the Parental Rights and Responsibilities Act (PRRA) and the way in which debate over the act has create a border between the state and the child by privileging the judgment of parents to know what is in the best interests of children and criticizing state sponsored experts. They see the case as exemplifying a shift away from the welfare state's use of social responsibility and toward an emphasis on individual responsibility. Their case both represents a critical practice of the investigation of judgment and provides concerns for those interested in the welfare state.

Finally, Maurice Charland concludes the second section of the volume with his "Property and Propriety: Rhetoric, Justice and Lyotard's *Differend*." Weaving together tales from the history of rhetorical theory with fictive and "not so fictive" examples, Charland provides a close study of the various implications of Lyotard's concept of the *differend* for rhetorical theory and public judgment. While a seemingly simple concept at first and in theory, Charland's dazzling use of example forces one to begin to think through, perhaps for the first time, the ways in which the *differend* necessarily changes how we think of judges and judgments while simultaneously offering a "severe critique" of attempts to secure rhetoric's position by granting it an ethical epistemic function. It is a powerful explanation of the *differend*, and one needed in rhetorical studies.

*   *   *

We wax rhapsodic, speaking grandly of judgment as the passion of human affairs, thus perhaps neglecting its reasoning aptitude as we find it expressed in touchstones of Western traditions of thought. In antiquity, (e.g., Aristotle's *De Interpretatione*) and especially in the Enlightenment (e.g., Kant's *Critique of Pure Reason* and *Critique of Judgment*), judgment was crucial to systematic philosophies as a site on which questions of truth, knowledge, taste, and subjectivity could be productively engaged. More generally still, judgment served as the rubric under which Western thinkers struggled to come to terms with how the world of human concerns calls for timely and appropriate actions. In the main, judgment was posited as the *sine qua non* of human action, as the preface for and ground of human engagement with the world. Crudely put, judgment connects subject and object in an appropriate manner, rendering a state of affairs intelligible to a consciousness that then, in an informed manner, may proceed to make decisions about how to act (e.g., "it is cold today"—therefore—"I will wear a coat"). With varying levels of complexity, environments of judgment are more or less un/stable (e.g., it is one thing to decide to wear a coat because it is cold out, and quite another to go to war with a country half way around the world).

Recently, judgment has newly emerged as a highly contestatory site for philosophical, rhetorical, and cultural reflection. In a sense, judgment has always been the *telos* of rhetoric, as Thomas B. Farrell points out in his *Norms of Rhetorical Culture*. And recent battles in continental thought and American multiculturalist debates have raised the stakes of judgment considerably. The connection/distinction between "correct" thinking and "right" thinking, between means-thinking and ends-thinking, in contemporary cultural debate—from "high" philosophy to popular culture—locates judgment as at once battleground and prize. With popular discourses awash in discussions of Generation X, family values, and of the loss and return of civilities, judgment has once again become a vital cultural topic in addition to its being a more or less consistent and vital philosophical one. Judgment has been revived not only in the hallowed halls of the academy, but also in the vernacular and public discourses that constitute the battle over what "value" means, and what particular values will have cultural currency.

Deriving from the Latin *jus* (right) and *dicere* (to say), judgment links up and complicates many problems in contemporary rhetorical theory and praxis that go beyond philosophical speculation. Judgment pushes us into the problematics of everyday life. Because the "right" (*ius*) is modified or even structured by a sort of "eloquence" (*dicere*), rhetoric is a technology of power that may be irrespective of ethics: through persuasive discourse, one may justify the unjust, or make the just seem trivial. This formula for rhetorical judgment muddies what is clear in certain philosophies of existence. When Heidegger wrote of "the call of conscience" in *Being and Time*, he advised that we listen to the "right" voice, and that we hear it as it is and not as something else. The relationship between a "call" and a judgment in this case is symmetrical: I hear the call, and I respond. A "judgment call," however, implies not knowing exactly how to respond, not knowing if one has heard the call as such or something else—as when an umpire must call a strike or a ball when only doubt is in his mind. In this understandably difficult situation, where one must invent a judgment in lack of sufficient "objective" materials, we cannot underestimate the importance of understanding how action itself is made up of both hope and malaise, constraint and commitment.

References

Fitzgerald, F. Scott. 1925. *The Great Gatsby*. New York: Scribbners.

PART 1

Judgment and
the Theoretical Quagmire

1

Phronesis in the Gadamer Versus Habermas Debates

Michael Calvin McGee

I propose in this essay to write a rhetorical criticism of the now-famous debate between Hans-Georg Gadamer, a metaphysician who has sparked and informed resurgent interest in philosophical hermeneutics, and Jurgen Habermas, a Frankfurt School sociologist whose *Theory of Communicative Action* has influenced communication research as well as social theory. This is a partial critique in two respects: First, the debate extended over a number of years, from 1970 to at least 1981—and in Gadamer's view, it may well be going on still. Though my interpretations are informed by what happened subsequently, this essay is confined to the initial moment of clash, Habermas's review of Gadamer's magnum opus, *Truth and Method*. Further, although the debate centered on seven terms (translation, horizon, narrative, *phronesis*, prejudice, practice and power), I will discuss only *phronesis*, a kind of knowledge in Aristotle's architectonic usually translated as "practical wisdom" or "practical knowledge." Narrowing the topic is essential to control the length of the essay, and narrowing it this way emphasizes what ultimately became the central issue between Gadamer and Habermas.

Scholars in communication studies should be especially interested in this debate, and in this particular issue, for two reasons: First, the line that conceptually separates rhetorical and communication theory also separates Gadamer (who links hermeneutics to rhetoric) and Habermas (who links hermeneutics to his theory of communicative action). Second, the conception of *phronesis* speaks to an age-old problem of rhetorical theory, that of establishing a linkage between ethics and rhetoric in the context of which rhetorical and communication theory are something more than a discursive technology of power (see Self 1979). I will first provide a general overview of the debate, then describe Gadamer's development of *phronesis* in *Truth and Method*, and then explain Habermas's response to the concept. Finally, I will react to the problems created by Habermas's deflection of *phronesis*.

An Overview of the Debate

Gadamer's *Wahrheit und Methode* was first published in 1960. He produced a second edition in 1965. Habermas's review appeared a year later in Beiheft 5 of Philosophische Rundschau, a special issue on reason in the social sciences (Zur Logik der Sozialwissenschaften). This publication history appears ordinary enough, but it can be misleading, for Habermas's "reviews" are extraordinary in their skill, their intent, and their effects. You get a hint of this in following the publication history through the translation process: Habermas's review was rendered in English in 1970, in the journal *Understanding and Social Inquiry*; but Gadamer's book, perhaps the clearest and most powerfully persuasive text yet to appear in its tradition, was not brought into English until 1975, fifteen years after its first appearance. Not many people are committed to "philosophical hermeneutics"; but if you happened to be one of them, you might find it frustrating to concede that the clearest proof of *Truth and Method*'s power and influence is not the clarity or persuasiveness of its arguments, but Habermas's appropriation of its terms and deflection of them to bolster his development of a critical social theory.

The most striking feature of Habermas's reviews of literature is his intent in reading, his strategy of theory building. He is a voracious reader of anything and everything connected to the enterprise of social inquiry. And he is quite unabashed in confessing to piracy—not the sort of thievery we condemn as plagiarism, of course, but the bold, imaginative appropriation of parts of theories that strike his fancy and suit his needs. If "taking things out of context" were the great crime scholars sometimes pretend, we would never cross the artificial barriers of the disciplines, we would not cross-pollinate our practices with fresh insights "from the outside," and we would be the poorer for our condemnation of Habermas's ingenious pilfering. In fact, we appreciate appropriation. But even so, we cannot succumb to the practice totally, seduced by its creativity. We cannot let Habermas hide in the nonpartisan ethos associated with the academic genre "book review." He comes to every text with pillage in his heart, a set agenda well-described by Lawrence:

> Whatever authors Habermas happens to be discussing, his overriding concern is always to see how they relate to his interest in emancipatory social theory. . . . He is less concerned with textual interpretation, in the sense of doing full justice to the author's meaning insofar as this is amenable to philo-

logical expertise, than with judging the correctness and evaluating the worth of the author's meaning. That is, he is less worried about making a case for the accuracy of his interpretation of an author's meaning than about stating just what he thinks is to be taken seriously in that author's work. Habermas's great popularity—which so contrasts with the inherent complexity and difficulty of both his manner of thought and the objects of his concern—is due in no small measure to the way he goes beyond the interpretation that understands to the further interpretation that discriminates. We sense that Habermas is really encountering the authors he writes about; that he wants to appreciate the values they represent as well as to criticize their defects. We sense that he is willing to allow himself to be challenged by their words and deeds to the degree that they strike him as in line with the reality of the subject matter in which he is interested. (Habermas 1983, viii-ix)

Despite Habermas's tremendous success, and the waning even of neo-positivist social theories, he imitates Marx's strategy for dealing with intellectual orthodoxy by doing "reviews" written from the battlements as if he were besieged by a host of technical thinkers who will win the day if the world is not freshly informed of the limits of causal theories (McCarthy 1978, 137). He is not alone in adopting this persona, of course; the most usual starting point of literature I include in the name social theory is some sort of "positivist bashing." Ironically, what makes him unique is his acceptance of a version of one of the positivist's ideals, the modernist dream of finding a localized set of "universal" principles that would unify the diverse practices of social inquiry. His strategy is political, not just in the usual sense of intending ultimately to intervene in the world by "taking sides," but also in a likely unintentional, procedural way, a consequence of the rhetoric of his "reviews": Like the skillful politician, he defines "the middle ground" as his own position, and he tries to locate and occupy it by using the strategy of appropriation as politicians use the strategy of compromise, to give all contending factions their due in the context of a general theory of society which will at once contain them all and transcend them all.

Habermas's evolving theory is far too elegant to be fairly represented in such a reduction, but it is nonetheless accurate to characterize it in terms of its two overriding commitments which, as they influence his judgments of particular texts and arguments, become criteria of theory in general: (a) First, any acceptable social theory must contribute to the emancipation of both the thinker and humanity in general. The most prominent feature of society is its system of constraints, and the imperative duty of the social critic is to minimize the effects of those constraints which cannot in reason be eliminated. (b) Second, any acceptable social theory must be amenable to bringing "empirical-analytical" thinking (social science) and "historico-hermeneutic" thinking (human science) "under one roof." This coexistence would not entail choosing causal analysis over interpretive understanding, or vice versa, "but of criticizing any pretension to universal and exclusive validity on the part of either, and of finding some sort of higher synthesis in which both have a place" (McCarthy 1978, 140).

Though his twist on the subject greatly vitalizes the concept, Habermas also works within the Frankfurt tradition by centering the term communication in his elaboration of the "higher synthesis." His predecessors featured the term in working out their controlling base :: superstructure metaphor, showing that ideology is determined indirectly by economic arrangements through a series of intervening causes located in "the culture industry." Ideology is in this treatment a vendible commodity, or more accurately a by-product, of this century's industrialization of communication. Newspapers, magazines, films, radio and television programming all ostensibly sell information and entertainment while at the same time improving the quality of communication by giving more people access to more facts about and perspectives toward the world. In truth, the argument proceeds, the fundamental requirement of the economic and political system in which the communication industries exist (which is that people accept advanced industrial capitalism as the "natural" and necessary social system) distorts communication, preventing otherwise rational people from understanding the world in their own right and seducing them to reproduce systemic distortions in their own communicative activity. One object of critical social theory on the Frankfurt model, therefore, is to expose systematically distorted communication for what it is—which is to say, ideology (see Horkheimer and Adorno 1972).

Habermas's greatest accomplishment, in my opinion, has been his attempt to theorize an unargued presupposition of ideology criticism. He wants to do more than resolve "Mannheim's paradox" by showing how an ideology critic is able to "step outside" ideology long enough to apprehend the "true" state of affairs (see Seliger 1977, 133–41). Far more specifically, he suggests that our ability to recognize systematically distorted communication as such presupposes that we could recognize undistorted communication. Knowledge of this type involves more than just knowing the truth of the matter, for we require an account of the intentional transfer of meaning from one subject to another in full appreciation that both are limited to the perspective of their particular historical situation. We must be able to show how we can infer and reconcile truth, intent, meaning, subjectivity, and circumstance in communication even as it occurs. We need, in other words, a different sort of "communication theory" than we are presented with in the mainstream social and human sciences. In the social sciences, we are usually presented with a theory of communication that is merely descriptive, or perhaps worse, theory that justifies itself instrumentally (prescribing "how to" point a camera or argue a point of law in the courtroom in a "successful" way, which is to say in a way that profits and satisfies the demands of industries that depend on communication skills). In the human sciences, we are usually presented with a theory of communication that rationalizes aesthetic preferences, insisting that discourse exhibit certain qualities and enforcing this prejudice with a style of "criticism" that celebrates the canonical and/or the fashionable. The sort of theory to which Habermas aspires identifies and evaluates that which is presupposed or taken for granted in any act of communicating. It is like Austin's and Searle's speech act theory in this regard, or any philosophical theory of language developed in contemplation of practical action. Habermas insists on the term communication, however; and he thereby signals that he is interested in "speech-acts-doing-work-in-the-social-world" and "language" as it appears in functioning discourse. In the terms of a commonly accepted academic distinction, he wants a "philosophical" theory that will also have force in "scientific" inquiry.

Habermas is so tenacious and consistent in pursuing his agenda that we know several things about his "reviews" before we see them, whether they appear innocently in the "book review" section of a professional journal or in the first twenty pages of a book Chapter to contextualize a line he wants to add to his evolving theory of communicative action. He will write only about books that can be ransacked for terms and arguments useful in conceiving communicative action. He will not wholly approve of any book he picks up. He will instead maintain his persona as "critic" by resisting any claim a book makes to having stated a general theory of society. He will also resist any part of an argument that demurs from his understanding of the terms critical, ideology, theory, practical, and of course communication. With this context in mind, we should be able to follow Habermas's reasoning in appropriating Gadamer's term *phronesis*. We should also be able to understand his resistance to Gadamer's use of the term.

Phronesis

Perhaps the major difference between the ancient and modern life of the mind comes clear in considering where we look first to develop a general overview of a difficult problem. The problems How should states be governed? and How are political beliefs developed?, for example, are in modern times addressed in a disembodied way. We turn first to the conditions of governing and of believing, describing how things are and justifying our vision of what would result if they were different. Or we turn first to the tools of governing and of believing, describing how they are used, how they could be used, and, finally, how they should be used.

Both of these starting points neutralize the specific people who face the conditions and use the tools of governing and of believing. The supposition is that conditions and tools make all the difference: Though some people could make a slightly better or worse job of it, the limits of actual performance are set by the conditions to which they must respond and the tools they have at hand; hence, anyone, "Everyman," can in principle govern and develop beliefs as well as anyone else possessed of proper tools in similar circumstances. The question How should states be governed? translates as What is the structure of the ideal state?; and How are political beliefs developed? becomes What logical or psychological rules generate and justify political belief?

By contrast, the Greeks and Romans turned first to particular embodiments of government and of political belief. A description of forms of government or a judgment about which form of government is best was always grounded in the study of governors. Biography was an integral part of political theory in the ancient world; for, after all, the essential difference between monarchy and tyranny turns out to be the personality of the autocrat. Advice offered to those who governed rarely encouraged creation of a certain organizational structure, or even the passage of particular laws; rather, political leaders were urged to compare themselves with others who had governed, thus to model themselves after good leaders and to avoid the vices of bad leaders. Greeks and Romans wanted to neutralize both conditions and tools, not people. That is, the conditions of government and of belief are too uncertain to be reified into formal principles. The only thing predictable about government is that the unpredictable will occur; and people are therefore well-advised to keep their political commitments as flexible as possible. With regard to tools, the ancients emphasized the difference between technology and art in suggesting that the personal characteristics of tool-users determined the quality of what the tool produced. In the hands of charlatans or untalented pretenders, for example, rhetoric was a technology of power; but in proper hands, it was an art capable of generating and justifying prudent political beliefs and good government. The sheet-anchor of confidence in a government or in a set of political beliefs was the character and conduct of governors, or of those who "stand for" certain beliefs. Interestingly, in most ancient ethical theories, there is almost a "semiotic" relationship between morality and people, with morality ultimately consisting of the "meaning" established by the example of those whose lives "signify" it. Greeks named the specific quality of Being-exemplary and Being-authoritative ethos, and described it as the perceived integrity, trustworthiness, knowledge, and charisma of an individual person. Thus the question How should states be governed? becomes What sort of ethos should the ideal governor possess?; and the problem How are political beliefs devel-

oped? translates as What ethos should generate, guide, and justify political belief?

This difference crystallizes into one of the major issues separating
Gadamer and Habermas. It is "Gadamer's issue," I think, in the sense
that it is the one which could motivate him to leave the friendly confines
of philosophical hermeneutics to confront a major sociologist, who was
in most other respects an ally, on his own ground. The term at stake is
practical knowledge. As Bernstein suggests, Habermas and Gadamer are
commonly supposed to be "on the same side" in a multi-disciplinary attempt to recover practical knowledge:

In a number of different contexts we can discern how a variety of
thinkers have been led to a reinterpretation or appreciation of the tradition of practical philosophy in order to come to a critical understanding
of modern society. It is an underlying theme in the work of Hannah
Arendt and Jurgen Habermas, both of whom share Gadamer's concern
sharply to distinguish the technical from the practical. The attempt to
clarify and restore the integrity of practical reasoning surfaces in such
critical appraisals as Richard Rorty's *Philosophy and the Mirror of Nature*,
Alisdair MacIntyre's *After Virtue*, Hilary Putnam's *Meaning and the Moral
Sciences*, Jean François-Lyotard's *Just Gaming* and *The Differend*, Chantal
Mouffe's *Return of the Political*, as well as many books in the Verso series
Phronesis. Differences among these thinkers are as important as the common themes that run through their work. But I do think we are witnessing a new turn in the conversation of philosophy and in the understanding of human rationality where there is a recovery and appropriation of
the type of practical reasoning, knowledge, and wisdom that is characteristic of *phronesis*. (Bernstein 1982, 833)

From Gadamer's perspective, however, there is something fundamentally wrong in Habermas's understanding of practical knowledge. The
difficulty arises when Habermas appropriates the language of practical
philosophy, but then applies that language as if it were a technology.
Habermas turns first, in other words, to description of the conditions and
tools of what he calls practical knowledge, neutralizing the specific people
who must deal with those conditions and use those tools. His conception
of the "ideal speech situation" (1979, 1–68), for instance, is an attempt to
expose ideology ("systematically distorted communication") and to regulate (in the sense of "modeling") communicative action by controlling the
situation in which a communicative act takes place. Similarly, his idea of
"thematized validity claims" in communicative acts is a tool for discovering, in a mechanistic way, which acts do and do not follow the rules of
communication in the ideal situation. Habermas never explores the perspective of practical philosophy, as Gadamer understands it, because he
never describes the character and the conduct of the ideal communicator

in concrete historical circumstances. In fact, by disembodying practical wisdom, Habermas actually contributes to the spirit of our time that has subverted it. For Gadamer, practical philosophy is grounded irrevocably in a theory, not of the ideal condition or tool, but of the ideal person. In Rome, this theory developed into the vir bonus ideal of public life, that all Roman citizens should strive to be "good men" able to "speak well" when they were called upon to give advice in the public interest. In Greece, the impulse of practical philosophy developed into the vision of the *phronimos*, a person imbued with practical wisdom who is able to bridge the life of the mind and the life of the polis. Whatever is put into the term practical philosophy, whatever line of argument or angle of interpretation you choose to explore, you must begin by asking What does the vir bonus do?, or What is the character of the *phronimos*? if you want to understand practical knowledge from Gadamer's perspective.

In *Truth and Method*, Gadamer works only indirectly with the Roman ideal of vir bonus, early in the book as part of a discussion of Vico's description of sensus communis (19–33). The Greek ideal of the *phronimos* as worked out by Aristotle, however, can be taken as the key not only to *Truth and Method*, but to all of Gadamer's projects since 1960. Bernstein, for instance, picks up on Gadamer's argument that "if we relate Aristotle's description of the ethical phenomenon and especially the virtue of moral knowledge to our own investigation, we find Aristotle's analysis is in fact a kind of model of the problems of hermeneutics" (Gadamer 1982, 289). He characterizes Gadamer's philosophical career as proceeding in part from a "decisive intellectual encounter with Aristotle, an encounter to which he frequently refers and which was initiated by his participation in Heidegger's seminar on the Nicomachean Ethics" (Bernstein 1982, 824). Gadamer does not claim that Aristotle was concerned with what he calls "the hermeneutical problem," nor does he defer to Aristotle's "authority" on the question of interpreting what is meant by the term *phronimos*. Rather, he works out an elegantly complex, reflexive analogy which suggests that we can recognize the truth within Aristotle's conception of the *phronimos* because his need for the term then was the same as our need for the term now.

Gadamer tells us that if we are to understand what a text or a piece of tradition says then we must not seek to disregard ourselves and our hermeneutical situation. This is characteristic of the way in which Gadamer approaches Aristotle. For what Gadamer takes to be basic for our hermeneutical situation is that we are confronted with a world in which there has been a 'domination of technology based on science,' that there is a 'false idolatry of the expert,' 'a scientific mystification of the modern society of specialization,' and a dangerous 'inner longing in our society to find in science a substitute for lost orientations.' It is this problematic that orients Gadamer's questioning of Aristotle's text, for Gadamer's central claim is that there has been a forgetfulness and deformation of what praxis really is.

What enables us to understand Aristotle and appropriate the 'truth' of what he says is that we ourselves have been shaped by this effective history. It is not a nostalgic return to Aristotle that Gadamer is advocating, but rather an appropriation of Aristotle's own insights to our concrete situation. . . . We come to understand what Aristotle is saying and at the same time come to a deeper understanding of our own situation when we are sensitive to Aristotle's own confrontation with the 'professional lawmakers whose function at that time corresponded to the role of the expert in modern scientific society' (Bernstein 1982, 831).

The analogy comes clearer as its details are worked out. Gadamer sets out to understand the *phronimos* by coming to grips with the special knowledge Aristotle believed he or she exhibits. The difficulty is easy to see in the English language, for whereas the Greeks had four words to signify different kinds of knowledge *(doxa, techne, phronesis,* and *episteme)*, we have only three (opinion, belief, and knowledge). Worse, the Greek term doxa did the job of both opinion and belief, leaving us with the overburdened term knowledge to do the work of *techne, phronesis,* and *episteme*. The problem of understanding the special knowledge of the *phronimos* turns out of be a job of translating the Greek word *phronesis*, for which there is no handy cognate, while keeping it distinct from *techne* and *episteme*, which also have no clear English equivalent. If Gadamer is right, we may have no way at all to say *phronesis* except by keeping it in Greek—the ability in English to distinguish a phenomenon within the term may have been lost.

The difficulty does not lie in the space between *phronesis* and *episteme*. For Aristotle, *episteme* was knowledge about which we can be certain. It was necessarily true, and its truth could be demonstrated. In terms of a contemporary account of knowledge, *episteme* is scientific knowledge, and it always assumes the form of a scientific demonstration. Aristotle thought we could be scientific about a much wider range of subjects than most people now think possible. Ethics, for instance, was the "science of morality," in the sense that philosophers try rationally to demonstrate "the good" without regard for practical limitations that make it virtually impossible to really "be good" in everyday life. Thinking about morality in everyday life, as we can hope actually to embody it, limits morality to the realm of possibility. Knowledge of "the good" in the two places is so different that two different words are needed to signify it: The *episteme* of ethics, Aristotle argued, is the business of philosophy, and the *phronesis* of ethics is the business of politics. The distance between the two kinds of knowledge is the same as the distance between theory and practice. "The

good" may be contemplated in "pure" form only "in theory"; "in practice," whatever you know (*episteme*) about "the good" must be mediated,
or translated, into what can be achieved within the limitation of particular historical circumstances (*phronesis*). In Aristotle's architectonic, the
transformation of the *episteme* of ethics into the *phronesis* of ethics is the
business of rhetoric (which is to say, in truncated terms, rhetoric is the
bridge between philosophy and politics).

This neat scheme, which would allow us to capture *episteme* and
phronesis with the terms pure knowledge and practical knowledge, is
frustrated by a third kind of knowledge, *techne*, which might have the superior claim to practicality. In his Gorgias, for instance, Plato caricatured
rhetoric as "a knack like cookery" which could be treated perversely as a
technology of persuasion. People have a tendency to approve what they
think good and to disapprove what they think bad. The methods of persuasion work equally well whether or not what people think is good really is good; hence, rhetoric requires neither the *episteme* of ethics nor the
phronesis of ethics to produce its effects. If you practice it as a technology,
rhetoric actually displaces philosophy and politics, fostering an illusion
of the good and promoting a politics ignorant of its most fundamental
purposes: Aristotle makes the special nature of moral knowledge and the
virtue of possessing it particularly clear by describing a naturally debased variety of moral knowledge. He says that the *deinos* is a man who
has all the natural prerequisites and skills for this moral knowledge, a
man who is able, with remarkable skill, to get the most out of any situation, who is able to seize his advantage everywhere and finds a way out
of every situation. But this natural counterpart to *phronesis* is characterized by the fact that he exercises his gifts without being led in any way by
moral being and hence without inhibitions and without any orientation
towards moral ends. And it is probably more than accidental that such a
person is given a name that also means 'terrible'. Nothing is so terrible,
so uncanny, so appalling as the exercise of brilliant talents for evil
(Gadamer 1982, 288–89).

If you believe, as many 5th-century B.C. rhetoricians apparently
thought, that "being practical" is simply keeping the machinery of everyday practices in good working order, and once in a while improving their
efficiency, you have associated practical knowledge with *techne* rather
than *phronesis*, and you have taken the risk of becoming a *deinos* rather
than a *phronimos*. Because it involved a relatively subtle distinction between two meanings of practice, and because his stance on one of the major intellectual disputes of his time required him to insist that the structuration linking philosophy and politics was more than a technical
mediation, Aristotle methodically and carefully distinguishes *phronesis*
from *techne* in three respects:

1. *Phronesis* presents an aspect of wisdom that is missing in *techne*. The experienced cabinet-maker has thoroughly mastered the rules of a craft, and he or she can therefore have a better vision of what is to be created, and it can actually be produced more efficiently and exquisitely than a less experienced artisan could manage. But we do not describe technical mastery as wisdom, for it consists of habituated familiarity with the applications of a technology—cabinet-makers do not "decide" in exigent circumstances; in fact, virtually all of their "decisions" are determined by the possibilities of their *techne*. By contrast, the *phronimos* is "always already in the situation of having to act" in exigent circumstances. The image people have of what they ought to be, their conceptions "of right and wrong, of decency, courage, dignity, loyalty etc." are always presupposed in decisions they are called upon to make (Gadamer 1982, 283). Even in cases where it appears that the *phronimos* is obliged to use an established technology of good and evil (in law courts, for instance, where even "uncodified" rules of conduct "can be very exactly determined" and made "binding"), the special knowledge of the *phronimos* comes clear in his or her departure from what the rules seem to dictate—which is to say that a judge demonstrates wisdom in the act of softening or intensifying the effects of law, not in following the law as a cabinet-maker follows the rules of furniture fabrication (Gadamer 1982, 283–86).

2. *Techne* presents a different aspect of immutability than is found in *phronesis*. Because any technology is oriented toward the production of a particular product, the relationship between means and ends is constant. So there is no need to "go back to school" to relearn or re-evaluate a technique each time it is used to create a product. This does not preclude inventing a new technique of cabinetry, for instance; but (a) one is not required to invent unique applications each time a chest is built, and (b) when there is a new technique, it only needs to be learned the first time to be available as an option in the building of another cabinet. By contrast, the object of the *phronimos* is a process rather than a product. The good is manifest in everyday life in various degrees and in a myriad of ways; thus, everyday life cannot consist of a constant, immutable goodness. It is rather always in process, always moving toward the good, its never-quite-achieved telos. Further, no means of striving for the good always, in every situation, pushes everyday life toward the good. The *phronimos* must constantly "go back to school" to be sure that what resulted in a degree of goodness last time will have the same effects this time, in this particular circumstance. The two constants of the life of the *phronimos* are neither means nor ends, but (1) constant reappraisal of strategies for approaching goodness; and (2) similar reappraisal of the potential for good in the particular circumstances faced here-and-now (Gadamer 1982, 286–88).

3. *Techne* presents an epistemic aspect, while *phronesis* presents an ontic aspect. The craft of cabinetry is something a cabinet-maker knows, not something that defines his or her Being. If a cabinet-maker identifies with his or her craft—if it is a part of Being—it is always identification with products, and not with the technical know-how that made the product possible. The declaration "I am a cabinet-maker" prefaces a display of the finished work the cabinet-maker most admires. By contrast, *phronesis* is not just something the *phronimos* knows, but also and primarily what he or she is. We cannot put you in a classroom and teach you the recipe for courage; all we can do is put you in a situation where if you have courage, you will display it, make it manifest. This does not mean that you cannot learn courage, but that there is no set recipe for it—you may never know how you got that way, and when it becomes part of your Being, you will know it only in the same way, and insofar as, you know yourself. Further, the *phronimos* extends his or her Being into all situations and relationships. The cabinet-maker "is" a cabinet-maker only when using the principles of his or her craft to produce cabinets, not when attending a play or reading books or participating in the political process. By contrast, the *phronimos* is always displaying her or his *phronesis*—indeed, when *phronesis* is a part of your Being, you can hide it only with the same difficulty that you hide the less attractive features of your body. The *phronimos* "does not know and judge as one who stands apart and unaffected; but rather as one united by a specific bond with the other," as one who "thinks with the other and undergoes the situation" with the other (Gadamer 1982, 288).

Tracing Aristotle's distinctions among *techne*, *phronesis*, and *episteme* revealed to Gadamer that the same distinctions separated his conception of hermeneutics from his understanding of mainstream thinking in the sciences of this century, particularly the social sciences. Science has become more *techne* than *episteme* in the sense that truth is determined increasingly by the purely technological criteria of method. Most of the influential dialogues in contemporary science make separate questions out of truth and its application, supposing that the former is settled by the techniques of investigation, and holding that the latter is virtually unapproachable from within science. Sometimes application is treated as a question of ethical judgment or deliberative policy; at other times, the technical possibility of acting is supposed to be sufficient justification for action. Wherever in society we once would have looked to find an example of the *phronimos*, we find instead an expert whose ethos consists of credentialed mastery of the *techne* of his or her field. Integrity, trustworthiness, knowledge, and even charisma (in the example of so-called "celebrity scientists") are now very nearly functions of *techne*. The disappearance of the *phronimos* in 5th-century Greece led Plato to attack "sophists" who perverted rhetoric by treating it strictly as a technology of persuasion; and it led Aristotle to a reconception of rhetoric, to insistence that any who mediate ethics and politics be imbued with the qualities of the *phronimos*. If a critique and reconstruction of rhetoric was to be effective, the term *phronesis* had to be promoted. The disappearance of the *phronimos* in the 20th-century West implicates science as rhetoric was implicated in ancient Greece; and finding the proper critique of science, and proper principles for the reconstruction of science, requires our recovery of *phronesis* now, as Plato and Aristotle recovered it then. In short summary, because it is perverse to treat either rhetoric or science as merely a *techne*, we must rediscover *phronesis* and insist that all who presume to mediate ethics and politics, whether they do so with rhetorical or scientific *techne* of power, exhibit the morality of a *phronimos*.

If you follow Gadamer's analogy closely, it is clear that the Greek ideal of the *phronimos* represents one strategy that could be pursued to achieve the first of Habermas's ambitions for social theory, that of developing a theory to mediate dominant causal analysis and marginal interpretive understanding, some "higher synthesis in which both have a place" (McCarthy 1978, 140). Habermas, however, would have to conceive his critical theory as embodied, and his appropriation of *Truth and Method* suggests that he will not follow Gadamer in that direction. He is more interested in the results than in the details of Gadamer's analogy between the situation of Aristotle and that of a contemporary critic of scientific practice. The attractive result that he wants to borrow, of course, is Gadamer's claim that interpretation provides a unique kind of theory that is always already applied:

> The immanent connection of understanding and application can be seen in the examples of theology and jurisprudence. Both the interpretation of the Bible in preaching and the interpretation of positive law in adjudication serve simultaneously as guideposts of how to apply the evidence in a given situation. The practical life-relation . . . is not simply a subsequent corollary to the interpretation. Rather, the interpretation is realized in the application itself. Gadamer does not want to restrict the scope of this constitutive connection between understanding and practical transposition into life only to certain traditions that . . . are already institutionally binding. Nor does he want to extend it merely to the interpretation of works of art or the explication of philosophical texts. He persuades us that the applicative understanding of distinguished traditions endowed with a claim to authority provides the model for hermeneutic understanding generally. (Habermas 1970a, 351–52)

Notice how Habermas changes Gadamer's analogues by comparing a hermeneutics that is confined to Bible study and forensics to a generalized hermeneutics; and notice that the virtues of the new hermeneutics are the virtues Habermas believes should be characteristic of his remodeled critical social theory: Theories of knowledge underwriting current scientific practice must consider the problem of their application as "a subsequent corollary," but the theory of knowledge implied by hermeneutics would integrate scientific practice and the practices of everyday life. This is what Habermas believes good social theory should do. Nor should social theory deal only with practices which "are already institutionally binding"; nor should it seek generalizations in such superstructural phenomena as "the interpretation of works of art or the explication of philosophical texts." "Applicative understanding" is a model of understanding in general, and hence a model for critical social theory in specific. The comparison under construction in Habermas's appropriation of Gadamer's treatment of *phronesis* seems to be that theory is to practice as hermeneutics in general is to critical social theory.

Habermas's statement of the case misses what Gadamer would likely regard as the most crucial element in his discussion of the integration of application in interpretation, namely that the integration is achieved ontologically in the person of the *phronimos* as a consequence of his or her embodiment of moral knowledge gained through the interpretation of tradition and life. In Habermas's hands, Gadamer's encounter with Aristotle, including his struggle to understand *techne*, *phronesis*, and *episteme*, is ruthlessly truncated. We do not even see the sense in which the *phronesis* of priests and rabbis, of judges and juridical scholars, is the moral knowledge of the *phronimos*. *Phronesis* is translated unambiguously as practical knowledge, and it is then discussed as if it were an epistemological achievement which could be understood apart from its embodiments as a matter of philosophical or social scientific *techne*: Hermeneutic knowledge has three features in common with that political-ethical knowledge that Aristotle distinguished from both science and technical knowledge. In the first place, practical knowledge has a reflective form; it is simultaneously 'knowing oneself.' For this reason we experience mistakes in the areas of practical knowledge in ourselves. False opinions have the habitual form of false consciousness. Deficient insight has the objective power of delusion. The second aspect is connected with this—practical knowledge is internalized. It has the power to fix drives and to shape passions. In contrast, technical knowledge remains external. We forget technical rules as soon as we fall out of practice. Practical rules, once mastered, become by contrast components of our personality structure. . . . The third aspect becomes comprehensible at this point—practical knowledge is global. It refers not to particular aims that can be specified independently of the means for their realization. The action-orienting goals, as well as the ways in which they can be realized, are components of the same form of life. This is always a social form of life that is developed through communicative action. Practical knowledge orients by way of rules of interaction. These transmitted rules are acquired by training; but the historically changing conditions of their use call for an application that, for its part, further develops the rules through interpretation (Habermas 1970a, 352–53).

For Habermas, all the markers of the *phronimos* are psychological features, matters of personality over which "Everyman" has control. You recognize a component of practical knowledge as you recognize having been the victim of ideological belief, experiencing feelings of shame and anger on discovering that you once embraced racist or sexist opinions—simple reflection produces practical knowledge. The Being of the *phronimos* is explained in knowing that he or she has "internalized" practical knowledge and integrated it into his or her "personality structure." Practical knowledge is at last deflected completely away from Gadamer's analysis and refitted in Habermas's terms: Practical knowledge is always social knowledge. It guides everyday life through communicative action. It orients communicative action by means of identifiable rules. But the rules "apply" only as statutes "apply" in a legal proceeding. Rules of communicative interaction, like the rule of law, may be shaped—in fact must be shaped—to fit historical circumstances as they change.

"Socializing" the *Phronimos*

The *phronimos* seems to have disappeared in Habermas's appropriation of the term practical knowledge. In fact, however, he or she is interpolated in a conception of society that subtly shifts in the course of argument from association with the Greek term polis to association with the Roman notion of communitas. Habermas begins working this magic without explanation or transition, making an abrupt jump-cut from Gadamer's and Aristotle's account of knowledge in the perspective of an individual person to his own rendition of social knowledge. "Action-orienting self-understanding" is suddenly a characteristic, not of your person, but of the groups to which you belong:

> Hermeneutic understanding is structurally oriented toward eliciting from tradition a possible action-orienting self-understanding of social groups. It makes possible a form of consensus on which communicative action depends. It eliminates the dangers of a communication breakdown in two directions: vertically, in one's own tradition, and horizontally, in the mediation between traditions of different cultures and groups. If these communication flows come to an end and the intersubjectivity of understanding either hardens or falls apart, an elementary condition of survival is disrupted—the possibility of agreement without constraint and recognition without force. (Habermas 1970a, 353)

The idea of the *phronimos* clearly emphasizes that moral responsibility is an accomplishment of the individual person. Morality is anchored in, and authorized by, one's interpretation of the tradition (and one's simultaneous application of such *phronesis* to his or her own circumstances). Habermas changes the statement of the case by suggesting that morality is anchored in group consensus. Tradition and circumstance are interpreted in such a way that *phronesis* becomes a common property of a social group. The authority of an ethic thus derives from the power of groups over individuals. Insofar as we are committed to rationality, it is important that this power not be arbitrary, that it preserve "the possibility of agreement without constraint and recognition without force." "Recognition without force" entails a "flow of communication" between past and present—everyone in the group must see a truth in the common tradition of their own volition, not as a result of some act of overt or covert group power. "Agreement without constraint" entails a synchronic "flow of communication" among all group members—everyone must voluntarily accept the authority of an ethic in the living circumstances of their everyday lives. All this emancipation, of course, strikes a realistic thinker as absurdly Utopian. But Habermas believes that Gadamer's rendition of hermeneutic understanding makes such voluntarism possible in principle: Recognition without force is a "vertical" (diachronic) "fusion of horizons," an historical dialectic; and agreement without restraint is an "horizontal" (synchronic) " fusion of horizons" achieved in polite conversation. (Notice here an especially clear instance of the intensity with which Habermas has committed himself to "emancipatory" theories: "Breakdown" in either "flow of communication" disrupts "an elementary condition of survival." His own existence, and that of civilized society, is in the balance whenever abuses of group power disrupt or distort the bi-directional flow of communication.)

Habermas is clearly as concerned as Gadamer has been with the importance of recovering a good understanding of moral reason. Further, he accepts the general idea of the *phronimos* (though, as I suggested earlier, he prefers to use epistemological instead of ontological terminology). What he adds is a caveat that Gadamer in fact understates in *Truth and Method*: The Greek *phronimos* is recognizable only insofar as he or she is acting within the context of a powerful social group, the city-state or polis. You cannot document Plato's or Aristotle's personal encounter with tradition, nor that of any other 5th-century Greek. Such understanding must be inferred from a text that documents publication of the results of encountering traditions. The very idea of publishing, "making public," necessarily presupposes that a prior reflection has been translated into language that is intersubjectively "available" for general understanding. The question is, Who understands?, or Whose understanding should be recognized as practical knowledge? If we examine the quiet ruminations of Kant or Hegel, we can see an encounter with tradition only as publicized in essays made available for interpretation; but because they are so complex and hermetic as to require a group of expert readers as audience, what we learn from them must be identified as an elite kind of knowing (*episteme*). If we are focused on practical knowledge, we are concerned with the availability of traditions (indeed, of any and all sorts of knowledge) in the whole polis generally. Gadamer's (Aristotle's) and Habermas's *phronimos* both represent the polis, but we are not sure about the character of that representation, and therein lies an important issue: In Gadamer's view, he or she purely mediates, working sometimes as a teacher instructing the polis about moral lessons available in the tradition, and at other times as a political advisor or leader persuading the polis to a particular course of right action. In Habermas's rhetoric, the *phronimos* reflects or mirrors both actual and potential social consensus— that is, the intelligence, knowledge, wisdom, integrity, trustworthiness, and dynamism of the *phronimos* exist within society (as group consensus, set expectations) and are only evinced by an individual person (appearing to be talent or achievement).

What I think of as "socializing the *phronimos*" results in an interestingly complex problem of Being that Habermas represents as a "dialectic" of "group identity" and "ego identity" that reflects or produces a "brokenness of intersubjectivity": The dialectic of the general and the particular, which also obtains in the appropriation of traditions and the corresponding application of practical rules, shows once again the brokenness of intersubjectivity. That something like tradition exists at all involves an aspect of nonobligation—the tradition must also be revisable; otherwise what is nonidentical in the sustained group identity would be destroyed. Ego-identities can be formed and maintained in linguistic communication only if the related group-identity can constitute itself, vis-a-vis the collective other of its own past, as simultaneously identical with and different from it. For this reason the global generality of practical rules requires a concretizing interpretation through which, in the given situation, it is molded into a concrete generality that is intersubjectively valid (Habermas 1970a, 353–54).

In this sequence, "ego-identity" is awareness of self-in-group, your knowing that you are an independent person despite your identification with a group. "Group-identity" is awareness of group-in-self, your knowing that you are an embodiment of the beliefs and commitments of a group despite being literally a biological individual. Each human being of course carries both identities in him- or herself, manifesting now this one in this situation, now that one in another situation. In Habermas's scheme, *phronesis* is a feature of the group identity and consists of a common understanding of traditional beliefs and commitments. Neither group identity nor *phronesis* simply exist like a nose on a face or the law of gravity. Traditions are not absolutely binding on groups, but are revisable to meet the exigencies of new situations and to accommodate everyone's ego-identity. As traditions are in fact revised, we see a correspondingly new group identity and new conditions of ego-identity. This difference, Habermas claims, must be rationalized by an interpretation that shows how new group- and ego-identities are in fact species of the same genus. *Phronesis* thus embraces beliefs and commitments that are both the same and different simultaneously, having one aspect of global generality, and another aspect of concrete generality. So, for example, Americans are taught that each person has a right to dispose of his or her property in any way he or she pleases. They also learn another global generality, that all people are entitled to live anywhere they please, constrained only by their financial resources. Property rights are an important part of the American group-identity, therefore, and attitudes toward property (pride of ownership or the frustration of not owning your own house, for instance) are important features of most people's ego-identity. Ordinarily these two global beliefs do not conflict. But in the context of "open housing ordinances" written to ameliorate the "ghettoizing" effects of racism, two kinds of adjustment must be made: (a) A concrete generality must be developed to determine which of the global beliefs takes precedence when they conflict; and (b) both global beliefs must be reinterpreted in light of the new concrete belief, allowing "losers" in the first determination to adjust their ego-identities so as to still feel included in the term American. Habermas's term brokenness of intersubjectivity, in this context, indicates that the agreements or fusion of horizons which characterize social groups are never constant, settled, or seamless; they are rather "broken"—still a cohesive pattern to be sure, but one that is always unsettled by constant need of adaptation and revision.

The brokenness of intersubjectivity leads Habermas to a discussion of the different theoretical logics suggested by one's choice to understand global beliefs and commitments as practical rather than technical knowledge. A technical approach to the problem of "open housing" would assume that the proper global generalization has always already existed, in the Constitution (tradition). We need only to locate it and to articulate it as a matter of definition—"the right to own takes precedence over the right to sell," for instance. Developing concrete generalizations is a matter of "applying" the global definition, in the sense of "making it operational." The result is a set of invariant rules or procedures which can be "applied" in this and all future situations where property rights of owning and selling clash. "It is otherwise with practical rules," Habermas shows:

We compare them with traditional meaning-contents, which are only under-stood when we have arrived at a consensus about their significance; only then do they have intersubjective validity in a social group. Understanding becomes a problem in this case because both the binding definition of fun-damental predicates and the invariant rules of application are lacking. A prior understanding guides us in the search for states of affairs in which the meaning can be made precise; but this identification of the range of applica-tion qualifies in turn the semantic content. The global generality, which we must already have understood diffusely, determines the subsumed particu-lar only to the degree to which it is itself first concretized by this particular. Only through this does it gain intersubjective recognition in a given situa-tion; the recognition is tied to this situation. A new situation demands a re-newal of intersubjectivity through repeated understanding. And intersub-jectivity does not come to pass arbitrarily; it is, rather, the result of thoughtful mediation of the past with present life. (Habermas 1970a, 354)

The technical approach is wrong, first, because Americans did not in fact understand property rights to be a dialectic of selling and owning until the particular conflict over "open housing" developed. The global generality is made concrete, and thus understandable, because of the particular situations it might make clear. The capacity of the global gen-erality to determine the rules of application thus derives from the capac-ity of concrete generalities to determine the global genus of which it is a species. This confusion is a relationship of co-dependency and co-vari-ance, a circle which must be kept going round: If you break the circle by treating the concrete as constant, the Constitution (tradition) loses its ca-pacity to define the conditions of intersubjectivity, thus threatening group identity. If you break the circle by treating the global as constant, the Constitution (tradition) loses its capacity to be relevant in new situa-tions, thus setting ego identities over and against group identity (so that one might say, for example, "My America no longer exists if I'm not free to sell my own house for any price and to anyone I please" when he or she should be articulating the same interest in language that does not subvert group-identity: "Because I am an American, and because we be-lieve in property rights, I should not be forced to sell my house to the Joneses").

This relationship of co-dependency and co-variance marks practical knowledge as logically pre-scientific, Habermas claims; but "hermeneu-tic procedures" can nonetheless "enter into the social sciences" whenever it is necessary to account for "the unavoidably historical content" of even very general global "schemata of possible world-conceptions" (Haber-mas 1970a, 355). When you try to understand how liberty is involved in the ego- and group-identities of Americans, for instance, you must find a way to account for all varieties of liberty Americans recognize. Each variety of liberty is a "possible world-conception" in that it is recognized by virtue of our ability to "see a world" in the context of which the idea (and term) liberty "means" one thing and not another. So, for example, the "world" where liberty clearly means "freedom from" is more pessimistic and conscious of the possibility of oppression than is the "world" where liberty clearly means "freedom to" do certain things. An account which links all possible "world-conceptions" into a coherent "schema" (e.g., argument or story) can be neither arbitrary nor random because all understandings of liberty necessarily have "historical content." An arbitrary philosophical rendition of what liberty should be in the best of all possible worlds runs aground on our knowledge of what liberty has in fact meant in this most imperfect of worlds—the history of what has been meant by liberty constrains and works to subvert any ideal notion of what it could mean. Similarly, a random scientific survey of what people mean by liberty here-and-now is poorly-conceived because no "here-and-now" of liberty exists except in comparison to the there-and-then of liberty. Thus if you are interested in an accurate and useful account of liberty in the social sciences, you need some method or procedure to capture historical as well as cognitive content. Habermas recommends "hermeneutic procedures" for the job of describing either global *phronesis* (the tradition-defined category liberty) or concrete *phronesis* (the situation-defined conjuring of liberty in communicative action).

The *Phronimos* in Polis and in Communitas

Habermas's analysis of the logic whereby a "socialized *phronimos*" manages two "dialectics" (the tension between global and concrete ethical principles and the tension between ego- and group-identity) suggests that hermeneutics itself is a *techne*, a method or procedure of any social science concerned with categories that have historical content. And this, of course, puts him at odds with Gadamer, whose treatise defends Truth by opposing Method. Habermas narrativizes the conflict by portraying Gadamer as a disgruntled humanist attacking positivistic social scientists—and in the heat of battle overstating his case: Gadamer unwittingly obliges the positivistic devaluation of hermeneutics. He joins his opponents in the view that hermeneutic experience 'transcends the range of control of scientific method.' In the preface to the second edition of his work he sums up his investigations in the thesis 'that the moment of historical influence is and remains effective in all understanding of tradition, even where the method of the modern historical sciences has gained ground and makes what has become historically into an "object" that has to be "ascertained" like an experimental finding—as if tradition were foreign and, humanly regarded, incomprehensible in the same sense as the object of physics.' This correct critique of a false objectivistic self understanding cannot, however, lead to a suspension of the methodological distanciation of the object, which distinguishes a self-reflective understanding from everyday communicative experience. The confrontation of 'truth' and 'method' should not have misled Gadamer to oppose hermeneutic experience abstractly to methodic knowledge as a whole. As it is, hermeneutic experience is the ground of the hermeneutic sciences. And even if it were feasible to remove the humanities entirely from the sphere of science, the sciences of action could not avoid linking empirical-analytic with hermeneutic procedures. The claim which hermeneutics legitimately makes good against the practically influential absolutism of a general methodology of the empirical sciences, brings no dispensation from the business of methodology in general. This claim will, I fear, be effective in the sciences or not at all (Habermas 1970a, 355–56).

In this story, the disapproval of "positivistic" social scientists should count as a powerful critique of philosophical hermeneutics—Gadamer's object was, or should have been, to improve the academic reputation of hermeneutics among intellectuals who have long been conditioned to identify rationality with the scientific method. Gadamer in fact has discovered a way to resolve a consequential aporia in the logic of social science, showing how one might account for the historical content of beliefs and commitments that presently have force in social relationships. But he undermines his more general goal of salvaging the reputation of hermeneutics by his refusal to present this "know-how" as a "methodological" innovation. Gadamer's discovery is in fact a method, Habermas believes; but even if it were not, social scientists who need a way to account for history will appropriate it as "method" with or without Gadamer's approval. Science, and the association of rationality with method, is already an historically powerful tradition, so powerful that any assertion of hermeneutics must be in the context of science. One cannot now simply oppose scientific method, as one might speak out against a new proposal in a legislative assembly, for such an attempt will be taken as irrational, marginal, not to be taken seriously.

This whole line of reasoning is distinct from the thinking that came before it in that it is purely refutative, functioning more to justify Habermas's disagreement with Gadamer than to qualify and justify his appropriation of Gadamer's arguments. But notice further that the grounds of refutation have shifted from counter-statement to analysis of internal contradiction. In its first moments, the refutation relocated the *phronimos* in group consensus rather than in individual embodiments of *phronesis*. Working out details of this relocation resulted in a theory which purports to show how people in society rationalize traditional beliefs and commitments with present beliefs and commitments in such a way as to preserve the fundamental agreements that make society possible. This theory was abruptly treated as a method, and in its last moments the refutation shifts to a critique of motives that exposes a contradiction between arguing against method and establishing the truth (rationality) of nontechnical argumentation. Each argument flows smoothly into the next so that one hardly notices the shift of ground, until at last we put the beginning and ending of the sequence directly together: What in the world does "socializing the *phronimos*" have to do with strategies for opposing "positivistic" influences?

Apparently, the proper answer is "Nothing"; but this too quickly glosses the ground shift by treating it simply as Habermas's difficulty with the logic of refutation when it is in fact a symptom of what may be the most important issue to separate Gadamer and Habermas. The issue comes clear when we think about the ambiguity of the term society, and of our consequent need of one or more "possible world-conceptions" to manage the ambiguity. (To repeat an understanding mentioned earlier, a "world-conception" is a representation of the human life-world in the context of which phenomena mean one thing and not another. In this instance we are concerned with the phenomenon and term society.) Throughout *Truth and Method*, Gadamer was "thinking Greek," in the sense that he was attempting to describe the present through an analysis and interpretation of Aristotle's arguments, meanings, and intentions. From this angle, the world-conception disambiguating society is the Greek habit of seeing society as contained within the physical and symbolic walls of the polis. Throughout his review, Habermas is "thinking theory," in the sense that he is attempting to integrate Gadamer's claims into an interpreted body of literature defined by his appropriation of it to articulate and justify a general theory of society. From this angle, the world-conception clarifying society is the academic habit of treating society as mediated within texts that describe society more rationally, clearly, and accurately than anyone could experience it. In other words, society is as it is represented in a community of scientists. These two quite different orientations create an issue that can be crystallized in the problem, Should society be understood in the world conception suggested by the term polis, or in another suggested by the word communitas?

Polis is far and away the more clearly articulated conception, but even it is murky. We read so many of the taken-for-granted terms of our own context into the Greek word that we must begin by clarifying what did not exist in 5th-century Greece: There was no society, no communion, communication or community, no political system, and no legal system. I do not mean by this to suggest that nothing Greek could be sensibly referred to in these words—the polis was a society, of course, and you can learn a good deal about Greek rhetoric by believing that it was a theory of communication. But in fact, the Greeks did not live or think in these terms. A society in Greece was the polis, and the polis was a unique human group virtually unprecedented in contemporary experience. It was a small, local, integrated group that regarded as foreigners even people who spoke the same language, shared similar history, revered the same gods, read the same literature, and fought the same enemies. It was sovereign, recognizing no binding ties or authority beyond itself. The polis superintended every moment of Being in Greece, from the most private to the most public actions and thoughts. When given the choice between exile from the polis and death, Socrates chose to commit suicide. The sort of consubstantiality indexed by words derived from the Latin communitas was taken for granted in Greece; hence, rhetoric is a theory, not of communication, but of persuasion. There were laws and trials, of course, but none of them clearly distinct from other business of the polis. In periods of democracy, electorates and juries were the same people gathered in the same place for a different purpose. There were no lawyers, no professional judges, no settled, inviolable rules of evidence or procedure. There was only the polis and its citizens, neither of which were ever quite wholly distinct from one another. In our time, when nothing superintends the form of the state, the decision to institute a democracy, scientific socialism, or an Islamic republic is earth-shaking and "final," in the sense that we treat such decisions as made for all time. But in Greece, the polis was forever. Choosing this or that governmental form was a political move and not a constitutional commitment—the constitution of the polis was a settled matter, at least until the imperial period when expanding the consciousness of the polis became an issue.

The Roman term communitas gains currency in a context radically different from that of Golden Age Greece. Even in its republican period, Rome always was an expansionist state; but it did not expand by creating an organization greater than itself to manage conquests. That is, Rome grew by annexations, much as contemporary cities grow by incorporating the lands and population of lesser towns and villages. But, unlike contemporary incorporations, none of the Roman conquests (except Carthage, sewn with salt) ceased to Be when Rome assumed administration of them. The genius of Roman administration was its tolerance of local laws, languages, religions, and customs so long as no threat to Rome was manifest in them. Roman rule was thus never imposed so much as it was superimposed, "laid over" familiar local practices. People in Iberia or Gaul could enjoy that measure of "home rule" which derives from cultural solidarity—each was a "polis without sovereignty." And Rome was itself affected, becoming over time a "polis without cultural solidarity," vulnerable to such solidarity movements as Hellenism and Christianity. Your "companions" (societas) became a local concept: You could not "walk with" those who administered the Empire if you lived in the Provinces, and in Rome citizens could only "walk with" each other. Your capacity or willingness to engage other people in conversation became a marker distinguishing the local from the provincial (in one direction) and the local from the Imperial (the other direction), especially after the Christian revolution: You would not commune with those who worshipped different gods—even if it were possible to "speak or converse" with them, you would not communicate, or you would speak outside the religious community as if you were addressing strangers. And, from the opposite angle, you would accept as part of the community, you would agree to communicate and commune even with traditional enemies of the state if they were also Christian. "Rendering unto Caesar that which is Caesar's" divorced cultural solidarity from sovereignty in ways that were both helpful and hurtful to the Empire. The principle did increase people's tolerance for oppression, but it also created a pocket of resistance all but immune to Imperial interference. Dividing the polis into "spiritual" and "secular" domains irrevocably changed the nature of sovereignty, making it sensible to discuss conditions of community that were not self-evident in the very Being of the polis.

World-conceptions suggested by the terms polis and communitas create two possible analogies that could clarify society. If society is analogous to polis, it is an essentially "synthetic phenomenon"; that is, the proper perspective on society would allow us to see how all of human life becomes an integrated totalization. The remarkable thing about society would not be its diversity and complexity, but its fundamental coherence despite such diversity and complexity. Most of the important questions of social theory would be problems of identification: Is society formed when individuals give up their subjectivity to an artificial group identity? Or is society the fundamental condition and our conception that we are individuals merely an appearance? How does society manifest itself in each person? How does society change? Does it necessarily involve change in the self-conception of individuals? The American rhetoric of the "melting pot" would be a clear example of the vision of society from this perspective: Entering into our society is a personal ontological achievement involving your surrender of your native culture and ethnic inheritance. Anyone can "Be American," even the "tired, poor, and wretched" of another polis; but you need to identify with our history, speak our language, and adopt our homogenizing perspective on the world.

By contrast, if society is analogous to communitas, it is an essentially "analytic" fiction; that is, society is the mysterious vision of coherence among lesser human groupings that is never itself an object of scrutiny. We see institutions, movements, and other specific examples of community; we look at the coherence of parts of society and suppose that coherence of the whole is explained by some monomythic theory such as Marxism or its arch enemy Capitalism. Society is a sovereign term, but it is as the vision of Imperial Rome from the perspective of the provinces. From this perspective, the remarkable thing about society would not be its mysterious coherence, but the solidarity, or lack thereof, within its constituent communities. Most of the important questions of social theory would be problems of local solidarity: How do labor union members identify their interest and then influence other communities whose interests are different? How are people constrained by their history and by the groups to which they belong? How do groups come to be? What distinguishes organizations from institutions? What strategies or tactics are used to promote and to resist change? In the language Habermas uses, the rhetoric of virtually every "empirical-analytic" social inquiry would be a clear example of the vision of society from this perspective: Our job in this particular study is to uncover something about a single social formation considered in isolation. We hypothesize that what we learn will be consistent with this general theory of society that we have accepted because we find it persuasive. Or, we believe that what we learn is a piece of the puzzle that Someday Someone will put together with other bits of research to form an incontrovertible general theory of society.

The *phronimos* would likely be a different person doing different things in society figured through the term polis than in society figured through the term communitas. However, we can nonetheless make the two meanings of *phronimos* roughly equivalent: The *phronimos* in (polis)society embodies the highest ideals of (polis)society, and is thus uniquely qualified to hold in trust the power of (polis)society. The identification of the *phronimos* with the ideals of (polis)society is so complete that the two are virtually consubstantial—an act of the *phronimos* is an act of (polis)society. From the other angle, the *phronimos* in (communitas)society is an embodiment of the common beliefs and commitments that provide the solidarity of his or her community. The *phronimos* is uniquely qualified to represent the community in all dealings with sovereignty, whether that be finding a way to "render unto Caesar" or finding a way to resist "Caesar." Maintaining distance from power ("Caesar") is imperative: The cohesion of the community should derive from its solidarity, not even from its own sovereignty, and especially not from "Caesar's."

The two points of contrast here constitute a major issue between Gadamer and Habermas: With regard to what the *phronimos* does, Gadamer treats power as a "neutral" feature of society imbued with moral quality by the character of the *phronimos* or *deinos* who wields it. Habermas treats power as already imbued with moral character, the character of oppression; the *phronimos* in consequence refuses to wield it and "acts" by creating emancipatory theories of social relationships. With regard to who the *phronimos* is, Gadamer has in mind the practical administrative politician who exercises sovereignty in the name of the polis. Habermas has in mind the practical philosopher who mobilizes the cultural solidarity of academic social theorists against those ("in Rome") who exercise sovereignty. The *phronimos* is not sovereign, but is instead only a critic. All kinds of knowledge are distinguished by the "method" which authorizes their claim to truth. Scientists are "experts" in the application of the methods capable of producing *episteme*. "Humanists" are "experts" in the application of methods capable of producing *techne* of the arts. When we recover "practical philosophy," another class of scholars will be "expert" in the "historico-hermeneutic" methods capable of producing *phronesis*. Because it is his ambition and life's work, the *phronimos* in the end turns out to be Habermas himself, or more precisely Habermas's vision of himself having perfected the theory of communicative action and in the act of showing persuasively how to resist and ultimately purify systemic distortions of communication. Within this interpretation, the cultural solidarity of a community of practical philosophers stands over and against sovereignty as the spiritual stands over and against the secular.

Summary of Problems

Issues in influential debates, whether between presidential candidates or celebrity intellectuals, are framing and agenda-setting devices. Until the dialogue is expanded by a more extreme position, the space framed by opposing views becomes the ground for finding a middle way, perhaps achieving a synthesis, or maybe just choosing sides so that thinking may go on to another, consequent topic. For those who did not participate in the debate, therefore, each point of clash becomes a problem to solve, and all issues together constitute an agenda for thinking, in this case, about the possibilities of *phronesis*:

1. Gadamer and Habermas agree that the substance of moral reasoning is an interpretation of traditional beliefs and commitments applied to concrete problems in the present. This controversial agreement may inspire some to look for alternative sources of morality; but if your purpose is to see how far the frame established by this debate will get you, it is better to understand that reliance on tradition is a clear presupposition. The problem to solve has to do with the connection between people and their morality: Does *phronesis* exist apart from specific embodiments of morality? Are individuals "moral" or not by virtue of their own character and conduct, or by virtue of their desire to maintain a group-identity? If *phronesis* resides in social groups, who speaks for the group? Is every

member morally obligated to become a *phronimos*? Or are there special-ized members of the group who establish moral standards and lead the rest of us—in other words, Is *phronesis* mediated? and if so, By whom and with what result?

2. Gadamer and Habermas are agreed that there is a deficiency in the way social sciences have developed in the second half of the twentieth century. They are further agreed that the deficiency consists of inatten-tion to, or of an inability to address, the historical content of the phenom-ena and terms social scientists wish to account for. The problem to solve has to do with the location of the difficulty created by this deficiency: Is the difficulty global, in that people in general have created a culture that accepts expertise as a substitute for *phronesis*? Is the difficulty concrete, in that social scientists have created communities which devalue history and do not now possess methods up to the task of recognizing and ana-lyzing the historical content of their vocabulary? Should *phronesis* be characteristic of individual scientists, scientific communities, those who exercise the sovereignty of the state, or of everyone within society fig-ured through the concept polis? Is *phronesis* without sovereignty even a possibility?

3. Gadamer insists that the *phronesis* gained from hermeneutical reflec-tion has nothing to do with domination, but rather with willing subordi-nation:

> Hermeneutics in the sphere of literary criticism and the historical sciences is not 'knowledge as domination,' that is an appropriation as a 'taking posses-sion of,' but rather a subordination to the text's claim to dominate our minds. Of this, however, legal and theological hermeneutics are the true model. To interpret the law's will or the promises of God is clearly not a form of domination, but of service. They are interpretations—which in-cludes application—in the service of what is considered valid. Our thesis is that historical hermeneutics also has a task of application to perform, be-cause it serves the validity of meaning, in that it explicitly and consciously bridges the gap in time that separates the interpreter from the text and over-comes the alienation of meaning that the text has undergone. (Gadamer 1982, 278)

Habermas, on the other hand, uses most uncompromising language to condemn this attitude toward the authority of *phronesis* because it ap-pears similar to that which resulted in German National Socialism: "One is tempted to lead Gadamer into battle against himself, to demonstrate to him hermeneutically that he ignores that legacy [of German rationalism] because he has taken over an undialectical concept of enlightenment from the limited perspective of the German nineteenth century and that with it he has adopted an attitude which vindicated for us (Germans) a

dangerous pretension to superiority separating us from Western tradition" (Habermas 1970a, 358). The problem to solve has to do with one's
attitude toward sovereignty: Is the intellect sovereign? Or does sovereignty exist outside the "spiritual" life of the mind in the practical "secular" world?—in other words, Is the *phronimos* a "critic," a "servant of
Caesar," or perhaps both and neither, an "embodiment of the polis"? Is
our understanding of history always oppressive? Can yielding to the
"authority" of our understanding of traditional beliefs and commitments
never be emancipatory?

This agenda is as subject to modification as any other, but it would
seem to be worth pursuing in rhetorical and communication theory especially. We find ourselves at nether ends of intellectual history charged by
"outsiders" with fundamentally the same responsibility and consequent
burden of justification. In Aristotle's terms, rhetoric mediates ethics and
politics. In the Frankfurt School's terms, communicative action in general
(and mass communication, "the culture industry," in particular) mediates ethics and social practices either in an oppressive or an emancipatory way. Even in refusing this way of framing a discussion of *phronesis*,
our own rules of argumentation and debate demand that we respond, ultimately with a reasonable position.

References

Bernstein, R. J. 1982. "From Hermeneutics To Praxis." *Review of Metaphysics* 35:
    823–45.
Gadamer, Hans-Georg. 1975. "Hermeneutics and Social Science." *Cultural
    Hermeneutics* 2: 307–316.
_____. 1976. *Hegel's Dialectic: Five Hermeneutical Studies.* Trans. P. C. Smith. New
    Haven, CT: Yale University Press.
_____. 1976. *Philosophical Hermeneutics.* Trans. D. E. Linge. Berkeley: University
    of California Press.
_____. 1979. "The Problem of Historical Consciousness." In *Interpretive Social Sci-
    ence: A Reader,* ed. Paul Rabinow and W. M. Sullivan. Berkeley: University of
    California Press.
_____. 1980. *Dialogue and Dialectic: Eight Hermeneutical Studies on Plato.* Trans. P.
    C. Smith. New Haven, CT: Yale University Press.
_____. 1981. *Reason in the Age of Science.* Trans. F. G. Lawrence. Cambridge: The
    MIT Press.
_____. 1982. *Truth and Method.* Trans. G. Barden and J. Cumming. New York:
    Crossroad.
Habermas, Jurgen. 1970a. "A Review of Gadamer's *Truth and Method.*" Reprinted
    in *Understanding and Social Inquiry,* eds. Fred R. Dallmayr and Thomas A. Mc-
    Carthy, 335–363. Notre Dame, IN: University of Notre Dame Press 1977.
_____. 1970b. "On Systematically Distorted Communication." *Inquiry* 13:
    205–18.

_____. 1970c. "Towards a Theory of Communicative Competence." *Inquiry* 13: 360–75.

_____. 1973. *Theory and Practice*. Trans. J. Viertel. Boston: Beacon Press.

_____. 1975. *Legitimation Crisis*. Trans. Thomas McCarthy. Boston: Beacon Press.

_____. 1979. *Communication and the Evolution of Society*. Trans. Thomas. McCarthy. Boston: Beacon Press.

_____. 1982. "A Reply to My Critics." In *Habermas: Critical Debates*, ed. J. B. Thompson and D. Held, 219–83. Cambridge, MA: MIT Press.

_____. 1983. *Philosophical-Political Profiles*. 2nd ed. rev. Trans. F. G. Lawrence. Cambridge: MIT Press.

_____. 1984, 1988. *The Theory of Communicative Action*. 2 Vols. Trans. Thomas McCarthy, Boston: Beacon Press.

Horkheimer, Max and Theodor Adorno 1972. *Dialectic of Enlightenment*. Trans. J. Cumming. New York: Seabury Press.

Lyotard, Jean-François. 1988. *The Differend: Phrases in Dispute*. Trans. Georges Van Den Abbeele. Minneapolis: University of Minnesota Press.

Lyotard, Jean-François and Jean-Loup Thebaud. 1985. *Just Gaming*. Trans. Wlad Godzich. Minneapolis: University of Minnesota Press.

McCarthy, Thomas. 1978. *The Critical Theory of Jurgen Habermas*. Cambridge: The MIT Press.

Mouffe, Chantal. 1993. *The Return of the Political*. New York: Verso.

Self, L. S. 1979. "Rhetoric and Phronesis: The Aristotelian Ideal." *Philosophy and Rhetoric* 12: 130–45.

Seliger, M. 1977. *The Marxist Conception of Ideology: A Critical Essay*. Cambridge, UK: Cambridge University Press.

2

Judgment and the Problem of Agency/Accountability

A Postcolonial Critique
of Poststructuralist Theory

K. E. Supriya

> Do you know that you take a great deal too much upon yourself," is the angry rejoinder:
> "and that in the part of the world I come from, you would be called to account for it?
> —Charles Dickens (1985, 98)

The tension between humanist thought and poststructuralist theory has become a philosophical motor force driving critical thought in the humanities. More specifically, this tension has engendered the examination of the theoretical, political, and ethical relations among subjecthood or subjectivity, language as discourse, institutional practice, and human agency (Foucault 1979, 135–170; Spivak 1994, 66–68; Young 1990, 119–126; Weedon 1987; 74–106). In this essay I argue that a postcolonial critique of poststructuralist reformulations of humanist thought has important implications for the analytical, political, and existential domains of human judgment.

The conceptual location of this essay may be understood as the juncture of Western philosophical thought, postcolonial theory, the concept of judgment, and the entire matrix of power relations that constitutes historical and contemporary social relations. Such a location both occasions and engenders a particularly postcolonial critique of poststructuralist theory on the basis that the latter, in critiquing humanism, evacuates the conceptual and performative possibility of human judgment by negating human agency conceived in unique terms of human accountability for relations of domination in multiple lived contexts. In elaborating upon the relations between judgment and agency that underwrite this essay, I might point to two interrelated problems of agency that underlie my argument. The first problem is elucidated in Alcoff's article "Cultural Feminism versus Poststructuralism: The Identity Crisis in Feminism" in terms of the problematic of the domain of willed human action. Alcoff observes, ". . . this rejection of biological determinism is not grounded in the belief that human subjects are underdetermined but, rather, in the belief that we are overdetermined (i.e. constructed) by a social discourse and/or cultural practice. The idea here is that we individuals really have little choice in the matter of who we are, for as Derrida and Foucault like to remind us, individual motivations and intentions count for nil or almost nil in the scheme of social reality" (Alcoff 1988, 416).

Alcoff completes the summary about the poststructuralist notion of overdeterminism by observing that according to the theory individuals are synonymous with discursive-social constructions and consequently as constructs "our experience of our very subjectivity" is itself the effect of individual imbrication within and constitution through social discourse "beyond (way beyond) individual control" (416).[1] The second is my own attempt to think through the theoretical and strategic importance of the concept of human agency in power-laden contexts of human action and experience. This directly leads to the problem or rather question of human accountability for discursive and material relations of domination and subordination in ways that do not repeat the agent or individual-centeredness of humanist thought.[2] The argument that the Janus-faced problem of agency conceptualized as both human action and accountability, a problem that is raised but not resolved by poststructuralist theoretical critiques of humanist theories of the subject, is also the problem of human judgment is the crux of this essay. In seeking a philosophical solution to this problem, the essay navigates between the agential excesses of humanist thought and the agentlessness of poststructuralist theory through the critical apparatus of postcolonial theory. To this end, I present a particular exegesis of poststructuralist theory wherein I treat a corpus of rather complex and disparate theoretical work in terms of its basic conceptual elements.[3] Poststructuralist critiques of humanism are embedded within this exegesis. I then present a postcolonial critique of poststructuralist theory by both directly drawing from and critically engaging and extending extant arguments made by postcolonial theorists who have intervened in the field of poststructuralist theory. [4] In particular, I place emphasis on postcolonial theoretical critiques of the "Eurocenteredness" of poststructuralist critiques of human agency so as to demonstrate how the theoretical elision of agency within the latter runs the danger of eroding the notion of judgment in contexts that are constituted by the intersecting axes of nationhood, ethnicity, gender, and religion and manifest as human abjection and suffering.[5] I conclude the essay by both theoretically opening a space for recuperation and restoration of questions of human judgment into poststructuralist theory and providing an example of how we might navigate this complex and contradictory terrain in the face of a particular power-laden experiential and material context—women and violence. One way by which such a philosophical position may be characterized is that of critical ethical humanism.[6]

Prior to an elaboration of these themes and arguments, I want to say a brief word about how I approach the question of judgment within this essay. I do not come to the question of judgment in the first instance—that is, through Western philosophy and aesthetics, Western theology or Western political theory. Rather I arrive at it in the last instance through the intersecting and oppositional trajectories of poststructuralism and postcolonial theory. In other words, the problem and questions related to human judgment ensue from critical engagement with the tensions between these two critical paradigms within the humanities. In particular, poststructuralist-postcolonial theoretical debates around the question of agency, articulated to the particular notion of accountability, ineluctably leads to the analytical political, and existential problem of judgment in a social matrix that is constituted by and riven with power relations.

Critical Reformulation of Humanism

Poststructuralist theory has critically examined many basic assumptions of humanist thought. Poststructuralist critical intervention into humanism can be understood in terms of the question of the human or man as the willed social actor—the human, or within a Foucauldian critical terrain, "Man"—who is the authorial origin of consciousness understood as speech (Weedon 1987, 6–8). In *Feminist Practice and Poststructuralist Theory*, Chris Weedon argues that "This understanding of subjectivity is itself the product of the long development of humanist discourse through which the God-given socially fixed, unfree subject of the feudal order became the free, rational, self-determining subject of modern political, legal, social and aesthetic discourses" (78–79). Humanist thought conceptualizes the human or man less as subject of history than subject over history. In other words, the "human" in humanism is a rational centered agent of history. The critique of this notion of human lies at the heart of both structuralism and post-structuralism. In *White Mythologies: Writing History and the West*, Robert Young makes the far-reaching theoretical and historical claim that "Structuralism's so-called 'decentering of the subject' was in many respects itself an ethical activity, derived from the suspicion that the ontological category of 'the human' and 'human nature' had been inextricably associated with the violence of Western history." (Young 1990, 124). In the context of structuralism heralding the concept

of the subject of/in grammar, Young observes that "One way of addressing this difficulty (of the subject) was to redefine the self through the
model of the different grammatical positions which it is obliged to take
up in language, which disallow the centrality and the unity of 'I' assumed by humanism" (124). (Curiously enough, a radical political and
ethical concern with the violence of humanism, which ostensibly characterizes structuralist thought, nevertheless led to a theoretical and ethical
position where the subject of violence becomes the subject of language-
as-grammar). Poststructuralist theory shares with structuralism a theory
of human subjects as decentered by language. The point of departure of
the former from the latter may be understood in terms of the deferred
sliding signified subject who follows the discursive terrain of the sliding
signifier and deferral. I therefore turn to the consideration of the linguistic or discursive reformulation of humanism by poststructuralist theory.

The notion of the centered rational human being in humanism is displaced by the notion of the subject in language. This is the substance of
subjectivity, "the conscious and unconscious thoughts and emotions of
the individual, her sense of herself and her ways of understanding her relation to the world" (Weedon 1987, 32–33). The subject is conceptualized
as a constitutive effect of language as discourse within discursive fields.
Weedon observes ". . . forms of subjectivity are produced historically and
change with shifts in the wide range of discursive fields which constitute
them" (33). Subjectivities that are engendered by language and discursive forms of culture are thus complex, multiple and often contradictory.
In the context of gender identity, Weedon observes "Many women acknowledge the feeling of being a different person in different social situations which call for different qualities and modes of femininity" and further "Our sense of ourselves and of our femininity may at times be
contradictory and precarious . . . " (86–87). The notion of subject-effects
(as an effect of discourse) as opposed to the pre-linguistic or pre-discur-
sive subject has significant theoretical and ethical implications for the humanist conception of the agent. Most importantly, it produces the notion
of the decentered subject. The subject is no longer the center of knowledge and reason and action but conversely a positioned conduit of cultural discourses about self and society. The radicalness of the poststructuralist notion of the discursively-constituted subject is most felt when
humanism is deconstructively realized as a discourse which reflexively
produces the man/woman who reproduce humanism through their
thoughts and actions. Also the individual is reconceptualized as an
agentless embodiment of discourses that act through the individual.
However, within poststructuralist theory, these discourses are not free
floating systems of language or sign systems. Rather discourses are located within social organizations that may be thought of as institutions. I

therefore turn to the third most significant concept that undergirds post-structuralist critiques of humanist philosophy.

One of the most far-reaching claims about the power of institutions in producing individuals has been made by Michel Foucault in his detailed sociological analysis of modernity, power, and prison systems in *Discipline and Punish* (Foucault 1979, 195–256). Foucault's genealogical researches into the rise of a new form of power in modernity, a power that may be thought in terms of discipline and techniques, led him to the historical and sociological conclusion that the emergence of a new and different form of power (different from classical forms of sovereign power) was imbricated in a new and different form of social organization that may be understood as a network of institutions. Foucault describes institutions as: ". . . a multiplicity of often minor processes, of different origin and scattered location, which overlap, repeat, or imitate one another, support one another, distinguish themselves from one another according to their domain of application, converge and gradually produce the blueprint of a general method" (138).

Foucault finds this new architectural rationality to be a spatially expansive and expanding one, "They were at work in secondary education at a very early date, later in primary schools; they slowly invested the space of the hospital; and, in a few decades, they restructured the military organization" (138). The effect of the expanding domain of institutional power is the production of the disciplined and docile corporeal subject of modernity through discourses organized within a discursive field. Based upon Foucault, Weedon conceptualizes discourses as historically- specific languages that are organized within discursive fields that are both linguistic manifestations and manifest within institutions. Weedon observes: "Social structures and processes are organized through institutions and practices such as the law, the political system, the church, the family, the education system, and the media each of which is located in and structured by a particular discursive field" (Weedon 1987, 35).

According to Weedon, a discursive field may be thought of as a system of meaning wherein different discourses and discursive fields themselves compete with one another to control and regulate and/or liberate subjects in and from giving meaning to the world. (An example that has direct bearing upon the trajectory of this essay is the discursive field that is the institution of Western philosophy. Within this discursive field existential philosophical discourse about the individual who is never free from responsible action can be seen as an instantiation of a discourse that gives a particular meaning to being-in-the-world while Nietzchean nihilist discourse may be seen as an instance of a discourse that ironically and subversively liberates the individual from the carceral effects of making sense of self and the world on the premise that meaning has always been already evacuated by power). It is through discourses and their relative position within institutions, and institutions themselves, that produce and reproduce power relations in society.

The radical critique of humanist thought through poststructuralist theories of the relations among subjectivity, language as discourse, and institutions significantly changes the ways in which human agency may be thought of within Western thought. These changes may be encapsulated through three inter-related arguments that follow the conceptual contours of poststructuralist theory. First the agential individual, the individual who is free to act and acts upon self and other, is arguably a theoretical error that negates the function of discourse and institution in society. Following from this, first the Western individual is a subject of Western discourses. Second, discourses are the new agents of culture and society as they are constituted by the intersecting vectors of language or signifiers, meaning, and power relations. Discourses are the agents of control and liberation of society and therefore of individuals in society who are subject to and subjects of discourses. Discourses position humans as subjects. Third, institutions insofar as they are material loci of discourses are also implicated in the reproduction of power relations in society. Thus discursive agency, the agency of discourse, is imbricated in institutional agency, the agency of institutions. However, this theoretical, ethical, and political evacuation of the agency of the West has been the subject of critique by postcolonial scholars. I now turn to a consideration of these critiques which complicates the poststructuralist reversal of humanist thought by calling attention to the problem of agency specifically conceptualized as the agent of Western colonialism and imperialism.

Postcolonial Theory and the West

Postcolonial critical interventions into poststructuralist theory have been principally engendered by the context of the power relations between the center and periphery, imperialism and the margins of history and culture, colonizer and subaltern subjectivity (Bhabha 1994, 85–92; Mani 1992, 392–395; JanMohammed 1985, 59–64; Said 1979, 1–28; Spivak 1990, 75–112). These interventions and their implications for judgment may be systematized in terms of three theoretical critiques that may be thought concurrently in conceptual and historical-political terms. (I here organize them so as to provide thematic coherence). The first of these, an overarching claim, may be understood as a critique of, rather caveat against, a decontextualized reading and application of a theoretical paradigm that is rooted in the West and has been formulated through a perspective that is distinctively shaped by the unique historical and political contexts that have shaped Western intellectual thought both within and without the context of power relations with the margins. In "Cultural Theory, Colonial Texts: Reading Eyewitness Accounts of Widow Burning," Lata Mani particularly makes the contentious claim that the fault lines of poststructuralism are made evident when poststructuralist theoretical and critical tools are extracted out of the particular context from which they arose and applied to a vastly disparate and divergent historical and material context. Mani alerts that such a decontextualized use of poststructuralist theory only serves to reinscribe power relations that are putatively the critical object of such an intellectual and political exercise. Mani observes: "The analysis of colonial discourse has drawn some of its tools from structuralist and poststructuralist theory, specifically textual strategies for reading against the grain of colonial representations. However, such work often applies these tools to texts produced in radically different socio-historical conditions from that which poststructuralist theory in particular has sought to address. While poststructuralist theory emerged in the context of mass capitalist societies with highly developed superstructures the colonial state . . . achieved not hegemony but dominance" (Mani, 1992, 394).

Mani's far-reaching critique is repeated with an emphasis on the disjunction between the discursive and material axes of power. This critique is made by Abdul JanMohammed in "The Economy of Manichean Allegory: The Function of Racial Difference in Colonial Literature" where an anti-intentionalist reading of colonial discourse is repudiated in light of "actual imperialist practices" (JanMohammed 1985, 61).[7] JanMohammed argues against circumventing "the dense history of material conflict between Europeans and natives" by treating "colonial discourse as if it existed in a vacuum" (60). These claims against a decontextualized application of poststructuralist theories of discursive overdetermination and the loss of subjecthood provide an intellectual context for examining two other interrelated yet distinct postcolonial critiques of the elision of the question, or rather problem, of agency within radical Western philosophy.

One of these critiques may be understood in terms of a paradoxical decentering and recentering of the West. This critique is both made and can be extended through a series of highly nuanced claims all of which take as their starting point Gayatri Spivak's observation that poststructuralist theory is caught in a double bind of simultaneously announcing the end of the subject and, to borrow an expression from O'Hanlon, "sneaking through the back door" the West as Subject (O'Hanlon 1988, 189–224). The first of these claims may be thought in terms of what Clifford has characterized as a hermeneutical posture of suspicion wherein Spivak reads against the grain of poststructuralist theory of the decentered subject. In "Can the Subaltern Speak?" Spivak begins a devastating critique of the theory by observing: "Some of the most radical criticism coming out of the West today is the result of an interested desire to conserve the subject of the West, or the West as Subject. The theory of pluralized 'subject-effects' gives an illusion of undermining subjective sovereignty while often providing a cover for this subject of knowledge. . . . The much-publicized critique of the sovereign subject thus actually inaugurates a Subject" (Spivak 1994, 66).

A companion critique of poststructuralist theory made by Spivak may be understood as the self-reification of the West as sole speaking subject that ironically speaks about the death of speech (particularly of the critical intellectual). (Spivak's criticism may also be extended to make the polemical claim that the recentering of the West as Subject is attended and rendered possible by the decentering of the margins as subject-less—spaces without subjects—conceptualized in its double session as both people who have been subjected and people who become subjects).[8]

Importantly, Spivak calls attention to the temporal location of the emergence of the paradoxical poststructuralist theoretical and political dissolution and restoration of the Western subject. In political terms, the moment may be thought as the West's simultaneous negation and reification of its own subjecthood, on the back of the decentered subject-less margins, at precisely that conjuncture when the historical moment is imbued with the material effects of the exorbitance of the Western self *once* realized both as a philosophical discourse about the West as the sole agent and author of world history and politics and narcissistic political discourse about the Western self as being superior to the colonized other.[9] Historically speaking, the moment may be thought as post-colonialism and neo-colonialism/neo-imperialism attended simultaneously by a reckoning with the devastating effects of colonialism and global capitalism and the attendant international division of labor. Spivak observes of the theory: ". . . ignores the international division of labor, a gesture that often marks poststructuralist political theory. . . . the subject-production of worker and unemployed within nation-state ideologies in its Center; the increasing subtraction of the working class in the periphery from the realization of surplus value and thus from 'humanistic training' in consumerism; and the large-scale presence of paracapitalist labor as well as heterogeneous structural status of agriculture in the Periphery" (Spivak, 1994, 67).

Taken together Spivak may be extended to make the claim that such a perverse paradox works in the service of reifying the West as a subject which is ironically a non-agent as it is also a non-subject. On the other side of postcolonialism and global capitalism, the West remains a chimerical subject-effect/subject that cannot be held accountable for subjection against subaltern peoples.

The second interrelated postcolonial critique may be organized under the rubric of the twin impulse and imperative of deferral/disavowal

within poststructuralism.[10] This critique is critical to Edward Said's genealogical *ouevre Orientalism* where Said makes a compelling critique of
poststructuralist theoretical privileging of the omniscience and omnipo-
tence of Western discourses and institutions that results in the deferral
and disavowal of Western individual agency. To elaborate, while Said
draws quite extensively from Michel Foucault's notion of discourse in
mapping the discursive field and network of colonial institutions that
produced knowledge of colonial others, Said also distances his analysis
from the theoretical evacuation of the acting individual or author which
underpins a Foucauldian theory of discursive regimes. In other words
Said opposes the notion that the author is dead.

Said makes the incisive observation that a critique of the production of
knowledge about the Orient through the nexus of power/knowledge
must account for both the strategic formation of the texts and intertextual
relations that repeat the self-other binarism at both latent and manifest
levels and strategic location of the discourse including "the author's position in a text with regard to the Oriental material he writes about . . ."
(Said 1979, 22). The rationale for such an analytical framework may be
understood when Said definitively observes, "Yet unlike Michel Foucault, to whose work I am greatly indebted, I do believe in the determining imprint of individual writers upon the otherwise anonymous collective body of texts constituting a discursive formation like Orientalism"
(23). The authorial imprint is then realized as both authorial style and
voice. The textuality of authorship is then articulated to the materiality of
discourse within the field of power/knowledge through critical scholarship so as to map the effects of such a formation upon the other.

On the basis of these critiques of poststructuralist theory, critiques that
recuperate an authorial style and voice within a discursive-institutional
formation and signal the imperative of accountability in terms of the
agents and subjects of domination and subjugation in a global matrix of
power relations, I turn to the problem of judgment.

Judgment and the Problem of Agency/Accountability

I ironically return to poststructuralist, particularly poststructuralist feminist, debates on agency. The reasons are two-fold. First, poststructuralist
feminist theory has grappled with the problem of women's agency. In explicating these debates and their theoretical resolution, I want to examine
how the restlessness over the question of agency has been evident in areas of inquiry within poststructuralist theory. Therefore explication of
these debates might enable a review of how the problem has been articulated by those who are committed to the tenets of the theoretical framework. Second, such an intellectual exercise, one that seeks to examine

prior inquiry into the problem of agency within poststructuralism, is meant to make a compelling case for productive engagements with post-colonial theory on the premise that such scholarly work will yield a more complex theoretical and political understanding and resolution of the problem of agency engendered by dominant and critical poststruc-turalisms. The latter is itself based on postcolonial scholarship which fig-ures the history of colonialism and complex theories of the subject into the humanities in ways that cannot make the resolution of agency a facile intellectual task. (My claim, one that I will shortly develop, is that femi-nist poststructuralism tends to resolve the problem of agency in reduc-tionist humanist terms).

The problem of agency has been felt and articulated within feminist poststructuralism (Alcoff 1988, 405–436; Weedon 1987, 152–163). While Alcoff addresses and resolves the problem of agency in explicitly stated metaphysical or ontological and performative terms through the position of positionality, Weedon addresses the political and emotional stakes of theorizing agency in terms of a similar notion of female or feminist agency as a choice among competing subject-positions. To reiterate, Al-coff advances the notion of gender as position to resolve the tension be-tween an essential feminine agent of cultural feminism and a constructed gender-less subject of poststructuralist theory, what is characterized as the "tendencies I have outlined toward essentialism and toward nomi-nalism represent the main, current responses by feminist theory to the task of reconceptualizing "woman" (Alcoff 1988, 421). Alcoff addresses this tension as it engenders the crisis over the identity of being a woman, particularly in terms of women's "politics and choices." Alcoff advances a notion of positionality to rescue feminism from the pitfalls of theories of essential femaleness and discursive subjectivity. The notion of woman as a position is meant to serve as corrective to the two erstwhile para-digms within feminist thought. Alcoff observes, "Therefore, the concept of positionality includes two points: first, as already stated, that the con-cept of woman is a relational term identifiable only within a . . . context; but, second, that the position women find themselves in can be actively utilized (rather than transcended) as a location for the construction for meaning" (428).

Weedon addresses the political stakes in moving to a notion of agency conceptualized as a choice between different positions of womanhood of-fered by discourses in society. Weedon argues that women are agents in a patriarchal society insofar as they are the bearers of particular discourses about womanhood and manhood. Therefore women may be seen to be agents of both the reproduction and resistance to power relations. Wee-don observes "We (women) may embrace these ways of being, these sub-ject-positions wholeheartedly, we may reject them outright or we may offer resistance while complying to the letter with what is expected of us" (Weedon 1987, 86). Weedon thus claims that the particular ways in which women take up subject-positions within discourses of womanhood can have the effect of reproducing and resisting patriarchy and more generally, power relations in society.

The problem with these accounts of female or feminist agency may be understood both in terms of what such a notion of agency includes and excludes from theoretical consideration. In terms of the politics of inclusion, in seeking to make a space for humanist notions of will, determination, self-definition, and action, both these notions of agency collapse the subject and the individual. In some ways, they end where they begin, with humanism. First, the language of "choice" is replete with notions of the individual who is discursively and materially liberated to make selections at will from a range of subject-positions offered by society. Second, the notion of the individual who is capable of constructing meaning rather than "discovering" meaning borders on the notion of the individual who is before language and originates consciousness and identity. In terms of exclusion, neither of these accounts address the implications of female positional agency for agency conceptualized as accountability for reproducing and in resisting power relations, in other words for judgment in the context of power relations.

My argument then is, in Spivak's terms, to interrupt the rather reductive treatment of the problem of agency with the notion of accountability so as to address the problem of judgment/agency/accountability in ways that do not reduce judgment to either humanist notions of the free-standing individual or poststructuralist notions of the discursive-institutionally constituted position.

Accountability is a *double entendre* which contains in its interrelated duality the possibility for addressing the question of judgment, which in this essay takes the specific form of the question or problem of agency. Accountability in the first sense may be thought within a matrix of power relations and as a critique of these relations. It is a performative mode in which others hold the self accountable for the relations of power that inscribe the self and other. In a related fashion, accountability is also a performative mode in which others hold other "others" accountable for reproducing the relations between self and other. (My use of the tropes "self" and "other" is deliberate based on the abstract power of these terms). The discourses of anti/post-colonial resistance may be said to embody an aesthetic of accountability wherein self-other power relations become the focus of critique and transformation (Fanon 1967, 41–82; Anzaldua 1987, 1–23). Postcolonial theories of the "ambivalent" subject, a notion advanced by Bhabha in his attempt to both rescue dominant and critical theorization of the colonial other as a dialectical and absolute other of the colonial self and historically figure the irreversible colonial traces upon colonial subjectivity, has done much to address the accountability of others among themselves. Bhabha observes: "Then the colonial mimicry is the desire for a reformed, recognizable Other, as a subject of a difference that is almost the same, but not quite. Which is to say that the discourse of mimicry is constructed around an ambivalence: in order to be effective, mimicry must continually produce its slippage, its excess, its difference" (Bhabha 1994, 86).

Preoccupied with the effects of colonial power upon colonial identity and resistance to colonial power through identity as mimetic repetition, Bhabha falls short of explicitly raising the question that is of relevance to this paper—judgment of the mimic. (The notion of accountability has been rhetorically addressed by Aijaz Mohammed who observes that the colonized have never had a "myth of primal innocence" about their identities and practices). Nevertheless Bhabha's argument can be said to anticipate the problem of mimicry as accountability for mimicking power by those who were once the object and effects of colonial normalization.

In its second sense, accountability may be thought within a matrix of resistance and social transformation. Here, accountability becomes a rhetorical mode in which we rhetorically produce accounts of the relations between individuals-discourses-institutions in ways that resist and transform power relations, in ways that hold individuals accountable for and within discursive and institutional relations of power. (Spivak would argue that the latter is the discursive domain of postcolonial intellectuals in the West). Accounts may take a myriad of rhetorical forms. They may involve diverse epistemologies—social scientific, rhetorical, literary, cultural, hermeneutic, interpretive, critical, legal, performative, and aesthetic modes of knowing. They may be articulated as axiomatic statements, experiments, arguments, metaphor, allegories, narratives, myth, genealogies, archeologies, pyschobiographical maps, verdicts, stand-up comedy, and art. In reading both these notions of accountability in tandem, one can respond to postcolonial critiques of poststructuralist theories of agency and hence resolve the problem of judgment that is made evident by these criticisms. Individual authors who repeat and reproduce institutions and discourses of power through their own styles and voices may now be conceptualized within a politics of accountability. Individuals may also become authors of accounts that produce and reproduce a politics of accountability in ways that transform the relations between selves and others.

However poststructuralist theory warns against a reductive humanist notion of accountability, one where individuals are judged for "their" choices, actions, and emotions. I therefore conclude the essay by gesturing towards a position from which we might engage in the performance and rhetoric of accountability. This position may be thought of as an epistemological position that ironically returns us to humanism albeit through the detour of poststructuralist and postcolonial theory.

Critical Ethical Humanism and Judgment

I place emphasis on the trajectory of the debate between humanism and poststructuralism which calls for a productive meshing of the two paradigms to produce a different position of knowing or *episteme* and political practice grounded in a critical ethical politics. This position and practice may be characterized as a critical ethical humanism. A critical humanism may be theoretically thought in terms of a poststructuralist reformulation rather than a rejection of the project of humanist theories of the subject and agent, the principles and politics of recognition and reflexivity.[11] (I say a reformulation rather than rejection both because poststructuralism runs the risk of theoretically undercutting itself if it poses the problem of humanism/poststructuralism as an either/or binary question and critical poststructuralism has been theoretically unable to completely eschew the discursive terms of humanism. Explicit acknowledgment of the theoretical problems that these debates have attempted to solve and review of the mode of their attempted resolution suggests that one may arrive at a different philosophical, theoretical, and political position than the either/or of humanism [risking the charge of theoretical "unhipness"] and poststructuralism [risking the charge of anti-humanism]).

This position of critical humanism theorizes human speech and action as being, to borrow a trope from Spivak, "irreducibly continuous" with discursive and institutional structures. Critical humanism may also be thought in terms of the intersecting concepts of recognition and reflexivity. Charles Taylor has nicely elucidated the concept of recognition as being critical to the search for a politics of resistance and transformation. Taylor observes: "The importance of recognition is now universally acknowledged in one form or another; on an intimate plan, we are all aware of how identity can be formed or malformed through the course of our contact with significant others. On the social plane, we have a continuing politics of equal recognition" (Taylor 1994, 81).

I take this notion of recognition in a different direction, away from authenticity and equality toward a different humanist epistemology. In other words, Taylor argues that what is critical to resistance and transformation is correcting the problem of misrecognition through recognition of identity. (Taylor's discussion is conducted in the context of internalization of deformed notions of selfhood by others in power-laden societies). I argue that the practice of recognition has relevance for a different humanism and therefore significant implications for judgment as accountability because within this new humanist *episteme,* judgment of humans ought to be guided by a politics of recognition of the irreducible continuity among humans, discourses, and institutions.

The concept of reflexivity has been defined by Hammersely and Atkinson as a particular feature of human action wherein the particular action continually calls attention to itself as such. According to Clifford reflexivity and epistemology exist as co-constitutive grounds, as reflexivity is the ground upon which humans come to know the world and knowing is the ground upon which human action-as-knowledge is reflexive. Reflexivity is an important concept within the *episteme* of critical humanism because it suggests that human judgment, as the space of accountability, cannot escape calling attention to itself as judgment and perhaps engenders judgment upon itself. In particular, an uncomplicated humanist position of judgment and/or a poststructuralist notion of the impossibility of judgment of humans *qua* humans call attention to themselves as either being produced through discourses within institutions in the case of the former and as being enacted by humans who are positioned within or against these discourses and institutions in the case of the latter. (I hesitate to use the term "outside" because of poststructuralist claims that there can be no "beyond" to discourse and institutions).

However, reflexivity is also theoretically important for a critical reformulation of humanism because it has a performative dimension to it which may be conceptualized in terms of self-reflexivity. Reflexivity signals the performative possibility of a self-reflexive practice of judgment. Such a practice of judgment might involve two concurrent actions. First, others are positioned within a space of accountability in ways that conceptualize continuity between individual and institutions through accounts. Second, the judging self is cognizant and perhaps deliberately calls attention to the ways in which the self is inscribed in a similar, yet different, set of constitutive relations involving the individual-institution axes and possibly through similar, yet different, accounts both within and without the context of judgment.

An ethical humanism may be best understood in terms of Young's summary of the intellectual critiques of the unethical excesses of modernist colonial humanism. Summarizing Sartre's Preface to *The Wretched of the Earth* Young makes two inter-related critiques. First Young argues that Western humanism was at best a contradiction because ideas of the ideals of humanness were generated at the same historical and political juncture as colonialism: "The formation of the ideas of human nature, humanity, and the universal qualities of the human mind as the common good of an ethical civilization occurred at the same time as those particularly violent centuries in the history of the world now known as Western colonialism" (Young 1990, 121).

Young encapsulates a related critique of humanism as being a contingent and partial humanism, ". . . the category of the human, however exalted in its conception, was too often invoked only in order to put the male before the female, or to classify others 'races' as subhuman, and therefore not subject to the ethical prescriptions applicable to 'humanity' at large" (123).In other words, Young argues that Western humanism was an intellectual project that was fraught with the binary of West/Other and human/non-human. The violent double play of human/non-human effectively rendered the project of Western humanism one that worked solely in the service of the West, by constructing the identity of the West as both human and superior in the great chain of (human) Being to non-Western ("non/sub") humans.

Young's critiques that may be read together as pointing to the evacuation of ethics within Western humanism, suggests the recuperation of ethics into humanism. Within ethical humanism, we may judge self and other within a discursive and material space of accountability by not starting at the premise or arriving at the inference that the other or self is sub- or non-human and therefore rejecting judgment of the other in terms that repeat the problems of humanism. Rather, the posture of ethical humanism is one which is characterized by a recognition that we are all humans. However an ethical humanism is only complete with its theoretical counterpart which is that of critical humanism. Thus an ethical humanist position might engender a practice of judgment that in seeking to redress the transgression of ethics by humans located within and by discourses and institutions accounts for these in the practice of judgment and in the process generates a different human-discourse-institutional continuum.

Critical Ethical Humanism in Contexts of Judgment

I return to the three domains of human judgment where such a position might register in the conduct of judgment. These include the theoretical, political, and existential domains of human judgment. The particular historical context within which I conceptualize critical ethical humanism in action is that of a context of human abjection, suffering, and pain—women and violence. I want to speak here about the woman who is figured by and figure of discourses of shame in the context of her experience of violence against her selfhood in the particular context of transnationalism and migrancy. I am specifically thinking about the woman who constructs her national, gender, and religious identity as a woman without shame; a shameless woman for ostensibly violating the discursive and corporeal codes of honorable womanhood because she has left the space of the home for shelter and spoken in public about the private in a different nation space—her husband and experience of domestic violence.

A critical ethical humanist analysis of judgment that is particularly directed towards an analysis of accountability for the reproduction of nationalist, patriarchal, and religious power relations through and by the woman who has experienced violence relations might begin by producing an analysis, an account, of the multiple discursive and institutional forces that have prevailed upon the identity of the woman to speak of herself as an other—a shameless woman/dishonorable woman. Such an account would map the vectors or lines of force among nationalist and religious discourses of honor and shame and ideal womanhood, familial discourses and practices of female childrearing, marital discourses and practices, popular cultural representations of women in the context of violence, national-religious communal discourses and practices in the context of violence, gender and nationalized economic and legal discourses and practices, political and cultural representations of natives and strangers, and the woman who experiences violence. The account points to diverse sites—human, discursive, and institutional—as reproductive of power relations and hence as sites of transformation of power relations. A typical analytical statement within the account may take the form of the critical social-scientific claim, "Battered women reproduce patriarchy" which would then be supported with evidence that juxtaposes the woman's discourses and practices with that of social discourses and institutions that position her (Supriya 1995, 244–259). The account might conclude with a critical component wherein transformative possibilities are examined through social scientific studies or literary criticism of Utopian allegories of change, revolution, social and human transformation.

The political dimension of critical ethical humanist judgment—of human accountability—in this context may be understood upon delineating two particular senses of the political. The first has been conceptualized by Grossberg, in the context of the intellectual practice of Cultural Studies, as the practice of intervention into a particular relation of power so as to transform it. My use of this particular inflection of the political is quite purposeful because it foregrounds the intellectual in the context of accountability, even though the practice of intervention can be said to have a broader interpretation extending to those domains where human actors confront power relations such as the reproduction of patriarchy by women who experience violence. The particular ways in which intellectuals can partake in a politics of accountability in this particular context may be articulated by critically extending Spivak's critique of the poststructuralist injunction against the speaking intellectual, to a similar context of power and silence. Spivak argues, metaphorically and empirically, that in the contemporary moment of post/neo-colonialism it is imperative for postcolonial intellectuals, located in centers of economic and political power, to speak for/about the subaltern who is located outside the

center and in its margins produced by economic and political coloniza-
tion. The battered woman, who has thus far been the empirical context
for my exploration of the possibilities for a critical ethical humanist approach to judgment as accountability, bears a metaphoric resemblance to
the subaltern who is the subject of Spivak's researches and her discursive
and material conditions are similar to the particular geo-economic-politi-
cal determinations adumbrated by Spivak. I say this because the woman
who experiences violence in a transnational migrant context is figurally
and empirically both located in the margins of the economic and political
institutions of the center and marginally positioned by discourses of
colonial or nativist constructions of the gendered other. On the premise
that postcolonial intellectuals in particular and the specific intellectual, in
a Foucauldian sense, in general may need to intervene in the particular
relation of power wherein the battered woman herself reproduces patriarchal power and the power of a social order on the margins of which she
is located (albeit *sans* intention) and that one such interventionist practice
may be that of making a judgment on accountability, I proceed to examine the relevance of the critical ethical humanist position for such a practice in this context. Intellectuals may practice a politics, in the interventionist sense, of accountability by speaking in a different and similar
sense than the one suggested by Spivak. In a different sense, Patti
Lather's discussion of a praxis approach to research is useful because it
illuminates how intellectuals, specifically as researchers, can engage in
dialogue with the other in the course of conducting research in power-
laden sites in ways that "encourage self-reflection and deeper understanding on the part of the persons being researched" (26). Intellectuals
may thus engage in a dialogue and meta-dialogue about accountability
with the other in ways that enable self-reflection about the human-dis-
course-institution-power relations continuum. Similar to Spivak's position of "speaking for the subaltern," critical intellectuals may produce accounts of accountability through political commentaries wherein the
woman who inflicts discursive violence upon herself is also positioned in
relation to the Center. Political actors such as activists and counselors, in
the context of domestic violence, may also position themselves in the political space of accountability through discursive and material practices
such as advocacy in the context of discourses of shame and honor and
therapeutic discourse such as counseling which focuses on accountability
in terms of the axis that has been discussed in this essay.

  The term political can also be nuanced through an ethical-legal discourse and in this sense is directly related to judgment. Drucilla Cornell's
sense of the ethical-legal imperative in terms of the good and right (or
conversely the not-good and not-right) is valuable as it suggests another
way through which self, others, discourses, and institutions can face each

other in the space of accountability in the context of domestic violence. (This dimension of the political becomes crucial when the context is extended to include the perpetrators of violence). How this particular political dimension of critical ethical humanism may be manifest is more the subject of the imagination than the other instances that have been the subject of this exploration. It may be spatially imagined in terms of a kinship-familial-communal model of judgment and the judge as a charismatic autocratic figure who is endowed with the ethical-legal authority to hold the human-discourse-institutional axis accountable. This may be done through the discursive production of accounts that may take the form of ethical-legal narratives and ethical-legal pronouncements of the good and the right, and their converse, in the context of violence and self-violence.

The importance of a critical ethical humanist position toward judgment as accountability is nowhere more felt than in the existential domain. Sartre's particular exposition of existentialism in terms of freedom from the world and responsibility for the world is edifying in this context, as the existential concept of responsibility of humans may be said to be the philosophical soulmate of accountability. As we live in our concreteness and act in the here- and- the-now of being and I might add becoming, we are continually faced with the capacity for human judgment and effects of human accountability on the one hand and on the other with the human, discursive, and institutional identities of ourselves and others. A critical ethical humanist position provides the philosophical conditions for the possibility for articulating one to the other in the conduct of quotidian life so that we may, in the process of judgment, exist in what Cornell calls a mimetic relation to our others, identifying with rather than as other.

I conclude on a critical ethical humanist note. The problem of judgment as in accountability is the problem of recognizing that humans and human actions are constituted in and through discourse and institutions, including those we may deem to be instances of irony, perversity, depravity, and cruelty. And it is precisely such a position that will also enable us to transform and liberate humanity from the excesses of both reification and disavowal of human agency.

Notes

1. Alcoff resolves the problem of displacement of agency by discursive determinism through a notion of "position" that is the space, experience, and human action constituted by the contradictory forces of discourses and willful human location against, within, and between discourses.
2. The latter leads to a politics of blaming the subject-individual in contexts where history, discourse, and material conditions considerably complicate reduc-

tion of social problems to the plane of human accountability. One example is the contemporary political controversy over women within the U.S. welfare state wherein women who are beneficiaries of welfare are held accountable for depleting the economic and physical resources of the state and taxpayers.(Pollitt 1994, 11).

3. There are many different ways of systematizing poststructuralist theory. Within the field of postcolonial theory itself there are markedly distinct inflections of poststructuralist theory; for e.g. Spivak foregrounds the concepts of the heterogeneity of the "power/interest/desire network" and the discourse of the Other while Bhabha places emphasis on the concept of the discursive constitution of colonial subjectivity through theories of ambivalence and hybridity. My paraphrase of poststructuralism abstracts the founding elements, prior to its historical extensions and extensions, which as I will shortly demonstrate engenders a theoretical and political crisis in power-laden contexts that require human judgment.

4. My move to circumvent postcolonial critiques of humanism is purposeful. The particular trajectory of this essay is meant to both avoid redundancy—as texts such as Robert Young's *White Mythologies: Writing History and the West* (1990) is a command postcolonial critique of humanism— and systematize arguments that are dispersed over a variety of theoretical and historical registers.

5. In this essay power, domination, subordination, intersecting axes of identity, and human suffering are treated as metaphoric and metonymic concepts.

6. An alternative conceptual formulation of this philosophical position is a poststructuralist humanism or a humanist poststructuralism. However I treat poststructuralism as equivalent with a critical and ethical intellectual project. (Further a synthetic approach has been rendered problematic within critical theory).

7. JanMohammed particularly wrestles with Bhabha's theory of the ambivalence of colonial discourse. However, this critical engagement is embedded within a more general critique of Bhabhas' rejection of Said's claim that in the colonial context the colonizer may be seen to possess colonial power over the other.

8. Another interpretation of Spivak's critique of poststructuralism is that the latter is itself a Western discourse that has been engendered at a particular historical juncture from particular institutional spaces by particular subject-individuals. (For if poststructuralism is taken to its logical extreme it begins to face its own limit as a social discourse. Spivak can be seen to interrupt the intellectual move to treat poststructuralism as a space outside of discourse and poststructuralist intellectuals as purveyors of a non-discursive truth about the subject).

9. The former argument is made by Snead and the latter by JanMohammed.

10. By deferral I do not mean a Derridean linguistic notion of *deferance*; rather I mean the word in a performative sense that might seize upon language as a vehicle for deferral of the question of accountability.

11. Both these concepts are arguably consonant with poststructuralist theory. As I will shortly demonstrate these concepts emerged in the humanities at the nexus of the confrontation among social scientific, humanist, and critical thought.

Bibliography

Ahmad, Aijaz. 1989. "Jameson's Rhetoric of Otherness and the 'National Allegory.'" *Social Text* 17: 3–25.

Alcoff, Linda. 1988. "Cultural Feminism versus Post-Structuralism: The Identity Crisis in Feminist Theory." *Signs: Journal of Women and Culture* 13: 405–36.

Anzaldua, Gloria. 1987. *Borderlands/La Frontera: The New Mestiza*. San Francisco: Aunt Lute.

Beiner, Ronald. 1983. *Political Judgment*. London: Methuen.

Bhabha, Homi. 1994. *The Location of Culture*. New York: Routledge.

Clifford, James. 1988. *The Predicament of Culture: Twentieth Century: Ethnography, Literature, and Art*. Cambridge: Harvard University Press.

Cornell, Drucilla. 1992. *The Philosophy of the Limit*. New York: Routledge.

Dickens, Charles. 1985. *The Mystery of Edwin Drood*. London: Penguin Classics.

Fanon, Frantz. 1967. *Black Skin, White Masks*. Trans. Charles Lam Markham. New York: Grove Weidenfeld.

Foucault, Michel. 1979. *Discipline and Punish: The Birth of the Prison*. Trans. Alan Sheridan. New York: Vintage.

_____. 1990. *The History of Sexuality, Volume 1: An Introduction*. Trans. Robert Hurley. New York: Vintage.

Grossberg, Lawrence. 1993. "Cultural Studies and/in New Worlds." *Critical Studies in Mass Communication* 10: 1–22.

Hammersley, Martyn & Atkinson, Paul. 1993. *Ethnography: Principles in Practice*. London: Routledge.

JanMohammed, Abdul. 1985. "The Economy of Manicean Allegory: The Function of Racial Difference in Colonialist Literature." *Critical Inquiry* 12: 57–88

John, Mary E. 1989. "Postcolonial Feminists in the Western Intellectual Field: Anthropologists and Native Informants?" *Inscriptions* 5: 49–74.

Khab, Mazhar Ul Haq. 1972. *Purdah and Polygamy: A Study in the Social Pathology of the Muslim Society*. Peshawar Cantonment: Imperial.

Lather, Patti. 1986. "Research as Praxis." *Harvard Educational Review* 56: 257–77.

Mani, Lata. 1992. "Cultural Theory, Colonial Texts: Reading Eyewitness Accounts of Widow Burning." In *Cultural Studies*, ed. Lawrence Grossberg et al., 392–408. New York: Routledge.

O'Hanlon, Rosalind.1988. "Recovering the Subject: Subaltern Studies and Histories of Resistance in Colonial South Asia." *Modern Asian Studies* 22: 189–224.

Pollitt, Katha. 1994. "Subject to Debate." *The Nation*, 11: 45.

Said, Edward. 1979. *Orientalism*. New York: Vintage.

Sartre, Jean-Paul. 1956. *Being and Nothingness*. New York: Washington Square.

Sawicki, Jana. 1991. *Disciplining Foucault: Feminism, Power, and the Body*. New York: Routledge.

Schacht, Richard. 1975. *Hegel and After: Studies in Continental Philosophy Between Kant and Sartre*. Pittsburgh: University of Pittsburgh Press.

Snead, James. 1990. "Repetition as a Figure of Black Culture." In *Out There: Marginalization and Contemporary Culture, ed.* Russel Ferguson et al, 213–232. London: MIT Press.

Spivak, Gayatri, C. 1990. *The Post-Colonial Critic: Interviews, Strategies, Dialogues*, ed. Sarah Harasym. New York: Routledge.

_____. 1994. "Can the Subaltern Speak?" In *Colonial Discourse and Postcolonial Theory: A Reader*, ed. Patrick Williams & Laura Chrisman. New York: Columbia University Press.

Sunderrajan, Rajeswari. 1993. *Real and Imagined Women: Gender, Culture, and Post-colonialism*. New York: Routledge.

Supriya, K. E. 1995. "Speaking Others, Practicing Selves: The Representational Practices of Battered Immigrant Women in *Apna Ghar* (Our Home)." *Women and Performance: A Journal of Feminist Theory*, 7–8: 241–266.

_____. "Confessionals, Testimonials: Women's Speech in/ and Contexts of Violence." *Hypatia: A Journal of Feminist Philosophy* 11: 92–106.

Taylor, Charles. 1994. "The Politics of Recognition." In *Multiculturalism: a Critical Reader*, ed. David Theo Goldberg, 75–106. Oxford: Blackwell.

Weedon, Chris. 1987. *Feminist Practice and Poststructuralist Theory*. Oxford: Blackwell.

Young, Robert. 1990. *White Mythologies: Writing History and the West*. London: Routledge.

3

Decentering Judgment

Toward a Postmodern Communication Ethic

Martha Cooper

At least since Aristotle, the intersection of politics, ethics and rhetoric has been an interesting location for scholarly investigation. From the perspective of Aristotle and his followers, communication was a means of influence, the power of which was more palatable if exercised from a position of virtue; virtuous rhetors could guide their audiences to judgment.[1] Postmodernity challenges this view by claiming power as inevitable and virtue as variable, thus questioning the very possibility of shared grounds for judgment. This essay responds to that challenge by proposing a model for communication ethics that includes, but decenters, judgment. The essay begins with a brief problematization of judgment as it relates to rhetoric and ethics in postmodernity. Then I elaborate a model for communication ethics. From a postmodern perspective, I argue that communication is a means of ethical action, necessitated by the fact that power is embedded in all interactions. Because both power and ethics are enacted through communication practices, those practices should become the focus for understanding the interplay between power and ethics. The model for a postmodern ethic is grounded in the primacy of discourse common to much postmodern thought; hence, I describe both the impulse for ethical action and alternative responses to such an impulse in communication terms. Following an illustration of the model, I turn once again to the concept of judgment and speculate about how a postmodern communication ethic can assist in reconceptualizing grounds for judgment.

Judgment and Rhetoric in Postmodernity

For centuries rhetoricians have taken for granted that the relation between rhetoric and judgment is one of means to ends. As Thomas Farrell explains, rhetoric is an act that "contests the realm of the problematic, even as it aims to facilitate judgment based on persuasion" (Farrell 1993, 33). Farrell's observation is based on a long tradition that views rhetoric as the practice of argument or persuasion, a practice that is assumed to facilitate a process of deliberation such that judgment can be rendered.[2] Aristotle, of course, distinguished among types of oratory by reference to the type of judgment[3] required of the hearers (Aristotle 1954, 1358b). As a *telos* of rhetoric, judgment provides a way to restore order to otherwise confusing and contentious situations in which alternatives proliferate and animosities among diverse points of view fracture communities and immobilize concerted action. Put simply, the judgments facilitated by rhetoric help people to decide on courses of action, to resolve disputes, to choose among alternatives. From classical and modern approaches to rhetoric, the function of judgment may be seen as variable, but the grounds for judgment are taken for granted as audiences are assumed to know and accept the values and first principles that motivate their actions.

Postmodernity poses a challenge because the very ground for judgments seems to have split apart beneath those who would judge. Richard Harvey Brown explains that if we take seriously the notion that reality is rhetorically enacted, then "it is harder to isolate any general or transcultural standards of judgment" (Brown 1994, 29). Clifford Christians observes that "in the late 20th century the paradigm of immutable and universal morality has been generally discredited. . . . Transhistorical certitude has been replaced by philosophical relativism, that is by the presumption that moral principles have no objective application independent of the societies within which they are constituted" (Christians 1997, 4–5). At best, the values and first principles serving as grounds for judgment appear to be partial, belonging only to specific times and places. At worst, such grounds for judgment seem only canonized preferences that secure the privilege of those who occupy positions of power. Christians continues: "Nihilism (no moral truths exist) and skepticism (moral propositions cannot be justified) are prevalent responses as well" (5).

While judgment is a primary telos for modern conceptions of rhetoric, many postmodern perspectives make emancipation, or social change, the primary end toward which rhetoric strives. From these perspectives, persuasion and practical argument are less important than critique or "critical rhetoric."[4] However, as numerous scholars have observed, effective critique requires some prior ground for judgment. From this view, grounds for judgment become the launching pad for critique, and without such grounds the emancipatory goal suffers. For example, Benhabib explains that "strong versions" of postmodernism "place in question the very emancipatory ideals of the women's movements altogether" and thus endanger the coherence of feminist critique (Benhabib 1992, 213). Similarly, Cloud argues that postmodern political theory, especially post-Marxism that is undergirded by "ethical and political relativism," removes important standards for judging political actions and thus renders critique impotent by obviating any such thing as "correct analysis" (Cloud 1994, 234). Thus, for the postmodern rhetorician, the problem posed by postmodernity is the potential loss of grounds for judgment from which to launch a critique.

Nowhere is the problem of the loss of grounds for judgment clearer than in discussions of communication ethics. Numerous scholars have addressed the problems for moral agency and ethical judgment that arise once postmodern perspectives that eschew universals are embraced (e.g., Benhabib1992; Baumann 1993; Caputo 1993; Flax 1995). Christians captures the problem in these graphic terms: ". . . how can we argue that bombing a federal building in Oklahoma City is wrong, that the wanton slaughter of Rwandese in a refugee camp is morally outrageous, that killing journalists in El Salvador is despicable, that ransacking the earth's ecosystem is evil? On what grounds are terrorists condemned for trying to achieve political ends by assassinations? How can we despise Hitler or praise the protectors of Anne Frank?" (Christians 1997, 16)

These questions make clear the discomfort we feel from postmodern turns toward relativism, nihilism, and skepticism and clarify the urgency many sense about recuperating grounds for judgment. They explain why those writing about recuperating judgment often find themselves writing about "moral obligation," "moral traditions," and the "ethics of rhetoric" (e.g., Benhabib 1992, 140; McDaniel 1993, 161; McKerrow, 1993, 120; Sloop and Ono 1993, 144).

It is tempting to recuperate judgment by returning to the classical notion of *phronesis*, or practical wisdom, developed by Aristotle and to argue that acceptable grounds for judgment will emerge from a rhetorical process. However, such a move overlooks the taken-for-grantedness of grounds for judgment in the classical tradition. As Charland points out, "*phronesis* is not the answer because it's limited to one community standard," that which benefits those who are privileged and in power (Charland 1991, 71–73). Still, some scholars advocate a universal ground for judgment that is rooted in rhetorical tradition; for example, Clark (1996) suggests embracing an Isocratean imperative "to serve the community" as the basis for rhetorically-informed critique in postmodernity. Still others believe that transhistorical "protonorms" do exist and thus advocate grounding judgment in a commitment to such human values (Christians 1997). Others advocate more transitory and perspectival bases for judgment to facilitate critique. Ono and Sloop maintain that "a commitment toward a contingent telos must exist as a sustained critical *praxis* for those engaging in critical rhetoric" (Ono and Sloop 1992, 48) and advocate making judgments on the basis of envisioned traditions, or consequences (Sloop & Ono 1993; Sloop and Ono 1997). Some advocate temporary and conditional adoption of the agendas of politically engaged groups such as women, people of color, or classic Marxists; Benhabib, for example, advocates acceptance of only a "weak" version of postmodernism and continued adherence to a feminist agenda (Benhabib 1992, 203–241).

Another alternative to recuperating judgment is to decenter judgment from the moral landscape—to suspend judgment, to set aside the need for grounds for judgment at least temporarily. Jane Flax (1995), for example, advocates "responsibility without grounds." She explains that "there may be more effective ways to attain agreement or produce change than to argue about truth," thus opening the possibility of ethical rhetoric that is neither grounded in nor aimed toward judgment (161). She continues: "Each person's well-being is ultimately dependent on the development of a sense of tolerance, empathy, friendly concern, and even benign indifference to others" (163). In a similar vein, Mark McPhail (1996) advocates a turn toward nonargumentative discourse as an ethical and moral response to postmodernity (124–128) even as he declares that "the issue most at stake in the debate between modernism and postmodernism [is] *judgment*" (125). This essay takes a similar tack.

While the urgency for rehabilitating the grounds for judgment in a postmodern world seem clear from Christians' questions, there is I believe a similar urgency for establishing the possibility of a postmodern communication ethic that is not tied exclusively to judgment. Put differently, I believe that we can at times benefit from suspending judgment—judging less frequently—and in so doing, we can also act as moral agents. To elaborate this argument, I advance a model for communication ethics (Figure 3.1) grounded in the primacy of discourse common to much postmodern thought. While the model includes a concern for judgment, I intentionally decenter judgment in order to open possibilities for ethical action that are not dependent on judging. In particular, I posit two alternatives that emerge less from traditional rhetorical frameworks that privilege judgment and more from contemporary postmodern and feminist perspectives for rhetoric that privilege identification, tolerance and empowerment. These alternatives to judgment are not necessarily substitutes for judgment; we may still wish to judge at times. On those occasions when judgment is desirable or necessary, aspects of the postmodern communication ethic I will outline may inform our judgment.

A Model of Postmodern Communication Ethics

Before detailing the model it is necessary to set the ground for the task at hand. My concern is with describing communication ethics, as distinguished from ethics of communication. While modernist conceptions of ethics might begin with principles drawn from religion, political theory, or other sources, a postmodern perspective toward ethics will begin with communication. Best and Kellner observe that postmodern theory generally privileges discourse as a philosophical starting point for understanding social interaction (Best and Kellner 1991, 26–27). Observing that reality is socially constructed through symbolic action, postmodern theorists investigate culture and society in terms of sign systems, their codes, and discourses. Foucault and others treat discourse and discursive practices as constitutive of knowledge, power, and ethics. Similarly, discourse becomes the site for struggles over meaning, power, and appropriate relations between self and other. The postmodern emphasis on discursivity—communication—thus provides a key for understanding ethics from a postmodern perspective. The central question is: what communication practices create ethics?

Central to my position is the persistent observation in postmodern thought that an ethical, or moral impulse—variously referred to as "obligation" (Caputo 1993; Lyotard 1988) or "conscience" (Bauman 1993; Hyde 1994) is inevitable. Such a sense of obligation, or call to conscience, occurs when the voice of an Other who is experiencing the repressive effects of power is heard (Levinas 1989).[5] The vortex for ethics thus is the call of a marginalized Other, an Other who has been consigned to such a narrow space of existence that he or she is oppressed. Perhaps the classic case of such a call is that of the Jews during the Nazi terror in Germany. Similarly, the plight of African-Americans subjected to discrimination or the stories of torture of women and members of political minorities throughout the world embody the call of the marginalized other. In more limited and sometimes less dramatic fashion, a simple request for help from an elderly person whose needs are neglected in the nursing home or a student whose creative ambitions seem stymied by the bureaucratic force of the university may constitute a calling. Moreover, we may experience an ethical impulse even when the oppressed Other is silent through either an empathic projection of a call from ourselves or through perception of a call from that small, still voice that many associate with the divine. For example, if we witness the hurling of a racial epithet or see the desecration of a cherished symbol, we may project a call from an unseen Other as we empathize with the pain they may feel. As we ponder the options of a child in the projects, or think of the unemployed man living in a once-booming but now-industrial-ghost town, or read about

Marginalized Other
(Calling)

Discourse Ethic
(Questioning)

Deliberation
Argument
Judgment

Ethic of Care
(Responding)

Empathy
Narrative
Identification

Ethic of Resistance
(Affirming)

Detachment/Connection
Ritual Celebration
Tolerance/Empowerment

FIGURE 3.1   Dynamics of Postmodern Communication Ethics

the plight of a battered wife, or consider the desolation of a child caught in a custody battle, we may sense that "something is not right," that "something needs to be done." That sense acts as a call from the marginalized Other.

How to answer that call of the Other, how to widen the space in which and from which the Other exists, is the fundamental problem of communicators who wish to act ethically. Postmodern thought suggests three alternatives: a *discourse ethic*, an *ethic of care*, and an *ethic of resistance*. The first two ethics—a discourse ethic and an ethic of care—are responsive to the call of the marginalized Other and have as their telos the empowerment of that marginalized Other. However, these two ethics are vulnerable to the inevitable will to power recognized by postmodern perspectives. Hence, a third ethic of resistance is necessary to temper potentially elitist effects of these first two ethics. An ethic of resistance functions to empower a marginalized Other by allowing that Other to create/recreate the self. These ethics entail three distinct communication practices—*questioning, responding,* and *affirming*—that at their best empower the marginalized Other but if used excessively merely perpetuate or recreate disempowered relationships. I will examine each alternative in turn, commenting on its potential for answering the call as well as the dangers associated with its excess.

Discourse Ethic: Questioning

A *discourse ethic* answers a call by encouraging *questioning*. By suspending taken-for-granted assumptions—what some call "questioning" (Porter 1993; Scott 1990) and others term "skepticism" (Bauman 1993)—postmodern critics answer the call of conscience and enact their obligations. Following the work of Nietzsche, Foucault, and Heidegger, Scott argues that ethical thinking takes place through questioning: "a process of thinking that diagnoses, criticizes, clarifies by means of questions, destructures the components of meaning and power that silently shape our lives together, and also questions the values and concepts that have rule-governing and axiomatic power in our culture" (Scott 1990, 7–8). The notion that questioning can advance the cause of ethics by inhibiting blind obedience to predominant values reflects a belief that "the postmodern perspective . . . means above all the tearing off of the mask of illusions; the recognition of certain pretenses as false and certain objectives as neither attainable nor, for that matter , desirable" (Bauman 1993, 3).

Questioning embodies an ethical guideline that advises communicators to subject all assumptions to scrutiny, to take nothing for granted without probing its implications. To ensure such an exercise of skepticism, communicators are advised, among other things, to avoid polemics (Foucault 1984b), to gain access to the data banks (Lyotard 1984), and to construct an ideal speech situation (Habermas 1975) in which any statement may be analyzed for its intelligibility, truth, truthfulness, and appropriateness. The discourse ethic is appealing for its scope of advice. It elevates the ethical potential of one genre of discourse (argument) while condemning another (polemic). It elaborates guidelines for evaluating the substance of talk (comprehensibility, truth, truthfulness, and appropriateness) that would allow easier assessment of what is and is not ethical. It even provides suggestions for how to reconstruct contexts for communication such that ethical discourse will more likely take place (provide open access to information). Thus, the communicative practice entailed by questioning is argument, a practice that is assumed to lead through a process of deliberation to judgment.

But almost from the start, a discourse ethic loses its luster because of its ambiguous relationship to the ethical impulse of responding to the Other. On its face, a discourse ethic responds to the Other only indirectly by questioning the oppressor. At its best, a discourse ethic would ensure equal access and opportunity for all interested parties to engage in questioning, thereby combating oppression by analyzing prevailing assumptions. As Benhabib (1992) suggests, in a postmodern world short on universal truths but brimming with diversity, deliberation in the form of dialogue is essential for arriving at judgments that take into account multiple perspectives. However, as I have argued elsewhere, too often the powerless are excluded from the sphere of discourse in which such questioning may occur, silenced by the absence of ideal speech situations (Cooper, 1991). Perhaps this is so because questioning every background assumption is a luxury rarely afforded oppressed people. Perhaps only the privileged have the time and resources to deconstruct, analyze, and endlessly question. Moreover, a commitment to questioning sometimes can fall into an infinite regress and symbolically annihilate those subject to questioning thus seeming less a call to conscience than a leap into nihilism. If the only check against such a move is the civility offered by something like Habermas' ideal speech situation, then we must question the grounds for appropriateness. Can these be other than predominant values of the privileged? Again it seems that the discourse ethic cannot escape the power of privilege.

An Ethic of Care: Responding

Another alternative that emerges is a more direct response to the call of the Other, an *ethic of care* that emphasizes *responding* rather than questioning. An ethic of care counsels concern for human relationships that can be enacted by reaching out for, and responding to, an Other with compassion and love (Noddings 1984; Kristeva 1986; Gilligan 1987; Wood 1994). Emerging from feminist approaches to communication and moral development and in accordance with standpoint theory, an ethic of care extolls the communication practices of marginalized groups. Responding is a practice of the subordinated—requiring little in the way of elite resources, but involving specific skills. Wood explains that "entailed in being responsive are specific abilities, including deciding to focus on another, responding to others as a means of affirming their presence and value, and listening and observing carefully in order to discern what it is that another means by her or his behaviors" (Wood 1994, 107). Hence, communicators are advised to listen and to paraphrase, to encourage the Other to tell his or her story. Narratives evoked through responsiveness provide a basis for understanding and action that are rooted in the everyday experience of relationships. Sullivan and Goldzwig explain that a feminist postmodern ethic "foregrounds the role of personal experience, context, and relationships in moral decision-making" (Sullivan and Goldzwig 1994, 204). By sharing stories and empathizing, communicators ultimately achieve a state of identification that promotes connection and community. At its best, the responsiveness of an ethic care confers a voice on the oppressed Other, using "the power of presence" to hear him or her into speech (Cooper 1994). Thus the communicative practice encouraged by responding is narrative, a practice that leads through a process of empathy to a state of identification.

Responding, however, can be just as problematic as questioning when it functions to further a disparity in power. With the role of caregiving comes the potential for a certain degree of power as the recipient of care becomes dependent on the caregiver for nurturance and support. A respondent may maintain a certain critical distance, encouraging another to talk, while remaining silent about his or her story. By hearing the Other into speech, the respondent may become the confessor, investing him- or herself with the mystique and interpretive power that frequently accompanies that role (Black 1988; Foucault 1988). At its extreme, "the gentle touch of love becomes an iron grip of power" (Bauman 1993, 103). In responding to the Other, the caregiver's maternal or paternal impulses can smother the Other. Foucault (1981) described this as the domination typical of pastoral power; Bauman explained that it blackmails its objects into obedience while lulling its agents into self-righteousness (Bauman 1993, 103).

Both questioning and responding are ethical communication practices that can alter prevailing power relationships. In the case of questioning, the superior in a superior-subordinate relationship is subject to scrutiny thereby potentially narrowing a disparity of power. In the case of responding, the subordinate in a superior-subordinate relationship receives attention again providing a potentially equalizing effect. However, both practices can also exacerbate power imbalances either by reinforcing elitist values and denying legitimacy to others in the case of a discourse ethic, or by establishing a relationship of obedience and authority between the Other and the one who responds in the case of an ethic of care.

An Ethic of Resistance: Affirming

One way to avoid the domination that can result from either excessive discourse (questioning) or excessive care (responding) is by following a third *ethic of resistance* that encourages *affirming*. An ethic of resistance calls for maintaining a space for subjects to position themselves as freely choosing subjects even in the face of oppressive practices and discourses that threaten to marginalize or otherwise constrain them. Foucault advanced the notion of resistance in his discussions of power and ethics (Foucault 1980; Foucault 1984a; see also, Richters 1988, 627; Biesecker 1992, 356–358). Laclau and Mouffe (1985) develop the idea of resistance in their discussion of radical democracy. To assert and maintain a posi-

tion that is larger or more central than that offered by an oppressor requires detachment from the oppressor (a sort-of disobedience) as well as
some attachment or connection to a life force both outside and within the
self. Caputo describes disobedience: "Sometimes responding to the call
of the Other requires the most searing, disturbing disobedience to the
law" (Caputo 1993, 120). Starhawk describes the impact of disobedience:
"Systems of domination are not prepared to cope with fearlessness, because acts of courage and resistance break the expected patterns"
(Starhawk 1987, 14). She continues, however, by describing a second
sense of resistance as creation: "Creation is the ultimate resistance, the ultimate refusal to accept things as they are" (26). An ethic of resistance is
thus concerned with how subjects constitute themselves, especially with
how one creates or recreates a self that is not defined or positioned by an
oppressor (Foucault 1984a; Rajchman 1986; Cooper 1991, 40–43). Foucault's chronicle of technologies that create the self are suggestive of particular communication practices that create resistance (Foucault 1988).
Similarly, Nancy Fraser's discussion of "needs talk" as a form of resistance is useful (Fraser 1989, 161–187). Common to both is the notion that
resistance depends on communication practices that are communal and
self-affirming.

When we affirm the self by reference to other relationships we illustrate what might be called the intertextuality of the self. Affirmation occurs in personal rituals (e.g., journalling, praying, meditating, actually
saying affirmations). Affirmation also occurs in collective rituals (e.g.,
singing "We Shall Overcome," marching, participating in a candlelight
vigil, engaging in liturgical demonstrations that emphasize connection to
the divine, engaging in pagan rituals that demonstrate connection to the
earth). While the power *to* resist may emerge from ritualistic communication practices that celebrate the self or connection of self with the divine,
the power *of* resistance emanates from its communal nature. Starhawk
explains that "the dispossessed, to survive, . . . know the power of the
common bonds of culture, of song, of ritual, of drum and dance, of heal-
ing to sustain hope and strength to resist oppression" (Starhawk 1987,
18). To avoid the sullenness and hyperactivity encouraged by the decline
of modernity, Borgmann advocates a postmodern turn to "genuine celebration"—celebrations that reflect reality, community, and divinity
(Borgmann 1992, 126–138). Resistance ultimately leads to tolerance and
empowerment. This is so because when otherwise marginalized people
resist they gain a voice and in doing so present their alterity within the
world; they are empowered and difference is by necessity tolerated.
Borgmann underscores this idea in his description of a satisfying postmodern community: "If there is a universal principle of postmodern political discourse, it can only be this: Let everyone speak in the first per-

son, singular and plural" (Borgmann 1992, 144). Similarly, McPhail rests his case for a rhetorical education on "the importance of having a voice, and the ability to tolerate the opinions of others" (McPhail 1996, 132). Thus, affirming entails a communicative practice I term ritual celebration that works through a paradoxical process of detachment and connection, leading eventually to tolerance and empowerment.

Elsewhere, I have explained how an ethic of resistance can correct for the flaws of a discourse ethic by placing primary emphasis on what type of subject is created through discourse that emphasizes questioning (Cooper 1991, 40–43). Does discourse create a participative citizen? Or a passive client or disinterested observer? An ethic of resistance can work similarly as a corrective for the excesses of an ethic of care. Porter explains that ethics have to do with positioning, and advises that "an important component" of a postmodern ethic is that "it has to be especially sensitive to the ways in which communities can marginalize as well as provide identities for individuals" (Porter 1993, 218–219). The pivotal question for caregivers becomes: how do I position the one to whom I respond? Does my responsiveness create a dependent subject who is beholden to my authority or does my responsiveness create an autonomous subject who may exercise choice and is capable of influencing the caregiver?

Despite its corrective potential, however, an ethic of resistance can impede empowerment if its practices are taken to extremes. Preoccupation with self affirmation can divert attention from structural change that may be promoted by the questioning common to a discourse ethic. Dana Cloud warns that "collective, public struggle is subverted" by new age, resistance theory because "its spiritual idealism leads to a definition of action as withdrawal and isolation" (Cloud 1994, 236–237). She continues: "Instead of taking the power discovered through consciousness-raising practice (whether it be individual or group) and organizing a confrontation with the state or corporation, on this argument one simply waits for everyone to come to the same realization, and automatically the world will be a better place" (237). While actual disobedience, as suggested by Caputo (1993) and Starhawk (1987), probably avoids this problem, it is possible for an ethic of resistance to result in withdrawal and isolation. Turning toward the divine and connecting with a like-minded community may produce a homogenous and parochial outlook that insulates one from the call of Others who are not part of that self-affirming community, thus subverting sensitivity to diversity that is so common to postmodern perspectives generally. That sensitivity to difference, of course, returns our attention to the call of the marginalized Other.

There is a dynamic tension between the three ethics common to postmodernism. We may think of that tension in terms of a pyramid (as illustrated in Figure 1). The vortex for ethics is the call of a marginalized

Other. That call may be answered either by a discourse ethic that questions prevailing values or an ethic of care that responds to the Other. In the move away from the Other and toward the questioning of dominance common to a discourse ethic, the potential for an Other to assert him- or herself may be limited. On the other hand, in the move toward the Other encouraged by the responsiveness of an ethic of care, the caregiver may assume a position of privilege. A third ethic, one that may be practiced by the Other her- or himself is necessary to check the movement of either the questioner or the responder. That ethic is an ethic of resistance; it provides a base for the pyramid. Within such an ethic, the Other both resists dominant values that oppress or marginalize and resists positioning that maintains privilege and subordinates the Other. Enacting such resistance empowers the Other by creating or recreating a self that is no longer defined or positioned by someone else. Communication practices that manifest disobedience to prevailing values and positioning *and* create the self anew thus become the focus of an ethic of resistance. The ethical imperative for all interested parties is to attend to what types of selves are created through communication when we respond to the call of the Other.

Illustration of the Model: Sexual Harassment

Sexual harassment is a distinctly communicative practice shot through with ethical questions. There can be little doubt that sexual harassment is a communication practice in that harassment occurs when a perpetrator engages in a set of communicative behaviors that are experienced and interpreted by a victim as offensive. Leaving aside the question of legality, harassment also entails ethical considerations. For the perpetrator, there is an overlooked ethical obligation (assuming that we agree that harassment is an unethical display or assumption of power). For the victim, there is an experienced breach of ethics. For the casual or practiced observer, there are questions about how to react to an incident of harassment. Moreover, harassment is a communication practice that is particularly useful for examining postmodern ethics in that it pivots around the issue of power. A harassing act functions so as to render the receiver powerless while playing on the power of the sender. If a receiver experiences harassment, he or she feels smaller, reduced, marginalized as a human being, as if his or her range of choice as a human being is limited. If another witnesses such a reduction, that other may feel the pain of the marginalized person almost as if the victim had called out in pain. Hence, in that moment of reduction and marginalization, a call—voiced or silent—is emitted that seems to demand attention.

Consider the following example. Standing in the department office, I overhear a colleague telling our secretary about his class that day. His voice is proud; his face is smiling: "I gave my class good advice today. We were listening to business reports. One of the students—a real, good-lookin' girl—ended her report with her address and phone number. When she sat down, I said, 'I hope you men wrote that number down. It may be the only way any of you will ever get that number, and she just gave it to you for free.'"

He is clearly self-satisfied. Our secretary smiles weakly. I bristle. In the instant it takes for me to turn to leave, I make a complicated ethical choice. During a series of fragmentary moments of self-reflection over the next few days, I examine that choice. It was a choice surrounded by issues central to communication ethics. It was a choice that easily illustrates the model for a postmodern ethic described earlier.

I easily interpreted my colleague's pronouncement to his class as harassment even though I had no contact with the woman I projected to have been victimized. Immediately upon hearing the story, I had assessed it as a story about sexual harassment. My colleague was clearly responding to his female student largely on the basis of her sex and attractiveness rather than her intellectual abilities or competence. He was calling attention to her romantic/erotic availability in a way that likely embarrassed her and reinforced the different and unequal status of women and men in his class. His language positioned her as an immature "girl" and his male students as mature "men." His comments, addressed to "you men," clearly excluded any other women in the class and manifested a heterosexist bias to boot. As professor he clearly occupied a position of power and authority in his classroom, while his students—especially his female students—were consigned to a narrow and disempowered position as objects of romantic pursuit. Moreover, the plot and structure of his story invited our (female) secretary and me to experience a similarly disempowered position if we retained our identities as "woman" as we listened, thus extending the reach of his initial act to create a sexist environment outside his classroom as well. In short, I had heard a call that begged for response.

We can now explore how each of the three ethics described above can come into play regarding sexual harassment generally and in regard to this particular case. The *discourse ethic* recognizes the power imbalance in the event and questions the background assumptions regarding gender relations. Any particular instance of sexual harassment necessitates calling the offender's communicative behavior into question, questioning what is taken for granted. A system of adjudication featuring deliberation about who can say what to whom with what effect comes into play, leading eventually to judgment about who was harmed and how to correct the wrong. In the case described earlier, I could have called the question in a number of ways. I might have asked: "Why did you treat your student that way?" "Have you ever suggested that the women in your class take down the phone number of a particularly attractive male?" "Are you assuming that attractiveness is more important for women than for men?" And so on. We might have engaged in dialogue about gender roles in the classroom. We might have argued about whether or not this was a case of harassment. We might have reached some judgment together. The student in question had apparently not called the question. Though she might have, the obvious power differential between her and her professor made such action unlikely. Perhaps at a later time, in the office of the Ombudsman, she might file charges and thereby initiate a questioning process; but such an act is unlikely and underscores the lack of an ideal speech situation. I am in a better position to question, but of course I am a woman and I have less seniority and I am reasonably sure that dialogue will be less likely than polemic should I initiate questioning. Instead, I imagine inventive ways in which I might question more generally, and apart from this particular incident, thus showing a preference for another ethical alternative.

An *ethic of care*, on the other hand, recognizes the pain of the victim by listening to the story of the victim (in actuality or in an observer's imagination), providing a safe place wherein the story may be told. In the narration one begins to empathize and through the sharing of story the experience is named and thus becomes an object for care and consideration. Eventually, the result is identification with the victim such that the problem of harassment is given voice. By hearing the call and sharing stories, a connection (empathy) is made with the one who called. While the student in this case was not present, I could imagine the caring role easily. There have been plenty of similar cases in which I heard the story from the student's point of view. I would listen, offer my support, probably ask the student if there was anything she wanted me to do that might be helpful. Perhaps I would even share a similar incident from my own experience. We would bond, at least to some degree, and the student would leave happier than she had arrived. If I was competent as a listener, the aggrieved student would feel respected and repositioned into a more powerful location. As I imagine how I might have cared, I enlarge the space occupied by the victim who was belittled through the harassment of my colleague and renew my commitment to respect my own students. But, the student is not here. I could lend an ear to my secretary who seemed to express at least temporary pain at my colleague's story, but the caring alternative seemed limited in this case.

The *ethic of resistance* recognizes the hurt of harassment and finds a way to resist the harassment by detaching from the harasser while at the same time finding connection to others or to the divine such that the self is empowered. The receiver of the harassing message resists the positioning provided by the harasser and assumes a different stance. To find an alternative stance, the receiver must find a position vis-a-vis some connection other than that provided by the harasser. I have no way of knowing whether the student in this case resisted. Nor do I know if our secretary resisted. But I am intimately familiar with my own resistance. As I returned to my office, I thought about my colleague, an older man from a different generation who probably thought he was being charming by openly complimenting his student. While I knew that I could call his behavior into question, I knew that for me to continue to interact collegially with him I needed to take care of myself rather than trying to discipline him. I needed to decenter judgment from my horizon of moral action. I also knew that my sense of self did not depend on him. I reminded myself of my worth, that I was mature and a whole person who could not be diminished easily. And I reminded myself that I was a woman—not a disempowered, marginalized inferior person, but a mature, empowered woman. I knew I would just keep being my professional self, sometimes questioning, sometimes responding, probably always being enigmatic to my colleague. I was able to remind myself of these matters in part because of my connection to communities of women and concepts of the divine that regularly rehearse my self worth and the self worth of others.

My analysis in this case has thus far concentrated on my ethical choices as one who hears the call. The same ethical choices are available, at least to some extent, to the one who calls; however, her most likely option is resistance. She could call the question by bringing charges (discourse ethic) or she could seek comfort with a sympathetic listener who might share her pain (ethic of care), but regardless (and especially if neither of these resources are available), the receiver must gather herself via resistance. Her resources for resistance are in affirmations, typically provided through ritual that celebrates her connection to the divine or to a community of similarly situated people. To accomplish such affirmation, she must detach from the pain-projection of the harasser (which will be called again into existence should she decide to bring charges) and from the concrete care of an other (which may leave her dependent on that other's warmth and support). Instead, the receiver must find for herself way(s) to resist. If she brings charges that still gives power to the harasser; if she seeks comfort that gives power to her comforter. She also probably wants just to be (apart from either relationship—negative with the harasser or positive with the comforter). The way to call herself into being is resistance that recreates herself as empowered.

What is the "right" thing to do when you are harassed? All three ethical responses are useful. Sometimes we can bring charges, sometimes we can seek comfort, sometimes we can avoid/detach by affirming our worth in other venues. Calling the question may move toward structural change. Empathizing helps to break the spiral of silence. Resisting may enhance tolerance and allow us to get along while *actively* presenting difference. So resistance may be a way of acting without a telos of change. All three are necessary in the long run of accumulated events, life spans, and cultural periods. However, in the moment of any particular episode of interaction, one of these responses may be more fitting than another; what a shame if we were to ascribe moral force only to one of them!

Conclusion

A postmodern approach does not abandon ethics in favor of power, but recognizes that because power is inevitable so is an ethical impulse. Once we recognize that power and the potential for oppression is afoot, we can respond to the call of the Other with communication practices that offer the possibility of reconfiguring the relationships between the center and the margin, between the oppressed and their oppressors, between ourselves and others. The postmodern emphasis on discourse suggests three alternative and interconnected approaches to ethics. The *discourse ethic* answers a call by encouraging *questioning*. The communicative practice entailed by questioning is *argument*, a practice that is assumed to lead through a process of *deliberation* and to lead to *judgment*. However, making judgments is not the only route to ethical behavior in a postmodern world. We can pursue other ends and still embody ethical actions, still check the power of oppression. The *ethic of care* answers a call by encouraging *responding*. The communicative practice entailed in responding is *narrative*, a practice that leads through a process of *empathy* to a state of *identification*. The *ethic of resistance* answers a call by encouraging *affirmation*. The communicative practice entailed in affirming is *ritual celebration*, a practice that works through a paradoxical process of *detachment* and *connection* leading eventually to *tolerance* and *empowerment*.

Understanding these three ethics and their attendant communication practices provides a means for moral action that includes, yet goes beyond, judgment. In other words, there exist possibilities for moral action that do not entail judgment—namely in those actions that promote identification, tolerance, and empowerment. However, in those cases where judgment is still preferred, the workings of these three ethics may offer some insight for reformulating the grounds for judgment in a postmodern world. As explained at the beginning of this essay, the very problem posed for judgment by postmodernity is the recognition of multiple perspectives in place of universal truths. Benhabib observes that, "If there is one commitment which unites postmodernists from Foucault to Derrida to Lyotard it is the critique of western rationality as seen from the perspective of the margins, from the standpoint of what and who it excludes, suppresses, delegitimizes, renders mad, imbecilic or childish" (Benhabib 1992, 14). This postmodern concern for multiple perspectives is at the heart of the impulse for ethical action described in this essay. That impulse suggests the importance of the Other, and thereby implies a value for perspectives other than our own, especially perspectives that are marginalized. This value accorded to the Other, to multiple perspectives, can supply a basis for judgment in a postmodern world. However, as Benhabib observes and Clifford Christians explains, to embrace such a value as a basis for postmodern judgment requires recognition of that value as an intentional commitment rather than as an immutable truth.[6] The postmodern commitment to the Other, then needs to be understood as just that—as a commitment; any other grounds for judgments thus also rest on intentional commitments rather than universal truths.

While a commitment to the Other and thereby to multiple perspectives is primary, the three ethics described earlier suggest other possible commitments that might ground judgment from a postmodern perspective. While typically a discourse ethic suggests a commitment to civility, an understanding of the dangers of a discourse ethic may encourage commitment to accessibility and equality. While an ethic of care commonly carries a commitment to compassion, the dangers of excessive care may encourage commitment to mutuality and reciprocity. And while an ethic of resistance pivots around commitments to self and community, its dangers suggest possible commitments to action and engagement.

In her discussion of postmodernity, Jane Flax explains, "To take responsibility is to situate ourselves firmly within contingent and imperfect contexts, to acknowledge differential privileges of race, gender, geographic location, and sexual identities, and to resist the delusory and dangerous recurrent hope of redemption to a world not of our own making" (Flax 1995, 163). We need not cling to modernist universals nor leap into nihilistic rejection of all judgment. Nor must we always seek judgment as the only means of moral action. As this essay suggests, there are other moral options when we find ourselves in those imperfect and contingent contexts described by Flax. When we are the ones who hear the call of distress, we may question those in charge or comfort those in distress or join those in distress through communal celebration that promotes tolerance and empowerment. When we are the ones in distress, we may choose to go into battle by calling the question or we may seek relief by asking for comfort, but always we must bolster ourselves and resist oppression by affirming ourselves. When we are not in distress we can be open to question, be willing to care, and be ready to engage with the voice within and with others. Our choices of which action to take can be grounded in a commitment to respect and value the Other and the multiple perspectives represented by the Other.

Notes

1. I am using the term "judgment" here to signify an act of forming an opinion after deliberation. Such acts may include determinations on moral grounds as well as formal opinions issued by authorities invested with special powers (e.g., the judiciary, religious officials, etc.); however, I do not intend to limit the definition of judgment to those special cases. I understand judgment to be a communication act that is declarative and expressive and that depends on a prior communication process most usually described as deliberative. Although this essay does not address the notion of judgment as a quality (e.g., "she has good judgment; he has poor judgment"), it may be helpful to note that persistent engagement in the act of judging may lead to impressions about one's judgment.

2. I use both terms (argument and persuasion) here only to signal to the reader an inclusive orientation that could treat these terms interchangeably. I do not intend to perpetuate either the conviction/persuasion duality common to eighteenth century scholarship or the reason/emotion dichotomy common in many twentieth century treatments of rhetoric. I do intend to suggest that rhetorical theorists have typically conceived of rhetoric as occurring through the use of arguments that engage both mind and heart and aimed to influencing both belief and behavior.

3. Aristotle distinguished deliberative from forensic oratory on the basis of the type of judgment required of hearers. He noted that epideictic oratory placed hearers in the role of observer rather than judge, an important distinction that reveals judgment is not the only legitimate end for rhetorical discourse. For an interesting treatment of the ends of rhetoric in both the Classical and contemporary periods, see Ceccarelli 1997.

4. Perhaps this is clearest in the case of McKerrow's notion of "critical rhetoric." McKerrow argues that the task of the rhetorician is "to constantly challenge the status quo to be other than it is," to enhance "the possibility of change through critique," both critique of domination—ideology critique—and critique of freedom—self-reflexiveness about power in everyday relations (McKerrow 1989; McKerrow 1991, 75).

5. Following Buber, Freire, and Levinas, Christians (1997) locates our obligation to the Other in the primal experience of relationships, an experience that he asserts exists in contraposition to modernist dichotomies and an experience that elevates the sacredness of life to a protonorm (7–8).

6. Christians (1997) uses the term "protonorm" to refer to a transhistorical commitment that can serve as the basis for ethical judgment. He advances the notions that life is sacred and relationships are central as constitutive of a protonorm of human solidarity. According to Christians, without such a "protonorm on behalf of human solidarity, history is but a contest of arbitrary power" (16).

References

Aristotle. 1954. *Rhetoric*. Trans. W. Rhys Roberts. New York: Modern Library.

Bauman, Zygmunt. 1993. *Postmodern Ethics*. Oxford: Blackwell.

Benhabib, Seyla. 1992. *Situating the Self: Gender, Community, and Postmodernism in Contemporary Ethics*. New York: Routledge.

Best, Steven, and Douglas Kellner. 1991. *Postmodern Theory: Critical Interrogations.* New York: Guilford.

Biesecker, Barbara. 1992. "Michel Foucault and the Question of Rhetoric." *Philosophy and Rhetoric* 25: 351–364.

Black, Edwin. 1988. "Secrecy and Disclosure as Rhetorical Forms." *Quarterly Journal of Speech* 74: 133–150.

Borgmann, Albert. 1992. *Crossing the Postmodern Divide.* Chicago: University of Chicago Press.

Brown, Richard Harvey. 1994. In "Reconstructing Social Theory after the Postmodern Critique." *After Postmodernism: Reconstructing Ideology Critique.* Eds. Herbert W. Simons and Michael Billig. 12–37. London: Sage, 1994.

Caputo, John D. *Against Ethics: Contributions to a Poetics of Obligation with Constant Reference to Deconstruction.* Bloomington: Indiana University Press, 1993.

Ceccarelli, Leah. 1997. "The Ends of Rhetoric: Aesthetic, Political, Epistemic." *Making and Unmaking the Prospects for Rhetoric.* Ed. Theresa Enos. 65–74. Mahwah, NJ: Erlbaum.

Charland, Maurice. 1991. "Finding a Horizon and *Telos*: The Challenge to Critical Rhetoric." *Quarterly Journal of Speech* 77: 71–74.

Christians, Clifford. 1997. "The Ethics of Being in a Communications Context." *Communication Ethics and Universal Values.* Eds. Clifford Christians and Michael Traber. 3–23. Thousand Oaks, CA: Sage.

Clark, Norman. 1996. "The Critical Servant: An Isocratean Contribution to Critical Rhetoric." *Quarterly Journal of Speech* 82: 111–24.

Cloud, Dana. 1994. "'Socialism of the Mind': the New Age of Post-Marxism." *After Postmodernism: Reconstructing Ideology Critique.* Eds. Herbert W. Simons and Michael Billig. 222–251. London: Sage.

Cooper, Martha. 1991. "Ethical Dimensions of Political Advocacy from a Postmodern Perspective." *Ethical Dimensions of Political Communication.* Ed. Robert E. Denton, Jr. 23–47. New York: Praeger.

_____. 1994. "Postmodernism, Feminism, and the Ethical Subject." *Conference Proceedings of the Third National Communication Ethics Conference.* Ed. James A. Jaska. 305–308. Annandale, VA: SCA.

_____. 1997. "A Feminist Glance at Critical Rhetoric." *Making and Unmaking the Prospects for Rhetoric.* Ed. Theresa Enos. 99–106. Mahwah, NJ: Erlbaum.

Farrell, Thomas B. 1993. *Norms of Rhetorical Culture.* New Haven: Yale University Press.

Flax, Jane. 1995. "Responsibility without Grounds." *Rethinking Knowledge: Reflections Across Disciplines.* Eds. Robert F. Goodman and Walter R. Fisher. 147–167. Albany: SUNY Press.

Foucault, Michel. 1980. *The History of Sexuality.* Trans. Robert Hurley. New York: Vintage.

_____. 1981. "Omnes et Singulatim: Towards a Criticism of 'Political Reason.'" *The Tanner Lectures on Human Values II.* Ed. Sterling M. McMurria. 225–254. Salt Lake City: University of Utah Press.

_____. 1984a. "On the Genealogy of Ethics: An Overview of Work in Progress." *The Foucault Reader.* Ed. Paul Rabinow. 340–372. New York: Pantheon.

_____. 1984b. "Polemics, Politics, and Problematizations." Trans. Lydia Davis. *The Foucault Reader.* Ed. Paul Rabinow. 381–390. New York: Pantheon.

_____. 1988. "Technologies of the Self." *Technologies of the Self: A Seminar with Michel Foucault*. Eds. Luther H. Martin, Huck Gutman, and Patrick H. Hutton. 16–49. Amherst: University of Massachusetts Press.

Fraser, Nancy. 1989. *Unruly Practices: Power, Discourse and Gender in Contemporary Social Theory*. Minneapolis: University of Minnesota Press.

Gilligan, Carol. 1987. *In a Different voice: Psychological Theory and Women's Development*. Cambridge: Harvard University Press.

Habermas, Jurgen. 1975. *Legitimation Crisis*. Trans. Thomas McCarthy. Boston: Beacon.

Hyde, Michael J. 1994. "Conscience and Rhetoric." Paper presented at Third National Communication Ethics Conference. Gull Lake, MI. 15 May 1994.

Kristeva, Julia. 1986. "Stabat Mother." Trans. Leon Roudiez. *The Kristeva Reader*. Ed. Toril Moi. 160–186. New York: Columbia University Press.

Laclau, Ernesto, and Chantal Mouffe. 1985. *Hegemony and Socialist Strategy*. Trans. W. Moore and P. Cammack. London: Verso.

Levinas, Emmanuel. 1989. "Ethics as First Philosophy." Trans. Sean Hand and Michael Temple. *The Levinas Reader*. Ed. Sean Hand. Oxford: Blackwell.

Lyotard, Jean-Francois. 1984. *The Postmodern Condition: A Report on Knowledge*. Trans. Geoff Bennington and Brian Massami. Minneapolis: University of Minnesota Press.

_____. *Peregrinations: Law, Form, Event*. New York: Columbia University Press.

McDaniel, James P. 1993. "Responsibilities: Speculations on Rhetoric and the Ethico-Political in Postmodernity." *Argument and the Postmodern Challenge: Proceedings of the Eighth SCA/AFA Conference on Argumentation*. Ed. Raymie E. McKerrow. 159–161. Annandale, VA: SCA.

McKerrow, Raymie E. 1989. "Critical Rhetoric: Theory and Praxis." *Communication Monographs* 56: 91–111.

_____. 1991. "Critical Rhetoric in a Postmodern World." *Quarterly Journal of Speech* 77: 75–78.

_____. 1993. "Overcoming Fatalism: Rhetoric/Argument in Postmodernity." *Argument and the Postmodern Challenge: Proceedings of the Eighth SCA/AFA Conference on Argumentation*. Ed. Raymie E. McKerrow. 119–121. Annandale, VA: SCA.

McPhail, Mark Lawrence. 1996. *Zen in the Art of Rhetoric: An Inquiry into Coherence*. Albany: SUNY Press.

Noddings, Nel. 1994. *Caring: A Feminine Approach to Ethics and Moral Education*. Berkeley: University of California Press.

Ono, Kent A., and John M. Sloop. 1992. "Commitment to *Telos*—A Sustained Critical Rhetoric." *Communication Monographs* 59: 48–60.

Porter, James E. 1993. "Developing a Postmodern Ethics of Rhetoric and Composition." *Defining the New Rhetorics*. Eds. Theresa Enos and Stuart C. Brown. 207–226. Newbury Park, CA: Sage.

Rajchman, John. 1986. "Ethics after Foucault." *Social Text* 13/14: 165–183.

Richters, Annameik. 1988. "Modernity-Postmodernity Controversies: Habermas and Foucault." *Theory, Culture, and Society* 5: 611–43.

Scott, Charles E. 1990. *The Question of Ethics: Nietzsche, Foucault, Heidegger*. Bloomington: Indiana University Press.

Sloop, John M., and Kent A. Ono. 1993. "Futuring Traditions: Making Postmodern Judgments." *Argument and the Postmodern Challenge: Proceedings of the Eighth Annual SCA/AFA Conference on Argumentation.* Ed. Raymie E. McKerrow. 143–148. Annandale, VA: SCA.

_____. 1997. "Out-law Discourse: The Critical Politics of Material Judgment." *Philosophy and Rhetoric* 30: 50–69.

Starhawk. 1987. *Truth or Dare: Encounters with Power, Authority and Mystery.* NY: HarperCollins.

Sullivan, Patricia A., and Steven R. Goldzwig. 1994. "Constructing a Postmodernist Ethic: The Feminist Quest for a New Politics." *Differences That Make a Difference.* Eds. Lynn H. Turner and Helen M. Sterk. 203–211. Westport, CO: Bergin & Garvey.

Wood, Julia T. 1994. *Who Cares: Women, Care, and Culture.* Carbondale: Southern Illinois University Press.

4

Judgment and Jouissance

Eliot, Freud, and Lacan Read Hamlet

Susan Schwartz

"The intense feeling, ecstatic or terrible, without an object or exceeding its object, is something which every person of sensibility has known; it is doubtless a subject of study for pathologists."
—**T. S. Eliot (1919, 146)**

"After all, the conflict in Hamlet *is so effectively concealed that it was left to me to unearth it."*
—**Freud (1942, 126)**

"It would be excessive, perhaps, if I were to say that the tragedy of Hamlet took us over the entire range of those functions of the object. But it definitely does enable us to go much further than anyone has ever gone by any route."
—**Lacan (1959, 29)**

"It's *not* my mother!"(Freud 1984, 437). So says the analysand in Freud's essay "Negation" when she repudiates his suggestion that the person in her dream is indeed her mother. The inversion of the statement, an act of judgment on the patient's behalf, gives Freud access to her unconscious. The patient's rejection of the analyst's interpretation provides him with a clear indication of the "not-me" that has been repressed. In this discussion of T. S. Eliot, Freud and Lacan's readings of *Hamlet*, I will be exploring the relation between negation and the textual unconscious as it appears at the moment of literary judgment. Their failure to account for the function of Hamlet's mother in the play both determines their literary judgments, and indicates the change in the position of the maternal/feminine in the shift from a modernist to a postmodern aesthetic. Freud, Eliot, and Lacan stake their authority on putting meaning in the place of the inexpressible: law and order in the place of the unknowable desire of the mother. In each literary judgment there is a negation of the maternal figure in the play which points to the repressed content of the critical text.

Freud argues in "Negation" that judgment is the effect of two stages in the process of decision making. The first stage determines whether something possesses or does not possess a particular attribute. Here judgment is under the auspices of the pleasure principle. The original pleasure-ego wants to take into itself the good and expel the bad. The second stage of decision-making tests whether or not something exists in reality. Developing out of the pleasure-ego, the definitive reality-ego decides whether a representation in the ego can be rediscovered at the level of perception in the external world. Judgment leads from thinking to acting. The precondition and aim of reality-testing for the subject is to refind an object that has been lost, an object that has once given him real satisfaction. A negative judgment is "the intellectual substitute for repression . . ." (Freud 1984, 438), according to Freud. The symbol of negation is the means by which the subject can liberate himself from both his subjection to the unconscious and the imperative of the pleasure principle.

Where Freud explores the relation between pleasure and reality, Lacan opposes pleasure and jouissance, the term that denotes exactly the excessive excitation, the painful pleasure, that the pleasure principle aims to prevent.[1] Pleasure is the product of a decrease in tension and is thus on the side of the law that is grounded in the prohibition against incest. In contrast, jouissance in its very excessiveness, its lack of limit, is disruptive and anxiety provoking. Lacan asserts in *The Ethics of Psychoanalysis* that the fundamental desire is incestuous, the pre-oedipal subject's desire for the mother, for the jouissance sited in her body (Lacan 1992c, 67). For this reason, jouissance is located in the Other and the pleasure principle functions to ensure that the "desire for the mother cannot be satisfied because it is the end, the terminal point, the abolition of the whole world of demand, which is the one that at its deepest level structures man's unconscious" (Lacan 1992c, 68).

In other words, the prohibition against incest is the very condition of speech.[2] In order to take up his place in the symbolic order the subject must sustain a loss by renouncing a mythic enjoyment. The prohibition against incest (Lacan's Name-of-the-Father) that institutes symbolic law produces desire in the place of lack, and desire, like pleasure in this instance, functions as the barrier to jouissance. If pleasure is on the side of the symbolic and meaning, jouissance is on the side of the real and the unspeakable. The primary effect of the signifier is to repress the (maternal) thing that promises the subject fulfillment. The paternal metaphor (the Name-of-Father) must take the place of the unknowable, intolerable desire of the mother. But this process always produces a residue, something that cannot be represented. In these readings of Shakespeare's play, a jouissance associated with Hamlet's mother is that which cannot be represented. It functions as the limit to literary judgment.

For generations of critics, *Hamlet* has been considered an unruly text. Critical response to the play points to the incoherence of literary judgment. For example, in his essay on *Hamlet*, Coleridge testifies to the enduring fascination of the play which, he suggests, is derived from the "inconsistencies" (Coleridge 1951, 457) evident in Hamlet's character and behavior. Coleridge notes the divide in Hamlet between "the impressions from outward objects and the inward operations of the intellect" (457). He refers to the "unpleasant perplexity" of the queen's character (472), but above all, his emphasis falls on something "out of its place" (467) in the play. This dislocated element suggests a symptom, a return of the repressed which is a site of both jouissance and anxiety. The literary judgments under discussion here double as diagnoses and employ a rhetoric of pathology. They are determined by complementary desires: to regulate (what exists in reality and what does not) and to exclude that which is perceived to be in excess (what to take in and what to expel). There is a residue remaining after the operation of judgment upon the text, an incompatible idea that literary judgment represses.

Freud, Eliot and Lacan's discussions of *Hamlet* were published in 1900, 1919 and 1959 respectively. A certain anxiety of influence informs the desire for originality that impels the essays. Each writer self-consciously unveils truths about the play which, he maintains, no previous commentator has seen. Freud discusses *Hamlet* in his seminal work, *The Interpretation of Dreams*. As the inversion of *Oedipus Rex* the play is integral to the founding myth of psychoanalysis. Eliot was in the early stages of his career as critic and his essay on *Hamlet* (originally entitled "Hamlet and his Problems") was included in his first collection of essays, *The Sacred Wood*. Only Lacan was already well-established when he tackled *Hamlet* in the 1958–59 Seminar VI, *Desire and its Interpretation.* It is pertinent to note that this was synchronous with the papers "The Signification of the Phallus" (1992a) and "Guiding Remarks on a Congress on Feminine Sexuality" (1982a), the latter considering the relation of feminine sexuality to language. Each reading focuses in very specific ways on the constitution of gendered subjectivity and on the nature of desire in the play. David Harvey's comment that "modernity and postmodernity derive their aesthetic from some kind of struggle with the *fact* of fragmentation, ephemerality, and chaotic flux" (Harvey 1989, 117) is pertinent to both the tension between judgment and jouissance in these analyses and to a change in the coordinates of judgment in the shift from the modern to the postmodern.

Where Eliot would like to find in *Hamlet* the unique but alienated self of high modernism and concludes that his inability to do so is Shakespeare's failure, Lacan sees in the figure of Hamlet a divided subject

mortgaged to the signifier. Freud bridges the positions. Insofar as he locates the founding myth of psychoanalysis in the repressed of the play
and employs it as a support for the scientific nature of psychoanalysis, he
can be seen to belong to revolutionary modernism. But despite this valorization of science and his claim for universality, Freud's discoveries
clearly opened the way for a postmodern understanding of sexuality as
representation. Even so, each literary judgment finds its limit in relation
to a specifically maternal jouissance. The interpretation of the position of
the mother in the play is thus a crucial determinant not only of the readings but of the changing place of the maternal/feminine in modern and
postmodern criticism.[3]

Eliot's modernist aesthetic of unity and universality demands that
tragedy should be "intelligible, self-complete, in the sunlight" (Eliot
1972a, 144). This is cause enough for him to recoil from the disordered
maternity he sees in *Hamlet*. The contaminating effect of the mother femi-
nizes the play in the sense that it fractures the unity of the drama. While,
as Koestenbaum notes, "Fantasies of maternity buttress male modernism" (Koestenbaum 1989, 122), these are fantasies of male birth which
doubly exclude the feminine.[4] In Eliot's judgment, Shakespeare's language fails to adequately represent Hamlet's relationship with his
mother. She is the traumatic maternal "thing" who rends the fabric of
tragic fantasy. For Freud, it is the peculiarity of the task that is the problem. Hamlet cannot kill Claudius because he identifies with him in his
desire for Gertrude. Lacan points to another peculiarity—the ghost's insistence that Hamlet not harm his mother when avenging his father's
murder—and he focuses on the relations of Hamlet, Gertrude and Ophelia to the phallic signifier. While the mother is cast as an omnipotent
Other in the play, for Lacan *Hamlet* is a tragedy of mourning for the phallus as lost object, a tragedy played out at one remove in Hamlet's relation
to Ophelia. Lacan is concerned primarily with the phallus and its relation
with fantasy and desire. This focus is compatible with modernist preoc-
cupations, but Lacan's discussion anticipates the importance that jouissance and the disruptive presence of the real in the symbolic will have in
his later work.[5] It is noteworthy that of the three writers, only Lacan directly addresses the language of the play.

Eliot: Feminizing *Hamlet*

In his essay "The Perfect Critic," published the year after "Hamlet," Eliot
explicates the fundamental relation that informs his critical rhetoric: the
interdependence of judgment and the aesthetic. In "a really appreciative
mind," Eliot writes, perceptions "form themselves as a structure; and
criticism is the statement in language of this structure; it is a develop-

ment of sensibility" (Eliot 1967a, 15). This statement exemplifies the function of judgment in which the ego of the critic is shored up by the dual processes of the affirmation of perception and the denial of that which is threatening. Indeed, negation is Eliot's critical mode. For him, judgment functions as a means of expulsion. He draws attention to *Hamlet*'s defects and his acerbic reference to Shakespeare's inadequate characterization of the mother terminates his analysis. The weakness in the play is structural: the drama is unbalanced for the emotion it generates exceeds the facts as they are given. Hamlet is immobilized by his disgust at the evidence of his mother's desire. She is too present in the effect of her guilt and not present enough in terms of her significance, inciting an excess of response in Hamlet which her negative status does not warrant. Eliot's judgment, impelled by a desire for critical mastery, for an objective and thus consistent aesthetic, asserts both the failure of Shakespeare's imagination—"why he attempted it at all is an insoluble puzzle" (1972a, 146)—and the ineptitude of prior interpretations.[6]

Critical judgment is referred to as an *admission* in the opening sentence of Eliot's brief essay on *Hamlet*: "Few critics have ever admitted that *Hamlet* the play is the primary problem, and that Hamlet the character only secondary" (Eliot 1972a, 141). Eliot's rhetoric suggests that the truth of *Hamlet*'s deficiencies as drama has been concealed by critics. He distinguishes himself from the aberrant judgments of his illustrious forbears, Goethe and Coleridge, valorizing instead minor critics who, following the example of seventeenth and eighteenth-century commentators, focus on the play rather than its protagonist. Eliot asserts that *Hamlet* is "superposed upon much cruder material which persists even in the final form" (142). His negative assessment of Shakespeare's play is unequivocal: *Hamlet* is "an artistic failure" (143), and the terms in which he makes his judgment are telling. Unlike any other of Shakespeare's works, *Hamlet* is "puzzling, and disquieting" (143); it has "superfluous and inconsistent scenes" (143); "versification is variable" (143) and "Both workmanship and thought are in an unstable position" (144).

In his diagnosis of the play's pathology, Eliot institutes a new critical term: the "objective correlative": "The only way of expressing emotion in the form of art is by finding an "objective correlative;" in other words, a set of objects, a situation, a chain of events which shall be the formula of that *particular* emotion; such that when the external facts, which must terminate in sensory experience, are given, the emotion is immediately evoked" (Eliot 1972a, 145).

Eliot's deployment of a quasi-scientific rhetoric as legitimization for literary judgment has, as its corollary, the exclusion of the maternal/feminine, for that is the locus of the inexpressible. The commensurate relation between object and emotion is guaranteed by the master signifier "objective correlative." It closes the gap between internal and external, a function that is fundamental to Freud's understanding of judgment.

The scientific aesthetic supporting Eliot's dismissal of *Hamlet* is grounded in a fantasy of mastery and is couched in a gendered rhetoric that permeates Eliot's critical writings. In "Tradition and the Individual Talent" for example, Eliot maintains that it is through the depersonalization of the artist—his "self-sacrifice"—"that art may be said to approach the condition of science" (1972b, 17). He compares the creative process to a chemical experiment in which the poet's mind functions like a catalyst, forming new substances but leaving no trace of itself in their production. As if illustrating the scission between judgment and jouissance, Eliot writes: "the more perfect the artist, the more completely separate in him will be the man who suffers and the mind which creates" (18). Eliot's act of division is in fact a suturing. In this negation of the body of the artist— a body, like the textual body, that is feminized in opposition to the masculine mind—Eliot places the poet on the side of unity and universality.[7] The self that Eliot considers to be beyond the pale of poetry is the unconscious self; his formula is informed by a desire to keep the repressed in its place. Eliot's aesthetic judgment is buoyed by a modernist fantasy of science which enables the critic to participate, in full consciousness, "in the common pursuit of true judgment" (Eliot 1972c, 25).

The objective correlative Eliot elaborates in *"Hamlet"* is a move toward producing a formula that will "cover everything I wished to include, even if I included more than I wanted" (Eliot 1972c, 31). The desire for such an encyclopedic formula is a defense against the lack of control he saw evidenced both in *Hamlet* and in earlier critical responses to the play. For Eliot, the perfect poet-critic is the ideal father who can master both his desire and the feminized text in the making of "correct" aesthetic judgments. Eliot's critical practice exemplifies Harvey's observation that "Modernism . . . became preoccupied with language, with finding some special mode of representation of eternal truths" (Harvey 1989, 20); that modernists were concerned with locating "the true nature of the unified, though complex underlying reality" (30). This concern with control is fundamental to Eliot's criticism and its persuasive power is derived from his appeal to quantifiable "fact."

Why did Eliot choose *Hamlet* as both the vehicle for his correction of other poet-critics, and as the arena for the explication of the objective correlative and the promulgation of his literary doxa? Eliot's formula orders the literary text. It provides a structure which acts as a barrier against an unruliness associated with the maternal/feminine. For Eliot, Shakespeare "takes a character apparently controlled by a simple emotion, and analyses the character and the emotion itself. The emotion is split up into its constituents—and perhaps destroyed in the process" (Eliot 1967b,

168). This is the flaw in *Hamlet*. The play "is full of some stuff that the writer could not drag to light, contemplate, or manipulate into art" (Eliot 1972a, 144). But Eliot's criticism of the play is directed precisely at that "stuff." Something *has* been "dragged to light" and he finds it repugnant. For Eliot, there is a contaminant in the play, an exposed secret that is inexpressibly linked to the desire of the mother.

In Eliot's judgment, *Hamlet*, that feminized text fails because "Hamlet (the man) is dominated by an emotion which is inexpressible, because it is in *excess* of the facts as they appear" (Eliot 1972a, 145). Such a formulation suggests an unsymbolizable jouissance associated with the maternal. Eliot justifies his judgment by referring to Gertrude as too "negative and insignificant" (146) a character to arouse the degree of repulsion that Hamlet experiences. Hamlet's disgust exceeds its object; he cannot understand his feeling; he cannot objectify it and thus he cannot put it into words. There is even more at stake in this judgment. Eliot correlates Hamlet's "bafflement at the absence of objective equivalent to his feeling" and Shakespeare's "bafflement . . . in the face of his artistic problem" (145). Shakespeare cannot express the particularity of Hamlet's emotion in art for it is "inexpressibly horrible" (146). Similarly, Eliot's analysis is stalled. It terminates in the expression of horror at that which cannot be spoken. For Eliot, modernist mastery of the word is founded on the appropriation of literary creation by a scientific aesthetic. This relegates the mother and her traumatic desire to the repressed of the critical text.

Freud: Hamlet's Neurosis

In "Creative Writers and Day-Dreaming," Freud describes the "essential *ars poetica*" as the artist's "technique of overcoming the feeling of repulsion in us [the effect of the revelation of the artist's phantasies in his work] which is undoubtedly connected with the barriers that rise between each single ego and the others" (Freud 1985b, 140). That is, our pleasure in a work of art is contingent upon the artist's ability to disguise his phantasies and to present them within a formal aesthetic, a position resonant with Eliot's. For Freud, the "enjoyment of an imaginative work proceeds from a liberation of tensions in our minds" (141), an enjoyment under the auspices of the pleasure principle and thus dependent upon a clear barrier being drawn between the self and the artist/other. Freud foreshadows that this is not a complete answer to the question of the relation of pleasure to art but it offers insight into Eliot's reading of *Hamlet* and his application of the objective correlative. The "unpleasure" that *Hamlet* gives to Eliot appears to be an effect of both a return of the repressed, and an encounter with Shakespeare's failure to regulate his fantasy within a formal aesthetic. This failure disturbs the boundary between work of art and reader. Shakespeare's fantasies—like the fantasies of Freud's day-dreamer—carry the taint of shame. This shame, associated in Eliot's reading with the abject figure of the mother, threatens to contaminate the reader.

Suzanne Clark argues very persuasively for Freud's profound influence on the modernists' understanding of sexuality and the divided self. She locates an anxiety in Freud about the desire of the mother, one which leads to her repression in psychoanalytic theory. While agreeing that the mother is a site of anxiety for psychoanalysis, I will argue that Freudian theory develops in relation to the enigma of feminine sexuality: "What does woman want?" This is particularly evident in Freud's interpretation of *Hamlet*. The mother is the figure who determines all other relations and while maternal jouissance is the unspeakable limit of Eliot's judgment, it is the unspoken presence in Freud's analysis. The mother is significant because she is prohibited. Where Eliot imposes a formulaic grid upon the text in order to diagnose its disorder, Freud finds in *Hamlet* an order that affirms his formula for the Oedipus complex.

In his first exegesis on the play in *The Interpretation of Dreams*, the coordinates of Freud's judgment are clear. His reading both reiterates the truth of psychoanalytic principles and demonstrates the way psychoanalysis illumines the literary text. Freud reads *Hamlet* as an affirmation of the experience of the adult psychoneurotic who, as a child, was in love with one parent and hated the other (Freud 1965, 294). He confirms his analysis by reference to *Oedipus Rex*. This play's "universal power to move" is explained by Freud in terms of the validity of his hypothesis concerning the psychology of children (294). Demonstrating Freud's scientific modernism, the chain of events that unfolds in *Oedipus Rex* can be reduced to the status of a formulaic relation between three terms: "It is the fate of all of us, perhaps, to direct our first sexual impulse towards our mother and our first hatred and first murderous wish against our father" (296). Freud refers to the frequency with which male adults dream of having sexual relations with their mothers (297–98). Such dreams, he notes, are "accompanied by feelings of repulsion, so too the legend must include horror and self-punishment" (298). This is the limit of pleasure, the jouissance that irrupts in *Hamlet*, and Freud explains the difference between Shakespeare's treatment of the theme of the child's unconscious wish and Sophocles's, in terms of "the secular advance of repression in the emotional life of mankind" (298). What is made overt in *Oedipus Rex* is repressed in *Hamlet* and we are only alerted to the concealed element in the play though Hamlet's inhibitions.

Freud is intrigued by the way that critics "have remained completely in the dark as to the hero's character" (Freud 1965, 298), failing to correctly interpret Hamlet's motives. Their blindness is counteracted by psychoanalytic insight. Like Eliot, Freud rejects previous critical readings, including Goethe's, and posits his own: "the peculiar nature of the task" (299) is the cause of the problem. Hamlet cannot take vengeance on Claudius because, through taking his father's place with his mother, Claudius confronts Hamlet with the realization of the repressed wish of his childhood. As a result, "revenge is replaced in [Hamlet] by self-reproaches" (299). This "fact" confirms Freud's rather reluctant diagnosis of Hamlet's hysteria, based on the "distaste for sexuality"(299) revealed in his conversation with Ophelia. In this context, Freud draws an equivalence between Hamlet and Shakespeare, "For it is of course only the poet's own mind which confronts us in Hamlet" (299). But where Eliot uses this identification to indicate Shakespeare's failure as an artist, for Freud—like Coleridge—it speaks to Hamlet's (and Shakespeare's) universality.

Freud returned to *Hamlet* in his sketch "Psychopathic Characters on the Stage," written in 1905–6. Here he reaffirms his earlier reading, placing a particular emphasis on the universality of the repressed impulse evident in Hamlet that enables the spectator to identify with him: "it is easy for us to recognize ourselves in the hero: we are susceptible to the same conflict as he is" (Freud 1985a, 126). That is, the *masculine* spectator identifies with Hamlet's identification with Claudius's desire for Gertrude. There is a significant refinement to his interpretation here. Freud maintains that "a necessary precondition for this form of art [is] that the impulse that is struggling into consciousness, however clearly it is recognizable, is never given a definite name; so that in the spectator too the process is carried through with his attention averted and he is in the grip of his emotions instead of taking stock of what is happening" (126).

In connecting, at the point of unconscious identification, an unnamed impulse in the play with an incompatible and thus repressed impulse in the spectator, Freud is positioning the play as a distraction from a traumatic encounter with the unknown, that is, with unconscious desire. The truth of the play lies in what is *un*expressed and in this way art works as a means of defense for the spectator against his fear of castration. It is clear that where Eliot's negative judgment of *Hamlet* is grounded in the desire to defend art against emasculation, and himself as master of emotion from Shakespeare's lack of mastery on that count, Freud's judgment of the play's universal significance is determined by his desire to ground psychoanalysis in the universal truth of the Oedipus complex, and to assert the potency of his theoretical insight.

Freud refers once more to *Hamlet* in his 1914 essay "The Moses of Michelangelo." He extols the power of art to create in the receiver "the same emotional attitude, the same mental constellation as that which in [the artist] produced the power to create" (1985c, 254). He disparages

purely literary analyses of the play: "what a mass of differing and contradictory interpretative attempts, what a variety of opinions about the
hero's character and the dramatist's intentions! . . . And how many of
these interpretations leave us cold! So cold that they do nothing to explain the effect of the play and rather incline us to the view that its magi-
cal appeal rests solely upon the impressive thoughts in it and the splen-
dour of its language" (Freud 1985c, 255).

Here, the "mystery" of *Hamlet*'s effect is explained "at last" by the
Oedipus theme (255), that is, the son's desire for his mother and the con-
comitant threat of castration by the father.[8]

The significance of Freud's literary judgment lies in the attention he
gives to the prohibition of the original love object in *Hamlet*. In so doing,
he opens the way for Lacan's exploration of the function of desire in the
play and the crucial position of the mother as both object in, and subject
of desire. The Freudian wish (*wunsch*) is supplanted by Lacanian desire
and in addressing the place of the mother's unknowable desire in the
play—what woman wants—Lacan revises Freud and intimates a move
from a modern to a postmodern understanding of the decentered subject.

Lacan: Desire and Maternal Jouissance in *Hamlet*

In an extraordinary moment in his discussion, Lacan responds to charges
of "timidity" in his interpretation of desire in *Hamlet*, by declaring "I'm
just surprised that nobody's pointed out that Ophelia is O *phallos*, because you find other things equally gross, flagrant and extravagant, if
you just open [Ella Sharpe's] *Papers on Hamlet* . . . " (Lacan 1989, 20). Lacan distinguishes his interpretation from "the sort of hogwash that psychoanalytic texts are full of" (20). He is not taking Shakespeare *literally*:
Ophelia/*O phallos*? Gross! But we shall see that as object of desire, Ophelia, "that piece of bait," (11) is indeed the veiled phallus. Just as Eliot admits what few critics have ever admitted, just as Freud sees what no
other critic has seen, Lacan also take up a position of singularity. His
judgment is definitive: "The tragedy of *Hamlet* is the tragedy of desire.
But as we come to the end of our trajectory it is time to notice what one
always takes note of last, i.e., what is most obvious. I know of no commentator who has ever taken the trouble to make this remark, however
hard it is to overlook once it has been formulated: from one end of *Hamlet*
to the other, all anyone talks about is mourning" (Lacan 1989, 39).

Hamlet is a play about mourning because its protagonist repeats the loss
of the object in losing Ophelia. That is, the play is a re-enactment of the loss
of jouissance which is symbolic castration. The loss of the phallus is impe-
tus to the metonymy of desire and for an identification through fantasy
with objects that will continually compensate for that loss. Lacan locates in

the play the structure of fantasy that grounds his theory of the divided subject: desire as the desire of the Other. In Lacan's judgment, Shakespeare's
play retains its interest precisely because it articulates the function of the
object in desire (Lacan 1989, 28). His examination of the functions of the
object demonstrates the substitution of the paternal metaphor—the Name-
of-the-Father—for the unknowable and thus terrifying desire of the
mother. Although Lacan considers the play to be dominated by the mother
as Other, and although he makes it clear that Hamlet's desire turns around
the phallus *qua* object of his mother's desire, his treatment of her is cursory.
The jouissance of the mother is the limit of Lacan's judgment of *Hamlet*.

Unlike Freud and Eliot, Lacan addresses the language of the play directly. He explores Shakespeare's use of "ambiguity, of metaphor, puns,
conceits, mannered speech" (Lacan 1989, 33) the rhetorical figures
through which motives and meaning escape indirectly. Lacan reads *Hamlet* as explicating the structure of obsession—the annulment of the desire
of the Other—and the decline of the Oedipus complex "insofar as the
subject must mourn the phallus" (46). Lacan translates the Oedipal narrative into his own terms. If Oedipus's crime charts the relationship of the
subject to the Other, that is, to the place of the inscription of the law,
Hamlet is at the center of the inquiry into origins (42).

Where Freud refers to the "secular advance of repression in the emotional life of mankind" (Freud 1965, 298) as explanation for the submerg-
ing of the Oedipal dimension of the drama, Lacan, in existentialist mode,
adverts to a change in the relationship of "the hero to his fate" (Lacan
1989, 19), that is, to his unconscious. Where Freud evinces the modernist
desire for symmetries in his comparison of Sophocles's and Shakespeare's tragedies, Lacan privileges the play's points of dissymmetry. He
argues that, in contrast to Oedipus, Hamlet knows about the crime and
this knowledge explains his feigning of madness. Indeed, Lacan claims
that "feigning madness is . . . one of the dimensions of what we might
call the strategy of the modern hero" (20). Recognizing his position of
weakness (that is, his dependence on the Other) Hamlet must "be mad
along with everyone else" (20).

Lacan reads the play for the way it dramatizes the mobilization of desire around the object, with the fantasy as its reference point. Where
Freud's Hamlet is an hysteric, Lacan's Hamlet, enmeshed in the enigma
of his mother's desire, is the obsessive whom Brousse describes as confounding "the object of desire, the object which causes desire and the object the subject thinks the Other is demanding of him" (Brousse 1995,
110). In *Hamlet*, the (M)Other's desire is both too evident (her hasty re-
marriage to Claudius) and disturbingly enigmatic (how *could* she?). The
obsessive's strategy, like Hamlet's, is to avoid the encounter with the object of desire and to control jouissance.[9]

Lacan goes some way toward confronting the "horror" that terminates Eliot's account: the traumatic presence of the mother. The mother in *Hamlet* is the "primordial subject of the demand:" the omnipotent Other (Lacan 1989, 12). Her "fall"—her marriage to Claudius—is crucial to Lacan's analysis for it is the cause of Hamlet losing the way of his desire: "This fall, this abandon gives us the model that enables us to conceive that Hamlet's desire—this zeal with respect to an act that he so longs to carry out . . . — how this zeal flags. The dependence of his desire on the Other subject forms the permanent dimension of Hamlet's drama" (Lacan 1989, 13).

For Lacan, the unknowable desire of the mother is evident precisely in Hamlet's inability to choose between the idealized father and the debased Claudius; Hamlet's traumatic confrontation with the desire of the mother deflects him from his course. It is important to note that while Hamlet's relation to Ophelia is in the imaginary—she is the object at the end of the fantasy—his relation to the desire of the mother, the primordial Other, is in the real. Lacan's focus is on the subject's anxiety when confronted with what he is for that Other. Even so, while Lacan refers to the scene of Hamlet's meeting with his mother in her chamber, he does not consider the significance of the violence of Hamlet's repudiation of Gertrude's sexuality, an articulation of disgust which makes this one of the most disturbing moments in the play. Slavoj Zizek does address this point. He argues persuasively that for Hamlet, the Name-of-the-Father is not securely in place. Because Hamlet's mandate is supplemented by a request that he not harm his mother, the demand of the father is subordinated to her desire. He asks "What if she really *enjoys* her filthy promiscuous relationship with his uncle?" (Zizek 1989, 120). Hamlet cannot take up his place in the social order as the true son of his father because the jouissance of the mother marks the point where interpellation necessarily fails (121).

For Lacan, what is out of place in *Hamlet*? The phallus is not where it should be in the Oedipal structure and as a consequence Hamlet's position in the social order is dislocated. In Lacan's judgment, Gertrude's desire for the phallus embodied by Claudius paralyzes Hamlet. Lacan understands Gertrude's attachment to Claudius in terms "of something present inside her, like an instinctive voracity. The sacrosanct genital object . . . appears to her as an object to be enjoyed [*objet d'une jouissance*] in what is truly the direct satisfaction of a need, and nothing else" (Lacan 1989, 13).

Even though he stipulates Gertrude's attachment to Claudius in terms of need, Lacan's reference to her "instinctive voracity" suggests an urgency pertaining to the real of the drive. Brousse makes a comment that is pertinent to the position of the mother in *Hamlet*: "Lacan deals with the drive and desire when he represents the mother as the real Other. Thus he describes the real Other, but also the Other of language. Now when the real Other is demanding, when it is in the field of speech, then in a way it is in the field of language without being barred. It is real, but you could say it is brought into the symbolic" (Brousse 1995, 109).

Reading Lacan's analysis of *Hamlet* though the concept of the real as it is developed in his later work, it could be argued that what is not recognized is the way the jouissance of Hamlet's mother perforates the symbolic field of the tragedy. Hamlet vilifies his mother because her age and her choice of love object reveal her desire as excessive. The maternal figure is the traumatic embodiment of an unbarred Other, an Other who contains the object and thus, in relation to the mother, Hamlet is dislocated, he does not have a place. Echoing Eliot, Ellie Ragland-Sullivan writes in reference to the play: "the paradoxical *raison d'être* of literature is an effort to bring to light this veiled object that, in life, catches the ordinary conscious subject unawares .... " (Ragland-Sullivan 1988, 37). The bringing to light of the object is disturbing and this uncanny, traumatic dimension of *Hamlet* helps explain the play's endurance. Something happens in *Hamlet* that is not reducible to the signifier. Thus while desire, as desire for the phallus, is foregrounded in Lacan's account of the play, the antinomy between desire and jouissance, desire as a defense against the trauma of jouissance is not explored. This gap intimates precisely the potency of jouissance to expose the inconsistency in the symbolic order.

Lacan's *Hamlet* is a tragedy of desire that begins with Ophelia's account of Hamlet's aberrant behavior after his meeting with the ghost, behavior that he considers to be indicative of Hamlet's "estrangement" from Ophelia (Lacan 1989, 21). "Estrangement" is a pathological moment in which "something in the fantasy wavers and makes the components of the fantasy appear" (22). That is, the fantasy which is located on the unconscious circuit crosses over to the level of the message, the signified. Lacan associates this moment with Freud's uncanny, that is when "something which ought to have remained hidden . . . has come to light" (Freud 1985d, 354). This experience is profoundly disorienting for "the imaginary limits between subject and object change" (Lacan 1989, 22). Lacan argues that Ophelia, as object, is the endpoint of Hamlet's fantasy; she takes the place of what Hamlet is symbolically deprived: the phallus. It is the negativity— the exposure of the lack that constitutes the subject—that becomes manifest in Hamlet's encounter with Ophelia. As the object in desire, she takes the place of what is concealed, that "something secret and hidden" (28) which is the subject's sacrifice of his "pound of flesh" to the signifier (28). When the fantasy becomes unbalanced, Ophelia as the exteriorized phallus is transmogrified. Annulled as love object, Ophelia becomes repugnant, contaminated with an obscene maternity. Lacan notes that "Hamlet speaks constantly of one thing: childbearing" (Lacan 1989, 23), but he does not explore the traumatic significance of the maternalization of Ophelia. He refers to the ambiguity of Hamlet's "Get thee to a nunnery," where nunnery also signifies a brothel, but he does not connect this with the jouis-sance associated with the mother in the play. I am considering this elision of maternal desire as a concealment—that which must not be brought to light—a concealment which reveals the jouissance of the mother as limit.

As his discussion draws to a close Lacan returns again to the mother: "Claudius' real phallus is always somewhere in the picture. What does Hamlet have to reproach his mother for, after all, if not for having filled herself with it? And with dejected arm and speech he sends her back to that fatal, fateful object, here real indeed, around which the play re-volves" (Lacan 1989, 50).

Lacan plays here with the ambiguity of "real" with regard to the phal-lus—for it is and is not the biological organ—and adds a further twist. In his final paragraph, Lacan quotes Hamlet's words in reference to Polo-nius's corpse: "The body is with the king . . . but the king is not with the body" (Lacan 1989, 52), and suggests that the word "king" be replaced by the word "phallus" as an indication that the phallus is indeed a ghost and is thus "bound to nothing" (52). But there is more than word play at stake here. While Lacan maintains that "the phallus is everywhere present in the disorder in which we find Hamlet each time he approaches one of the crucial moments of his action" (49), the phallus is not commensurate with it. As we have seen, in his focus on the subject's relation to the symbolic phallus in his interpretation of desire in *Hamlet*, Lacan lets fall the ques-tion of Hamlet's traumatic encounter the jouissance of the (M)Other. By representing Gertrude's sexuality in terms of a purely phallic enjoyment, he does not consider the effects of the very excess implicit in his own use of the term "voracity" and the effect of that excess upon Hamlet. While at-tention is drawn to the place of the mother, her real effect in the drama is not addressed. Judgment appears to be a defense against impossible ma-ternal jouissance. If the king is a thing of nothing and the phallus is indeed a ghost, something real remains and is not accounted for. It is not until 1972 in his writing on feminine sexuality that Lacan will begin to develop the notion of a supplementary jouissance, that is, a non-phallic enjoyment, and the possibility that we are not subject only to the play of the signifier but rather, "we are played by jouissance" (Lacan 1982b, 142). This later de-velopment is not unproblematic, as Jacqueline Rose argues. Lacan's at-tempt to define a specific mode of feminine enjoyment risks collapsing into the very notion of feminine essence that the non-universalizing of "Woman" is designed to avoid (Mitchell and Rose 1982, 137). Neverthe-less, this move is indicative of Lacan's constant interrogation of claims to knowledge. His emphasis on the very disturbing nature of maternal jouis-sance in *Hamlet*, even with the reduction of this disturbance to the mother's relation to the phallus, moves towards a postmodern reading of the disruptive nature of feminine desire. It draws attention to the lack in the Other, the absence of a single signifier for the feminine sex and thus, the non-totalization of the signifying field.[10]

The Limit of Judgment

Included in Eliot's 1917 collection *Prufrock and Other Observations*, is a short prose poem entitled "Hysteria" (Eliot 1963, 34) that offers some insight into the valorization of masculine form over feminine content in the modernist aesthetic. The speaker is "drawn in" to a woman's uncontrollable laughter and is "lost finally in the dark caverns of her throat, bruised by the ripples of unseen muscles" (34). He only saves himself by "concentration" and "careful subtlety" (34). Eliot's poem anticipates the need for an objective correlative, a formula for the escape from an unbearable emotion. This poem also recalls another traumatic encounter between a man and a woman's throat, that referred to by Freud in his dream of Irma's injection (Freud 1965, 138–53). Here a formula is offered as a means of protecting Freud from anxiety. In his analysis of the dream narrative the implications of the function of the formula are exposed. When Freud looks into Irma's throat he sees large patches of whitish-gray scabs and is alarmed that his treatment may be at fault (140). The formula "Trimethylamin" acts as an antidote for Freud because it offers him a way out of responsibility for mis-diagnosis by making Irma accountable for her continuing illness. As we have seen, Lacan also offers a formula for dealing with the intolerable desire of the mother: the paternal metaphor, the Name-of-the-Father.

A juxtaposition of Freud's formula, Eliot's objective correlative and Lacan's metaphor illumines the contested position of the maternal/feminine within the modern. Freud is anxious that his treatment is inadequate and wants responsibility to be attributed to Irma: "If [the pains] were her fault they could not be mine" (Freud 1965, 141). There must be an absolute differentiation between the analyst and the hysteric upon whose cure the success of psychoanalysis as a science depended. Eliot was concerned that women poets threatened the rigor of the modernist aesthetic. In the original version of *The Waste Land* he satirizes women poets in the figure of Fresca, a poetess of "unreal emotions, and real appetite" (Eliot 1971, 27). Significantly, Eliot's attack on Fresca is directed at her body. As Koestenbaum points out, Eliot "must separate his verse from hers because . . . hysteria and poetry spring from the same source" (Koestenbaum 1989, 134). That is, if those are the faults of a woman writer, they can't be his. Fresca complains: "I've much to say —/But cannot say it" (Eliot 1971, 23). The woman writer is absolute Other for the male modernist; modernism is grounded in the repression of the maternal/feminine.

For Lacan, the Other, is the place of the subject's dislocation. As Samuel Weber explains, it is a negative place occupied by various instances: first by the mother as that utterly Other in the sense of that demand for love;

then by the father as the forbidding, castrating instance which also introduces the Law; and finally by the phallus "itself," as the selfless, self-effacing mark that bars the place and splits the subject (Weber 1991, 148).

The Other is the place of the incompatible idea which emerges into consciousness in the form of a negation: "It's *not* my mother." I have argued that negation operates in these literary judgments to relegate Hamlet's mother, embodiment of a traumatic and dislocating jouissance, to the repressed of the critical text. She is figured by Eliot as inexpressibly disgusting; by Freud, as the prohibited and thus repressed object of desire in the Oedipal configuration; and by Lacan as a figure whose unknowable desire is canceled by the Name-of-the-Father. In each of these analyses maternal jouissance is the residue of literary judgment and thus marks its limit. Jouissance is judgment's incoherence. It is that point where truth is intimated not by modernist formulae, but by the point of rupture, the failure of words to say it all.

Notes

1. See Evans discussion of the history of Lacan's use of the pleasure principle (Evans 1996, 148–149) and of the term jouissance (Evans 1996, 91–92).

2. Lacan makes the point even more strongly in his essay "Subversion of the Subject": "jouissance is forbidden him who speaks as such" (Lacan 1992b, 319).

3. Linda Hutcheon notes the paradox that while postmodernism distinguishes itself from the myth of "élitist romantic/modernist originality and unique genius" (Hutcheon 1988, 26), postmodern interrogation "is totally dependent upon that which it interrogates (42). This comment is pertinent to the place of the maternal/feminine as the Other of the masculine modernist aesthetic, and the valorized qua marginal Other of the feminist postmodern.

4. This is literally evident in "The Perfect Critic" when Eliot refers to the creative process as "the expulsion, the ejection, the birth" (Eliot 1967a, 6). It is pertinent that Eliot had started working on *The Waste Land* in 1919, the same year that he wrote his essay on *Hamlet*. As Koestenbaum notes, in its original form Eliot described it as "a scrawling chaotic poem," (Koestenbaum 1989, 124) requiring Pound's regulative masculine intervention.

5. As Zizek comments, "the shift from the Lacan of the symbolic to the Lacan of the real is the shift from modernism to post-modernism" (Zizek 1995, 205).

6. Indeed, for Eliot "*Qua* work of art, the work of art cannot be interpreted; there is nothing to interpret; we can only criticize it according to standards, in comparison to other works of art; and for 'interpretation' the chief task is the presentation of relevant historical facts which the reader is not assumed to know" (Eliot 1972a, 142).

7. Suzanne Clark develops this line of argument in her defense of the transgressive potential of the maternal/feminine against the masculinist and essentially conservative modernist aesthetic.

8. Freud returns once more to *Hamlet* in "Dostoevsky and Parricide," written in 1927–28, and again the emphasis changes. Because Hamlet's repressed wish to

kill his father is carried out by someone else, "The forbidden motive of sexual rivalry for the woman does not need, therefore to be disguised. Moreover, we see the hero's Oedipus complex, as it were, in a reflected light, by learning of the effect upon him of the other's crime" (1985e, 454). Hamlet is paralyzed by a sense of guilt, but this sense is "displaced on to the perception of his inadequacy for fulfilling his task" (454).

9. See Colette Soler's discussion of the obsessive's relation to desire and jouissance (Soler 1995, 269–270).

10. See Rose's discussion of the later developments in Lacan's understanding of feminine sexuality (Mitchell and Rose 1982, 48–57).

References

Brousse, Marie-Hélène. 1995. "The Drive (II)." In *Reading Seminar XI: Lacan's Four Fundamental Concepts of Psychoanalysis*. The Paris Seminars in English, ed. Richard Feldstein et al., 109–117. New York: SUNY Press.

Clark, Suzanne. 1991. *Sentimental Modernism*. Bloomington: Indiana University Press.

Coleridge, Samuel Taylor. 1951. "Hamlet." In *Selected Poetry and Prose of Coleridge*, ed. Donald A. Stauffer, 457–475. The Modern Library College Editions. United States of America: Random House.

Eliot, T. S. 1963. *Collected Poems 1909–1962*. London: Faber and Faber.

_____. 1967a. "The Perfect Critic." In *The Sacred Wood: Essays on Poetry and Criticism*. London: Faber.

_____. 1967b. "Dante." In *The Sacred Wood: Essays on Poetry and Criticism*, 159–171. London: Faber.

_____. 1971. *The Waste Land: A Facsimile and Transcript of the Original Drafts Including the Annotations of Ezra Pound*. Ed. Valerie Eliot. London: Faber and Faber.

_____. 1972a. "*Hamlet*". In *Selected Essays*, 141–146. London: Faber and Faber.

_____. 1972b. "Tradition and the Individual Talent." In *Selected Essays*, 13–22. London: Faber and Faber.

_____. 1972c. "The Function of Criticism." In *Selected Essays*, 23–34. London: Faber and Faber.

Evans, Dylan. 1996. *An Introductory Dictionary of Lacanian Psychoanalysis*. London: Routledge.

Feldstein, Richard et al. 1995. *Reading Seminar XI: Lacan's Four Fundamental Concepts of Psychoanalysis*. The Paris Seminars in English. New York: SUNY Press.

Freud, Sigmund. 1965. *The Interpretation of Dreams*. New York: Avon.

_____. 1984. "Negation." In *Metapsychology*, Vol. 11, Penguin Freud Library, ed. Angela Richard, trans. James Strachey, 435–442. Harmondsworth: Penguin.

_____. 1985a. "Psychopathic Characters on the Stage." In *Art and Literature*, Vol. 14, Penguin Freud Library, ed. Albert Dickson, trans. James Strachey, 119–127. Harmondsworth: Penguin.

_____. 1985b. "Creative Writers and Day-Dreaming." In Art *and Literature*, Vol. 14, Penguin Freud Library, ed. Albert Dickson, trans. James Strachey, 129–141. Harmondsworth: Penguin.

_____. 1985c. "The Moses of Michelangelo." In *Art and Literature*, Vol. 14, Penguin Freud Library, ed. Albert Dickson, trans. James Strachey, 249–282. Harmondsworth: Penguin.

_____. 1985d. "The Uncanny." In *Art and Literature*, Vol. 14, Penguin Freud Library, ed. Albert Dickson, trans. James Strachey, 335–376. Harmondsworth: Penguin.

_____. 1985e. "Dostoevsky and the Parricide." In *Art and Literature*, Vol. 14, Penguin Freud Library, ed. Angela Richards et al, trans. James Strachey, 435–460. Harmondsworth: Penguin.

Harvey, David. 1989. *The Condition of Postmodernity: An Enquiry into the Origins of Cultural Change*. Oxford: Basil Blackwell.

Hutcheon, Linda. 1988. *A Poetics of Postmodernism: History, Theory, Fiction*. New York: Routledge.

Koestenbaum, Wayne. 1989. *Double Talk: The Erotics of Male Literary Collaboration*. New York: Routledge.

Lacan, Jacques. 1982a. "Guiding Remarks for a Congress on feminine Sexuality." In *Feminine Sexuality: Jacques Lacan and the École Freudienne*, ed. Juliet Mitchell and Jacqueline Rose, trans. Jacqueline Rose, 86–98. Houndsmill: Macmillan.

_____. 1982b. "God and the Jouissance of The Woman." In *Feminine Sexuality: Jacques Lacan and the École Freudienne*, ed. Juliet Mitchell and Jacqueline Rose, trans. Jacqueline Rose,137–148. Houndsmill: Macmillan.

_____. 1989. "On Desire and the Interpretation of Desire in *Hamlet*." In *Literature and Psychoanalysis: The Question of Reading Otherwise*, ed. Shoshana Felman, trans. James Hulbert, 11–52. Baltimore: Johns Hopkins University Press.

_____. 1992a. "Signification of the Phallus." In *Écrits: A Selection*, trans. Alan Sheridan, 281–291. London: Routledge/ Tavistock.

_____. 1992b. "The Subversion of the Subject in the Dialectic of Desire." In *Écrits: A Selection*, trans. Alan Sheridan, 292–325. London: Routledge/ Tavistock.

_____. 1992c. *The Ethics of Psychoanalysis 1959–1960*. The Seminar of Jacques Lacan. Book 7. Ed. Jacques-Alain Miller. Trans. Dennis Porter. London: Routledge.

Mitchell, Juliet and Jacqueline Rose, eds. 1982. *Feminine Sexuality: Jacques Lacan and the École Freudienne*. Trans. Jacqueline Rose. Houndsmill: Macmillan.

Ragland-Sullivan, Ellie. 1988. "*Hamlet*, Logical Time and the Structure of Obsession." *Newsletter of the Freudian Field*. 2: 29–45.

Soler, Colette. 1995. "Hysteria and Obsession." In *Reading Seminar XI: Lacan's Four Fundamental Concepts of Psychoanalysis*. The Paris Seminars in English, ed. Richard Feldstein et al., 248–282. New York: SUNY Press.

Weber, Samuel.1991. *Return to Freud: Jacques Lacan's Dislocation of Psychoanalysis*. Cambridge: Cambridge University Press.

Zizek, Slavoj. 1989. *The Sublime Object of Ideology*. London: Verso.

_____. 1995. "The Lamella of David Lynch." In *Reading Seminar XI: Lacan's Four Fundamental Concepts of Psychoanalysis*. The Paris Seminars in English, ed. Richard Feldstein et al. 205–220. New York: SUNY Press.

5

More than Meets the Eye

An Exposé on Patriotic Libido and Judgment at the Level of the Image in American War Culture

James P. McDaniel

Snapshots: Fragments of Western Democracy's Family Album

In a marvelous passage that performs quick but vast remembrance and nuanced interrogation of Western history's violent mythos, J. Glenn Gray situates the erotic mystery of war at the level of the image and the enigma of "likeness," a single notion that maintains tensions between similarity and difference:

> There is a familiar Greek myth about the goddess of love, Aphrodite, becoming the mistress of Ares, the god of war, whose youth and passion captured her heart, though she was the bride of Hephaestos, who forged the weapons and armor of the gods. The two of them spent many sweet, illicit hours together, and one of their children was the beautiful Harmonia, another the ever-youthful Eros. The liaison between love and war, familiar early in Western history, might occasion more wonder and reflection than it usually does. How can it be that these two, outwardly so unlike, have any attraction for each other at all? What is the source of this affinity? Is the attraction really an adulterous one, as in the myth, or is it more legitimate than the early Greeks wanted to believe? How durable can we expect the liaison to be between love and war? Questions like these arise almost spontaneously when I begin to reflect on modern enactments of the Aphrodite-Ares story in World War II. (1959, 60–61)

Glenn's penetrating and transhistorical questions regarding whether or not the attraction between love and war is adulterous or legitimate, normative or perverse, temporary or permanent, has been decisively answered by the twentieth century's most brilliant rhetorical theorist, the Freud-oid Kenneth Burke. His judgment is posed as final, yet also is a bit surprising. Says Burke: war is a "derivative condition" of "the order of love," "a *perversion*" (1950, 20). To complicate the judgment of war as perversion, he also maintains that war may be regarded "as a 'special case of peace'" (1950, 20), recognizing that what war "is" depends largely on how it gets rhetorically constructed, imagined, justified, and so forth. Though war may be troped as hell, purification, retribution, compensation, or even passion, its cross-hatching of violence and love seems fundamental. Burke goes further to recommend that we gain purchase to war most fully when we recognize that it is the desire for communion gone awry, submission of the other to our desire by force in the name of whatever good. While perhaps not a democratic practice in any orthodox sense of the term, war nevertheless performs the politics of *e pluribus unum* at a hysterical pitch. It is the seamy side of democratic desire for community. Burke advises: "You will understand war much better if you think of it, not simply as strife come to a head, but rather as a disease, or perversion of communion" (1950, 22).

Punning a bit off the Latin root *communis*, the "common," we might add the obvious: that war also is a perversion of communication and community that displaces symbolic interaction and negotiation in favor of brute force. Yet the perversion of communion that is war may paradoxically create unity, *communis*, by constituting a field of difference against which the ground of identity may most vividly appear. A commonplace of politics, contemporary and historical, has always been: when there is trouble at home, find trouble abroad, go to war. Community may eruptively appear as a sort of miracle conjured by ritual killing, sacrifice, a sense of exterior threat, and rhetorical displays of judgment between "us" and "them." This procedure of (symbolic) sacrifice is summed up by the communicative practice of "scapegoating." Strange as it may on first blush seem, or perhaps it may not, communities have historically coalesced around a discharged otherness, or what Bataille (1991) has provocatively called an "accursed share." Just as identification may be compensatory to division, so too division may be the paradoxical substance of identification—"social cohesion through victimage" (Burke, 1965, 284–285; see Ivie, 1980, 279–281).

The presumption someone or something "must" be sacrificed to forge identification reveals the seamy side of the Western mythos in all its violence, desire, and often (self)destructive eroticism. Drawing from one of Beethoven's great erotic compositions, we may ask: *Es muss sein*, "must" it be? Milan Kundera would perhaps respond that "*Es könte auch anders sein*"—"It could just as well be otherwise" (1984, 35). That it *may* be and *has*

been is certain. Rhetorics of victimage and scapegoating are culturally effective, and may derive from the *différance* of language from itself (see Derrida, 1973, 129–160) coupled with the drive for erotic self-transcendence:
the capacity for one term to stand in for another, substituting or displacing
it in favor of a new matrix brought into being by the shifting of signifiers.
Along with linguistic substitutions come affective shifts. Says Burke: "substitution is a prime resource of symbol systems" which accomplishes
"catharsis by scapegoat (including the 'natural' invitation to 'project' upon
the enemy any troublesome traits of our own that we would negate)"
(Burke, 1968, 18; see Burke, 1957; Ivie, 1980; Keene, 1986). The other may be
construed in this vocabulary as a screen of desire for our own violent projections, in which love and war intermingle or are even consubstantial. The
war-love identification suggests one of the West's most tantalizing and disturbing images: the two-backed beast, an image of sexual union that yokes
together the erotic and the morbid in tender violence.

   Such reflections on the liaison between love and war—and the clash
and blend of the illicit and the sanctioned, the obscene and the decorous,
the perverse and the normative—at the level of the image bring pornography quickly to mind. "Traditional" pornography renders the act of love
in terms of violence, even of warfare, where the guiding desire is scripted
not merely as the defeat of the enemy but her destruction. I presume that
it is now a bygone point to argue that the "art of love" as it gets conveyed
in pornography is transcoded as an "art of war," replete with its
weapons, explosions, cries of victory and defeat, heroes, villains, casual-
ties, and even technologies of "combat." War is the counterpart to love.
While illicit and perverse from a number of perspectives, traditional
pornography also legitimates male desire and the objectification of
women, thus supporting a solidly American normative libidinal economy. Pornographies of war render violence in erotic terms, wherein "the
enemy" replaces women as other. And if we accept that "traditional"
pornography is coded for male pleasure, and moreover by patriarchy, we
should recognize soberly that the pornography of war is coded for patriotic enjoyment. Further, just as traditional pornography must be understood as constitutive rather than merely symptomatic of cultural habits,
so too the pornography of war must be understood as generative of patriotic beliefs, attitudes, values, and behaviors. Just as traditional pornography may stimulate sexual activity, at whatever cost to the
viewer/voyeur, the pornography of war may locate libidinal activity
in/for/with one's Country or MotherLand. Both sorts of pornography
may be read as creating environments of judgment that make it possible
for (male-patriotic) subjects to erotically enjoy violence against the (fe-
male-enemy) other.[1] Through repetition as much as through affective
force, each sort of pornography works toward the naturalization of a set

of relations and performances that are in fact contingent. And each pornography rehearses the "murder" of the other as an act of "love."

So it is that the other is absolutely instrumental to desire, both as possessing its object-cause, e.g., a trait the self can identify with or wish to have, and as barrier or bar, e.g., an unknowable quantity: a provocation and a denial. Communicative practices, of both visual and verbal orders, are inscribed by and structure relations to the other—as liminal boundary, internal inconsistency or blight, exotic locus of enjoyment, accursed share, and so on. The other must be retained in some way or another for the subject to go on desiring, the nation to go on loving-hating (itself), and, most generally, for self-identification at whatever level to occur. Without the other, identity would have no ground—an object-less passion. Rhetoric may be construed as a manipulation of props and figures that gives shape to the stage of human passion, directions to the drama of desire. Put a bit differently, the other is the crutch on which the drives lean; rhetorics of identity and difference locate the other as a site of desire through which enjoyment may be accessed. To dislocate or destroy it, or to achieve complete satisfaction with respect to it, would be to stop desiring—to "fall down." In short, it would be death. Lacan's thesis that all desire manifests the desire to desire reinforces the absolute necessity of the other as a location of enjoyment, and a source of life (Zizek, 1991b; see Hegel, 1977, §§360–366; Kojève, 1969, 38–70). Further, for Lacan the other has a "captivating value" at the level of the ego/*imago* because it "enables man to locate precisely his imaginary and libidinal relation to the world in general. That is what enables him to *see* in its place and to structure, as a function of this place and of his world, his being" (1988, 125). Zizek goes so far as to say that nations provide sites of otherness for one another, so that nationalist political consciousness may figure itself reflectively from an alterior perspective:

> Why was the West so fascinated by the disintegration of Communism in Eastern Europe? The answer seems obvious: what fascinated the Western gaze was the *reinvention of Democracy*. It is as if democracy, which in the West shows more and more signs of decay and crisis and is lost in bureaucratic routine and publicity-style election campaigns, is being rediscovered in Eastern Europe in all its freshness and novelty. The function of this fascination is thus purely ideological: in Eastern Europe, the West seeks for its own lost origins, its own lost original experience of "democratic invention." In other words, Eastern Europe functions for the West as its Ego-Ideal (*Ich-Ideal*): the point from which West sees itself in a likable, idealized form, as worthy of love. (1993, 200)

The other provides for the subject, and even for a nation: a point of view or external-referential location that allows him to see himself otherwise—to transcend his particularity; to excite himself beyond himself in passionate moments of self-overcoming; a locus for kairotic inventions of identity out of difference.[2]

The pornographized other would seem peculiarly significant in this respect, for it supplies a spectral fantasy that excites and mediates desire. This other, preserved by the image in scenes of erotic and symbolic death, may be perpetually returned to when the subject wishes to be aroused. Because always contingent and transient, even whilst masquerading as necessary and permanent, rhetorics of identity and difference refigure the other, and subjects' relations to/with it. Thus, the other may be destroyed on one level only to be preserved or sublimated on another. Sublimation and preservation are (always incomplete, imperfect) defenses against death, and are effects of what McGee has been calling for years the *rhetorical impulse*—a will-to-invent and transcend material-symbolic limitations.

This defense occurs profoundly, but not without problems, in the making of images. In the famous essay "The Ontology of the Photographic Image," André Bazin speculates that the deep origins of photography are to be found in the Egyptian practice of mummification, where what is lost to the ravages of time is preserved visually and materially. Mummification, "by providing a defense against the passage of time . . . satisfied a basic psychological need of man, for death is but the victory of time." It also strives to accomplish the victory of Thanatos over Eros. Mummification thus may be understood as a simulated conquest of Eros over Thanatos, virulence and sex over impotence and death. Bazin goes on to say: "To preserve, artificially, his bodily appearance is to snatch it from the flow of time, to stow it away neatly, so to speak, in the hold of life. It was natural, therefore, to keep up appearances in the face of the reality of death by preserving flesh and bone" (1967, 9). And yet simultaneously, the desire to preserve as it is accomplished by the (photographic) image also admits of radical loss, for an image "makes" a subject into an object and without words confesses its incomplete defense against the inevitable. Inscribed in the wrapping of mummies, the making of an image, is the deep pathos of memory and desire.

The defense of desire against the ravages of time at the level of the image is an impossible yet alluring cultural practice that reaches back not only to Egyptian civilization, but also to the Greeks. Indeed, we might speculate that the early development of rhetoric as a civic art was in part motivated by the desire to create semblance of Beauty in the face of death. A lesson to be learned from the ancient Greeks: rhetoric not only is a way of life, it may be an art of Eros. Of course, rhetoric may also be an art of death or Thanatos. The one implies the other as dialectical counterpart, and the cross-hatching of the erotic and thanatopic may be seen to constitute the whole field of human affairs. Eros and Thanatos offer basic coordinates for judgment. From interpersonal to organization communications and beyond, creating one out of many or many out of one—both identification and division—is perhaps *the* basic function of rhetoric. And for a person or even a people to believe that they are part of "something larger," a unity, is a judgment that performs the operation of Eros; rhetoric may cultivate this structure of belief.[3] Human sexuality and finitude, life and death, regeneration and decay, identification and division, plenty and lack, supply a deep reservoir and basic topological structure for all symbolic action (see Burke, 1950; Lacan, 1985; McGee, 1975). Plato's idea, articulated in the *Philebus*, that it "is bad to arrive too quickly at the one or the many," features that we have a *choice* in conceptualizing our (collective) existence (Peters, 1994, 117). The gap between the one and the many, and the choice between them, is a rhetorical exigency constitutive of democratic deliberation and judgment. The democratic culture of ancient Athens, faced with the fragmentation of Greek culture into competing city-states, was profoundly riddled by a loss of identity—an impending death—which encouraged rhetoricians like Isocrates to begin mummifying the corpse of Greece into a spectral Panhellinism. He erected an image to direct Hellenic desire toward unification, in a manner both similar to and different from what Plato performs in the *Republic* via the trope of Utopia. Though but an illusion created with words, an image planted seed-like in the mind, this representation of Greek unity was to goad democratization. Democracy is a promise, perhaps even a vow, made in the face of contingency; it is an aporia (see Derrida, 1992). It may be regarded as the joining of many into one, a symbolic union of competing identities whose contingency is generative of the struggle for mutual recognition, love, and justice (see Hegel, 1977; Peters, 1994; Zizek, 1993). With the rhetorical invention of Panhellinism, the present of ancient Greece was to be judged by a possible future, whose beauty was (merely) imagined. Democratic judgment arises here from a lack, that which is not, and a plenitude, that which may be. Its fundamental faculty is the imagination, and textual type the image. Its temporal structure is precisely *possibility* (see Poulakos, 1984) rather than actuality, which requires no judgment for it is self-present. Democratic rhetoric, and judgment, are exercises of aesthetic imagination—radical inventiveness rather than scientific discovery.

Democracy, imaginary beauty, desire, and rhetoric are deeply intertwined in Greek philosophical speculation as well. In Plato's scheme, the desire to possess the Beautiful for all time is an impossible urge which nevertheless keeps the human machine operating, desiring—forever striving toward an impossible object, and, consequently, forever lacking the Beautiful. The desire to possess the Beautiful for all time is inscribed

visually and materially in "real" or earthly beauties, which are in fact
merely shadows on the wall of Plato's cave: images, place-holders for
and other-than the Beautiful itself, which does not appear as such but
rather abides in the realm of the Pure Forms. At the "origin" of systematic Western thought and the cradle of democratic culture, a series of images props up a way of thinking and life paradoxically resistant to the
image. A rhetoric of tropes supports a metaphysics which privileges
mimesis, or literal correspondence between word and thing, but which
also requires rhetoric's image-making aptitude to leap beyond itself toward Utopia and the realm of Pure Forms. And so it is with various
Christian traditions, where the manufacture of images produces at once
signs of God and also human arrogance in the form of idolatry: human
representations, both visual and verbal, overshoot or undershoot the
Real. Lack (desire) and plenitude (jouissance) mark representations of the
Ultimate Subject, i.e., God. While much may be accomplished at the level
of the image, the image cannot comprehend God's absolute otherness, a
truth which led the prophet Isaiah to complain: "Their land is full of
idols; they worship the work of their own hands, that which their own
fingers have made" (Isaiah 2:8; Peters, 1997, 9). Lacking the real object of
desire, God, images seek (and always fail) to fill the void. Thus, they are
simultaneously present and markers of absence. The simultaneous requirement (which Bazin renders as the deep psychological need) for and
distrust of the image is inscribed by the double play of desire, and the
perilous situation of the other as its object-cause. Worship of works made
by human industry—a form of commodity fetishism—may be expressed
by the formula: "loving things as persons and using persons as things"
(Peters, 1997, 9), a passion particularly well-supported by the image, and
a passion that in turn may generate violent conflict.

In this chapter, this passion is located at the level of the image in a series of photographs and advertisements from the war culture of 1940s
America. Storytelling, citation, critical textual analysis, visual illustrations, and speculation combine to make up the strategies of the chapter.
Rather than merely "reading" rhetorically, the chapter *performs* rhetorically, activating as many modes of proof and suggestion as are available.
It aims at discovering and creating what Dilip Gaonkar terms (1990), in
his critique of Michael Calvin McGee's theory of rhetoric as performance,
a "'felt quality' of social life" (308; see McKerrow, 1993)—to delight, trouble, move, and even instruct. Thus, perhaps more and less than an argument, this chapter aims at exposé—a performance in the rhetoric, politics, and ethics of visibility. Working first through a psychoanalytic
phenomenology of the gaze which harvests questions of guilt, perversity,
desire, and accountability from unlikely sources—fictional narrative,
photography, popular movies about war, a painting by René Magritte,

testimony, a Nazi love song—we ultimately will read/view libidinal investments into and out of specific visual texts from *Life* magazine and other popular texts as markers of patriotic pornography, wherein the desire for the other is inscribed as an erotic death drive. What judgments do these investments and their textualization in patriotic porno encode for, impose on, and elicit from their viewers? How is enjoyment of sexualized aggression, hatred, and death constitutive of and directed by the patriotic libido? And how can we traumatically render visible the obscene enjoyment of patriotism in a productive, even therapeutic way, which may ultimately call us to provisionally embrace its obscenity? The chapter concludes with meta-critical reflections that speculate on an *affective turn* in ideology critique and social theory, which might issue from the realm of rhetoric.

Tales of the "Guilty" Soldier

Now people want to be admired by those and admire those who have something good in the way of honors or from whom they happen to be greatly in need of something those people have in their control, as lovers [want love or sexual favors]; but they aspire to the rank of those [they regard as] like themselves, and they take account of prudent people as telling the truth[.] . . . [P]eople feel more shame before those who are going to be with them and those watching them, because in both cases they are "in" their eyes.

—Aristotle, *Rhetoric* (1384a.16–18/146)

The quest for virtue and admiration, Aristotle says, is punctuated by lack: that which the subject does not possess but desires to. Shame interrupts the quest for virtue, rendering visible a flaw in the subject "in" the eyes of the other. One is always being gazed at in public, Aristotle implies, judged as shameful or shameless according to what may be seen. A poetics of hiding seems immanent. Guilt may be grasped as a defense against shame, a motive to keep secret or hidden that which, if rendered visible, could be held against the subject. What happens when guilt is willfully rendered visible? What is at play when a guilty subject tells a tale, or his tale is told, publicly? Aristotle seems to believe that the basic motive force of such storytelling is either justice or slander. He does not appear to believe that the two may be practically related. "Professional jokers and comic poets," Aristotle says, are "slanderers and talebearers" who, with questionable integrity, hold actions of others up to public judgment (*Rhetoric*, 1384b.20–21/146–147). Let us follow the example of a more impious judge or *phronimos* than Aristotle was: Kenneth Burke, who advises that, "whatever poetry may be, criticism had best be comic" (1959, 107), perhaps even talebearing slander.

There is a funny tale about a soldier who, fighting on the American side during the Korean War, was repeatedly wounded in battle, sent to military medical units, decorated for his valor, and returned to the front lines.[4] A puzzle for the doctors who stitched him back together time and again, only to see him return for war, this soldier's courage and unswerving resolution to keep fighting became a mythic enigma. What kind of man was this? How did he come by his pathological bravery? Yet there was something more immediately odd about this soldier, which supplied additional spice to these questions: he had a nervous tick or twitch around the eye. When asked about this tick or twitch, the soldier revealed the "secret" of his bravery and unswerving resolution. His returns to battle were repeated attempts at death, a strange form of suicide. The nervous tick or twitch around his eye was the result of a psychotherapist's suggestion that he localize a certain traumatic guilt, derived from battle, at a physical level. As it turns out, the traumatic guilt, of which the tick or twitch was a motor discharge, resulted from the fact that he was Korean—a Korean killing Koreans who *looked* like him.

Judgment of the other as enemy, threat, incarnate evil, savage, superhuman, monster, machine, or animal, supplies for the military subject (and for citizens on the homefront) an obvious equipment for living, and for killing (Ivie, 1980)—an equipment particularly unavailable to the Korean soldier of our anecdote. For when this soldier was in battle, killing the enemy, a relation of similarity and likeness remained intact. Paradoxically, and at the extreme ends of this narrative, the Korean soldier who wanted to die or commit an odd sort of suicide repeatedly was killing "himself," a *doppelganger* self, an image of and in his own likeness. Race was a master trope of his scopic field, a nodal point quilting visual signifiers in a way that ran counter to the rhetoric of war available to other (white and black) soldiers fighting on the American side, anchoring his judgment of the enemy as like rather than different from him in an embodied, material way.

Lacan offers purchase to this fictional Korean's guilt and his paradoxical returns to the battlefield, in a manner that takes us beyond this analysis and into trickier, more troublesome issues. Says Lacan: "In the scopic field, everything is articulated between two terms that act in an antinomic way—on the side of things, there is the gaze, that is to say, things look at me, and yet I see them. This is how one should understand those words, so strongly stressed, in the Gospel, *They have eyes that they might not see*. That they might not see what? Precisely, that things are looking at them" (1978, 109).[5]

With the eye, there is looking, which exhibits the subject's command of the scopic field. With the gaze, there is an eerie reciprocity, a simultaneous looking and being-looked-at (Zizek, 1991a, 109–110). There is an ethical distinction here, which we can illustrate quickly with reference to an everyday phenomenon. Husbands often say to their wives, after staring at another woman, "I was just looking!"[6] They wish to be let off the hook, almost a priori forgiven, because the relation they have to the other is "merely" at the level of the image, an exercise in fantasy. The other remains a blind object. An instance of gazing would be quite different, for that which in the look was merely an object-other now becomes a subject who looks back. With the gaze, the subject is the object of the desire of the other, for the gaze belongs to the other.[7]

The enigma of the Korean soldier now transcends the domain of guilt, and moves us uncomfortably into perversity.[8] Presumably unlike most of his compatriots in war, this soldier recognizes the moment of the gaze. It is not simply that he "sees" them as being "like" him. He is *seen*. This is a moment of profound communicative intersubjectivity, which Hegel (1977) refers to as mutual recognition—a moment of reciprocity that puts a halt to the master-slave dialectic and which stalls the desire for combat. While his compatriots have eyes yet might not see human eyes looking back at them, this Korean soldier does. And yet he kills, is wounded, is healed, is praised and glorified, and returns to kill more. If his own death were truly his desire, that would be an easy enough matter. But no—he feels somehow compelled to return to a scene in which the other is returning his gaze, suspending his judgment of the other as Other, registering the pull of its desire. This is a theater of pain, repeated pain, which tells us that his avowed desire (to die) is in fact, as the repressed kernel of his own narrative, a disavowal of his desire: to inflict pain; to be seen inflicting pain by a subject capable of recognition; not to die, but to kill. To be guilty, perhaps even to enjoy public shame. This conscientious warrior is perhaps the scariest sort of all, reminding us of Zizek's (1991b) twist on the crucifixion (where Christ cries out, "forgive them Father, for they know not what they do!"), a twist which alerts us to the fact that they know what they do but do it anyway. This is why Pilate and Judas are such heinous figures in the Western imagination: their actions outstrip, go against the teeth of, their best judgment. They are perverts who act knowingly, and for the enjoyment of profit (rendered to them by the Military State apparatus).

Perverse enjoyment performs a link between knowledge, action, and judgment, which in Christianity is absented, i.e., the Roman soldiers who took part in the crucifixion know not what they do. Consequently, their actions are forgivable. They are spared God's judgment. Orwell's *1984* gives us a good hard look at the difference between those who know not and those who know. For Orwell, not knowing (false consciousness) appears to be the test for the ideological. Another test, which zooms in on a contiguity of knowing, doing, and enjoyment takes us elsewhere, i.e., from false consciousness to perversity. Zizek tells a tale, based on an interpretation of a photograph, which is directly relevant:

> Where can we grasp 'enjoyment as a political factor' at its purest? A famous photo from the time of Nazi anti-Semitic pogroms shows a frightened Jewish boy driven into a corner and surrounded by a group of Germans. This group is extremely interesting in so far as the facial expressions of its members render the entire scale of possible reactions: one of them 'enjoys it' in an immediate, idiotic way; another is clearly scared (perhaps he has the premonition that he might be next); the feigned indifference of the third conceals a freshly awakened curiosity; and so on, up to the unique expression of a young man who is obviously embarrassed, even disgusted, by the entire affair, unable to yield wholeheartedly to it, yet at the same time fascinated by it, enjoying it with an intensity that surpasses by far the idiocy of immediate pleasure. *He is the most dangerous*: his quavering indecision exactly corresponds to the unique expression of the Rat Man's face noticed by Freud when the Rat Man was relating the story of the rat torture: 'At all the more important moments while he was relating the story his face took on a very strange, composite expression. I could only interpret it as one of horror at pleasure of his own of which he himself was unaware.' (Zizek, 1994, 1)[9]

In the event this example remains too arcane, or the interpretation embedded in it too uncanny, one need only reflect briefly on the practice of "hazing" common to many university "Greek" organizations. Young men and women perform "shameful" acts in the presence of their peers, and yet the Law that constitutes the symbolic apparatus of the organization requires these actions. The result, of course, is not merely "guilt-by-association," but rather its negative or inverted image: *association-by-guilt*. The knowing discomfort of "pledges," their troubled enjoyment of the hazing ritual, is not only expected but is in fact hoped for, since it is the visible trace of guilt that will bind the subject to the collective. It is not the radical *duping* of subjects that this ideological operation performs, it does not aim at "false consciousness," but rather an encroachment of perversity (knowing-doing the shameful; performing for the enjoyment of the Other; making oneself an instrument of the Other's jouissance).

Those who robotically perform the will of the Big Other, or Big Brother, are not so frightening as those who do so with the intimation or even knowledge that what they do is perverse. They render themselves as objects of Its enjoyment, thus reversing the formula of fantasy Lacan set out some time ago ($\$\lozenge a$, or the barred subject in relation to a fantasized object of desire) into the formula for perversity ($a\lozenge\$$, the barred subject as a fantasized object in relation to the Big Other's jouissance).[10] According to Lacan, "the subject here makes himself the instrument of the Other's *jouis-*

sance" (1977, 320).[11] Racially incapable of participating in the patriotic fantasy that the enemy is radically Other, the Korean soldier nevertheless performs beyond the call of duty and receives many honors. Through a series of episodes that appear as "accidents" or "chance happenings," he becomes a hero; a figure of praise that props up the machinery of war his desire presumably works against. Simultaneously, he is a pervert of the scariest sort, and embodies an uncanny linkage of heroism and cowardice, the normatively valued and celebrated and the perverse. He is also, to some extent, an exemplary product of the war culture's patriotic assembly line—a Korean who kills Koreans "for" America. So too with the German boy who indecisively yet robustly procures the enjoyments of enmity and aggression: he will be an excellent Nazi, the most dangerous of all, according to Zizek: a patriot who is seen doing that which he has considerable qualms about (and unthinkable enjoyment in) publicly, in the eyes of those he aspires to be admired by. Solidarity-in-guilt, judgment-in-jouissance.

The manufacture of soldiers, war machines whose judgment of the other as radically Other and not-human, is accomplished by a stunning range of communicative performances and daily practices, some of which they look at as spectators (such as Capra's *Why We Fight* films) and others which they more actively participate in (such as drills, joke-telling, and everyday conversation). These performances—which may routinize and streamline judgment of the other as radically Other—provide relatively stable defense mechanisms against paralyzing affects, such as guilt and fear, and an equipment for living whose vestiges are carried with them residually, perhaps for life. One soldier, recounting his participation in the gang rape of a Vietnamese woman, claims that he did not perceive his actions at the time as the violation of another human being, but of a "gook." The sexual aspect of the act was displaced by its violence at the level of the spectacle, or so he says. He did as his comrades did, and they presumably watched him do it just as he presumably watched them. Yet something remained embedded in his memory, and thus his experience, of the event which troubled and agitated him (later in life)—a blemish on an otherwise "pure" event of war, so clean in its brutalities, so allegedly sexless in its rapes.

The framing and saturation of the military subject's scopic field thus may be incomplete, a stain or spot may appear, leaving a trace of the desire of the other—a place from which the other gazes back at the subject (see Zizek, 1991a, 125–126; Lacan, 1978, 104). This stain, spot, or trace of the desire of the other problematizes the notion that military subjects don't see the eyes looking at them when conducting the ugly business of war, that they don't in fact know what they're doing but do it anyway. The stain, spot, or trace of the desire of the other renders highly suspect the idea that their training has secured and completed a judgment of the other as radically Other. The Korean soldier, the German boy, and the American rapist—all express in one way or another a hesitation or indecision about their knowledge and action. In admittedly different ways, each of these subjects stands squarely within the visibility of the patriotic gaze and its judgment. Though perverse, they are to be judged as shameless, for their actions are beheld "in" the eyes of those they aspire to be like. At least two questions remain: What accounts for such perversity? How is it practically constituted?

Roughly contemporary films that tease out the manufacturedness of aggressive patriotic judgment zero in on the gap which separates the military subject from the discourses and practices that make him. In *Full Metal Jacket*, we see how a fat, kind, young, even child-like, and fragile human being (nicknamed by the drill sergeant, "Private Pyle") becomes the ultimate war machine while other, presumably tougher, men maintain friction between knowing and doing—they do what they are told, but they don't necessarily do so based upon knowledge that it is right, good, or even necessary. It is ordered. And yet the military code has a place for this doubled subjectivity—that of the simultaneous dupe and non-dupe, wherein one cannot use an order to shield oneself from accountability: because it is a priori demanded that you know what you're doing, merely following orders does not suffice; but not following orders is unacceptable. Indeed, the military code doubles back on itself, making its subjects responsible both for following orders and for being accountable for their own actions "as if" they were strictly voluntary. The double injunction or articulation of two Laws: one may be persecuted for not following orders, and, at the same time, for following them. There are two Laws within the military code: the public law, which is visible to the naked eye, and what Zizek (1994) calls its dark superego, which lingers like a specter just beyond visibility yet which also is known. Thus, far from constituting a threat to the war machine or the factory of ideology, knowledge supplies the foundations for a collective guilt that is stronger than any reasonable attachment to others. The subject is judged, both by others and by himself, as guilty. Pyle, however, remains up to a certain point innocent, for he knows not what he does. The other military subjects are guilty, for they know what they do. In a very interesting moment of the film, which almost marks a transition from innocence to guilt, Pyle is assaulted whilst sleeping by his peers—beaten with bars of soap wrapped in towels. The motive behind the beating was Pyle's ineptness, his incapacity to obey the letter of the Law: the entire group of trainees was punished for his errors, and now they punish him (to avoid further punishment). The group consolidates in the beating of Pyle, in an avoidance of pain, and Pyle does not report the beating. The public Law has been violated with the beating of Pyle, yet it also has been supported by an illegal enjoyment: solidarity-in-guilt, peace-in-violence. So well does Pyle learn his lesson that he dramatically transforms from an innocent into a well-tuned machine. Problematically, Pyle comes to believe in only one Law. Transcending both innocence and guilt, Pyle becomes an abomination: he embodies the Law, and thus embodies its contradictory imperative. It is not at all paradoxical, therefore, that Pyle comes to constitute a threat to the American war machine, because he has reversed the relationship which he (qua military subject) really ought to maintain between knowing and doing. While the usual formula for ideology would suggest that what the ideological state apparatus "wants" is subjects who know not what they do, thus making actions of the military subject merely extensions of the war machine and not theirs at all, in fact its obscene desire is that subjects know precisely what they do, and thus situates the subject as guilty subject of the Law. Pyle very literally no longer knows what he is doing, so absorbed has he become in the military code, for it has been materially beaten into him. The ideological operation of the Law, and its dark superego, left nothing untouched: both body and mind had been submitted utterly, which paradoxically equates with the Law's failure. Something must be exceed the Law for it to function properly, and Pyle's excesses all were reigned in and submitted. As "perfect" subject of the Law, Pyle in fact is an abomination, and is portrayed finally as insane. His aggressiveness in the end is turned against the military machine, the "perfect" subject goes against the Law, turning it on itself, killing the drill sergeant and himself with a rifle in the presence of several other privates—in the "John," no less, which is where all privates and Pyles/piles (of shit) truly belong. All signifiers have come home here, attaching themselves to a perfectly sensible field of reference that irrupts in a moment of madness. As Lacan says, the Real is what returns to its place. In this scene, the Real has returned to its place indeed. The Law has produced its own obscene inversion—Pyle has become the perfect military subject and killing machine—featuring "at this point of failure," to borrow the words of Zizek, how "the public Law is compelled to search for support in an illegal enjoyment" (1994, 54). This illegal enjoyment is the perverse action-in-knowledge or praxis of military subjects who know what they are doing and do it anyway, and who, thus, are the Law's always already guilty subjects. Instead of viewing ideology the old-fashioned way as "false consciousness" or "non-knowledge," now we grasp it as perversity. And, further, we recognize that the cohesiveness of military intersubjectivity and community hinges not on false consciousness or non-knowledge but on a collective guilt that circulates at the level of the image as an open secret: again, the military subject knows what he does, does it anyway, and sees others doing the same, is seen by others doing the same, and sees himself being seen by others . . . ad nauseam, into expanding circles of reflection that quickly take us to the nether regions of intersubjective recognition. The circuit of looking and gazing here travels far, perpetually deferring desire, but not judgment. The subject of the Law is judged, both by specific others and by the Big Other: Guilty! Guilty because the hot and fricative relation between knowledge and action is not ideologically lubricated, or cemented in a final way, by "false consciousness." All is in plain view and simultaneously concealed, like a sandwich in a plastic bag. It is this clear or translucent envelop which holds subjects together in knowing-guilt, not in dark or bedazzled false consciousness. Zizek offers two analogies that may flesh out this somewhat elusive point:

> Let us return to those small-town white communities in the American South of the 1920s, where the reign of the official, public Law is accompanied by its shadowy double, the nightly terror of Ku Klux Klan, with its lynchings of powerless blacks: a (white) man is easily forgiven minor infractions of the Law, especially when they can be justified by a 'code of honor'; the community still recognizes him as 'one of us'. Yet he will be effectively excommunicated, perceived as 'not one of us', the moment he disowns the specific form of *transgression* that pertains to this community—say, the moment he refuses to take part in the ritual lynchings by the Klan, or even reports them to the Law (which, of course, does not want to hear about them, since they exemplify its own hidden underside). The Nazi community relied on the same solidarity-in-guilt induced by the participation in a common transgression: it ostracized those who were not ready to take on the dark side of the idyllic *Volksgemeinschaft*: the night pogroms, the beatings of political opponents—in short, all that 'everybody knew, yet did not want to speak about aloud'. (Zizek, 1994, 55)

It is precisely this grainy slippage between knowing (better) and doing (otherwise) that renders the perverse constructedness of the military subject's scopic field, and guilty-judgment, itself part of the field of visibility. As with the uncanny surrealist paintings of René Magritte, who between 1940 and 1945 joined the French resistance to Hitler, the frame itself often is envisioned in what often appears to be a realistic scape. Indeed, as with "The Human Condition, I" (1934), and many other of Magritte's works, the framing of vision appears most powerfully when it is on the verge of vanishing, its obscene or meaningless "blank spot" painted over. The canvas here, propped up by an easel, appears as a window onto the real. It is placed before a window overlooking a pastoral scene, and what is painted on the canvas almost perfectly fills in the gap in the pastoral that it would presumably block: if a viewer looked out the window from behind the painting—and the viewer of the painting proper doubles as the viewer of the painting-within-the-painting—the "unfinished" image on the canvas would not obscure what is beyond it but would provide its double or supplementary image, supplying the illusion that it is not a painting at all but rather another window looking out the window. Yet a slight unpainted portion stands out in all its unmarked vividness—a rough, unfinished spot. This is an eruption of the Real into the Symbolic, the unmarked into the marked, which draws attention to the peculiar constructedness of visibility in a potentially traumatic moment of recognition. It is a rupture in the ideological field; a protest reminding us that the imaginary *is not* the real even if it appears to be. Nevertheless, this rupture/protest may serve to congeal knowledge around a blank-spot so that *praxis* emerges guilty: knowing, unknowing, still acting "as if..." The presence of the unmarked may be traumatic, and may never be fully repressed. With Magritte, this is so by design, and so too it is with the framing of the military subject's scopic field: the framing itself is framed as a surplus or "more than" which meets the eye/I. With both, Edenic innocence and non-knowledge is compromised and rearticulated on another plane, conveying guilt to the subject who knows and still acts as if s/he didn't. The unmarked is obvious to the eye, and yet subjects may go on acting as if it weren't.[12] If in the eyes of the Law ignorance does not exclude the subject from judgment, knowledge would seem to locate the subject squarely in the domain of guilt, even shame. But in the former lies the possibility for solidarity, whereas shame would seem to be sovereign—a rather lonely occupation.

The guilty-judgment is structurally present even at this micrological level of scopic identity-formation as a terrible bonus or supplement, reminding us of Captain Willard's matter-of-fact and yet chilling utterance early in *Apocalypse Now*: "Every man gets everything he wants. I wanted a mission." Willard's desire makes him good company for military intelligence, desirable. He surrounds himself with hypocrisy, willfully making himself an instrument of its excessive and cannibalistic jouissance. Guilty. While on leave, all Willard can do is drink himself into oblivion, and reflect on the paradoxes of the military subject: when in Nam, all he can do is think of home; and when at home, all he wants is to return to the jungle. The military subject's relation to himself is always extimate, strange, and simultaneously intimate and familiar. The basic trait of this lifestyle: the desire to desire; desire without object. In this catch-22, Willard's desire falls on the side of the jungle, toward the religious passion of a mission. And a mission he got, yet at the terrible price of knowing full well before hand that the man he was going to kill—Colonel Walter Kurtz (Marlon Brando)—was a brilliant, extremely well-educated, and "perfect" killing machine. No matter: Willard's deepest desire was to return to the jungle, away from his wife and home, where he/things no longer made any sense. Only a confrontation with the jouissance of the Other, and in his recognizing gaze, would do. Yet this confrontation produced an unhappy bonus, a stain on the screen of enjoyment, which brought Willard (played by Martin Sheen) to want and accept no more missions. The encounter with Kurtz is an encounter of Willard with an *imago* or imaginary reflection of himself, reminding us of the Korean soldier who killed Koreans. Part of Willard (and not the best part, to be sure) was left behind with the corpse of Kurtz. Willard's career ends with this murder. One plausible interpretation is that he lost his religion. He had seen too much, too many stains and spots, and, consequently, knew too much to keep on acting as a military subject. Another interpretation would suggest that Willard confronted in his mission and encounter with Kurtz precisely the *unmarked*, a gap in the symbolic economy of military *praxis*—a traumatic eruption of the Real, unspeakable, and unrepresentable. Willard confronted his own desire, lack: a hole in the symbolic order. But he also confronted an excess, jouissance: more than the symbolic order may contain. The gap, in which Kurtz stands, the place that he occupies, is precisely the unmarked territory of military Law: the constitutive void in its system of justice. As with Magritte, this gap or void doubles as a surplus conveying the simultaneous idiocy and urgency of ideological illusion. Either way we slice it, i.e., arguing that Willard came to "know too much" *or* that he confronted the obscene jouissance of idiotic non-knowledge at the core of the Law, we appear to land in the same place: the simultaneity of lack and plenitude, knowledge and idiocy, desire and jouissance, at the heart of the Law and the scene of judgment. Not only are these apparently competing interpretations of *Apocalypse Now* plausible and in fact deeply intertwined, they each speak directly to the doubledness of judgment at the level of the image: too much, not enough, a surplus (of lack). Willard's guilt, which produced solidarity with military brass aplenty, finally sinks into shame. Willard finally sees himself as Other, appears as strange "in" his own eyes, as Aristotle puts it. But whose eyes does Willard see himself through to make this judgment? Of course, the gaze belongs to the "madman," Kurtz, the subject who had gone beyond the Law by becoming the Law. Through the eyes of the supreme subject/Law, Willard recognizes his own perverse il/legality. Rather than seeing himself as a self-identical reflection of himself, he recognizes at once a hole and a dark bonus.

The appearance of this surplus or "more than" in the form of a gap, stain, spot, or trace of the Other's jouissance—which cuts against the grain of ideological discourse—is discovered by Zizek at the level of sound, and more particularly music, in Fassbinder's film *Lili Marleen*, a film that takes us to a period we will shortly be spending some time with, the milieu of World War Two. In this film, Zizek argues, the manufacture of public judgment is revealed in all its clanky dissonance, shattering the ideological illusion that Nazi totalitarian power is a "natural" movement of world history, and thus should be embraced with passion and pride by the German *Volk*. The unmarked/unheard is conjured *via negativa* by the overmarked/heard, by ideological overexertion. Zizek's interpretation is stunning and provocative:

> during the film, the popular love song of the German soldiers is replayed to exhaustion, and this endless repetition changes a lovely melody into a painfully disgusting parasite that fails to release us even for a moment. Here, again, its status is unclear: totalitarian power (personified by Goebbels) tries to manipulate it, to use it to capture the imagination of the tired soldiers, but the song escapes its grasp like a genie released from a bottle. It begins to lead a life of its own—nobody can master its effects. The crucial feature of Fassbinder's film is this insistence on the utter ambiguity of "Lili Marleen": a Nazi love song promulgated by all sorts of propaganda devices, certainly, but at the same time, on the verge of transforming itself into a subversive element that could burst from the very ideological machine by which it is supported, and thus always in danger of being prohibited. Such a fragment of the signifier permeated with idiotic enjoyment is what Lacan, in the last stage of his teaching, called *le sinthome*. *Le sinthome* is not the symptom, the coded message to be deciphered by interpretation, but the meaningless letter that immediately procures *jouis-sense*, "enjoyment-in-meaning," "enjoy-meant." If we consider the role of the *sinthome* in the construction of the ideological edifice, we are compelled to rethink the "criticism of ideology." Ideology is usually conceived as a discourse: as an enchainment of elements the meaning of which is overdetermined by their specific articulation, i.e., by the way some "nodal point" (the Lacanian master-signifier) totalizes them into a homogenous field. . . . But when we take into account the dimension of the *sinthome*, it is no longer sufficient to denounce the "artificial" character of the ideological experience, to demonstrate the way the object experienced by ideology as "natural" and "given" is effectively a discursive construction, a result of a network of symbolic overdetermination; it is no longer enough to locate the ideological text in its context, to render visible its necessarily overlooked margins. What we must do (what Gillian or Fassbinder do), on the contrary, is to *isolate* the *sinthome*'s utter stupidity. In other words, we must carry out the operation of changing the precious gift into a gift of shit (as Lacan put it in his Seminar XI), of experiencing the fascinating, mesmerizing voice as a disgusting, meaningless fragment of the real. (1991a, 128–129)[13]

The effect of this operation, says Zizek, is "estrangement," which in the example of *Lili Marleen* "dissolves totalitarianism as an effective social bond by isolating the heinous kernel of its idiotic enjoyment" (129). Estrangement may rip the tapestry of ideology, register a dissonance-within-harmony, thus opening a space for critical rhetoric, judgment, and social change. To this articulation of estrangement, ideology, rhetoric, judgment, and social change, we will return at the conclusion of this chapter, under the rubric of criticism as a performance of the return of the repressed—a rubric that can be summed up by the paradoxical phrase, now available to the popular imagination, and ceaselessly toyed with by Zizek (1991a) and Lacan (1988), "back to the future!" With the return of the repressed, the hard nut of American patriotic enjoyment is traumatically cracked, compelling us to recognize the terrible in the past as propellant toward the future.

Incentives on Patriotism and Perversity: Disavowing the Other's Desire; Knowing and Doing

"Life as a means to knowledge"—with this principle in one's heart one can live not only boldly but even gaily, and laugh gaily, too! And who knows how to laugh anyway and live well if he does not first know a good deal about war and victory.

—Nietzsche, *The Gay Science*, §324[14]

American democratic patriotism during the Second World War was organized around a heinous kernel of idiotic enjoyment which nevertheless remained an open secret of the scopic field, structuring judgment of the other as radically Other through a variety of visual techniques and caricatures. Since the full range of techniques for so doing can't be surveyed here, we will focus on those which render the Japanese war machine in animalistic-sexual terms for patriotic aggression and enjoyment. The interpretive thrust here suggests that the visual rhetoric to be examined created an environment of judgment or way of seeing that supported an erotic fear of the enemy-other, a sort of pornography of war which both citizens and the media industry participated in creating. This structuring of judgment was oriented toward making the hating and killing of Japanese subjects seem not only easier, but indeed enjoyable, justifiable, and even necessary.

In 1942, a drawing was submitted to a "This is the Enemy Contest," and later "was exhibited at New York's Museum of Modern Art and reprinted in Life" (Dower, 1986, 189). In it, a Japanese soldier slouches forward toward the frontal boundary of the picture, as if advancing on the viewer. The portrayal of his carriage mirrors a large array of visual techniques employed to render the Japanese soldier as monkey or gorilla, featuring a curved spine and awkward or incompetent bi-pedalism. The left side of the body is thrust forward, so that the shoulders are not squared toward the viewer, the left arm hanging loosely toward the ground. Unlike the simian or gorilla portrayals that were so prevalent in the popular press and perhaps in military literatures, this image suggests that the curvature of the spine, the bent knees, and the hanging arm, are fundamentally linked to sexuality and aggression rather than merely an expression of physiology. For the Japanese soldier clearly is human, even though his carriage, features, and style, mark him as different and perhaps obscene: an eerie combination, sexually charged, of human, animal, and alien. The eyes in particular are strange, set far apart and not focused in one place: they seem to look in several directions at once: outward, toward the outside of the picture and at the viewer, and simultaneously to what for the viewer is an unseen aspect of the scopic field constituted and framed by the picture. His awkward and slouching movement result from carrying a "naked white woman" (Dower, 1986, 189) on his back, and a pistol in his left hand.

In 1943, "a British graphic was used to illustrate . . . [an] article in the New York Times Magazine" (Dower, 187). Like the "This is the Enemy" picture, it caricatures a Japanese soldier's manner of carriage, except that here the figure is rendered as a giant gorilla who, King Kong-like, carries women in his right hand through a desiccated warscape. The left hand props up the giant gorilla figure, knuckles to the ground. The eyes, behind small round spectacles, this time are remarkably close together, and seem to focus beyond the scopic field of the picture (slightly downward and to the viewer's right).

Here, in these two images, the patriotic impulse is libidinally articulated *via negativa*— as a defense against an obscene threat combining sexual, bestial, and aggressive attributes: a defense which significantly responds to the idea of woman-as-property. As *sinthome*, or idiotic enjoyment-in-meaning (jouis-sense), we might recognize that these pictures are constructs of the patriotic imagination, which performs a visual judgment and fantasized projection of the other as radically Other; not as hindrances to its desiring operations, but as fuel. This judgment and fantasized projection encodes both patriotic desire and fear at the level of the *imago* in a way that registers, according to Dower, "sexual fears underlying the Yellow Peril and anti-'colored' sentiments" (189), and "the perception of the Japanese as super-men . . . alongside the images of apes and lesser men" (187). Established through visual rhetoric as object-cause of patriotic desire, such visualizations of the other at the level of the image creates a scopic field of judgment which supports exterminationist policies and actions, including the dropping of atomic bombs on Hiroshima and Nagasaki. Against the sheerly verbal and realist arguments made by scholars of the Second World War, particularly Robert Newman (1994), who argue for or against the bombings of Hiroshima and Nagasaki based upon interpretations of "cost-gains" analyses of an invasion campaign, or upon readings of Truman's diaries, a turn to visual rhetoric enriches the problematic. The choice between one and many is qualitative, not just quantitative. I do not wish to claim that Newman's argument is necessarily wrong, nor even that the bombings of Hiroshima and Nagasaki were, either. But in addition to the usual claim—that the bombings saved both American and Japanese lives—we should take into account that the visualizations of Japanese subjects supported the bombings, whereas alternative images would not have. Unlike popular representations of Germans, who were often portrayed as 'sick' or mentally ill people led by an ego-maniacal Führer, the American media industry represented the Japanese as abominations. Whereas sickness may be cured, abomination cannot. Thus, a link may be forged between image and judgment that suggests the visual rhetoric of war was intimately connected to military policies. The pornography of war excited patriotic libido, leading up to the (anti)climactic atomic explosions high above two Japanese cities, putting an end to the hot war and announcing the beginning of the Cold War.

The rhetoric of representation employed in these pictures, and others, habitually renders Japanese subjects as either sub- or super-human—as possessing a surplus, or as lacking. Such sub- and super-human representations articulate the alien *jouissance* of the other as the basis of racism. As super-humans, Japanese subjects/soldiers possess capacities beyond those of "normal" human beings, i.e., Anglo-Americans, and for that reason register as threatening. As sub-humans, Japanese subjects/soldiers lack that which "normal" human beings have, et cetera, and thus register as threatening. In this double-bind, Japanese subjectivity is always already imperialist subjectivity: subjectivity that lacks (desires) and that overflows (in alien jouissance), and consequently seeks either fulfillment or release by spreading disease-like across geographic and libidinal boundaries. As a strategy of representation, with consequent judgments, this rhetoric of enmity, in which the Japanese are Other, doubles as a rhetoric of racism more generally. This perspective on the pictures Dower treats in *War Without Mercy* takes us beyond what the "pictures themselves say," and toward their circulation of enjoyment and anxiety, which explains their incredible power to render judgment. Patriotic, and racist, judgment is marked by a certain indecisiveness between desire (lack) and jouissance (plenitude) in the Other, which is resolved by the application of a both/and rhetoric: at once more and less than human, more and less than meets the eye/I of patriotic Americans.[15]

As ideological critique, Dower's "reading" or "use" of visual images leans heavily on the assumption that these images at once accomplished the naturalization of the judgment that the other was radically Other, and, as part of that naturalization process, put their own constructedness or imaginary status under erasure through a sort of rhetorical *softening*. Says Dower: "The linguistic softening of the killing process was accomplished most often through two general figures of speech: metaphors of the hunt, and of exterminating vermin" (86). I would invert Dower's claim to say that the rhetorical *hardening* of the killing process was accomplished, not through primary metaphors, but through articulations of alien desire and jouissance in sub- and super-human renderings of Japanese subjects. The proliferation of these figures, presumably and paradoxically, rendered them so ordinary as to seem transparent, real relations to the Real itself and not imaginary ones (see Althusser, 1971). The threatening and alien desire and jouissance of the Other was materialized visually, as though it were merely a reflection and not a rhetorical construction. Such is the uncanny power of the image: to be made, and to pose as a "natural" object or mimetic reflection thereof. The most powerful rhetoric, as John Lyne and Michael Calvin McGee have argued (1987), erases its own rhetoricity, producing the illusion that it is a transparent window onto reality—not a judgment call, in the sense of an active and tricky engagement with the undecidable, but a "called" judgment, in the sense of an always already imposed or prefigured reality which the image mimetically reflects. In response to this mimetic reflection, presumably, subjects "know not what they do," for their response to the image is called for. There is no tick or twitch at the eye, no guilt, but only patri-idiotic enjoyment, *sinthome*—interpellated or "called" judgment.

Now we have located the force of Dower's argument about the rhetorical construction of judgment at the level of the image in American 1940s war culture, and have shored up its chief limitation: it puts minimal accountability on subject-consumers of the images, and (rightly, perhaps) puts the burden of racist representation on the State and the media industry. And yet . . . It neglects the possibility that the visual rhetoric of war, no matter how incredibly expansive and powerful, nevertheless revealed itself as *sinthome*, suggesting a troublesome thesis already explored speculatively but in some detail above through anecdotes and fragments of popular texts. Namely, though with complacent resistance to the knobby visual rhetoric of war, that Americans (soldiers and civilians) knew what they were doing and did it anyway—that, like the love song in *Lili Marleen*, these images overflowed the scopic field's frame, bringing the frame itself into eerie visibility, so that subjects had to (at best) repress the dissonance. Can this unlikely, unpatriotic thesis be defended? Certainly, a somewhat less ambitious argument regarding the fricative relation between knowledge and action can be substantiated, though it is a less surprising (but no less troubling) one. Nevertheless, it puts us through a useful detour to our question, which perhaps cannot be answered at all, that can be looked at but not touched: a provocation only.

The less ambitious argument: There was an image industry in the U.S. that circulated patriotic desire and aggression through public communications, and this industry was just as systematically ideological in character as other patriotic propaganda (for example, the Nazi "documentary" *Triumph of the Will*). Whether or not or to what degree it *accomplished* the manufacture of public judgment via images of the other, as radically Other, however, is almost impossible to say at this point in history. (For who knows what agencies to locate ideological accomplishment in? The paranoid answer, of course, is: in all of them.) It was endeavored; this has already been demonstrated in plenty, on both scholarly and popular orders of critique. Yet even this "endeavor" is only problematically linked to the will or judgment of individual subjects, who in fact may be seen to obey the call of the Big Other, and who traverse the circuit of guilty association in a perverse spirit. What we are after is maximum accountability at all levels, and yet are faced with subjects who do not perhaps know what they are doing. Non-sense, jouis-sense, appears to be the driving force that structures patriotic desire.

The story behind Frank Capra's seven *Why We Fight* "documentaries" (1942–1945) is an interesting case in point that will return us to question whether or not the scopic field of American patriotism might have been doubling back on itself, placing knowledge and action in fricative contact. John Lucaites (1986) has argued that these films manufacture and reaffirm American liberal and patriotic values in their portrayals of the Other. They rhetorically materialize threats to the American way of life, and to democracy more generally. Lucaites' interpretation, which is absolutely correct, suggests that the material reality of war, and the very psychological motives for war, is inseparable for their rhetorical construction. In Lacanese, the "real" of war is always already symbolic. To make sense of the madness of war, to justify war, a translation of jouissance into desire is necessary. The mediary between war's real and symbolic manifestations, of course, is the imaginary. And in film, it is precisely the image, which renders intelligible judgment on global-military affairs. Behind the image, of course, and at the very scene of its making, we find a strangely hollow core of non-knowledge and idiocy. Let us tell the tale behind the making of the *Why We Fight* documentaries.

Capra, a Hollywood director, was called into Army Chief of Staff George C. Marshall's office, and was asked to create "a series of orientation films for viewing by American troops" (Dower, 15). Capra allegedly declined, claiming that he'd never made a documentary film before, and thus lacked the know-how. Marshall replied: "Capra, I have never been Chief of Staff before. Thousands of young Americans have never had their legs shot off before. Boys are commanding ships today, who a year ago had never seen the ocean before." Capra replied, promising "the best damned documentary films ever made" (Capra, 1971, 327). The results of this endeavor included massive audiences numbering in the millions, systematic government involvement in the production and "editing" of manuscripts, and, consequently, an Academy Award in 1942 for Prelude to War.

We must pause here to remark on the strange and simultaneously familiar reversal of knowledge and action in his accounting for how he came to make the *Why We Fight* documentaries, and in his account of how Chief of Staff Marshall persuaded him to make them. In both cases, we have a claim of non-knowledge not only covering for but moreover demanding action. With Marshall, we have: "I don't know what I'm doing, but I do it anyway—and basically nobody else involved in the military does either—therefore, so should you!" To which Capra in effect responds: "OK . . . I don't know what I'm doing, but neither does anybody else, therefore I will do my very best, which will be nothing short of excellence!" Everybody now knows that nobody knows what they're doing, yet all (are called to) act as if they do. (Is this not the structure of perversity, which leads Walter Kurtz, in *Apocalypse Now*, to his disgusted embrace of military hypocrisy and madness, and which, initially goads Willard to accept the mission to kill him?) Again: this empty performance, visible as an open secret, secures the pound of flesh which binds military subjects cohesively together in repressed guilt. And again, as with the Korean soldier in our opening anecdote, we move from guilt to perversity precisely because of the manifoldly inverted relation between knowledge and action. Though at first it appears as if the soldier is going to battle to kill (because he's guilty), and then to die to put an end to guilt, his motivation remains radically uncertain, cueing us in to the perverse kernel of his enjoyment, which consists exactly in having other Koreans (those whom he recognizes and recognize him, in the Hegelian sense) witness his killing of Koreans. And the Korean soldier makes public his tale, the core of non-sense that he knows to be goading his actions. So too with the image of the entire military apparatus as it emerges in the exchange between Capra and Marshall: why they're doing "it" (i.e., being Chief of Staff, making documentaries, commanding battleships, killing Japanese, whatever) is retroactively established precisely by an absence of motive, which Edgar Allan Poe terms the "spirit of perverseness": "it is in fact a mobile without motive, a motive not *motviert*. Through its promptings we act without comprehensible object; or, if this shall be understood as a contradiction in terms, we may so far modify the proposition as to say, that through its promptings we act, for the reason that we should not [i.e., because there is no motive, and no comprehensible object to orient action toward an end.—JPM] In theory, no reason can be more unreasonable; but, in fact, there is none more strong. . . . It is a radical, a primitive impulse—elementary" (Poe, "The Imp of the Perverse," cited in Zizek, 1994, 98–99).

Elsewhere, in "The Black Cat," Poe asks: "Have not a perpetual inclination, in the teeth of our best judgment, to violate that which is *Law*,
merely because we understand it to be such?" (cited in Zizek, 1994, 98).
Zizek argues that we should recognize in the rhetoric of perversity a mirror image of Kant's articulation of aesthetic experience, expressed in the
Critique of Judgment as "purposefulness without purpose." The experiences of beauty and of perversity appear to be of the same family. The
categorical imperative of jouissance, if Kant had invented one, would
likely have been enjoyment for enjoyment's sake—enjoyment without
utility, without Law, and without judgment—no questions asked. And
Poe seems to insist that perverse inclination outstrips judgment, over-
comes the questioning voice of conscience and Law, and is marked by a
disavowal. Zizek explains that perversion "is defined precisely by the
lack of a question." And yet this lack of a question remains at the level of
the ego/*imago*, where one sees what one does and, on this condition, proceeds to act knowingly. There is a slippage in Zizek's theory of perversion, for on the one hand there is a lack of a question, but on the other is a
knowing disavowal (which implies the presence of indecision, a question, logically prior to judgment and action). Zizek *avec* Zizek: "The pervert possesses an immediate certainty that his activity serves the enjoyment of the Other" (1991, 181 n. 10). Perhaps this slippage between
question and certainty is inevitable when trying to lay hold of perversion. Let us stick with the strict Lacanian formula, which Poe grasps most
immediately as a wicked flight from judgment: not exactly the lack of a
question, but the disavowal of lack in the other. Aesthetic experience
(purposefulness without purpose) translates into a mode of political action, which aims at expediency and enjoyment leaning on certainty without knowledge: perversion. Inflected this way, we might find the conjunction of the aesthetic and the political in Capra's *Why We Fight*
"documentaries" to be precisely perverse, from origin to end, or cause to
effect: from the meeting with Chief of Staff Marshall all the way to the
theater and beyond.

Situated in this discussion of the perverse inversion of knowledge and
action, Capra's documentary, *Know Your Enemy—Japan* is especially interesting just as its title now seems particularly ironic. This film was re-
leased to the public on 9 August 1945—the very day Nagasaki was
bombed—and was recalled two weeks and one day later. Rather than
creating "knowledge" of the enemy's identity, habits, visual appearance,
and so forth, with which to ground and justify military action against
them, and to manufacture public consent, *Know Your Enemy* supplies
knowledge after ultimate action has already been taken. If anything,
then, it offers but a defense mechanism against guilt. Dower describes
this particular film as hurried, messy "patchwork," yet also as particu-

larly "vivid." He writes of one scene in particular: "Beneath its dazzling surface imagery . . . the message was simple, conveyed in a stark metaphor and a striking visual image. The audience was told that the Japanese resembled "photographic prints of the same negative." Visually, this was reinforced by repeated scenes of a steel bar being hammed in a forge" (19, reference deleted).

Let us push the interpretation further. This image/metaphor of radical collectivity—bureaucratic, mechanistic yet alive, almost that of the beehive—stands sharply against images of American individualism, uniqueness, and personal freedom, so prominent in the war culture and in the liberal ideology more generally. Against the back-drop of Pentagon "editing" of the script for *Know Your Enemy*—which included the firing of "leftist" Dutch film maker Joris Ivens, and the deletion of materials that suggested Japanese citizens were "ordinary humans victimized by their leaders" (Dower, 19)—this image/metaphor is particularly troubling. The reproductive economy established by this moving image of the hammer and the steel bar suggests that Japanese subjects are made mechanically, and not conceived sexually. Yet the moving image is itself sexual, a *mise en scene* metaphorizing reproduction mechanistically. It is an image/metaphor of sameness that overwrites any differences within Japanese culture. The (military) judgment encoded here suggests: "If you're going to kill one, you might as well kill them all, for there's no difference." They are not conceived of from sexual intercourse between individual human subjects, but rather by the State and its hermaphroditic hammer-forge mechanistic organs. Guilty! Of what? Precisely: of not registering as human subjects in the rhetoric of American individualism. A judgment against a whole people is metonymically enacted, supported by an image that articulates with other images circulating in the patriotic imagination. Here, the link between racism and nationalism becomes clear and troubling, for it is the nationalist/patriotic imagination that projects out of itself images of the other as radically Other, thus retroactively justifying its own fear and desire. Whereas Germans were often represented as ill, Japanese are here imaged as constitutionally Other. Metonymized as a single steel bar fashioned by a single hammer, and its rhythmic pounding, and as "prints of the same negative image," the desire of the other does not at all claim the viewer. Indeed, the desire that claims the audience is profoundly not "Japanese": it is American patriotic, sinthomatic desire—idiotic jouis-sense, which has been manufactured around systematically repressed alternative knowledge (e.g., that the Japanese "people" are "ordinary human beings" subjected to military intelligence and tyrannical rule). It is not the other's desire that is manifest in this image, but rather patriotic desire that 'calls' American subjects to their positions. The other has been rhetorically transformed into everything Americans don't want to be, yet perhaps are: a mass, a body politic, and prints of the same (negative) image. Scapegoating this accursed part of itself, America shines forth as a land in which 'I' and 'We' exist in perfect independence and simultaneous mutuality (see Hegel, 1977, §177). 'The people' (McGee, 1975) of America is rhetorically invoked and invented by an image of otherness with a political-military *telos*. Against the negative image of "them," an "us" emerges in all its mythic positivity.

The performative contradiction in this scene—it is, after all, nothing other than ideology purporting to unmask ideology, a hammer forging American patriotic consciousness—might return us to Zizek's discussion of the *sinthome* in *Lili Marleen*, but let us instead bear witness to another sinthomatic nugget of American patriotism from a few years before the *Know Your Enemy* film, at a time when the campaigns against the Japanese in Guadalcanal was receiving considerable attention from the image industry. We limit the immediate discussion to two examples that feature in a rather outright manner the heinous enjoyment of the patriotic imagination, and its (perhaps) simultaneous repression of traumatic self-recognition that (perhaps) kept the guilty-judgment at bay.

In an advertisement from *Life* magazine (February 1, 1943, 41), a schoolteacher sits behind a desk with pointer in hand, as if gently lecturing a schoolgirl. The desk bars the girl from the teacher—both are blond, fair-skinned, and blue-eyed—and a large globe sits on the desk to the rear of the picture. At the top of the picture, a large caption reads, "These are the things we are fighting for"; and at the bottom is printed: ". . . the right to teach the truth . . . not propaganda[.]"[16] This ad, for Community Silverware, substitutes patriotism for product, reminding American consumers that all Community's industry (skills and facilities) is bent toward making the war machine. Thus, instead of promoting silverware, Community is peddling patriotism, and using patriotism to (some day again) sell silverware. Additionally, the war (of American patriotism and capitalism) is being fought over, through, and with the bodies of children.

On the opposing page, we find excerpts from a book published by Oxford University Press, Gregory Ziemer's *Education for Death*. This book studied the Nazification of German children in graphic detail, and was the source of two films: "Walt Disney's short with the same title" and "RKO's feature-length drama, 'Hitler's Children'" (*Life*, February 1, 1943, 40). Four stills from the Disney film stand to the right of text excerpts from Ziemer's book. In the first, a woman (probably a mother) sits nervously and passively on a bed where a child innocently rests. The projected specter of a Nazi soldier performing a salute colors the room with shadow, an image cast threatening inward by a door he has presumably thrust open. In the second still, we see a classroom where German children (boys) salute an absurd portrait of Hitler grinning stupidly above the blackboard. The teacher stands in the center of the room, in front of rather than behind the podium, also saluting. In the third, a long line of young (but noticeably older) German males goose-step and salute stiffly in the midst of a cemetery adorned by crosses, which mark graves, helmets, and swastikas. In the fourth and final still, we see a row of Nazi soldiers decked out in the full regalia of war: helmets, muzzles, weapons, and a chain at the neck binding each soldier to the war machine itself.

Viewed side by side, the ads for *Education for Death* and Community Silverware constitute an allegory of the American patriotic ideological state apparatus which stands forth in all its in/visible obscenity and contradiction. On the one page, we have a critique of propaganda that borrows heavily from Aryan decorum; on the other, we have a critique of Aryan decorum. On both pages, we have *sinthome*—an idiotic enjoyment which neglects its own perversity: a Disney film for American children performing ideological operations it critiques in another culture, and an advertisement that raises truth above propaganda without substantive claims in the dictatorial style and blond, blue-eyed, fair-skinned elegance of Aryanism. All has become aestheticized, recalling the Kantian formula of purposefulness without purpose, which in turn recalls the formulas of perversity we access through Poe, Lacan, and Zizek—they know what they do, and do it anyway. (But do the children?) The call of judgment is neglected in favor of a judgment-call scripted, rewarded, and sanctioned by the Big Other. Is not perversity the formula for the political in its rawest sense? The well-known adage that, in politics, "once you know how to fake authenticity, all is yours," stands as our exemplar here. And so it is with the aesthetic, with truth raised over propaganda and, contradictory as it may sound, formal beauty and sublimity raised over substance: once you know how to fake beauty, all is yours. Here, image is indeed everything.

What is most troubling in these two advertisements is their focus on children and education, a focus or squinting of the eye which responds to the sexual overtones so absolutely constitutive of these ads, and, consequently, of the patriotic war culture. Children are peculiar figures which adults define themselves against, quite romantically, and thus we should realize that our belief in their innocence, pre-sexuality, and lovely ignorance is a romantic projection of our own desire. Troubling as it may be, the image industry not only creeps into their scopic fields, it aims to. We typically think of children as being outside of ideology, in all their freshness and innocence, which is why so many school systems remain ambivalent about bringing in computer technologies that can access digitized images that are pornographic, by one definition or another. Even while these technologies are crucial to educating competent subjects for the labor force, they also may tap into the seamy side of (American) desire, confronting children with images that direct libidinal pulsations in a way they're not presumably "ready for." The ads for the Disney film and for Community Silverware register the pull of patriotic desire in a similarly troubling way, purporting to unmask ideology with ideology, creating a virtual geography of judgment that places "truth" with America and "propaganda" with the other (Germany in this case). The ironic aspect of these ads remains an open secret, obvious and concealed at the same time.

Tropologically, these ads constitute a field of us-them divisions that directs the flow of desire. They perform the patriotic libido, supplying for the audience appropriate objects of desire and objects of repulsion. As part of this tropological operation, they encode normative judgments, yet require the collaboration of their audiences in a manner that reminds us of Aristotle's discussion of the enthymeme in his *Rhetoric*. The enthymeme is an "informal" mode of proof whose bite is supplied not by the text but by the audience. Thus, culpability extends from text to viewer in the articulation of patriotic libido. The assumption that the enthymeme evokes a proof already "in" audiences neglects how that proof "got there" in the first place. By tracking enthymematic judgment at the level of the image, we get some clue.

In the ad for *Education for Death*, next to the Disney stills we have three text excerpts from Ziemer's book that coerce the enthymematic response according to the pulsations of American patriotic libido. Each of the excerpts has strong sexual overtones. In the first, Ziemer recounts having heard "a chorus of screams and yells" that came from "A group of twelve year old girls[.]" The girls yelled: "Grab her, grab the dirty little thing." The girls caught their prey, and "rubbed her face in the sand, kicked her exposed rear and spat on her." Ziemer discovered that what he had thought was some sick game the children played was in fact a scene of punishment. He questioned the group of girls. "The excited girls yelled answers at me from which I gathered that their victim, Anna, was: a rascal, a pig, an evil-smelling thing, a culprit, a criminal, an unpatriotic German unfit to wear the Nazi uniform." Ziemer goes on:

> I learned that this girl had "insulted" Marie's sister. She had said that it was wrong for the sister to have a baby. This talk about babies, bandied back and forth by little girls bewildered me. I asked, "What's wrong with Marie's sister having a baby?"
>
> I was informed that nothing was wrong. That was just it. Marie's sister was doing just what the Führer wanted all German girls to do. She wasn't married but that certainly didn't matter. She did not have to be married to have a baby. Just then the *Gruppenlieterin* came up. She advised the girls that they had done their duty well, but that she would punish Anna. As they disappeared over the hill she had little Anna by the hair.

In the other two excerpts from the book, Ziemer recounts how he discovered a young boy of ten "staked out" over an ant hill as part of a training exercise in which he played the role of spy, and Ziemer recounts how a young boy of nine with pneumonia nevertheless wished to "die for Hitler" so that his father would be proud of him. In the final excerpt, a doctor treating the boy exclaims: "Now do you see what I mean? . . . He wants to die. What is this strange ideology that can even pervert the instincts?"

Read alongside the stills from the Disney film that borders it on the right, and next to the ad on the opposing page for Community Silverware, these excerpts create a rhetoric of opposition and division fundamentally linked to the sexual. In this rhetoric, several "unstated propositions" (Gronbeck, 1995) about children, sexuality, and knowledge are advanced in a way that regulates the circulation of patriotic desire or, rather, that regulate the circulation of desire toward a patriotic, Americanist ethnocentrism which provides warrants for hating and killing "the enemy" (in this case, Germans) based upon differences in libidinal cathexes. These propositions not only purport to correspond with the empirical world, but also make that world available and meaningful to viewers/readers. The propositions, enthymematically encoded, double as judgments.

Unstated Propositions	*Enthymematic Judgments*
1. Children are (and should be) innocent.	1. German children are guilty.
2. Children are (and should be) ignorant of sex.	2. German children are aware.
3. American education of children aims at truth.	3. German education of children aims at ideology.
4. American education respects the life instinct (Eros).	4. German education respects only the death drive (Thanatos).
5. American libidinal economy is normative.	5. German libidinal economy is perverse.

The list could go on for some time, for the mechanism operative here, i.e., differentiation, implies a full range of distinctions between Americans and Germans that reach well beyond this particular text. An entire weave of intertextuality might here be explored, which would show how judgment and enthymeme facilitate one another by recourse to reservoirs of cultural meanings that have been rhetorically activated in/by the ads. But let us instead press a plausible interpretation of the libido-rhetoric circulating in the ads, which registers between Americans and Germans, us and them.

The master trope of this us-them field of di/vision, its animating tension, is exactly perversity. Its double or shadow figure is normativity. By constituting the Germans as perverse, this rhetoric simultaneously accomplishes the constitution of Americans as normative/normal. Germans introduce knowledge where it doesn't belong, which excites patriotic American agitation and arousal. Germans procreate outside of wedlock to produce military subjects, insist that their male children become men as soon as possible, punish and torture one another performing a will not theirs but the Other's (e.g., the Führer's) and take enjoyment from these actions. They are perverts all. The first still from the Disney film may be viewed as an Oedipal scene, complete with father, mother, and child, where father is a German soldier come to direct his son's desire away from mother and to Mother Land. A component of becoming a patriotic German is castration anxiety. It is an invasion scene, too, rife with imagery of penetration and fear/desire. The boy in the bed is prematurely called to duty, at once castrated and sexualized by the appearance of the father's/soldier's looming shadow. Against this field of perversity, an image of "Americans" shines forth in all its obscene purity—a conjured illusion, a manufactured illusion, and a brilliant effect of rhetorical abracadabra. (With this in mind, regard the angelic beauty and peacefulness on the teacher's face in the Community Silverware ad, and the little girl's wide-open mouth, waiting to gobble up the "pure" knowledge the teacher is implied to possess: she holds the pointer, the phallus, the truth.) The viewer/reader of these sorts of texts has their desire attached to the patriotic machine, and is rewarded. It is precisely because the audience "fills in" the unstated propositions and "supplies" the enthymematic judgments that they may experience the idiotic jouis-sense of patriotism. Paradoxically, of course, what gets filled in or supplied by the audience was there all along. Their enjoyment, apparently spontaneous, an effect of interpretation is in fact anticipated by the text. Zizek explains: "*enjoyment itself, which we experience as 'transgression,' is in its innermost status something imposed, ordered*—when we enjoy, we never do it 'spontaneously,' we always follow a certain injunction" (1991b, 9). Again, formulas for perversity creep up on us: Poe's notion of mobile without motive; Kant's idea of purposefulness without purpose; and Lacan's thesis that perversity consists in making oneself subject to the jouissance of the Big Other.

When the American audience fills in or fleshes out the unstated propositions and enthymematic judgments here, and everywhere, they are recognized as subjects of the patriotic war machine, thus becoming simultaneously objects of "its" desire. They recognize themselves in the desire of the Other (e.g., Uncle Sam's smoldering eyes, as in the "I Want You!" posters for enlisting military subjects) when they do what "it" wants. In this light, we may wish to believe that the enthymeme is not so much supplied by the audience as it is placed there to be called on again by the Big Other. This suggests that "it" (the Other) is already in "you" (the subject). It is for this reason precisely that Lacan puts a bar through the "S" of the subject (\$), for it is different from itself, split by a resident alterity. So it is that the subject is always already marked by the desire of (and lack in) the Big Other—a lack designated by the cancellation of the Other as a self-present and complete locus of enjoyment, which Lacanian algebra renders thusly: Ø. Uncle Sam, in this case, wants something from the subject, suggesting the formula, \$◊Ø: Uncle Sam lacks, asking subjects to fill the void with patriotism, while simultaneously promising to fill the void in them with patriotism.[17] Both the subject (S) and the Other (O) lack, are incomplete, and thus are barred (\$, Ø). Yet both promise to fill the void, paradoxically, with that which they require from the other. The signifiers are empty, in search of fulfillment: absence in search of presence, desire in search of (an always already lost) object.

When the subject is "called" by the Other (Uncle Sam), they are also being "reminded" that they have not yet performed their duty, i.e., the subject has not yet enlisted in the armed services. And even if they have enlisted, the desire of the Other is unquenchable: there is always "more" to do for Uncle Sam. Uncle Sam's disapproving eyes stare menacingly, his finger points, articulating what Zizek would call a "'guilt feeling' of a purely formal, 'non-pathological' . . . nature, a guilt which, for that very reason, weighs most heavily on those individuals who 'have nothing on their consciences'" (1994, 60). This "non-pathological guilt" coincides with "innocence," for, strictly speaking, the subject has not "done anything." The advance made in the theory of ideology by taking into account the articulation of lack in the subject (\$) and the Other (Ø) takes us beyond Althusser (1971), for it demonstrates the way in which the subject is always already "interpellated" and judged by the structure of signification (Law): the lack in both subject and Other is not merely an "effect" of symbolic processes of ideological operations; it is instead the mark of the uncanny, unbidden, traumatic, and eruptive Real. The "I Want You!" poster thus may be seen to materialize a void or lack with which the subject identifies in a moment of "non-pathological guilt."

\$◊Ø: Lacan appropriates these mathemes, and develops his formulae, to suggest an analogy between psychic operations and general traits of signification, common to all symbol systems, including set theory and other "scientific" attempts to grapple with the problem of indeterminacy. The elementary lesson of set theory, on the Lacanian view, is that lack circulates even at the level of mathematical articulation: a set may "contain" itself, thus posing as complete and self-identical, but this implies a set of sets and a set of sets of sets, *ad infinitum*. Self-identity, as in the phrase "war is war" (a set which 'contains' itself), is meaningless; a relation to alterity is re-

quired to render identity meaningful, e.g., "war is hell," "war is a derivative condition," "war is a perversion," and so forth. The "essence" or
"identity" of war is conferred by a negative reflection. Notice that, included in the rhetorical meeting of war with its own identity, i.e., as other-
than-war, is a judgment. They key, common to all manners of signification,
is that this lack drives efforts at totalization and marks the nether boundary of judgment. It is not a robust presence existing "outside" of signification that orients such efforts, but rather a resident void. This void, around
which the drive in its endless aim circles, also may be understood as the
absence which calls for and de-limits judgment.

Patriotism is a peculiar habit or way of filling the void, materializing
Nothingness, and rendering judgment. By sketching what America and
Americans *are not*, the ads for Community Silverware and *Education for
Death* supplement America's and Americans' lack by visualizing the alien
jouissance of the Other as perversity. The flowers of American normativity blossom from 'unclean' yet incredibly rich soil (imported from Germany). American patriotic desire finds fulfillment in the jouissance of the
Other. Love (of country) is purchased by a negative judgment on the
Other (country, and the sexual/epistemological practices which constitute it). Thus, the ads materialize the Nothingness around which the patriotic libido in its endless aim circulates.

Japanese Skulls—Sublime Objects of Ideology

*Contrary to the commonplace, according to which, in pornography, the other (the
person shown on the screen) is degraded to an object of our voyeuristic pleasure, we
must stress that it is the spectator himself who effectively occupies the position of
the [degraded] object.*

—Zizek, *Looking Awry* (1991a, 110)

In 1945, a psychoanalytic critic observed that Japanese aggression was
deeply rooted in unsublimated aspects of the phallic stage, and unre-
solved anxieties regarding castration. The results, she argued, concerned
an obsession with cleanliness, wherein women and foreigners figured as
filthy, and wherein the fantasy of an ultra-clean male/father goaded aggressive political culture (Silberpfennig, 1945; see Dower, 130). It was
convenient, and even popular at the time, to discuss Japanese aggression
with the relatively fashionable tropes of libido provided by psychoanalysis. But no such discussion of American military action and political culture seemed invited, even though libido-rhetoric was omnipresent in
popular magazines, public address, and cultural practices of the time.
Sexually charged images saturated the political culture of 1940s America.
Perhaps they were so omnipresent that they were invisible, vexing our

assumptions about image politics, e.g., being "visible" is the first step to recognition.

The simultaneous application and disavowal of libidinal tropology in the manufacture of patriotic war culture at the level of the image in American culture cannot be grasped anywhere more powerfully than in a full page photo that appeared in the same edition of *Life* as did the ads for Community Silverware and the Disney film. The centerpiece to a photo-essay on Guadalcanal and the Battle of the Grassy Knoll, this image demands that we pay careful attention to how patriotic libido articulates the other in sexual terms that ultimately must be disavowed in order to defend against the perverse, heinous enjoyment that is the hard kernel of patriotism. The simultaneous application and disavowal of the sexual is expressed in terms of contradictory impulses in the public justification of war by Daniel Pick in his magnificent study, *War Machine: The Rationalisation of Slaughter in the Modern Age.*

> Almost without exception . . . the writers I study are men, and often men for whom war evidently raises troubling questions of sexuality and gender, even though, at the same time, war is frequently said to resolve them. . . . The nation is itself often gendered as female; yet women apparently count little in the economy of chivalrous battle. War is the fault of women. War is born from the womb of the state. War is the testing ground for virility but it disturbingly produces 'feminine' hysteria amongst the men. War is either very good or very bad for racial reproduction. War is the mechanical human beast. War is the runaway train upon which interminable crimes of passion are committed. War erupts from a secret French steel tube thrusting out beneath the sea and henceforth England is no longer virginal. (1993, 2–3)

Pick's hypotheses about what war "is" are intriguing, and recommend that we will understand brutal conflict and its public justification more richly if we attend to issues of sex and gender. Most interesting of all, Pick implies how the rationalization of slaughter may hinge on doubling the other as masculine-feminine. With this doubling the enemy-other is not judged as either/or but as both/and masculine feminine. Thus, it may generate heternormative desire, fear of the castrating (M)Other, homophobic fear and homoerotic desire, aggressiveness, and generally destructive eroticism. An exemplar of this doubling is to be found in a *Life* magazine image, which will name "Skull Fuck," a startling piece of patriotic pornography.

In another image that employs the skull figure, the presence of a woman looking at a Japanese skull squelches the doubling function and figures the skull as a castrated (but still sexual) site of enjoyment, which also mediates patriotic desire. The gaze of the woman channels desire heterosexually beyond the materiality of the skull—which does not appear as threat, but rather as instrument or Thing—and toward symbolic Eros. We will refer to this photo as "Mediated Skull Fuck," which one may view in Paul Fussell's book *Thank God for the Atom Bomb and Other Essays*.

In each of these images, the skull of the (Japanese) other is a trophic and eroticized object through which American patriotic enjoyment may be heinously procured through aggressive, violent sexuality. They are pornographic and patriotic at the same time. With "Mediated Skull Fuck," we have soft-core, and with "Skull Fuck," we have hard-core porn. In addition to providing enjoyment, these images instruct. They are aesthetic and political objects at the same time, and they are rhetorical agencies that say a million words, as the cliche goes, without saying any. Therein lie their terrible splendor, expansive aptitude, and awful danger.

The caption to "Skull Fuck" tells us that what we see is "A Japanese soldier's skull . . . propped up on a burned out Jap tank by U.S. troops. Fire destroyed the rest of the corpse." "*Propped up*"? "It" has been *rammed* onto that pipe. That Japanese soldier's helmet has been tilted back on his head like a bonnet, or else its placement is a happy accident. "By" U.S. troops? Somebody particular performed this feat, yet this somebody is absorbed into the U.S. war machine's collective body—is now figured not as a 'he,' but as an extension of It. "Fire destroyed the rest of the corpse"? Disavowal; immanent guilt. The judgments encoded in the caption, for the audience to enthymematically supply or fill in, put minimal agency and responsibility on particular military subjects (they, as individuals, are not guilty of anything, for they have patriotically performed their duty).

They know not what they do, and they do it anyway? Or do they know exactly what they do? These questions require a judgment call of the most perilous sort, and in the richest sense of the terms judgment and call, for we realize that a judgment call would place blame in a very problematic way that makes us think of that odd set of phenomena called "war crimes." To insinuate notions of criminality into the discourse and practice of war is difficult, at best, as we know from the Nuremberg trials and the Oliver North scandal. In both cases, the perverse rears its ugly head, and is masked by excuses ("I did what I was told to do!"). Yes, but . . . Let us hold out for the thesis, which doubles as a very brutal judgment against the discourse and practice of war: yes, they know what they do. And they do it anyway. That they/we "have to" neglects the greater questions: should we? Can we not? We must at least ask, and keep asking. Rodney King, who wonders aloud, "can't we all just get along?" raises the question of humanity, judgment, and peace at a fundamental level of experience that became a horrible pornography of intra-cultural war featuring the "repressive state apparatus" at work on a black man.

How much idiotic and perverse enjoyment was accessed there, in those perpetually replayed and edited video clips, by perverts in America, and all over the world, I hesitate to ponder. So too we should hesitate—which is to say plunge into with considerable anxiety—at the fact that what the King beating and its televisuality began to do was to locate blame at the level of the State (e.g., "it" is racist to the core), but that this location of blame did not hold up in a court of law. And the judgments that were verified for some by the beating—black men are drug-abusers, animals, dangerous, and thus must be beaten and subdued, killed if necessary— should awaken us to how the patriotic imagination revolves around an other who we simultaneously hate, fear, desire, eroticize, and so absolute and problematically seem to need. "We" project "it" to know who we are.

The "it" which mediates our self-knowledge is a blank spot, occupied by a strange object, and filled in with our desire. "Skull Fuck" raises the question of judgment at a feverish pitch that threatens us with a Siren song of our own making. I don't know whether we should recognize the photographer (Ralph Morse) as a critically minded genius, a guy who was at the right (or wrong) place at the right (or wrong) time, a patriotic dupe creating the pornography of war, or what. How we should account for his performance of patriotism or the critique thereof, is itself a judgment call that won't be decisively answered here.

In "Skull Fuck," the enemy-other has been radically feminized, yet remains threatening. As a motivational apparatus, the image simultaneously tropes the other as an object of desire (which we see as something to fuck, or that always already "fucked"—in both senses of the term, i.e., sexually engaged and doomed), and as an object of fear which acts like a subject (which we see as something to destroy, even though it is already destroyed, i.e., "fucked"): alluring and intimidating at the same time, something that is demolished yet which lives hauntingly on like a nymphomaniac ghost. The helmet is "worn" bonnet-style, the mouth gapes in a double feature of agony and ecstasy. The Japanese war machine is portrayed as masculine, robustly so. Tank nozzles stand at varying degrees of erection, gigantic in the background of the photo, and in close proximity to the gaping mouth. This is a scene of oral-vaginal enjoyment, a projection of the patriotic imagination. The gaping mouth invites fellatio, yet retains the capacity to bite. It is the *vagina dentata*, a seductive (feminine) lure and a profound (masculine) threat. It transforms war into sex, and sex into war, in a circular manner. From Eros to Thanatos and back again.

The doubledness of "Skull Fuck" as a tropological scopic field makes easy divisions into "us" and "them" camps problematic, for it implicates American audiences who are caught in the act of gazing just as it almost catches U.S. troops and a *Life* magazine photographer in the act of staging the photo. The judgment it encodes too is doubled—the enemy is a sexual object, and a threatening subject: a death mask and a site of oral-vaginal enjoyment. But, even though problematic, "Skull Fuck" nevertheless operates rhetorically to justify American military action, and does so in highly erotic-thanatopic terms. The placement of the skull amongst the phallic signifiers makes visible, or rather actively constitutes, Japanese perversity in a way that is highly homo-erotic (the skull and the tank nozzles belong to the Japanese; yet they also have been appropriated by American soldiers). Though the skull has been feminized, it still is masculine—at once passive and alluring (e.g., "come fuck me") and at the same time active and threatening (e.g., "I will bite you!"). The erotic pull of the other brings the audience into a fantasy, which culminates in aggressiveness, destruction, and death. Already destroyed, the enemy-other (at once masculine and feminine: the *vagina dentata*) must be ceaselessly and mercilessly demolished. Its promise is never completely fulfilled or nuptual consummated. This is a powerful rhetoric of war and enmity. That it is staged, that this scene was made, by Americans and for Americans, remains an open secret: it is in plain view, yet is simultaneously repressed, massaged by the language of the caption, which places action elsewhere (e.g., on "fire" rather than on military subjects).

"Mediated Skull Fuck" is similarly staged or posed, and is a scene of erotic inscription which shows the utility of a Japanese soldier's skull for the patriotic libido. Like the cranium in "Skull Fuck," this skull has in a sense become U.S. property, for whatever use it may be put to. In response to an ex-marine that denied that U.S. soldiers took such obscene trophies, Paul Fussell also puts the Japanese skull to use. He writes, as if to the ex-marine:

> It also was a sailor who was the kind donor of the famous Japanese skull "found on New Guinea" and sent in 1943 as a souvenir to his girlfriend in Phoenix, Arizona. . . . [T]he girl [is] meditating pensively on the skull in a full-page photograph, thus bringing to its several million patriotic readers the good news about Japanese skulls being collected in the Pacific. It is notable that the girl in the photograph is neither ghoul nor a tramp. She is dressed in a nice suit and tasteful earrings, with her hair worn up. The photographer has posed her at a desk where she is said to be writing a thank-you note to her generous boyfriend. Perhaps she is answering his message, which he has written in ink on the top of the skull. The tone of the photo and caption is one of calm normality, without a trace of irony or outrage. (Fussell, 1988, 49)

While the photo disavows irony and outrage, Fussell does not. And yet he for some reason labels the woman in the photo a "girl," desexualizing her: "neither ghoul nor tramp." Perhaps Fussell is being ironic, fleshing out the barely repressed sexuality of the scene. Neither ghoul nor tramp, but perhaps a pervert? Nevertheless, his choice (and lack thereof) here is suggestive of the difficulty entailed in making the sexual contents of war photos explicit or public. The discourse of libido, often construed as so very private, has entered into the public sphere, and yet has not registered as an obscenity. It "looks" quite normal, the audience disavows the erotic register and instead views it as "good news," a possibility much more troubling than the photograph itself. As with "Skull Fuck," in "Mediated Skull Fuck" the other functions as an object of desire whose grotesque material appearance is transformed pornographically into a symbolic sexual prop for patriotic libido and enjoyment. We must now unlock the mechanism by which the obscene object is transformed into an object of American desire, and lacuna jouissance.

Speaking of the drives in Seminar VII, Lacan argues that the sort of transformation we are here discussing is precisely sublimation. Sublimation, he says, "raises an object . . . to the dignity of the Thing" (1992, 112). Sublimation, according to Lacan, performs a diversion of the drives towards socially valued objects. Simultaneously, sublimation functions as a constitutive force in determining just what is valuable or ethical, and links the ethical with perversion via psychic-rhetorical processes. How is this link to be established? Let us proceed with a series of propositions:

When we raise an object to the dignity of the Thing (*das Ding*), we invest it with libidinal energy and desire "it," yet we have "made" "it" and thus find in "it" a reflection of our own desire. The object-become-Thing, in other words, does not exist independent of the subject's desire: the Thing marks the subject's desire to desire. For Lacan, sublimation does not involve a change in sexual aim but a change in the position of the object within the structure of the fantasy, i.e., through sublimation subject may become object (as in perversion) just as the object may become Thing. The object becomes the sublime object (the Thing) because of the linguistic nature of the drive: the change of the object in itself is made possible because the drive is marked with the articulation of the signifier. This linguistic nature of the drive suggests that objects of desire are always already inscribed by a lack, for they are (merely) fantasized projections of the subject. The subject projects fantastically not because overfull, as though displacing an affective surplus. The subject projects fantastically because s/he is lacking. The sublimation of object into Thing expresses this lack creatively, transforming or transubstantiating materials into symbols. The disavowal of sublimation as a creative, linguistic, fantastic operation, also is a disavowal of lack in the other/object. To assume plenitude in the other/object, to assume that it in itself provokes my reaction and desire, is to neglect my responsibility for its manifestation to my consciousness. To disavow lack in the other is thus simultaneously a disavowal that the other desires, i.e., is a subject and not an object, a person and not a Thing. As it turns out, disavowal is the formal mechanism of perversion, which Lacan discusses in terms of the "specular relation" of recognition (1988, 221). The pervert disavows lack, their desire is "caused" by a presence— such as, for example, a Japanese skull—and their enjoyment is structured in a fixed mode of jouissance in which the other's desire/lack is disavowed. Though fixed, the mode of jouissance particular to perversion also is delicate, and Lacan argues, relatively easy to topple. It is "fragile, at the mercy of an inversion" (1988, 221).

We can see in "Skull Fuck" and "Mediated Skull Fuck" an object being raised to the dignity of the Thing in a way that supports patriotic judgment: for example, that the other is not human, is a threat to humanity, and thus must be annihilated. To reiterate a claim made earlier, this way of seeing the other (as object-become-Thing) may be regarded as the formal basis of racism, grounded in a rhetorically structured/constructed relation to the Other's jouissance; the Other remains mute. But this way of seeing (and not seeing) the photos neglects an element that Lacan argues is essential to perversion: namely, its communicative, intersubjective structure. The particular perversion in these photos is sadism, i.e., taking pleasure in the other's pain. Even after death, reduced to a body part, the other peculiarly lives on as a site of spooky enjoyment. Without at least a modicum of resistance-participation from the other, without at least a trace of the other's status as subject and not merely object, perverse-sadistic enjoyment could not be accessed. Says Lacan:

> One thing is certain—the sadistic relation can only be sustained insofar as the other is on the verge of still remaining a subject. If he is no longer anything more than reacting flesh, a kind of mollusk whose edges one titillates and which palpitates, the sadistic relation no longer exists. The sadistic subject will stop there, suddenly encountering a void, a gap, a hollow.... Is it not true that most sadistic manifestations, far from being taken to extremes, remain rather on the threshold of execution—playing the waiting-game, playing on the fear of the other, with pressure, with threat, keeping to the forms, more or less secret, of the participation of the partner. (1988, 214)

Lacan goes on to say that, without the gaze of the other, "desire sinks into shame" (1988, 220).

Shame runs counter to the patriotic libido, which at all costs wants to enjoy itself, perhaps with just a taste of guilt, and the mechanism that defends against it is disavowal. Yet now we must make the argument that this disavowal is imperfect, incomplete. As a perverse economy, the rhetoric of the scopic fields of these photographs must be grasped in all its fragility. Were the perverse economy not fragile, malleable, were it permanent and stable, the war mentality would rule public consciousness of the other. Perhaps it does. Changing images of the Japanese enemy-other after the dropping of the bombs on Hiroshima and Nagasaki, however, suggest that America and its media industry are quick to replace one perversity with another—to move from a violent sexualization of the other toward its deflation and domestication. A tame and vaguely uncomfortable chimp replaces King Kong images, and we see no more eroticized skulls. Neither would have a place in a mode of jouissance that had shifted from war to peace. What was done in the name of justice or goodness yesterday looks like shameful activity with the dawn of a new morning. The temporality of libido, and of shame, is not linear or regular. It is fragile and herky-jerky. So too are its rhetoric, and its judgments. The other is judged in terms of excess and lack, masculinity and femininity, super- and sub-humanity— both/and/all/none: gorilla, simian, chimp, alien, insect, vermin, human, machine, vagina, mouth, virile, impotent: a proliferation of signifiers marking the profound undecidability of the Other. The excessive jouissance of the Other defies signification, and goads it on. Thus, while offering relatively stable and powerful platforms for patriotic judgment, imagings of the Other also are fragile and replaceable.

This fragility is most easily understood when we recognize that, yanked out of their historical context and placed in an academic book, the affective force of the photos is contingent on their context of production and consumption. In 1943, a woman in Phoenix, Arizona looks straight through a Japanese soldier's skull and into the love relation (which is a reflection of her own desire). Or rather, her gaze bounces right off it in bedazzled jouissance. The skull serves as a mirror, really, more than it does a window, not allowing visual access to itself. How can this presumably grotesque, dross object function erotically in the libidinal economy of the subject? Lacan reminds us of something important here: "Perverse desire finds its support in the ideal of an inanimate object" (1988, 222), yet this object cannot be "seen" as merely an object, otherwise the pervert gets precisely what she doesn't want: to experience the gaze of the other and be claimed by their desire, and as a consequence of this challenging claim, to see her own desire sink into shame. Americans did not want to see a human being looking back at them, not with the full force of their desire. As some audiences of this photo look at it, they perhaps look at it with her eyes, through her eyes. More generally, perhaps, audiences were encouraged to look through the eyes of love, thinking of loved ones fighting and dying overseas. As Burke pointed out, love and war are of the same order, and what connects them is precisely perversion. Yet the perverse gaze on the skull in the photo disavows this connection, and in 1943 the skull and the photo were perhaps looked on with enjoyment. Today, many look at it with alarm and disgust, and almost always with deep and uncomfortable puzzlement.[18] The skull looks back at us, registering the pull of the other's desire, and confronting us with projections of our own making. Lacan's tweaking of the Gospel echoes: They have eyes that they might not see; there are eyes that see us; God, the absolutely Other, is watching.

In 1943, the Japanese skulls functioned as what Zizek (1989) would term "sublime objects of ideology"—objects whose materiality, shape, and reality are radically sublimated. "Sublimation," says Zizek in *Looking Awry*, "is usually equated with desexualization, i.e., with the displacement of libidinal cathexis from the 'brute' object alleged to satisfy some basic drive to an 'elevated,' 'cultivated' form of satisfaction." Freud makes this identification between sublimation and desexualization in *The Ego and the Id*, and in *Leonardo da Vinci and a Memory of his Childhood*: sublimation directs sexual energy toward allegedly non-sexual aims, e.g., work, art, sport. Following Lacan, however, we might insist that the sublimation of Japanese skulls performs the exact opposite function: it raises objects to the dignity of Things, not in a cultivated or desexualized manner, but indeed in a deeply erotic way rooted in the objects' profound ugliness/beauty. Zizek explains that the sublime object/Thing may be materialized in "an ordinary, everyday object that undergoes a kind of transubstantiation and starts to function, in the symbolic economy of the subject, as an embodiment of the impossible Thing, i.e., as materialized Nothingness." "This is why," Zizek goes on to say, "the sublime object presents the paradox of an object that is able to subsist only in shadow, in an intermediary, half-born state, as something latent, implicit, evoked: as soon as we try to cast away the shadow to reveal the substance, the object itself dissolves; all that remains is the dross of the common object" (1991a, 83–84). In a later work, Zizek clarifies this point with reference to Lacan: "What Lacan means by sublimation," he says, "is shifting the libido from the void of the 'unserviceable' Thing to some concrete, material object of need that assumes a sublime quality the moment it occupies the place of the Thing" (1994, 96).

The sublimation of Japanese skulls does not desexualize them, or render them as castrated/destroyed enemies, as passive/perverse viewings of both photos, recommended by their captions, would suggest. Rather, it transforms them into Things for perverse patriotic enjoyment, and judgment. As sublime objects of ideology, the Japanese skulls materialize the Nothingness which patriotic libido would fill: they mark its condition of im/possibility. They evoke the libido, are cathected objects whose sexual force is cloaked in the shadow of "drossness." When we attempt to cast away the shadow of drossness, a mundane purveyor of victory, we are left with gritty objects that reveal the elusive substance of patriotic enjoyment, and quickly vanish again. As the woman in "Mediated Skull Fuck" gazes at/through the Japanese skull, what does she see but an object raised to the dignity of Thing? And what does this object do, but revert to its drossness, serving merely as a tablet or novel stationery for the inscriptions of a lover? The activity of the subject viewing the skulls—which is to say in the case of "Mediated Skull Fuck," the viewing of viewing of skulls—is thus punctuated by the idiotic blindness of patriotic enjoyment, an identification of the subject with the Big Other through the agency of the sublime object. Hariman offers an insightful comment which, though a discussion of perversion in *Gravity's Rainbow*, applies here: "Perversity models the act of mind fundamental to the complex act of identification; the decision that is supposed to accompany empathic substitution can only be found and celebrated if it is preceded by vicariousness, by 'antisocial and mindless pleasures.' Perversity has also been used to introduce, order, and judge a problem of interpretation, specifically, the use to which the book will be put in accepting or denying oneself as a historical agent" (1979, 56). If we substitute the word "book" with "photographs," Hariman's discussion of perversity becomes highly relevant to our discussion of images of Japanese skulls. For it focuses us on the dual possibility of acceptance and disavowal—of history, agency, judgment, and perversity—encoded in every object of interpretation. The Japanese skull is not an exception. We may view it today as a sublime object of ideology in American war culture of the 1940s—a normativized perversion in which love and war, Aphrodite and Ares, bed down together, making a two-backed beast under the translucent covers of patriotism.

Returning the Repressed; (Re)Turning the Screw; Giving the Perverts Their Due

The war came as a great relief, like a reverse earthquake, that in one terrible jerk shook everything disjointed, distorted, askew back into place. Japanese bombs had finally brought national unity to the U.S.

—*Time*, 15 December, 1941[19]

If we consciously desire to profit from violence, we can no longer reach the heights of frenzy and lose ourselves in it. Violence, the core of eroticism[,] leaves the weightiest problems unanswered. We have achieved awareness by pursuing a course of regular activity; every element has its place in the chain of consciousness and is distinct and intelligible. But by upsetting the chain through violence we revert to the extravagant and incomprehensible surge of eroticism. So we experience something blinding and overwhelming, more desirable than anything else, which defies the conscious appraisal, we bestow on all the other facts of our experience. Human life, therefore, is composed of two heterogeneous parts that never blend. One part is purposeful, given significance by utilitarian and therefore secondary ends; this part is the one we are aware of. The other is primary and sovereign; it may arise when the other is out of gear, it is obscure, or else blindingly clear: either way it evades the grasp of our intelligence. Hence the problem has two sides. Conscious understanding wishes to extend its range to include violence, for such an important part of man's make-up must not be neglected any longer. And on the other hand violence reaches beyond itself to lay hold of intelligence, so that its satisfactions, brought to the surface of consciousness, may become profounder, more intense, and more compelling. But in being violent we take a step away from awareness, and similarly by striving to grasp the significance of our violent impulses we move further away from the frenzied raptures violence instigates.

—Bataille, *Eroticism: Death and Sensuality* (1986, 192–193)

Whether or not, or to what extent, the woman in the photo was a pervert, we are not positioned here to say decisively, but the fixed mode of jouissance of American patriotic culture certainly was perverse. Yet even this judgment may be judged variously, experienced otherwise. Nietzsche would probably have reveled in it, and laughed gaily. *Time* editors expressed, as if for all of America, relief. Bataille might have located in patriotism's fixed mode of jouissance either an inscription of the erotic unconscious, over which we exert no control, or a purposeful attempt to profit from and enjoy violence. To sacrifice violence in the names of purpose, consciousness, and peace, is to divorce us from half of our humanity. But perhaps a good divorce indeed is better than a bad marriage. Bataille appears to refuse the choice between one or the other in favor of enjoying thoughts of both—an enjoyment which propels his pen, and a postponement of judgment which appears to make continued reflection possible.

It is hard to judge patriotism, and its perversity. It was perhaps a necessary, or at least felicitous, perversity that lubricated the step from (non)knowledge to action for Americans during the Second World War. And for Japanese. And for Germans. And for Russians. Without the pornography of war, perhaps the 'Good War' would have been even more difficult to fight than it already was. However heinous patriotic enjoyment may be, perhaps it is an obscene enjoyment requiring occasional and illicit embrace. Ares and Aphrodite, no matter how different, join in passion, making the two-backed beast of Eros and Thanatos, love and war. Is their joining a perversion? This is, of course, a judgment call of the trickiest sort. It leads us to question: is the rhetoric of patriotic perversity endemic to all war cultures? In a media culture that thrives on eroticizing violence, aggression, and even death, is not perversity—and even that perversity called war—a predictable and even desired outcome? Finally, and most troublingly, we must ask: is not the eroticization of war absolutely central to not only its justification, but to its very practice (by military subjects) and its public representation (for people on the home front)? In this chapter, I have argued, implied, wandered around, and exclaimed my answer to these questions: yes! But because perversity is a fragile libidinal economy, and because it is rhetorically constructed, the possibility of representing war, enmity, and conflict more generally otherwise is quite real, even if it seems simultaneously impossible. If the hyper-erotic rhetoric of war, enmity, and conflict constitutes, projects, and regulates the circulation of desire at the level of the image for an entire culture, I suspect that humanely portraying the other and their lack (desire) would make it much more difficult to fight wars, to justify wars, and to so perversely enjoy wars.

Yet if we press the analogy of pornography and certain sorts of images of the enemy-other, a thesis emerges that takes us beyond the Enjoyment Principle governing patriotic enjoyment as we have so far understood it: the pornography of war may be necessary to rouse a person, a people, and even a nation to action in times when action is particularly difficult to take. Presuming that some wars are "good," and World War Two was after all "The Good War," perhaps it is necessary to seize the means of persuasion wherever they are to be found—to get it up how one can, so to speak. If psychoanalysis tells us anything with respect to rhetoric and public affairs, it tells us that we find the means of persuasion in the gap between subject and other—in the nexus of desire, jouissance object, and linguistic transformation. This gap may be sutured with love, often at the expense of justice; or with justice, often at the expense of love. Where "One death is a tragedy," according to Stalin, "a million deaths is a statistic" (cited in Peters, 1994, 137). Yet the argument may be made obversely, as it was by U.S. military intelligence pondering an invasion of Japan which the bombings of Hiroshima and Nagasaki made unnecessary: let a relative few die so that many may live (see Newman, 1995). In both arguments, however, judgment falls against the anonymous or other (whether they are many or few) and in favor of the known or loved. Even if, as Lacan argues (1985), the Eros of "the One" is strictly speaking an objective impossibility, it is an impossibility which registers as real passion in discourse and historically material life—the mark of a lack/surplus which goads symbolic action, creating a feeling of proximity that may transcend questions of possibility and impossibility. However illusory, false, or deceptive we may construe it *a la* Lacan, the Eros of "the One" has material force even if it is but a strictly symbolic or imaginary rhetorical construction. The threat of Thanatos, which Lacan understands as a symbolic counterpart of and bar to Eros, "is the reduction to dust" (1985, 138)—the splitting of one into uncountable many. In the gap between one and many, anonymity and intimacy, justice and love, otherness and sameness, Eros and Thanatos, rhetoric issues.[20]

In this chapter, I have placed sublime images from 1940s American public culture that engage Eros and Thanatos provocatively in conversation with psychoanalytic judgments of war. The "of" here cuts at least two ways at once, suggesting that psychoanalysis facilitates seeing and judging war and its pornographies in a provocative way, and also that war itself returns the favor as a mirror of desire which makes judgments on "us." War is a reflection of our ownmost possibility, and perversity—the very rottenness of our quest for perfection. Just as this chapter has sought to bring back traumatic episodes of an American past through a psychoanalytic reading machine put to work on patriotism's (and perhaps even democracy's) family album, so too the faces and episodes in this fable look back at us, constituting the potential for an awful recognition. At issue has been not only patriotic memory and desire, but also (implicitly at least) the prospects for altering representational tactics before, during, and after conflicts. Possibilities have become visible, even if we ultimately will choose not to act on them. Critique expands the inventory of choice, of hope, and of historical burden.

The methodological guide here has been the belief that productive criticism ought to perform a return of the repressed, should make the unconscious conscious, so that we can establish more reflective relations with ourselves and with others. Criticism should be prescriptive, and not merely descriptive—rhetorical in both senses of the term: an anatomy of textual power and response, and a contentious *praxis* oriented toward the cultivation of "possible worlds" more just than the ones we find in the past, the present, and even in imaginings of the future (see Fisher, 1987, 64; Kirkwood, 1992; Poulakos, 1984; Turner, 1980). Such should be our "commitment to *telos*" (Ono and Sloop, 1992), our ethic and aesthetic of performative criticism. Rather than beginning with a "finished text," performative criticism stitches together "text fragments" (McGee, 1990). Performative criticism thus is an art of creation, perhaps more than it is an art of discovery. One might even say that it is a praxis of sublimation reflective on its own politics, disavowals, and perversions. Its force is to be felt at the nexus of rhetoric, aesthetics, ethics, and politics more than at the level of analytic judgment. Its "reason" is practical rather than pure, to borrow a distinction from Kant. Its purpose may be to delight and move, to estrange and familiarize, but always its *telos* ought to be toward the cultivation of choice and possibility. For those who want, or feel they need, more certainty or decisiveness, let them have religion or the promises of fortune cookies that ensure "today you *will* . . . " and "tomorrow you *will* . . . " The key temporal coordinate of performative criticism is neither "will" nor "won't." It is *may*, which emphasizes potentiality and possibility rather than determinism or necessity. But the ethical leap that animates performative criticism is made from *may* to *should*, even if the last word is punctuated with uncertainty in the form of a question mark. Above all, criticism should be an exercise in *risk*.

As with any other sort of performance, in criticism desire circulates. If, as Lacan says in Seminar VII (1992), the ethics of psychoanalysis is summed up by the phrase, "don't give up your desire," we might fill out the other side of this ethics: "don't disavow the desire of the other!" This double injunction of desire should mark the *telos* of any critical rhetoric purporting to critique both domination and freedom (Charland, 1991; McKerrow, 1989; Hariman, 1991; Ono and Sloop, 1992). Ultimately, if taken "all the way," this double injunction may place us in a zone of the undecidable, where judgment reaches its limit with unspeakable jouissance. As Susan Schwartz has put it in her chapter on "Judgment and Jouissance": "Jouissance is judgment's incoherence. It is that point where truth is intimated not by modernist formulae, but by the point of rupture, the failure of words to say all."[21]

Performing the critique of ideology may extend beyond explaining why people "know not what they do" toward judgment's incoherent jouissance; from describing how ideological interpellation dupes subjects, to cracking the hard nut of the perverse enjoyment deriving from knowing at some level what you're doing and doing it anyway, in a manner that places the subject in the position of witness in a litigational scene.[22] Perhaps the subject will break into tears during testimony, or will be unable to speak. Instead of hearing these outbursts of inarticulateness as insignificant, we may register them as symptomatic/*sinthomatic*. In the former case, with describing the duping of subjects, we access minimal accountability, whereas in the latter responsibility, obligation, and duty are to be found just about everywhere, in every eye/I. In the former, we consistently locate power with the Big Other, thus neglecting complicity at the level of individual knowledge-action—a complicity whose primary incentive, I have argued, is enjoyment: a textually complex effect/affect of what we have termed libido-rhetoric. A shift to the critique of ideology as *jouis-sense* may accomplish much in this respect, outstripping both postmodern hyper-determinism and skepticism (Ono and Sloop, 1992, 50), as well as chilly modernist hope-in-reason. Such a shift in emphasis would likely turn critics to questions of desire, comfort, enjoyment, pleasure, and to their opposites—questions which Aristotle devoted an entire book of his *Rhetoric* to, and which unfortunately lay flat on the page for most contemporary readers of that ancient treatise on persuasion and human affairs. The judgments critics might make on discourses and actions in numerous communicative contexts, informed by an *affective turn*, might be supplied with considerable bite. I hesitate to propose yet another turn in the human sciences: the critical turn, the discursive turn, the rhetorical turn, the linguistic turn—so many turns are being advocated that we should feel dizzy. In fact, the 'turn' I suggest really is a *return*—not merely to Aristotle, or to Freud for that matter, but to that seamy side of love and passion and desire the Greeks called *mania* ('madness'). The (re)turn has been with us for a long time, more or less repressed. We find *mania*, a sublime version of jouis-sense, perhaps, in religious experience, inter/personal intimacy, the formation of groups, and the constitution of entire peoples. Rather than thinking of affective life and libidinal economy as aspects of existence that remain secret or shadowy to human subjects and communities, social critics and theorists might instead press hard the claim that, even in these presumably murky affairs, subjects are to some degree responsible to and for their enjoyment. And certainly, the media industry is, and public address more generally. The judgments of critical rhetorics should not be shy about this. The Christian dicta that we should not judge lest we be judged implies guilt present in every human being, which must be responded to with silence. Psychoanalysis is much harsher than religion in this respect, for in Christianity we are taught to follow the divine example of Christ, who would forgive all, whereas in psychoanalysis forgiving itself may be viewed as a pathology and indeed a perversion that denies the desire of the other and of the self in the name of Eternity—an other-worldly ethic of deferred desire, a Reality Principle founded upon endless waiting for and deferral of pleasure (see Marcuse, 1955)

In contemporary America, a host of critical rhetorics emerging from the Hollywood culture industry are being produced that offer a comic corrective to the eroticization of war and violence, an eroticization profoundly played out in the media manufacture of the Persian Gulf conflict. Let us risk the following interpretation, and focus attention on the affective pulse of American political culture as it rose and fell historically approaching the Gulf conflict. Leading up to this conflict, on a quick and long view, was a period of intense frustration—the Cold War. During that time, American patriotic libido was highly active in imagining conflict with the enemy-other, Russia, but could not satisfy its bloodlust in actual combat. The stakes had become far too high. The fantasy of war did not disappear, however. Rhetoric of the "evil Empire" constituted America's radical Other as being always out of reach, but also always in close proximity. Im/potent, America endured the Cold War as if waiting for something to happen. And when U.S. troops were sent to battle "for democracy" in Vietnam, they were sent half-castrated, as the story goes, "with one arm tied behind their backs." The culture of melancholia, which may be characterized by an incapacity to put to rest an object of impossible significance or even to admit its radical loss (see Abraham and Torok, 1994, 125–138), persisted. The Persian Gulf offered a dark continent for an explosion of patriotic desire for an America just waiting to reclaim its gonads after years of profound sexual-political frustration. Melancholia became mourning, i.e., the frustrations of Vietnam and the Cold War were ritually worked out, lost objects rediscovered and put to rest. From melancholia to mourning, from mourning to symbolic feast—an eruption of libidinal activity (see Abraham and Torok, 1994, 107–124). Is this not the basic pattern of frustration-feast that characterized American culture from the Cold War to the Persian Gulf conflict? The return of lost objects was a major theme of American intervention in the Gulf. There, the rhetoric of rape and victimage was applied to Iraq's invasion of Kuwait, thus suggesting that America was masculine and, in the courtly style, was duty-bound to avenge the violent/sexual theft of feminine innocence and chastity. This theft was given religious and perverse dimensions in American public address of the time. George Bush repeatedly mispronounced Sadam Hussein's name, calling him "Sadam" (Satan) and "Sodom." At a time when Bush was thought to be something of a wimp, even though he had combat experience, this aggressive sexualization of war masculinized Bush nicely, playing heavily to American biases about gender, experience, and leadership. Bush could not only get the military machine organized and moving in the Middle East without the full support of Congress; he could stand up on his own; he also could "talk dirty." Not only could he conduct action in an urgent contemporary context, he could (in so doing) retrieve the lost virulence of a deeply frustrated America, overcoming the culture of melancholia that had persisted since the anticlimactic conclusion of World War Two. Avital Ronell (1993) goes so far as to argue that the Gulf conflict may be read as transference of autobiography into history, wherein George Bush projected memory and desire onto the geography of the Middle East. Lost objects, troubling memories and unfulfilled desire could be through this transference put to rest. But this autobiography of Bush's obeys the contours of the West's story more generally, so it is difficult to decide whether autobiography is history or history is autobiography. For both Bush and the West more generally, a new perversity/pervert had been found in Hussein/Iraq—a body (politic) that required no mourning or melancholia. Against the "pure," "virtuous," and quite heterosexual imagery rhetorically and retroactively attached to Bush by his own televised performances—and by extension to America, even to the West—Hussein was repeatedly shown with little boys, patting their heads; and the strange fanaticism of Iraqi women, decked out in "strange" Islamic fashion and trilling their tongues, became an American commonplace. With these images of difference, the strangeness of Iraqi people was placed in an ethnocentric idiom of sexualized conflict that enabled the West (America in particular) to gaze back on itself as virtuous, pure, and good. This narrative of chivalry and courtly love, in which Iraqis are sexualized as fanatical perverts stripped of decorum, supplied motivational force for U.S. policies and actions in the Gulf. How strange and yet familiar it is to look back and to see democracy so forcefully constituted against the screen of the other's (symbolically manufactured and condensed) perversity.

The manufacturedness of this libido-rhetoric was plain as day, but also oddly invisible. An amazingly effective open secret. That it didn't last long is an issue to be taken up another time. A wide portion of Americans enjoyed it tremendously, and ventriloquized it with considerable relish, repeating all the slogans of American politicians (e.g., "Sadam is Hitler!"), perhaps with eyes glazed over, perhaps not (see Reese and Buckalew, 1995). So common did this libido-rhetoric become, that Hollywood made excellent spoofs of the Gulf conflict with Charlie Sheen (the *Hot Shots* series), which also played on the hyper-masculinity of the *Rambo* series, which in turn drew from the culture of angry discontent and melancholy residual from America's failed repression of the trauma of Vietnam. All of the performances of libido-rhetoric articulate intertextually with one another are marked by history. Films like *Independence Day* and *Canadian Bacon* portended to reveal the tragi-comic savagery of technologically advanced political and cultural formations, and how heavily they lean on an Other to serve as constitutive threat and support. The invasion of aliens from outer space constitutes an exterior threat which binds the world together in a ridiculously portrayed "global village," of which America is of course the center (*Independence Day*). Sadly, *Independence Day* was merely received as a poor epic, when its more radical thrust as a representation of American patriotic libido and sinthomatic idiocy was effectively evacuated. Audiences focused on the spectacular special effects, and viewed it as an aesthetically pleasing but substantially lacking action flick. Viewers actually cheered at the strangest moments, when the enemy-other was annihilated, instead of laughing at rather brilliant critique of the absurd manufacture of patriotism. Potentially critical and estranging rhetoric was transcoded as commodity. And few people know of *Canadian Bacon*, which spoofs the American patriotic impulse to find an enemy in order to bolster affective connections between "the people," the State, and its leaders. In the wake of drooping public opinion polls, the American President (Alan Alda) is advised to find an enemy. Several figures are toyed with in an absurd slide-show, featuring the likes of Hussein and Khomeni, but none fit the bill. Finally it is decided that the former Soviet Union should be wooed for enmity. Representatives are helicoptered to the White House for pizza and conversation. When the White House proposal is made, asking for at least the paraphernalia of enmity, the foreign ambassadors laugh at the Americans, claiming that national health care reform has sapped their funds for military build-up, or even its simulacrum. The democratization of the former Soviet Union had been costly, leaving no room for defense budgets. At the height of absurdity, as the foreign ambassadors prepare to enter the helicopter for home, the U.S. Press Secretary tackles a Soviet state official, begging him for enmity. At the sublime extremes of comedy, the White House selects Canada as enemy. Public opinion skyrockets. Farce ensues. A brilliant critique. The comic corrective to the eroticization of war and the attraction-repulsion construction of the other in mass mediated (and always political) communication, is simply not enough.

If Lacan is correct when he points to the instability of perversity, to its rhetorical constructedness and thus malleability, then we must engage in a critique of perversity that is tragic in character, even if it has moments of levity and a taste for discovering the idiotic. Even if he is not correct, and perversity is a stable way of life that keeps the guilty-judgment at bay for the sake of pleasure and comfort and decisive action, its mechanisms should be raised to the level of consciousness as we study the rhetoric of patriotism, judgment, and war. Such a tragic critique would suppose that human beings are incredibly susceptible to perversity, regardless of whether it is fragile or stable—it is, in Lacan's words, "an existential possibility" just waiting to be explored (1988)—and that the most devastating, consequential perversion of all is war. War is the tragic perversion of communion—is, to borrow a turn of phrase from Burke, love in reverse. In tragedy, the contest between heroic will and destiny is loaded in favor of destiny. So it is with the tragedy of war. Its seductive, erotic lure speaks to something deep within us. We must recognize in patriotism the seamy identification-fantasy of radical affective attachment to country and others, and how this identification-fantasy is propped up on dead bodies of enemy-others we have systematically fetishized. The fetishization of enemy-others helps make us want to kill, and enjoy the imagery of destruction (see Keene, 1986). Thus it is, finally, that we must turn our gazes within, to the demonic Other that lurks there hungrily gobbling up the patriotic pornography of war, realizing that the "enemy" I see in *Life* magazine, on the television, at the cinema, and indeed on the battlefield, is a projection of my own passion.

The danger of this imperative is that, in circumstances of urgency and terrible ethical appeal—in the face of naked aggression, brutal inhumanity, and so forth—we will pause, or perhaps stand paralyzed in stunned recognition at the horror we see in ourselves. Perversion makes ugly, even evil action possible. Most disturbing of all, it makes such things *enjoyable*. It yokes nobility and savagery together in violence and love. Of all the ugly things of which political cultures are made, patriotism is perhaps the ugliest, most passionate, erotic, hateful, and powerful of all. And if war is hell—a sexy place as well as a place of damnation and pain—then fire must perhaps sometimes be fought with fire. We are now beyond good and evil, beyond judgment, and so I must conclude with a final round of speculation.

We can critique patriotism in times of peace with relative luxury, even if it perturbs patriots. As the recent *Enola Gay* exhibition and the controversy that surrounded it demonstrated, patriots are apparently easily perturbed. To destabilize the fragility of their love of country, to reveal their pornographies of war to the public eye as pornographies, as the Smithsonian bordered on doing, is not so difficult a thing as some make it out to be (see Nobile, *Judgment at the Smithsonian,* 1995). As an abstract concept or distantly located historical formation, I am quite comfortable cracking the nut of perverse patriotic enjoyment. It is a much more difficult thing to realize that the fragility of patriotic perversity holds together the lives and memories of veterans, and that critique implicates them, opens old wounds, and creates new ones. It is little wonder that they so enjoy bashing the Left, revisionist historians, and draft-dodgers. In critique of our own luxury and perspective, we might ask: what is the heinous enjoyment that structures ideology critique, and marks the *telos* of critical rhetoric? To raise this question does not take the bite out of the critique of patriotic libido, enjoyment, and its habits of judgment. It opens it to critical self-reflection. Critique too may be perverse. Thus, having already returned the repressed, and (re)turned the screw of patriotism, let me close by giving perverts their due.

Thanks to and in collaboration with John Lucaites, I've been watching Capra's *Why we Fight* documentaries in preparation for further studies in the rhetoric of patriotism, war, and libido. There's a scene from *Russia Goes to War,* in which a tattered group of Soviet men take an oath together to avenge the loss of friends, family, lovers, land, and a way of life to German invasion—a violent penetration of Mother Russia. Their oath ascends from the highly personal ("my" things) to the highly collective ("our" things), finally to a sublime moment that implies both "my" things and "our" things are "Its" things, where "It" refers to Russia. These men are not soldiers, and do not appear to be much of a match for Nazi stormtroopers. Purposefulness without purpose, these men go to fight in the name of Russian patriotism—a love of Country that transcends individual or even collective properties ("mine" and even "ours" become "Its": objects/properties are raised to the dignity of Things). It is a powerful and perhaps even noble perversity that drives them to their deaths, a fixed mode of jouissance in which each man becomes a function of Its enjoyment, which now will be taken in revenge: a tragic revenge whose ethics we should perhaps not so quickly judge.

Could it be that quick judgment is itself the basic trait of enmity's erotic mystery? Yes. No. Maybe. The desire to render fast, decisive judgment may be read as the drive toward identification that marks the liminal horizon of human passion. The ultimacy of death, the enjoyments of enmity, and the capacity to kill in the name of whatever good, are lures which fix the gaze menacingly on the other so that life may be preserved, mummified, and made symbolically permanent. So long as people believe in the good, the true, and the beautiful—so long as we believe in and require hierarchies of value—war too will be mummified, a permanent possibility always waiting to be revived. If we have life without value, we have life "deprived of something" (Lacan, 1978, 212)—life that is lacking. If we have value without life, we have, strictly speaking, nothing at all—properties without relation. The question, Which shall it be, life or value?, puts the subject who wants it all in an aporetic predicament of judgment, an "either/or" double bind (see Kierkegaard, 1959). Lacan designates this choice between existence and value, marked by the linguistic function of the word "or," "the *lethal factor*" (1978, 213). War is a way of establishing value that hinges ultimately on death. Between two sacrifices—value *or* life—and situated squarely in the play of the lethal factor, judgment awaits making. Or else it awaits execution.

Notes

I wish to thank Cherie Bayer, Barbara Biesecker, Dieter Boxmann, David Cochran, Margaret Dorsi, Nicki Evans, Robert Hariman, Bob Ivie, Bill Lewis, John Lucaites, Roopali Mukherjee, David Nellmark, Kim Schultz, Allen Scult, Jennifer Tecklenburg, Robert Terrill, and students in my course in political communication at Indiana University and in social theory at Drake University for their generous conversations as I thought and went through various stages of research and writing. I would like to thank Michael Curtin, Director of Cultural Studies at Indiana University, for his advice and assistance, and for allowing me to use the resources of the Smith Research Center. John Sloop too was generous, particularly with deadlines and friendship. Michael Calvin McGee was my most contentious and careful reader and passionate partner in conversations of inquiry approaching the last draft. Susan Schwartz contributed so much to this chapter, from first draft to last, and to my life more generally, by way of criticism, advice, and example, that the least I can do is dedicate it to her in friendship. Of course, responsibility for this chapter rests with the author.

1. Erotic enjoyment in the pornography of war does not necessarily require the feminization or emasculation of the enemy. Indeed, the hyper-masculinization of the enemy as a rhetorical tactic represents the enemy as a radical threat to the MotherLand, to Lady Liberty, and other feminized notions of nationality and conflict. As I will argue later, "chivalric" or "courtly" action provides a narrative frame for the justification of war that features the enemy as masculine, aggressive, and without decorum. The key is that the enemy is represented *sexually*, and that sexuality offers a topos for navigating and creating the rhetoric of war. See Pick, *War Machine* (1993). Hariman's conception of political style is applicable

here, too (1995). Drawing from him, we might say that the rhetoric of war may assume various discursive forms, or be expressed according to the habits of a particular political style. The present essay, in Hariman's vocabulary, aims at critiquing the habits of the patriotic style as an affectively/politically charged *praxis* of rendering judgment.

2. Needless to say, it is not the other who does the gazing in these scenarios. Rather, the other supplies a placeholder for the eye/I of the subject or nation from which it looks at itself as if in wonder, enjoyment, horror, and so forth. Thus, to speak of the other as an external entity is not precise in this context. The other is eaten, is "inside" the subject or nation, in a manner of speaking.

3. As I emphasized above, drawing from Burke, rhetorics of Eros or identification also often are compensatory to Thanatos or division. Lacan takes this insight a somewhat different direction to argue that the quest for "the One" of *e pluribus unum* is always already failed because the lack in the subject/other cannot be filled. McGee, conversely, finds in the human urge for meaningfulness a magnetism that may be rhetorically activated. We should notice that the difference between the psychoanalytic (Lacan) and rhetorical (McGee) positions on the Eros of communication is figured rather deterministically by the former and openly by the latter. We might hazard the following interpretation: where Lacan is skeptical of symbolic-erotic magnetism for structural reasons, McGee is skeptical for political ones.

4. I was reminded of this tale by John Lucaites when I one day sat in on his graduate seminar in rhetorical theory at Indiana University. Lucaites told a version of this story in part to illustrate how fundamental rhetoric are to knowledge, as a way of seeing that in part structures the possibilities of action. Its popular origin is from an episode of the television series, *M*A*S*H**.

5. Lacan's discussion of the look, the gaze, and recognition (Seminar I) is highly indebted to Sartre (1966) and his phenomenology of anxiety and the existence of others in *Being and Nothingness*. The Lacan of Seminar XI, however, makes a departure from Sartre to emphasize that the gaze as object of the drive is a matter of making oneself seen rather than being looked at. The later Lacan dovetails with Aristotle, and the discussion of shame offered in the *Rhetoric*. For Aristotle, the gaze (of the other) as object of the drive concerns prestige, recognition, honor, and other public virtues. Both the later Lacan and Aristotle seem to insist that the gaze contains a judgment, which offers incentive for "ethical" (or at least publicly esteemed) action. But Aristotle does not at all grasp the motives for actually doing the shameful publicly, whereas Lacan does. We might say that Aristotle's psychology of rhetoric fails to comprehend the circulation of perversity in public life as a force of social cohesion. Performing shameful, yet paradoxically sanctioned, actions in public is a way of articulating what I will discuss, via Zizek, as "solidarity-in-guilt."

6. This sort of situation, of course, is not gender specific (e.g., wives "look" too). Nor does it require matrimonial contract. It is a broad-based communication phenomenon. Theodor Reik (1968, 406–411) nevertheless argues that the cultural-structural properties of the look-event feature the objectification of women, so that the "way" women are looked at (both by males and females) is substantially different than the "way" men are looked at.

7. As in psychoanalysis, the status of the other in rhetorical theory remains provocatively unstable. In an article for an *Encyclopedia of Rhetoric and Composition: Communication from Ancient Times to the Information Age*, Biesecker and McDaniel (1996) locate the prospects for social change in this very instability, albeit with many an elision and collusion, e.g., desire is implicitly equated with jouissance (a conceptual error); femininity with multiplicity (an unargued essentialism); otherness with self-difference (a reduction); doing is not adequately or meaningfully differentiated from acting (another conceptual error?); nor are the central problems of rhetoric and philosophy practically distinguished (a form of theory fetishism); and so forth. Much is packed into this small article, so much that insufficient space is devoted (or was available) for unpacking. They say: "The question of the relation of self and other is the inaugurating question of Western philosophy and rhetoric. From Parmendies' inquiry into the problematics of the one and the many regarding the unity of Being, through G.W.F. Hegel's formulation of self-consciousness and identity, and to the litany of thinkers working within and against the dialectical tradition, the history of the thinking on the relation of self and other registers the movement from being (ontology) through knowing (epistemology), through doing (ethics) and, finally, to acting (rhetoric)" (488). Notice the emphasis on *thinking* and *thinkers*. A more practical orientation is called for with respect to theorizing the other rhetorically. The potential relations to the other move between polarities of alterity and reciprocity, difference and similarity, familiarity and strangeness. The other is potentially a friend, a lover, a neighbor, an enemy, an object, and so on. The key is that what the other "is" depends largely on rhetorical construction, negotiation, and adaptation. The Being of the other, when viewed from the side of the subject, requires a judgment (which may be "right" or "wrong," "good" or "bad," but which always is consequential). When viewed from the side of the other, the other is subject and the subject is other. Throughout this chapter, I employ "other" with a little "o" to signify actually desiring others (e.g., Japanese and American soldiers, civilians, and generalized particular entities). I use the term "Other" with a big "O" to signify a certain anonymity, a lacuna of alterity not reducible to an individual person or even group. In the Lacanian idiom, particularly in Zizek, the "Big Other" registers functions of the (political) unconscious. But also, the Other refers to the radical difference of a particular other: the other becomes/is Other when they are regarded as alien. We will have to rely ultimately on contexts of usage to establish the conventions, rather than on a general grammar.

8. Whereas Freud seems to locate perversity strictly in the realm of sexuality, Lacan appears to extend it to apply more generally to enjoyment that is willfully against the grain of the Symbolic order, i.e., the Law. For this reason, we needn't judge perversity to be "wrong" in the parochial sense of the term, for the Law itself may be perverse.

9. Emphasis in text; reference deleted.

10. Lacan's algebraic formulas are explained in considerable detail by Rapaport (1994), and by Zizek (1991b). Perhaps they are but an absurd remnant of positivism that Lacan picked up in order to "scientize" psychoanalysis. I will unpack a few Lacanian formulas later in the chapter. The formula for perversity in particular is difficult. Michael McGee has asked me, Where and how does Lacan/Zizek prove that perversity is possible? In quick response to this question, we might

say: the very idea of normative culture proves it by establishing and enforcing differences between acceptable and unacceptable, appropriate and inappropriate, objects for libidinal cathexes. This does not get at the hard edge of the question, however, which asks in addition: how do we judge perversion in anything other than a culturally relative vocabulary? What norm is supposed in rendering the judgment that a practice is perverse? Is psychoanalysis (merely) after normalizing certain pleasure principles? Does psychoanalysis possess a utopian impulse, and if so what is it? Whereas the work of Herbert Marcuse (1955, 1964) is rather unambiguous about this, that of Lacan and his followers, particularly Zizek, is not. At the close of this chapter, I attempt to recuperate the utility and perhaps, even, the troublesome ethicality of perversion. But McGee's questions remain.

11. A distinction must be made between desire and jouissance. On the Lacanian view, desire marks lack, whereas jouissance is excessive. It is interesting to note that in Plato's discussion of love in the *Symposium*, love is discussed as the child of two parents: lack and plenty (desire and jouissance?). Manifestations of enmity, such as jealousy or possessiveness—e.g., the other desires that to which I cling and desire, and thus reminds me that what I "have" in the beloved is not, strictly speaking, "mine"—may be seen to emerge from the very genealogy of love.

12. On the "unmarked," see Phelan, *Unmarked: The Politics of Performance* (1994).

13. Emphasis in text; references deleted.

14. I cite this passage from Derrida's essay "Interpreting Signatures," in Michelfelder and Palmer (eds.): *Dialogue and Deconstruction* (1989, 66).

15. Both/and rhetoric will be implicitly contrasted to, and situated as derivative of, either/or rhetoric at the conclusion of this chapter. The fetishization of both/and-ism in contemporary leftist political theory and *praxis*—which purports to admit radical difference—in fact may be read as an evasion of judgment. Both/and rhetoric avoids the hard choices of situated political life in favor of a utopic, radically democratic culture marked by the absence of hierarchy. As Lacan (1978) points out, signification peculiarly circulates around an absence or hole punched in the symbolic order by the word "or." Judgment is not just a consequence of signification that may be outstripped, therefore: it is a permanent, unavoidable feature of signification. Judgment "happens" (see Caputo, 1993).

16. Ellipses in text.

17. This provides a model for the theory of ideological interpellation that is properly Lacanian. Althusser's try at such a theory (1971) missed by a bit (see Zizek, 1994). Althusser misses the double-lack of at the scene of interpellation: not only does the subject lack/desire, so does the Other. For what would a State be without people, or vice versa?

18. The skull photographs were shown to a World History class at Drake University in the Spring of 1997 as part of a lecture I delivered on the *Enola Gay* controversy and the status of public memory in America. They were responded to with disbelief. Several students doubted that they came from *Life* magazine, and implied that I'd made them myself or gathered them from secret military archives. Similar responses were registered by people in numerous settings, some academic and others not. None looked at or through the photos with obvious enjoyment. This, of course, is at best dubious evidence.

19. I cite this from Roeder (1993, 153).

20. I draw here heavily from John Peters' discussion of "The Gaps out of Which Communication is Made" (1994).

21. Susan Schwartz, "Judgment and Jouissance: Eliot, Freud, and Lacan Read *Hamlet*." I quote this essay from a manuscript version of a book chapter that will appear in John M. Sloop and James P. McDaniel (eds.), *Judgment Calls* (Boulder: Westview Press).

22. As with Lacan, we do not here imply that another possibility does not exist. Yet there appears to be something absolutely irreducible about the lethal factor. For example, the linguistic function of the term *and* may be said to mark an alternative possibility of judgment/action. With *and*, for example, we might get both life *and* value. Such is the aim of emancipatory politics, from Hegel's master-slave dialectic to abolitionism in America to present day struggles of women's movements and beyond. Yet we should notice that the outcry of the oppressed, or the undervalued, often is attended by quasi-patriotic or -matriotic slogans: *Give us value or give us death!* (We hear in such outcries startling echoes of early American patriotism, e.g., *Give me liberty or give me death!*) On the way to the both/and, the either/or aporia establishes the value of values. It is an ultimate form of expression and choice, a bias on which the subject of judgment is situated. See Kierkegaard, *Either/Or* (1959).

References

Abraham, Nicolas and Maria Torok. 1994. *The Shell and the Kernel, Volume I*. Trans. and ed. Nicholas T. Rand. Chicago: University of Chicago Press.

Althusser, Louis. 1971. *Lenin and Philosophy and Other Essays*. Trans. Ben Brewster. New York: Monthly Review Press.

Aristotle. 1991. *On Rhetoric: A Theory of Civic Discourse*. Trans. George Kennedy. New York: Oxford University Press.

Bataille, Georges. 1986. *Eroticism: Death and Sensuality*. Trans. Mary Dalwood. San Francisco: City Lights Books.

_____. 1991. *The Accursed Share, Volume I: An Essay on General Economy*. Trans. Robert Hurley. New York: Zone Books.

Bazin, André. 1967. *What is Cinema? Volume I*. Trans. Hugh Gray. Berkeley: University of California Press.

Biesecker, Barbara and James P. McDaniel. 1996. The Other. In *Encyclopedia of Rhetoric and Composition: Communication from Ancient Times to the Information Age* (pp. 488–490), ed. Theresa Enos. New York: Garland Press.

Burke, Kenneth. 1957. *The Philosophy of Literary Form: Studies in Symabolic Action*. Rev. edition. New York: Vintage. First edition published in 1941. Baton Rouge: Louisiana State University Press.

_____. 1959. *Attitudes Toward History*. Rev. second edition. Boston: Beacon Press.

_____. 1965. *Permanence and Change*. Indianapolis: The Bobbs-Merrill Company. First published in 1954.

_____. 1968. *Language as Symbolic Action*. Berkeley: University of California Press.

_____. 1969. *A Rhetoric of Motives*. Berkeley: University of California Press. First edition published in 1950.

Capra, Frank. 1971. *The Name Above the Title: An Autobiography*. New York: Macmillan Co.

Caputo, John. *Against Ethics: Contributions to a Poetics of Obligation with Constant Reference to Deconstruction*. Bloomington: Indiana University Press, 1993.

Charland, Maurice. 1991. Finding a Horizon and *Telos*: The Challenge to Critical Rhetoric. *The Quarterly Journal of Speech* 77: 71–74.

Derrida, Jacques. 1973. *Speech and Phenomenon and Other Essays on Husserl's Theory of Signs*. Trans. David B. Allison and Newton Garver. Evanston: Northwestern University Press.

_____. 1992. *The Other Heading: Reflections on Today's Europe*. Trans. Pascale Anne-Brault and Michael B. Naas. Bloomington: Indiana University Press.

Dower, John. 1986. *War Without Mercy: Race and Power in the Pacific War*. New York: Pantheon Books.

Fisher, Walter. 1987. *Human Communication as Narration: Toward a Philosophy of Reason, Value, and Action*. Columbia, SC: University of South Carolina Press.

Fussell, Paul. 1988. *Thank God for the Atom Bomb and Other Essays*. New York: Summit Books.

Gaonkar, Dilip. 1990. Object and Method in Rhetorical Criticism: From Wichelns to Leff and McGee. *Western Journal of Speech Communication* 54: 290–316.

Gray, J. Glenn. 1959. *The Warriors: Reflections on Men in Battle*. New York: Harper and Row.

Gronbeck, Bruce. 1995. Unstated Propositions: Relationships Among Verbal, Visual and Acoustic Languages. In *Argumentation and values*, ed. Sally Jackson (pp. 539–542). Annandale, VA: Speech Communication Association.

Hariman, Robert. 1979. *The Public Temper of* Gravity's Rainbow. PhD thesis, The University of Minnesota, directed by Robert L. Scott.

_____. 1991. Critical Rhetoric and Postmodern Theory. *The Quarterly Journal of Speech* 77: 67–70.

_____. 1995. *Political Style: The Artistry of Power*. Chicago: University of Chicago Press.

Hegel, G.W.F. 1977. *Phenomenology of Spirit*. Trans. A.V. Miller. New York: Oxford University Press.

Ivie, Robert. 1980. Images of Savagery in American Justifications for War. *Communication Monographs* 47: 279–294.

Keene, Sam. 1986. *Faces of the Enemy: Reflections on the Hostile Imagination*. San Francisco: Harper and Row.

Kierkegaard, Soren. 1959. *Either/Or*. Trans. Walter Lowrie. New York: Doubleday.

Kirkwood, William. 1992. Narrative and the Rhetoric of Possibility. *Communication Monographs* 59: 30–47.

Kojève, Alexandre. 1969. *Introduction to the Reading of Hegel: Lectures on the* Phenomenology of Spirit. Trans. James H. Nichols, Jr. Ed. Allan Bloom. Ithaca: Cornell University Press.

Kundera, Milan. 1984. *The Unbearable Lightness of Being*. Trans. Michael Henry Heim. New York: Harper and Row.

Lacan, Jaques. 1977. *Écrits: A Selection*. Trans. Alan Sheridan. New York: W.W. Norton and Company.

_____. 1978. *The Four Fundamental Concepts of Psycho-analysis* Trans. by Alan Sheridan. New York: W.W. Norton.

_____. 1985. God and the Jouissance of the Woman. In *Feminine Sexuality: Jacques Lacan and the école freudienne*, eds. Juliet Mitchell and Jacqueline Rose (pp. 138–148). New York: W.W. Norton.

_____. 1988. *The Seminar of Jacques Lacan, Book I: Freud's Papers on Technique 1953–1954*. Trans. John Forrester, ed. Jacques-Alain Miller. New York: W.W. Norton and Company.

_____. 1992. *The Seminar of Jacques Lacan, Book VII: The Ethics of Psychoanalysis*. Trans. Dennis Porter, ed. Jacques-Allain Miller. New York: W.W. Norton and Company.

Lucaites, John. 1986. *The Vital and Stable Dimensions of Discourse in the Mobilization for War: A Case Study of "Why We fight."* Paper presented at The Southern Speech Communication Association Convention, Houston, Texas.

Marcuse, Herbert. 1955. *Eros and Civilization: A Philosophical Inquiry into Freud*. Boston: Beacon Press.

_____. 1964. *One-Dimensional Man: Studies in the Ideology of Advanced Society*. Boston: Beacon Press.

McGee, Michael Calvin. 1975. In Search of 'the People': A Rhetorical Alternative. *The Quarterly Journal of Speech* 61: 235–249.

_____. 1990. Text, Context, and the Fragmentation of Contemporary Culture. *Western Journal of Speech Communication* 54: 274–289.

McGee, Michael Calvin and John Lyne 1987. What are Nice Folks Like you Doing in a Place Like This? Some Entailments of Treating Knowledge Claims Rhetorically. In *The Rhetoric of the Human Sciences: Language and Scholarship in Public Affairs* (pp. 381–406), eds. John Nelson, Allan Megill, and Donald McCloskey. Madison: University of Wisconsin Press.

McKerrow, Raymie. 1989. Critical Rhetoric: Theory and Praxis. *Communication Monographs* 56: 91–111.

_____. 1993. Critical Rhetoric and the Possibility of the Subject. In *The Critical Turn: Rhetoric and Philosophy in Postmodern Discourse* (pp. 51–67), eds. Ian Angus and Lenore Langsdorf. Carbondale: Southern Illinois University Press.

Michelfelder, Diane P. and Richard E. Palmer (eds.). 1989. *Dialogue and Deconstruction: The Gadamer-Derrida Encounter*. Albany: State University of New York Press.

Newman, Robert. 1995. *Truman and the Hiroshima Cult*. East Lansing: Michigan University Press.

Nobile, Barton J., ed. 1995. *Judgment at the Smithsonian: The Bombing of Hiroshima and Nagasaki*. New York: Marlowe and Company.

Ono, Kent A. and John M. Sloop. 1992. Commitment to *Telos*—a Sustained Critical Rhetoric. *Communication Monographs* 59: 48–60.

Pick, Daniel. 1993. *War Machine: The Rationalisation of Slaughter in the Modern Age*. New Haven: Yale University Press.

Peters, John. 1997. Beauty's Veils: The Ambivalent Iconoclasm of Kierkegaard and Benjamin. In *The image in Dispute: Art and Cinema in the Age of Photography*, ed. Dudley Andrew (pp. 9–32). Austin: University of Texas Press.

_____. 1994. The Gaps of Which Communication is Made. *Critical Studies in Mass Communication* 11: 117–140.

Phelan, Peggy. 1993. *Unmarked: The Politics of Performance*. New York: Routledge.

Poulakos, John. 1984. Rhetoric, the Sophists, and the Possible. *Communication Monographs* 51: 215–226.

Rapaport, Herman. 1994. *Between the Sign and the Gaze*. Ithaca: Cornell University Press.

Reese, Stephen D. and Bob Buckalew. 1995. The Militarism of Local Television: The Routine Framing of the Persian Gulf War. *Critical Studies in Mass Communication* 57: 40–59.

Reik, Theodor. 1968. *Of Love and Lust: On the Psychoanalysis of Romantic and Sexual Emotions*. Fifth printing. New York: Farrar, Straus, and Giroux.

Roeder, George H. 1993. *The Censored War: American Visual Experience During the Second World War*. New Haven: Yale University Press.

Ronell, Avital. 1993. Support our Tropes: Reading Desert Storm. In *Rhetorical Republic: Governing Representations in American Politics* (pp. 13–37), eds. Frederick M. Dolan and Thomas L. Dunn. Amherst: The University of Massachussetts Press.

Sartre, Jean-Paul. 1966. *Being and Nothingness: An Essay on Phenomenological Ontology*. Trans. Hazel E. Barnes. New York: Washington Square Press.

Schwartz, Susan. Forthcoming publication. Judgment and Jouissance: Eliot, Freud, and Lacan Read *Hamlet*. In *Judgment Calls*, eds. John M. Sloop and James P. McDaniel. Boulder: Westview Press.

Silberpfennig, Judith. 1945. Psychological Aspects of Current Japanese and German Paradoxa. *Psychoanalytic Review* 32.1 (January): 73–85.

Turner, Victor. 1980. Social Dramas and Stories About Them. *Critical Inquiry* 7: 141–168.

Zizek, Slavoj. 1989. *The Sublime Object of Ideology*. London: Verso.

_____. 1991a. *For They Know not What They Do: Enjoyment as a Political Factor*. London: Verso.

_____. 1991b. *Looking Awry: An Introduction to Jacques Lacan Through Popular Culture*. Cambridge: The MIT Press.

_____. 1993. *Tarrying with the Negative: Kant, Hegel, and the Critique of Ideology*. Durham: Duke University Press.

_____. 1994. *The Metastases of Enjoyment: Six Essays on Woman and Causality*. London: Verso.

PART 2

Case Studies in
Judgment Calls

6

"Had Judas Been a Black Man ... "

Politics, Race, and Gender in African America

Karen L. Dace

Watch these mono-issue people. They ain't gonna do you no good. I don't care who they are. And there are people who prioritize the cutting line of the struggle. And they say the cutting line is this issue, and more than anything we must move on this issue and that's automatically saying that whatever's bothering you will be put down if you bring it up. You have to watch these folks. Watch these groups that can only deal with one thing at a time.
—**Bernice Johnson Reagon**

In her 1981 speech to the West Coast Women's Music Festival, veteran civil rights worker Bernice Johnson Reagon (1995, 546) admonished her audience to attend to the needs of every coalition member. One faction cannot and should not be permitted to assume greater importance than others. Competition is dangerous, even foolish. The concerns of one sub-group should not be promoted or perceived as more significant or urgent than any other sub-group. When this happens, when the coalition be-comes single-minded or "mono-issued," it is inevitable that those who must wait their turn suffer in the interim. One wonders whether the dominant group ever reaches that point at which it will be adequately satisfied to allow others within the group to address their concerns and issues.

That African American and European American world views differ is no surprise. Recent surveys demonstrate this point well. While the ma-jority of European Americans polled by the Gallup Organization in 1997 "see little need to be concerned when it comes to opportunities for blacks in jobs, education and housing" fifty-nine percent of the African Ameri-cans polled were quite concerned (Staff 1997, A11). Forty-five percent of the African Americans reported being discriminated against "in situa-tions outside their homes" at least 30 days prior to taking the survey.

That statistic jumped to seventy percent when "limited to black men" (Staff 1997, A11).

Forced to function in a system that never meant to include their voices or bodies, African Americans have worked to "preserve black social order under circumstances of white literal attack and symbolic assault" (West 1994, 37). It is within this framework, this reality, that African American judgment operates. The struggle, then, has many prongs. While attempting to create and preserve this social order, African Americans do so recognizing that others refuse to or cannot see racial injustice. Added to this situation is the additional burden of the African American male. Viewed by many European Americans as a threat to society, he is celebrated and encouraged within an African American community that interprets his situation quite differently. For example, it is unlikely that European Americans would conceive the need for a Million Man March, however many within the African American community recognized that need. It is upon these standards that judgment is made within the African American community. Behaviors must be such that they ensure the continuation of the culture and protect its members. As men are judged to be most threatened, they require greater attention and concern than women within the culture. This essay suggests that individuals and factions within the African American community both interpret and plan actions with this knowledge.

Consequently the essay suggests the African American community has failed to heed Reagon's advice. Rather than incorporating the concerns of all members in the struggle for equality and fairness, the voice and needs of its women play second fiddle to that of the men within the culture. The speed with which the community moves to address, "fight" for, and defend its members varies. Men garner support and women receive little assistance when threatened by persons or organizations from either the dominant or African American culture. Mike Tyson, Clarence Thomas and Mel Reynolds serve as examples of massive community campaigns which sought to aid them. Their examples are alarming when one considers the lack of support, coupled with the attacks, their "accusers" (Desiree Washington, Anita Hill and Beverly Heard) received from the community. The addition of Lani Guinier and Joycelyn Elders, African American women who were attacked by European American conservatives and some liberals, to the list is telling. The community offers equally weak support for African American women whose detractors come from outside the culture. Community members rally around men at the expense of women with little concern for the calibre of "charges" against either gender.

African American women have long recognized the danger and taboo of charging fellow African Americans with wrongdoing. Consequently,

Washington, Hill and Heard were labelled by many as traitors to the race. However, Guinier and Elders were not guilty of what many see as race treason. Yet, the community failed to establish a support base for Guinier and Elders equivalent to that formed for Tyson, Thomas and Reynolds.

Given a society in which African American men historically have been marginalized—the inability to get jobs when women could—as well as pervasive negative notions of African American men, community members developed a defense mechanism which governs the way judgments are made. African American women were hired in albeit subservient positions in an era where any job was better than no job. The plight of African American men made that of women less significant. Decisions about which causes and community members to support come out of this history. While such judgments are not always fair to every community member, the reason for the support of African American men at the expense of African American women is clear.

Gender and Support

The difference in community support for boxer Mike Tyson and rape victim Desiree Washington has been discussed more thoroughly elsewhere (Dace 1994). Although both were members of the National Baptist Convention, the largest black religious entity in America embraced Tyson with prayers, rallies and even a phone call to Washington requesting she not press charges. African American leaders—Jesse Jackson, Al Sharpton and Louis Farrakhan—voiced support for Tyson and doubt about Washington's charges. Washington was accused by Farrakhan of using the same game "sisters" have used over the years, saying "no" when they really meant "yes." During his incarceration, rapper Chuck D of Public Enemy fame, called for the release of political prisoner Mike Tyson. Washington was accused of helping destroy "one of our few black heroes."

The treatment accorded Clarence Thomas and Anita Hill has filled several volumes (e.g., Morrison 1993). As West (1994) explains, the African American community, obviously concerned about Thomas' ability to assume Thurgood Marshall's position on the Supreme Court, remained silent rather than publicly question their brother's qualifications. Such questions, West suggests, were asked within the community, at barber and beauty shops, in mosques and church pulpits. However, this discussion seldom made it out of the community. Some supported him in hopes that once in the life-long position Thomas would "be true to the game." This closing ranks mentality (West 1994) forced African Americans to publicly support Clarence Thomas in spite of their concerns about his character, professional record and charges of sexual harassment from Anita Hill.

The more recent conviction of Illinois Congressman Mel Reynolds on twelve counts of criminal sexual assault, sexual abuse, solicitation of child pornography and obstruction of justice (Sanz, Eskin, and Fisher 1995) serves as another example of divided community support. Perhaps Oprah Winfrey's comment to Reynolds' accuser Beverly Heard best reveals some of the African American sentiment. Winfrey explained that sixteen (Heard's age when Reynolds met her in front of her high school and initiated a sexual relationship) is not the same today as when the talk show host was that age. In other words, Heard was more like a adult woman when she had sex with Reynolds because the times have changed. An African American female caller to a Chicago radio talk show lessened the significance of Reynolds' behavior by explaining that in the past many people married earlier, "some as early as the age of 13." Hence, sex for someone Heard's age is not so alarming when one considers historical practices. Each day of Reynolds' trial supporters marched outside the courthouse, picket signs in hand, yelling their support for the congressman and disapproval of Heard. After his conviction some community members created a fund to pay Reynolds' mortgage which exceeded $3,000 monthly.

Community support of Thomas, Tyson and Reynolds far exceeded that given Hill, Washington and Heard. West's (1994) discussion of the closing ranks mentality is helpful in understanding the difference in treatment for African American men and women. In each of these cases, women were accused of being used by the white power structure. These women were viewed by many in the culture as pawns of European Americans whose chief goal is to destroy African American manhood. The notion of closing ranks is important in that it creates the impression of unity. African Americans come together to help and defend their own. Unfortunately, in the three cases above, only one side can be helped— Thomas *or* Hill; Tyson *or* Washington; Reynolds *or* Heard (West 1994, 37): "The idea of black people closing ranks against hostile white Americans reinforces black male power exercised over black women (e.g., to protect, regulate, subordinate, and hence usually, though not always, to use and abuse women) in order to preserve black social order under circumstances of white literal attack and symbolic assault."

In the three cases above, the closing ranks moves of community members dictated "saving" men and "sacrificing" women as African Americans united. The need to present a united front contributes to labelling women who accuse men of misconduct as traitors. The support of men over women is further explained by a cultural rule. It is strictly taboo for African Americans to publicly (read: in the presence of European Americans) discuss or accuse one another of improper behavior. As Pemberton (1992, 189) explains: "There are many hidden laws governing intraracial black behavior. One of the most important is the cardinal rule that says one does not complain about another black person to a white one, particularly a white person in a supervisory position. A black woman *absolutely* does not indict a black man in front of a white one, as this act is hopelessly entangled within a welter of images and symbols from slavery."

The closing ranks mentality circles the wagons around men rather than women. The rule against speaking out against African American men further justifies this exclusion of women from similar support. The need to close ranks in order to do battle in a "hostile country" (West 1994) which lead many members within the community to develop programs and campaigns to help Reynolds and Tyson, as well as remain silent over Thomas' appointment, explains the lack of support for their accusers. That these women broke a widely held cultural rule further explains their exclusion from community assistance. However illuminating this explanation is, it does not explain the treatment afforded Lani Guinier and Joycelyn Elders. Unlike Washington, Heard and Hill, Lani Guinier and Joycelyn Elders were not embattled with African American men. Indeed, their plight was more reminiscent of African Americans struggling within a "hostile country" which, following West's (1994) theory, should lead to a closing ranks move on the part of African Americans. It did not.

When Bill Clinton nominated Lani Guinier to head the civil rights division of the U.S. Department of Justice right wing politicians moved in for the attack. She was labelled a "quota queen," threat to white manhood. These attacks came in response to distortions of her academic writings which members of the press and conservative politicians insisted questioned fundamental aspects of American government, specifically majority rule. Although Guinier insisted again and again that she had never supported quotas and that she had no "quarrel with majority rule," rather she had the same concerns members of the Reagan and Bush administrations voiced about protecting the rights of minorities, the law professor was not given an opportunity to address charges against her. President Clinton withdrew her nomination without allowing Senate confirmation hearings, bowing to pressure from Republican and some Democratic senators including Bob Dole, Joe Biden and Orrin Hatch. Guinier's qualifications were not debated or suspect (unlike her legal predecessor Clarence Thomas). Rather, her views, which differed drastically from conservative politicians who questioned every Clinton appointment, made Guinier suspect among right wingers. As attacks from her opponents grew, African Americans failed to circle the wagons of support, a fact some have lamented.

According to Jesse Jackson the community was ill-prepared to rally around Guinier. The minister felt African American inactivity was the result of disorganization. The key to winning future battles, Jackson offered, rests in establishing a "national system of communication" (Warren 1993). His idea, the linking of pulpits, civil rights organizations and members of the black press (A29): "Blacks have suffered most from their lack of organization at times of crisis, when they have been unable to fight back effectively, he said . . . 'When Lani Guinier was in trouble, we did not have the capacity to transmit our word,' Jackson said. 'We must have the ability to push a button and connect the network.'"

Jackson's reasoning is curious at best when one considers the networks that enabled wide-range community support of other African Americans, especially Mike Tyson. The communication network already exists within the African American community which links politicians with pulpits with the media with various community leaders. With little notice, thousands filled black churches and convention centers to hear an assortment of leaders and ministers praise and support Mike Tyson. Although then-chair of the Congressional Black Caucus Kweisi Mfume defended black politicians, asserting that the Caucus had "been on top of this issue since day one" (Ross 1993), Eleanor Holmes Norton, the District of Columbia's delegate to Congress, blamed civil rights leaders for lack of attention. According to Norton, Guinier was without community support because many within civil rights circles assumed the White House "would sufficiently shore up Guinier": "'I've heard some of our colleagues in the civil rights movement complain they (the White House) put her out there and didn't get out there and defend her,' Norton said. 'It was our job to defend her. Particularly since this White House has been weakened in the last several weeks.'"

Jackson's explanation of an ill-prepared African American community does not ring true when the recent history of community action is considered. Eleanor Holmes Norton's summation is more revealing than it seems. The historical nature of African American gender relations, which includes pitting men against women and the myth of European American support for women at the expense of men, may have lead many within the community to assume, as Norton suggests, that another community would "take care" of Guinier—liberal European Americans. Hence, there was no need to gather together to defend Guinier.

Joycelyn Elders, once America's "top doctor," was forced to resign her position in President Clinton's cabinet as surgeon general. Her resignation came after a series of remarks which shocked and offended conservative and liberal politicians. She was in favor of sex education, abortion, corporal punishment, studying the feasibility of legalizing drugs, and eliminating the fear, ignorance and shame surrounding masturbation. The so-called religious right scared her. She thought they were self-righteous and dangerous. Although Elders never indicated teaching children how to masturbate; never said schools should distribute condoms to nine-year-olds, members of the press and several politicians reported differently. There was little in the way of public outrage when Clinton forced her resignation. Nor was there much community response when Vice President Al Gore explained Elder's suggestion of studying possible outcomes of legalizing drugs was "just stupid, ridiculous." The African American community remained silent on the surgeon general issue until Clinton announced Henry Foster as her replacement. Although Foster did not survive the battle to become the nation's top doctor, he enjoyed a wide-base of community support from the NAACP, Congressional Black Caucus, ministers and neighborhood counsels.

African American Women as Endangered Species

Beverly Heard, Anita Hill, Desiree Washington, Lani Guinier and Joycelyn Elders represent modern manifestations of the exclusion of women's concerns, issues and struggles from the African American agenda. This prioritization, which Reagon (1995) warned against over a decade ago, is rooted in historical practices which placed women in subordinate positions. There are at least three judgments which contribute to the exclusion of one half the African American population from the struggle for equality: racial reasoning as explicated by Cornel West (1994); the historical identification of blackness with masculinity which requires silencing women; and pervasive stereotypical depictions of African American women.

Judgment I: Racial Reasoning

Cornel West (1994) argues that African American captivity to the normative or white gaze creates space for a faulty reasoning practice, racial reasoning, which undermines any serious discussion of issues affecting the community. Because African American leaders employed racial rather than moral reasoning, they were forced to support Clarence Thomas' nomination to the Supreme Court amid serious doubts about his character and qualifications.

Racial reasoning consists of three progressive steps. The first requirement is the establishment of the "victim's" black authenticity. Using Clarence Thomas as an example, West (1994) explains the Supreme Court nominee offered himself as a true black man—he survived in racist Georgia. With his blackhood established, the second component, closing ranks within the community to assist Thomas was possible. There was a need to help him in his bid for the top court, protecting him from any detractors. The fundamental problem with racial authenticity and closing ranks for African American women is that they necessarily lead to the third and final stage—encouraging black cultural conservatism (37). African American cultural conservatism is patriarchal and homophobic in nature (37–38): "Most black leaders got lost in the thicket of reasoning and hence got caught in a vulgar form of racial reasoning: black authenticity→black closing ranks mentality→black male subordination of black women in the interests of the black community in a hostile white racist country."

Racial reasoning limited discussions to pigmentation and acceptance of a black phenotype in the form of Clarence Thomas (West 1994). Moral reasoning incorporates the political and ethical dimensions of blackness. According to West (1994), the opening up of reasoning to include these moral constructs would have enabled African Americans to attend to the less than authentic comments Thomas made about his sister Emma Mae whom he labelled a welfare queen in a speech before a conservative audience. Thomas neglected to note that his sister cared for an ailing aunt while unemployed as well as the fact that upon exiting the welfare system she held down two jobs, working until 3:00 a.m. (40–41): "The failure of black leaders to highlight his statements discloses a conception of black authenticity confined to black male interests, individuals, and communities. In short, the refusal by most leaders to give weight to the interests of black women was already apparent before Anita Hill appeared on the scene."

Notions of black authenticity within the racial reasoning framework necessarily leads to closing ranks at the expense of gender, class and sexual orientation issues (West 1994). Cultural conservatism within the African American culture necessitates the assertion of maleness over femaleness. Just as European American cultural conservatism incorporates racism, sexism and homophobia, African American cultural conservatism "means principally attacking black women and black gay men and lesbians" (42).

The process of racial reasoning and its component cultural conservatism illumine what happened to Hill, Washington and Heard, as well as Elders and Guinier within the African American community. As West (1994) notes, women in the first group were excluded due to the closing ranks mentality which forced the community to make a choice. A conservative framework makes no space for women when they are at odds with men. Complex judgments are rendered simple due to the absence of moral and political considerations of blackness. Thomas, Tyson and Reynolds required attention and support. Hill, Washington and Heard were judged to be part of the white power structure. When African American leaders closed ranks around Thomas, Tyson and Reynolds they simultaneously moved against Hill, Washington and Heard.

The effect of racial reasoning on Lani Guinier and Joycelyn Elders is threefold. First, according to the theory, black authenticity must be acknowledged. Clarence Thomas established himself as a genuine black man when he described his poor, racist Georgia upbringing. He solidified that authenticity when he labelled the sexual harassment hearings a "high-tech lynching." Similarly, Mel Reynolds characterized his charges and the subsequent guilty verdict as reminiscent of "the shackling of his slave ancestors" (Zook 1995). Community and church leaders invoked black authenticity for Mike Tyson. He was touted repeatedly as "one of our few black heroes."

Neither Joycelyn Elders nor Lani Guinier invoked black authenticity nor was it invoked for them by others. Without this invocation the next step, closing ranks, is impossible. While Thomas and Reynolds used black authenticity to solicit support, religious and political leaders used it to justify standing up for Tyson, Guinier and Elders refused or neglected to employ the strategy.

Second, had Guinier and Elders opted to play the race card, it is doubtful the African American community would have closed ranks around their causes. Closing ranks mentality is situated within a patriarchal structure establishing manhood over womanhood. It would be counter intuitive for a male power structure to make room for women. As West (1994) points out, the need to protect, subordinate and regulate women eliminated the possibility of equal attention and support for Elders and Guinier. The fact that Guinier and Elders did not play the race card (nor did Washington, Hill, and Heard) presents an interesting question. One wonders whether they viewed themselves as professional or women (or both). Or, did they neglect the strategy because the race card is not in the African American woman's deck?

Third, African American cultural conservatism offered no outlet for a program of support for Guinier and Elders. Because racial reasoning asserts manhood and subordinates womanhood, there is no space for a rally around African American women, even when they are attacked by the white power structure.

Male-skewed racial reasoning creates space for countless "hero" products like t-shirts bearing O.J. Simpson's and convicted rapists Mike Tyson's and Tupac Shakur's images. This same reasoning excludes similar products sporting African American female images. Kristol Brent Zook (1995) speculates "we'll never see the brothers on the corner peddling righteous images of Anita Hill or Joycelyn Elders" (89).

Judgment II: Black Equals Masculine

The colored woman of to-day occupies, one may say, a unique position in this country. In a period of itself transitional and unsettled, her status seems one of the least ascertainable and definitive of all the forces which make for our civilization. She is

confronted by both a woman question and a race problem, and is as yet an un-
known or an unacknowledged factor in both. While the women of the white race can
with calm assurance enter upon the work they feel by nature appointed to do, while
their men give loyal support and appreciative countenance to their efforts, recog-
nizing in most avenues of usefulness the propriety and the need of woman's dis-
tinctive co-operation, the colored woman too often finds herself hampered and
shamed by a less liberal sentiment and a more conservative attitude on the part of
those for whose opinion she cares most. That this is not universally true I am glad
to admit. There are to be found both intensely conservative white men and exceed-
ingly liberal colored men. But as far as my experience goes the average man of our
race is less frequently ready to admit the actual need among the sturdier forces of
the world for woman's help or influence. That great social and economic questions
await her interference, that she could throw any light on problems of national im-
port, that her intermeddling could improve the management of school systems, or
elevate the tone of public institutions, or humanize and sanctify the far reaching in-
fluence of prisons and reformatories and improve the treatment of lunatics and im-
beciles,—that she has a word worth hearing on mooted questions in political econ-
omy, that she could contribute a suggestion on the relations of labor and capital, or
offer a thought on honest money and honorable trade, I fear the majority of Ameri-
cans of the "colored variety" are not yet prepared to concede.

—Anna Julia Cooper (1969, 134–135)

In 1892 Anna Julia Cooper's (1969, 134–135), *A Voice From the South* lamented the status of African American women in the struggle for equality. More than one hundred years later, African American scholars including Cornel West, Angela Davis, bell hooks, Toni Cade Bambara and Michele Wallace echo Cooper's concern that the African American fight for justice, civil rights and subsequent nationalist movements equated black power and success with black male power and success. The subordination of women during reconstruction; diminishing of female contributions in the struggle to end slavery; that most of the community, if pressed, cannot name women who fought in the civil rights movement; attempted exclusion of women from the podium during the March on Washington; and the admonishment that women stay home and "teach the children" rather than attend the Million Man March communicate gender relevance within African American culture. According to West (1991), African American male power has been linked to the reduction of female power (107): ". . . one of the major means by which Black men are empowered is to have power over Black women. For people who feel already powerless, it becomes a form of competition to not occupy the bottom rung of the ladder."

Before Cooper's provocative book in 1892, Sojourner Truth expressed concern about the exclusion of African American women from civil rights movements. In 1867 she addressed the Equal Rights Convention in New York (Adrienne T. 1995, C5): "There is a great stir about colored men getting their rights, but not a word about colored women; and if a colored man gets [his] rights and not the colored women theirs, you see, the colored men will be masters over the women and it will be as bad as before."

Sojourner Truth's 1867 and Anna Julia Cooper's 1892 fears that the community refused to make room for the woman's voice continues as a concern of African American feminists in the 1990s. The silencing of African American women is a by-product of equating liberation with masculinity. This is so because although there are many areas which men and women share in the battle for rights, there also exist concerns which are uniquely male and uniquely female. However, defining the struggle in masculine terms excludes addressing women's issues. Women are required to toe the line, remaining silent when the movement overlooks their needs and concerns. Behavior to the contrary is interpreted as a lack of commitment to the community. Insistence on patriarchal values (hooks 1995), the required silence of African American women (Bambara 1970), and the refusal to acknowledge her needs and expertise (Cooper 1892) inform one another and enforce practices that equate the African American struggle with masculinity. In this environment, African American women learn to remain quiet in the interest of cultural unity (Bambara 1970, 102–103): "She is being assigned an unreal role of mute servant that supposedly neutralizes the acidic tension that exists between Black men and Black women. She is being encouraged—in the name of revolution no less—to cultivate 'virtues' that if listed would sound like personality traits of slaves."

"Black male and female refusal to consider the importance of eradicating sexism has ongoing negative consequences for black solidarity" (hooks 1995). It is within this sexist structure that Anita Hill, Beverly Heard, Desiree Washington, Joycelyn Elders and Lani Guinier exist. Such judgments question the "blackness" of Hill, Heard and Washington. The relevance of men and the consequent insignificance of women enabled community members to suggest that while Tyson might have been guilty of raping Washington, in the interest of the community she should withdraw the charges (Dace 1994). Similar arguments were made concerning Heard's and Hill's charges against Reynolds and Thomas, respectively. Their refusal to be silenced made Hill, Heard and Washington race traitors, unworthy of community support.

Equating blackness with masculinity made it impossible for African Americans to defend Lani Guinier and Joycelyn Elders. Within this patriarchal framework the plight of women is nonexistent. Only men suffer within a racist society; or, they suffer the most, warranting the most attention. When the African American struggle is synonymous with the struggle of black men (which the masculinization of blackness accomplishes), it may be impossible to perceive attacks on black women as attacks on blackness. African Americans were not moved to rally around Guinier and Elders because they were not black enough. To be black enough within a sexist framework means to be attacked by European Americans *and* to be male. While Elders and Guinier were threatened by the European American power structure, their gender prevented community support. The rhetoric surrounding the Million Man March is the most recent evidence of this masculinization of blackness.

Judgment III: Stereotypical Depictions of Women

> Called Matriarch, Emasculator and Hot Momma. Sometimes Sister, Pretty Baby, Auntie, Mammy and Girl. Called Unwed Mother, Welfare Recipient and Inner City Consumer. The Black American woman has had to admit that while nobody knew the troubles she saw, everybody, his brother and his dog, felt qualified to explain her, even to herself.
>
> —Trudier Harris (1982, 4)

Trudier Harris' (1982, 4) description of the labels associated with African American womanhood are crucial in understanding the lack of support women receive from the community. Patricia Hill Collins (1991) illustrates the defining and controlling power of the stereotypical notions surrounding African American women. Specifically, Collins contrasts the images of mammy and matriarch as ideals used to perpetuate racist notions and practices. Although these depictions are discussed as ways European Americans justify their treatment of African American women, these images play a part in restricting community support of women. The myth of the black mammy holds that she cares more for European Americans than she does for her own African American husband and children. The mammy's time and energy are spent seeing to the needs of European Americans at the expense of African Americans. Conversely, African American matriarchs are all powerful and consequently more masculine than feminine in that they run and rule their households with little interference from men (Collins 1991, 75):

> Taken together, images of the mammy and the matriarch place African-American women in an untenable position . . . becoming the ideal mammy means precious time and energy spent away from husbands and children. But being employed when Black men have difficulty finding steady work exposes African American women to the charge that Black women emasculate Black men by failing to be submissive, dependent, "feminine" women . . . In essence, African American women who must work are labeled mammies, then are stigmatized again as matriarchs for being strong figures in their own homes.

The third cultural system preventing support for Washington, Heard and Hill is the attaching of mammy status to them. As the myth goes, the mammy always holds whites in esteem, blacks in contempt. She attends to white desires at the expense of black needs. In this sense, she is a traitor to her own people in an effort to gain acceptance from others. African American discussions and evaluations of Hill, Heard and Washington took on this mythical characteristic. All were accused of self promotion within European American political, economic and justice systems. Many community members, for example, speculated about the amount of money Anita Hill would make and the number of job offers she might receive in exchange for accusing Clarence Thomas of harassment. Hill, Washington and Heard were characterized as being more interested in supporting white attacks on black manhood than being part of the community. Louis Farrakhan accused both Hill and Washington of being easily manipulated by the European Americans they so adored. Because mammies do not warrant support—they certainly don't need it from blacks, whites have their backs—there was no need for African Americans to rise to their defense.

Controlling images also curved African American willingness to assist Guinier and Elders. As an attorney/professor and physician respectively, these women represent prestige and power within the culture. Graduating from medical and law school are not easy tasks. This fact, coupled with the accurate belief on the part of most African Americans that these accomplishments are most difficult for people of color, fuels the perception that Elders and Guinier are strong African American women. Finally, they are both outspoken, forceful, authoritative and unapologetic in their communication. For many, Elders and Guinier are the perfect embodiment of the mythical matriarch. And, as the myth goes, a matriarch "don't need nothin' from nobody." She cares little for and needs nothing from European Americans and African Americans. Consequently, Elders and Guinier receive equally poor support from both European Americans and African Americans. Unlike Hill, Heard and Washington who were embraced by some European American women's groups, Elders and Guinier stood alone. This is "logical" considering the myth of the overly independent, matriarchal African American woman.

Prescription: Judgment Shifts

The faulty practice of racial reasoning (West 1994) masculinization of the African American struggle, and pervasive controlling images (Collins 1991) of African American women work together to preclude community support of women. These problematic cultural practices prevented African American leaders from establishing programs of support for

Anita Hill, Beverly Heard, Desiree Washington, Lani Guinier and Joycelyn Elders. The community was equally inattentive toward women involved in disputes with other African Americans or members of the European American political structure.

Racial reasoning, requiring the silence of African American women in
the interest of unity, and acceptance of European American originated
notions of black womanhood indicate the captive nature of African
Americans. West and hooks (1991) suggest most African Americans
never completely escape the white or normative gaze. Yet, that escape is
what is required, in part, to open African American communities to discussions of gender. Racial reasoning and defining African American culture in masculine terms lead to dangerous ideals of blackness. Zook
(1995) explains the concept of "black authenticity tricks us into equating
support for the Million Man March, or O.J. Simpson for that matter, with
support for black people, because anything else is considered race treason" (88). African Americans who opt out of championing the likes of
Simpson, Tyson, and Thomas are viewed as cultural outsiders and are
easily silenced by this rhetoric.

The need to close ranks around a mediocre Supreme Court candidate
(West 1994), make moves to silence women who are at odds with other
African Americans, and accept racist and sexist labels of embattled women
reveals just how closely African Americans attend to European American
conceptualizations and expectations. Such requirements and practices stifle
serious discussions. For example, West (1994) believes African American
leaders remained silent about the inadequacy of Clarence Thomas' nomination because on some level many accepted the European American suggestion that mediocrity was all African America had to offer (36): "Of course
some privately admit to his mediocrity while pointing out the mediocrity of
Justice Souter and other members of the Court—as if white mediocrity were
a justification of black mediocrity. No double standards here, the argument
goes, if a black man is unqualified one can defend and excuse him by appealing to other unqualified white judges."

The inclusion of women's concerns within the struggle for equality necessitates the eradication of the judgment that makes their presence incon-
sequential and annoying at best. This does not involve replacing heroes
with (s)heroes. Rather, an intelligent exploration of issues in moral and ethical terms might have prevented the endorsement of both Clarence
Thomas and Anita Hill. In their rush to defend Clarence Thomas, African
American leaders missed the boat on his participation in a political process
and party that has done more harm than good to their brothers and sisters.
They also failed to see that Anita Hill shared many of Thomas' views.
Cleage (1993) explains that discussions of Anita Hill seldom note her con-
servative political background (79): "She is found silent and surprised,

adrift in a white male world where Ronald Reagan and Oral Roberts signed her checks and Judge Bork was a personal hero."

Had African American leaders truly attended to the records of both Thomas and Hill rather than adopting the closing ranks mentality, they would have evaluated both accuser and accused differently (West 1994, 44–45):

> . . . both Thomas and Hill would be viewed as two black Republican conservative supporters of some of the most vicious policies to besiege black working and poor communities since Jim and Jane Crow segregation. Both Thomas and Hill supported an unprecedented redistribution of wealth from working people to well-to-do people in the form of regressive taxation, deregulation policies, cutbacks and slowdowns in public service programs, take-backs at the negotiation table between workers and management, and military buildups at the Pentagon. Both Thomas and Hill supported the unleashing of unbridled capitalist market forces on a level never witnessed in the United States before that have devastated black working and poor communities.

However, a judgment process that includes racial reasoning, exclusion of women from African American agendas and the racist images of African American women worked against community members seriously addressing these important issues.

African Americans must develop standards of judgment which dissect and discard the controlling images limiting female participation in the culture. The view of the African American female body as a sexual sign (hooks 1991) and women as mammies and matriarchs (Collins 1991) diminish opportunities for inclusion in cultural struggles. The matriarch and mammy are both selfless individuals. The former gives of herself for the betterment of her family; the latter serves others outside her family and community (hooks 1991, 155): "Collectively, many Black women internalize the idea that they should serve, that they should always be available to meet the need of someone else whether they want to or not."

It was that expectation that made the behavior of Hill, Heard and Washington inappropriate. As hooks (1991) explains, intellectual activity is viewed as irrelevant for African American women. Rather than being a sign of selflessness, participating in intellectual pursuits makes African American women selfish in the eyes of some community members. Hence, African American women like Guinier and Elders have no place within this framework.

That African American men are subject to pervasive and damaging representations is not disputed. In fact, the Million Man March, in part, was offered as a response to those images. The sea of African American men of all ages stood in defiance of every belief system which labelled them unruly, gang banger, drug dealer, drug addict, absentee father, and the like. African Americans more readily recognize and discuss male plight. For example, (Zook 1995, 86): "We live in an era in which the narrative of the Endangered Black Man resonates with increasing force among both women and men . . . But by exalting the persecutions of black men, the narrative elevates their particular truths to the mythical status of universal black reality."

The Million Man March is the most recent indication of the community's attempt to destroy such negative male images. African Americans, male and female, participated in the planning and speech making in an effort to recognize the diversity, intelligence, majesty and strength of African American men. Yet, there exists no comparable movement for African American women.

The Million Man March presents another challenge for African American women. As noted above, it is the most recent evidence of the masculinization of blackness. In 1963, African American women were not allowed to address the March on Washington crowd. In 1995, they were excluded from marching but after some cajoling permitted to assist in the planning and addressing march attendees. As impressive as this most recent act was (and it was indeed impressive and moving), the exclusion of women from the largest civil/human rights march in the history of the United States says much about whose issues are judged to be most pressing within the community. Such exclusion assumes African American women do not experience racist practices in America, at least not to the degree men do, as well as the idea that vicarious participation while at home teaching children is a sufficient substitute for both actual participation and uplifting. Further, the patriarchal suggestion that the Million Man March signalled the recapturing or reinstitution of male leadership within the community communicates the unequal status of African American women. Zook explained (1995, 86): "It wasn't banishment from the march that was so offensive . . . It was being told to stay home with the children, to be quiet and prepare food for our warrior kings. What infuriated progressive black women was that the rhetoric of protection and atonement was just a seductive mask for old-fashioned sexism."

Playing the "my plight's bigger than your plight" game does little to remedy anyone's challenges. As Reagon (1995) explained, it is impossible, futile and dangerous to prioritize needs in the struggle for equality. When cutting lines within movements are drawn, one faction suffers at what on the surface appears to be the advancement of others. In the African American culture this takes the form of promoting the needs of men at the expense of women. It makes it impossible for the community to rally around women when the assumption is that men are the most at risk and threatened. Prioritization of issues along gender lines eliminates the support of all women, even those like Guinier and Elders who can not be characterized (using faulty reasoning) as race traitors. The need to equate the black struggle with male struggle does more than render women invisible. It simultaneously promotes some men of questionable character. The presence of Clarence Thomas on the Supreme Court will haunt African Americans for years to come (West 1994). It was the cutting line, the masculinization of the struggle and the requirement of silence from women that enabled an African American phenotype with limited ties to the community to garner support. Labelling Thomas a Judas to the culture may be extreme. But his participation in activities and policies which harmed African Americans, women, as well as poor and working class people from all cultures, do little to suggest him as savior or someone warranting community endorsement. Finally, the requirement of silence in the interest of unity has always been one-sided. McKay (1992, 282) notes "there are no circumstances that require such a sacrifice of black men."

A New Judgment Premise: From Unity to Communion

Perhaps we need to let go of all notions of manhood and femininity and concentrate of Blackhood.

—Toni Cade Bambara

This new framework should be a prophetic *one of moral reasoning with its fundamental ideas of a mature black identity, coalition strategy, and black cultural democracy.*

—Cornel West

Racial reasoning, excluding women from conceptualizations of African Americanness and stereotypical images of African American women create a false sense of unity while simultaneously limiting the incorporation of all views and concerns in the quest for equality. The history of Africans in America makes the need to present a united front understandable. However, rather than moving African Americans toward social and political autonomy, unity secures their captivity to the normative or white gaze. As captives of the normative or white gaze, African Americans place European American point of view at the center of their activity. Instead of exploring and reflecting the diversity of African American voice, attending the normative gaze requires singleness of vision, opinion and voice as the community attempts to demonstrate power and commitment through unity. Such demonstrations of unity are for the benefit of European Americans. A united African American front signals to all outsiders that African Americans are in agreement, organized, and committed—they are a force to be reckoned with. Unfortunately, this attention to impression management forces the silencing of diverse voices within the community.

Unity necessarily limits the role and importance of all members of the community. Women's needs are judged either less significant or easily subsumed by those of the larger group. Such thinking enables African Americans the easy task of taking sides in disputes between men and women with the plight of men judged most significant. When African American men are attacked by forces inside or outside the community, procedures exist to support them. The reasons for lack of support for African American women caught in battles with African American men may be clear. But, how does one explain the lack of support for African American women who are threatened by forces outside of the community? The quest for unity, which requires stifling difference and gender, renders all women's issues irrelevant and nonexistent. In other words, because the unity framework makes the women's voices inaudible, it becomes difficult, if not impossible, to recognize her plight whether she is struggling with African Americans or European Americans.

African American judgment has been shaped by an oppressive structure that seemed to require unity at all costs. As African Americans banded together, that unified voice demonstrated commitment, faith and strength. Unfortunately, the need for one voice worked to silence many valuable contributions. Unity not only quieted women, it made their struggle invisible and impossible to perceive. The need to include rather than exclude all members of the community seems to suggest a shift in judgment—a move away from unity as a goal.

Toni Cade Bambara (1970, 103) and Cornel West (1994, 43) recommend rethinking our judgments about blackness in order to eliminate cultural practices that hinder the inclusion of all African Americans in the community's agenda. In the late Marlon Riggs's last film "Black Is . . . Black Ain't," bell hooks calls for a move away from unity and a move toward communion. Unity, hooks believes, requires a "flattening out of differences." African American women's concerns, needs and causes get flattened in the quest for unity. Communion, on the other hand, provides space for "a community of comrades who are seeking to deepen our spiritual experience and our political solidarity, and others of us seeking primarily to deepen our understanding of Black life and Black political experience (hooks and West 1991, 2). Together, Bambara (1970), hooks and West (1991) and West (1994) call for a way to judge and explore and be and address the challenges of African American identity that acknowledges, appreciates and accepts the diversity of blackness. This represents a move away from priorities, cutting lines, power moves and the faulty assumption that one faction's advances substitute for the success of others. When African Americans come to grips with what it means to be black in ethical and moral terms (West 1994) all are included, issues are thoroughly explored and no Judas—male or female—is championed.

References

Bambara, Toni Cade. 1970. *The Black Woman*. New York: New American Library.

Cleage, Pearl. 1993. *Deals with the Devil and Other Reasons to Riot*. New York: Ballantine Books.

Collins, Patricia Hill. 1991. *Black Feminist Thought: Knowledge, Consciousness, and the Politics of Empowerment*. New York: Routledge.

Cooper, Anna Julia. 1969. *A Voice from the South*. New York: Negro Universities Press.

Dace, Karen Lynnette. 1994, November. *Let's Set the Bitch on Fire: The African American Community's Response to Desiree Washington*. Paper presented during the annual meeting of the Speech Communication Association in New Orleans, LA.

Harris, Trudier. 1982. *From Mammies to Militants: Domestics in Black American Literature*. Philadelphia: Temple University Press.

hooks, bell. 1995. *Killing Rage: Ending Racism*. New York: Henry Holt and Company.

_____. 1990. *Yearning: Race, Gender and Cultural Politics*. Boston: South End Press.

hooks, bell and Cornel West. 1991. *Breaking Bread: Insurgent Black Intellectual Life*. Boston: South End Press.

McKay, Nellie. 1992. "Remembering Anita Hill and Clarence Thomas: What Really Happened When One Black Woman Spoke Out." In *Race-ing Justice, En-gendering Power: Essays on Anita Hill, Clarence Thomas and the Construction of Social Reality*, ed. Toni Morrison, 269–289. New York: Pantheon.

Morrison, Toni, ed. 1992. *Race-ing Justice, En-gendering Power: Essays on Anita Hill, Clarence Thomas and the Construction of Social Reality*. New York: Pantheon.

Pemberton, Gayle. 1992. "Sentimental Journey: James Baldwin and the Thomas-Hill Hearings." In *Race-ing Justice, En-gendering Power: Essays on Anita Hill, Clarence Thomas and the Construction of Social Reality*, ed. Toni Morrison, 172–199. New York: Pantheon.

Reagon, Bernice Johnson. 1995. "Coalition Politics: Turning the Century." In *Race, Class and Gender: An Anthology*, eds. Margaret L. Andersen and Patricia Hill Collins, 540–546. Belmont, CA: Wadsworth.

Ross, S. 1993, June 3. *Civil Rights Leaders Disappointed Guinier Dropped*. Associated Press Wire Service.

Sanz, Cythina, Leah Eskin, and Luchina Fisher. 1995, September 4. "Congressman Mel Reynolds Faces Prison as a Result of an Affair to Forget." *Time*, 55.

Staff. 1997, June 11. "Whites See More Pluses than Blacks. *The Salt Lake Tribune*, A11.

T. Adrienne. 1995, October 16. "Once Again, Black Men put Women in Back Seat. *The Washington Times*, C5.

Warren, Susan. 1993, July 25. "Jackson Calls for Organization of Fax Communication Network." *The Houston Chronicle*, A29.

West, Cornel. 1994. *Race Matters*. New York: Vintage Books.

Zook, Kristal Brent. 1995, November 12. "A Manifesto of Sorts for a Black Feminist Movement." *The New York Times*, 86.

7

The Fictions of
Racialized Identities

Marouf A. Hasian, Jr. and Thomas K. Nakayama

While many U. S. American citizens, scholars, and jurists espouse their belief that the nations should be ideally "color-blind," we are just beginning to realize that the complexities of race, class, and gender constructions militate against finding any quick fix legal solutions to culturally embedded conundrums. The recent debates over the Thomas Hearings, the O.J. Simpson verdicts, and the Rodney King trial are just the most recent manifestations of the contradictions that exist in a nation filled with tales of "separate but equal," racial "diversity," and political "opportunity." For most of the twentieth century, most U. S. Americans believed that the solutions to the nation's racial problems depended on incrementally removing the barriers that stood in the way of egalitarianism—including desegregation of schools, the freedom to travel, the removal of restrictive covenants, etc. Yet as the nation approaches the twenty-first century, it is witnessing the fragmentation of the Enlightenment dream of linear progress. Defenders of color blindness are being assailed for their complicity in maintaining the power of an edifice known as "whiteness." While critics for decades have been commenting on the social construction of "blackness," it is only in recent years that scholars have taken seriously the notion that "whiteness" is also in need of critique.

In place of classical liberal notions of neutrality and color blindness, we now hear the clarion call of many critics who claim that radical social change can only come from "race consciousness" and a recognition of the institutional nature of racism. These debates have also started to influence the ways in which academicians discuss the epistemic and ontological dimensions involved in identity formation, hegemonic power, and the taken-for-granteds of the everyday world. A variety of communities are now beginning to interrogate the sources, discursive spaces, and material realities that influence all of our perceptions concerning social relationships. From within such perspectives, not only our racial categories but the very pursuit of "race" is itself often a misguided and impoverished exercise.

While there are a variety of fruitful approaches that could be taken in understanding the intimate relationship that exists between racial rhetoric and power, we believe that it is importance for us to understand the particular ways in which individuals and communities have to confront the racial dimensions of legal and public classifications. As Davis (1991) has recently observed, seldom has the topic of racial definition "been emphasized in scholarly research and writing on race relations, black history, or civil rights" (ix). We believe that it is imperative that critical theorists and practitioners critique the ways in which "race" is socially, politically, legally, and rhetorically constructed in today's society. It is our contention that at this particular cultural moment, the intersection of race and power have become increasingly salient subjects both within and outside of the academia.[1] At the same time, both elite and vernacular judgments about "race" involve issues of identity, domination, and even property (Harris 1993).

Like many of the other essayists in this book, we are deeply concerned with the ways that ordinary citizens and cultural critics look at the concept of judgment, both epistemically and rhetorically. How do we decide both legally and publicly that we have the right to judge that a particular person belongs to a particular "race?" Can we choose our "race," or is that a matter of communal judgment? Should we even have such an entity as "whiteness" or "blackness' if we live in a colorblind society? These questions are especially important when particular "races" are valued/devalued and hierarchically organized, and one's lifelong opportunities and obligations are often influenced by these racial markers. At different historical moments, various communities have sought the mystic power and pleasure of whiteness or blackness, yet this status cannot always be self-ascribed. And the shifting valences attached to various racial colors can be maddening.

Take the legal case of the Malone brothers, Massachusetts residents who wanted to be members of the Boston Fire Department. In 1975, both of them identified themselves as "white," and they each did poorly on a civil service examination. Initially they were not accepted into the Department, but two years later, they self-identified themselves as "black." Because of a court-ordered affirmative action program, both Paul and Philip Malone could use the older test scores and be hired as "black" but not as "white" (Harris 1993, 1232–1233). For more than ten years, the Malones kept their jobs without any major trouble, but in 1987 a hearing officer made the legal determination that the Malones were not black and that they had falsified their records. For the next several years, authorities were embarrassed to find almost a dozen similar cases, and the Massachusetts courts were filled with discussions of "Black ancestry," "fair skin," "Caucasian facial features," etc. (Harris 1993, 1233). The Malones are of course not alone in their search for the power of a particular color or category.

In this essay, we extend the work of those scholars who are interested in understanding the political power of "whiteness" (Bernardi 1996; Frankenberg 1993; Frye 1983; Hall 1981; Haney-López 1996; Harris 1993; Nakayama & Krizek 1995; Roediger 1994; Sleeter 1994). It is not our intention to defend any essentially theoretical position which uncritically reverses the binaries that perpetuates the privileging of "whiteness" over "non-whiteness." Nor do we intend to provide our readers with forms of vernacular discourse that do not problematize the complexities of racial discourse. This will not be one more essay that calls for the inclusion of one more outgroup that needs to be included in the census or on affirmative action forms.

Instead, we would like to illustrate that the very search for accurate judgmental categories of race helps to perpetuate many of our racial problems. In other words, placing particular individuals in the "right" racial box on a form does not radically alter our understanding of the cultural imperatives that have fueled this search for "race" in the first place. In order to advance our argument about the relationship between "whiteness," power, and the judgments of social actors defending the "rule of law" in the United States, we divide this essay into four parts. In the first section of the manuscript we provide a critical genealogy of "whiteness" and focus on the rhetorical power of racial classification. This theoretical discussion is informed by our second segment of the paper, where we will recontextualize the case of Susie Phipps. In the third part of the essay we will talk about the strategic use of this case and other examples of "whiteness" in U. S. American public and legal discourse. Finally, we hope to provide a heuristic conclusion which outlines some possible directions for future research.

Genealogies of "Whiteness," Rhetoric, and the Power of Racial Judgment

The contemporary construction of "whiteness" as an invisible racial discourse that constructs invisible racialized subjects is but one aspect of a much larger racial rhetoric. Any genealogy of whiteness, of course, is never neutral, nor innocent. Our telling of the story of whiteness is embedded in our critical impulse to expose its workings, its maskings, and its embedded character in U.S. life.

While contemporary understandings of whiteness often emphasize its invisible character (Dyer 1988; Frankenberg 1993; Roediger 1991), whiteness has not always been an invisible rhetoric. From the beginning, racial rhetoric has been grounded in the foundations of the United States, in ways that are not necessarily invisible (Roediger 1994). The early requirement that voters must be white male landowners reflects the visibility of whiteness (and maleness and class positions). Far from being invisible, the salience of whiteness has always been marked by racial rhetoric in a myriad of ways, from the U.S. census to the creation of miscegenation laws.

The mere existence of miscegenation laws, however, did not ensure that interracial heterosexual relations would not occur. While these relations were not always consensual, their legacy is written into the fabric of the United States: "the longer a person's family has lived in this country, the higher the probable percentage of African ancestry that person's family is likely to have—bad news for the DAR, I'm afraid" (Piper 1997, 426). Yet the legacy of these interactions did not lead to the dismantling of whiteness, but instead to the reinforcing of the boundaries of whiteness.

The intense struggle that ensued from these earlier racial classifications is exemplified by the Irish American attempts to become classified as "white." A number of rhetorical strategies were utilized by Irish Americans to gain white privilege. Rather than posing any significant challenge to the ways that whiteness and U.S. racial rhetoric instantiate these problems, the Irish American claim to whiteness merely utilized the existent rhetoric to reconfigure their classification in U.S. American life (Ignatiev 1995; Roediger 1991).

The more recent turn toward an invisibility to whiteness emerges in large part from a social retreat from the rhetoric of segregation. Attempts to turn toward race-blindness, as part of a larger effort to eradicate racial segregation are best exemplified in the rhetoric of Martin Luther King, Jr. As a consequence of that struggle, white Americans retreated from an explicitly privileged position of white subjects to a less blatant, more insidious position of invisibility. This newly unmarked racial position, the white subject, became by default a universal subject.

For scholars interested in exploring the nexus between law and discourse, the Phipps case thus provides us with the opportunity of understanding the complex relationships that exist in the construction of "whiteness" in particular concrete settings. This Louisiana court case was charged to make a judgment of whether Susie Phipps could call herself "white" even though her birth certificate indicated that she was "black." A rhetorical analysis of the case would help to answer several intriguing questions:

1. What are the discursive practices and material constraints that hegemonically operate as limitations for individuals and communities who are interested in "self-identification?"

2. What are the political/legal/rhetorical implications for being classified as "white," "black," or other classificatory categories?
3. What would be the legal and rhetorical effect of jurisprudential changes that obliterated racial classifications?

In sum, "whiteness" is not only a racial category—it is also a powerful social, political, and economic marker, creating passports or closing doors. The historical struggles over which groups were accorded "white" status and which were not, particularly as exemplified in the Irish case, demonstrate the power behind these racial rhetorics. The history of the U.S. cannot be understood outside of these shifting rhetorics and the privileges enjoyed by those cloaked in the blanket of whiteness. As one observer of the Phipps proceedings would later note "she is emphasizing something we've said all along. It is a great advantage to be white in American society. It costs several thousand dollars a year to be black. Schools, clubs, economic advantages are still to this day much better if you are white" (Thompson quoted in Gilliam 1982, B1).

The Phipps case exposes the social and economic privilege that pertains to the whiteness. This essay explores this exposure for it highlights the significance of racial judgment in U.S. society.

Who Is "White" and Who Is "Non-White"?: Recontextualizing the Case of Susie Phipps

I'm not light, I'm white. Take this color off my birth certificate. Let people look at me and tell me what I am.

—Susie Phipps[2]

While there are many narratives that need to illustrate the pervasive power of whiteness, we focus attention in this essay on the story of Susie Phipps. We have chosen this particular case for several reasons. First, this fable illustrates the continuing influence that cultural genealogies have on our racial hierarchies and cultural perceptions. Second, this case illustrates some of the inherent difficulties that exist in foundational legal theories that attempt to eliminate discrimination by simply increasing the precision or accuracy of categories.[3] At the same time, this was a case that came to the attention of millions of journalists and lay persons, and many of these individuals became participants in a complex social drama. The media constructions of "race" that surrounded her court battle lasted for almost a decade, and during that time a variety of rhetors and audiences gave their views on the source of America's racial problems. Between 1982 and 1986, many of the major newspaper chains discussed the case,

and many different ethnic communities commented on the legal ramifi-
cations of the case for "white" and "non-white" U. S. Americans.

Susie Phipps' search for the elusive power of whiteness began in the
1970s. Countless newspapers would later report that she claimed that for
most of her adult life, Phipps believed herself to be white. After growing
up in Acadia Parish, Louisiana as Susie Guillory, she moved to Lake
Charles, where she eventually would meet her second husband, Andy
Phipps. Press accounts would later characterize the Phipps as well off,
and Andy was described as a construction tycoon, someone who made
millions building ships or working in the oil and fishing industries
(Trillin 1986, 62). In Susie's rendition of the tale, her troubles with the
state of Louisiana began when she went to New Orleans in 1977 to pick
up a passport.

In New Orleans, Phipps was told by a clerk for the Division of Vital
Records that obtaining the passport was going to be a problem because
Susie's self-designation of being "white" did not match the state's recording of Susie as black. The City of New Orleans had a certificate which
clearly showed that a Susie Guillory had been born in Acadia Parish in
1934, and the race of both parents had been marked "Col."—colored
(Trillin 1986, 62). Susie Phipps was quickly informed that if she was going to try to change this designation she was going to have to talk to
H.M. (Jack) Westholz, Jr., chief of the New Orleans section of the Office of
the General Counsel of the Louisiana Department of Health and Human
Resources. Phipps soon found that Westholz was someone who was reluctant to change the apparent judgment of Louisiana's legislature or the
markers of the past.

In most legal situations, changing information on a birth certificate is not
too difficult if it involves matters such as changing the spelling of a name
or the removal of clerical errors. But changing a state's final "race" designation on birth certificates is a difficult undertaking because many courts
have ruled that such records are important for health purposes, and this is
considered to be a "compelling" need that overrides any individual incon-
venience to the petitioner who disputes the legitimacy of this categorization. What made Phipps' situation even more difficult was in that in
Louisiana "the question of what constitutes blackness or whiteness has
been a matter of almost constant contention" (Trillin 1986, 62–63).

For centuries, the state of Louisiana has had a number of different legal
standards for racial categorization—at times there have been as many as 64
different racial gradations etched into the nomenclature of the law. These
prerequisite cases used a mélange of different methods to ascertain the
proper designation of "mulattoes" and other people of color. While French
and Spanish laws had an entire range of such categories, United States law
usually followed a European system of racial classification that involved

an application of either binary or tertiary designation—a person was either "white," "black," or "mixed." Since the time of the Louisiana Purchase, Louisiana has had to cope with issues raised by "the mating of the French and Spanish colonists with black slaves" (Jaynes 1982, B16). When this region became a part of the United States, it also inherited an augmentary recording system from the Catholic churches that maintained its own genealogical records. At the time that Phipps applied for her passport, there was a 1970 Louisiana law in effect that declared that "anyone with at least 1/32nd 'Negro blood'" could be classified as "black" ("Family" 1982, 3).[4] In the eyes of the Louisiana officials, the clear guidelines of the law meant that self-identification and the subjective beliefs of any one individual had little weight in comparison with the objectivity of the state.

Ironically, the 1970 Louisiana law that was used to judge Phipps was believed to have been a *progressive* improvement over the older Jim Crow laws that allowed simple "common" reports to serve as the determination of a person's race (Omi & Winant 1986, 162). In rural Louisiana, many officials were guided by notions of "common repute" (Harris 1983, A3), and before 1970 "a trace" of black blood meant that a person was "black in the eyes of the law" (Jaynes 1982, B16).[5] Under the newer 1970 law, a person's race depended in part on the designation on a birth certificate, and at least one of Phipps' parents listed her as "black." The state officials who kept Louisiana's vital statistics could therefore claim that they were doing a public service for the community by keeping accurate markers that correctly labeled a person's race.

As we noted above, there were multiple layers of ideologies that had been used to create this dense fabric which stood in the way of Susie Phipps request. Since the early nineteenth century, race purity statutes had been passed throughout the nation in an attempt to maintain the "separation" of the races. More modern rationalizations for such classifications include the need to keep accurate census records, and to ensure that the proper "races" are allowed to take advantage of affirmative action legislation.

Susie Phipps' attempt at becoming white thus involved more than simply rectifying the situation by altering the notations on a birth certificate. Nor was this simply a case that highlighted the lingering effects of a bygone era, where racial purity was considered to be a legitimate goal advanced in the name of public health and welfare. Many commentaries discussing the Phipps cased in the 1980s recognized the property rights that seemed to belong to anyone classified as "white" in U. S. society. As one commentator astutely observed, this was more than "a single eccentric's identity crisis" (Gilliam 1982, B1). These designations altered both the discursive social relationships and the material realities that can be obtained in this society.

Instead of simply complying with Susie Phipps' request, the state of Louisiana decided to allow the Vital Statistics Departments to defend Louisiana's laws. Many of the rhetorical strategies used by the state of Louisiana in denying Phipps the status of whiteness depended on both genetical and pragmatic types of arguments. The state began its defense of its racial designation by arguing that a white midwife who filled out Phipps' birth certificate had marked it as "colored" (Harris 1983, A3). Technically this meant that Susie Phipps had the burden of proof of showing why this notation had been erroneous. Using this standard of judgment, it would be up to Phipps to show not only that she was white—but that the person who had recorded her parents' designations of color had also been in error.

The attorneys for the State of Louisiana were aided by genealogists and vital recorders who spend thousands of dollars tracing Phipps' ancestors in an effort to show why the local municipalities had not been in error in categorizing Phipps as "black." Research purportedly showed that Susie Phipps had a great-great-great-great grandmother [Margarita] who was the black mistress of a Mobile plantation owner in 1760 (Harris 1983, A3; Jaynes 1982, B16). At one of the lower court trials, one genealogist told the court that Phipps was 3/32 black, and that under Louisiana law, anyone who was even 1/32 black was considered to be black. This meant that a person could legally be designated as "black" if they had even one great-great-great grandparent who was of African ancestry (A3). In most states at time, one's "race" was simply a matter of discovering what the parents had told the authorities to record on the birth certificate (Jaynes 1982, B16), but in the state of Louisiana the combination of laws regarding percentages of blood seemed to trump even the parents' designation. The state of Louisiana could theoretically claim that even if Phipps parents had represented her as "white," the genealogical records showed that genetically and legally she was in fact "black."

What make Susie Phipps' position at court even more difficult was the damaging oral histories that were collected from some of Phipps neighbors' who remembered that most of her ancestors considered themselves to be black. In the early lawsuits some of Phipps relatives would argue that they too had grown up "white," but the state countered with boxes full of depositions and other data that illustrated how even church records seemed to treat many of the Guillorys in Acadia Parish as if they were either black or "mulatto." Phipps now had to combat not only the state apparatus of racial designation and the power of genealogical charts—she now had to combat the social and public records of "whiteness" that went beyond the coercive powers of the state. In some Louisiana courts in the nineteenth century, "race" was considered to be something that could be ascertained using common sense, everyday notions of what a person looked like. This custom was known as the test of "common repute," and Phipps now found herself having to answer questions that depended on her personal memory and the collective judgment of several communities.[6]

In order to counter the state of Louisiana's genetical, legal, and pragmatic arguments, Phipps was allowed in court to take the stand and explain why she should be categorized as "white." She tried to claim that her own relatives had testified that they were white, that she self-identified her white, and that her own children were now designated as white. At both the trial and appellate levels, Phipps lost her case. In the eyes of the state of Louisiana, she remained black. Blood will tell.

The Pervasiveness of "Whiteness" in a Postmodern World

In classical liberal theorizing, racial reforms are obtained by lawyers, jurists, and laypersons who supposedly become increasingly "colorblind." Yet as we illustrated in our recontextualization of the case of Susie Phipps, the instantiation of this color blindness in U. S. legal discourse often involves attempts at refining, adding, or correcting racial categories. This allows the legal system to reify our notions of blackness and whiteness, where social prejudices are transmuted into categories that look natural, ordinary, and true. The legal actors involved in the Phipps case were not only embarrassed by the existence of outdated laws; they were also embarrassed by the public gazes which sometimes problematized and criticized the very existence of "race" as a legal classification in the first place.

Reactions to Phipps' attempt to change Louisiana's judgment of her racial classification varied. Louisiana state legislators, embarrassed by the press coverage that had been given to the 1/32 "Negro" blood rule, voted unanimously to repeal the law in June of 1983 ("Louisiana Wiping" 1983, 2). Employing the rhetoric of orthodox jurisprudential change, Democratic Senator William Jefferson of New Orleans confidently proclaimed that Louisiana's legislation had passed a bill that would "remove from the record that last discriminatory law" (2). Other critics were not so sanguine.

Some commentators argued that this was the chance for the nation to abolish some of the last remnants of slavery by totally abandoning the construct of "race." Dr. Dan Thompson, a sociologist at Dillard University and himself the great grandson of a white slave owner in Georgia, hoped that "her case will dramatize the foolishness of race as a criterion in our society. I would like to see this distinction abolished. I would like to see racial designation gone. When you apply for a job and somebody asks your race, it's demeaning. What the hell difference does it make?

You're an American citizen, period. Finally, I would say race does make a difference, and if I were her, by God, I'd try to get it changed, too, if I could" (quoted in Gilliam 1982, B1).

Thousands of Louisianans who had also faced the law's judgments concerning whiteness could readily identify with someone who wanted to change her racial identity.

Outside of the state of Louisiana, the Phipps case was used by some critics as a way of illustrating the poverty of both racial classifications and the rhetoric of "color blindness." One writer for *The Washington Post* noted that "Susie Phipps is doing what many blacks are doing—running away from being black . . . . You cannot escape the prison by pretending that you're free . . . " (Gilliam 1982, B1). Gilliam would go on to argue that "it sounds harsh and its a hard admission to make, for I'm as proud of the 60s revolution of black consciousness as anybody else. But it is a mistake to think it took us further than it did. Instead of tut-tutting Susie Phipps, those of us who have been fooling ourselves into thinking that something had changed fundamentally in America ought to be thankful for the reminder that it hasn't. . . . Every time a black person turns on television, he or she learns that if you're not white, you don't have much of a place in this society. It's more subtle than a century ago, but it's not all that different" (1982, B1).

Other commentators in the public sphere reacted to the Phipps cases by defending their own judgments that blackness was an important relational attribute and form of self-identification. Jaynes (1982), for example, noted that "the story, a story as old as the country, has elements of anthropology and sociology special to this region, and its message here in 1982 America, is that it is still far better to be white than black. Some New Orleans blacks are cheering the woman on. Her name is Susie Guillory Phipps. . . . 'I'm not light,' she said, pointing to her face. 'I'm white.' So say thousands of Louisianans with Negroes in their ancestry, while thousands of others, blue-eyed and light as day, consider themselves black" (B16).

In such recirculations of the Phipps narrative, individuals and communities could voice their concern about the continued power and resonance of "whiteness" in a society that only found color in the designation of the "Other."

Beyond Racial Judgments:
Toward the Abolition of Whiteness

Throughout this essay, we have tried to problematize existing legal and public judgments of "race" in U.S. American discourse. We have illuminated the ways in which racial fictions have been created at particular historical junctures in time, and then reified and empowered to regulate the lives of those who live under these racial rhetorics. The arbitrary character of 'race,' best exposed in its shifting rhetorics, remains a powerful rhetoric in U.S. society.

The recent controversy surrounding Fuzzy Zoeller's "joke" about Tiger Woods ordering "fried chicken" or "collards" at next year's Masters Tournament dinner points towards the enduring character of racial rhetoric in U.S. life. Whatever Zoeller really meant, the intricate weavings of racial rhetoric throughout our society leave us without an easy means to eradicate the significance of "race." Simply recognizing that "race" is a fiction, created over many years, will not release us from the grasp that this history has on us. We need to understand the complexities of racial judgments, to see our own complicity in allowing the concepts of race neutrality or color blindness to obfuscate our understanding of the power of whiteness.

By studying "whiteness" in general and the Phipps case in particular, we join in the conversation of those who researchers who are intrigued by legal judgments in general and racial classifications in particular. By studying the complexities of cases like Phipps, we realize that critics and members of the public need no longer treat whiteness as the absence of "race." At the same time, we believe that this example of a lived problematic illustrates that racial difficulties will not be improved by ignoring the various judgments that are made by the public or the press when it comes to the issue of "race." Tiger Woods, like Suzie Phipps, lives in a world that continues to categorize individuals as belonging to a certain racial category, regardless of self-identification or the social constructive nature of race. Such judgments are in need of constant criticism and interrogation.

It is therefore imperative that critics continually investigate the various manifest and latent meanings that are found in racialized texts—especially those that claim to be race neutral. The volatile history of such classifications insures that racial concerns will continue to alter the ways that we view everything from welfare to education, affirmative action to immigration reform. This is not simply a matter of inaccurately checking the wrong vital statistic box. As one critic observed at the beginning of the Phipps contest, this suit really spoke to the "emotion and psychology surrounding racism as much as to its politics and economics" (Gilliam 1982, B1). This confirms Harris's (1993) contention that whiteness is as much a property and living space as it is a racial designation.

In the short term, perhaps it is enough to point out the race consciousness of society or the need for particular marginalized groups to come under the ambit of civil rights protection through the creation of new categories to represent particular disempowered communities. But in the long run, the social construct known as "whiteness" will best be combatted by going beyond these strategic essentialisms. As Roediger (1994) explained, we will need the contest the very identities, histories, and powers of racial definition that gave rise to the categories in the first place. One small step in this process will involve self and communal reflexiveness that no longer take for granted the fictions of "race."

Notes

1. For an introductory discussion of the rise of whiteness studies within academia, see Stowe (1996).

2. This particular quotation from Phipps game from Gilliam (1982). We found it in most accounts of the case.

3. For example, in the nineteenth century, legal scholars believed that race relations would improve when the laws kept strict records of who was white, Indian, Chinese, and mulatto. Accurate record keeping was supposed to help control miscegenation and maintain racial harmony through the separation of the races. Today, some organizations believe that there would be less discrimination against multiracial communities if the U.S. census provided them with their own category.

4. For a discussion of the cultural significance of this ancient "no drop" rule, see Michaels (1994).

5. The person who helped pass the 1970 law was willing to talk to reporters but only if his name was not published. This New Orleans lawyer told reporters that at that time he had been representing another white family who had a child who was given a black birth certificate and someone "saw the name and it alerted him to the fact that the family had a trace of Negro blood" (Jaynes, 1982, p. B16). When the New Orleans lawyer traced the family genealogy, he found that the child of his clients might be "one two-hundred and fifty-sixth" black. Under the any trace rule this meant that the child was black.

When the lawyer went to the legislature to change the law, he ended up negotiating and "we finally struck the bargain at one thirty-second, and it sailed through. There was no debate" (quoted in Jaynes, 1982, p. B16). The unnamed lawyer summarized his motivation in 1970 by claiming that he was trying to help a white person get a white birth certificate. . . . Whatever you feel on the race question, it's a fact that white people don't want to be known as colored and maybe colored people don't want to be known as white (p.B16).

This type of reasoning fits within classical liberal notions of egalitarianism because it makes it looks as though legal troubles come when difference is taken for inferiority. This in turn obligates the legal system to maintain clear records and accurate racial designations in an attempt to negotiate the treacherous terrain between separatism and assimilation. Notice the ways in which forms of cultural amnesia also set in when there is no discussion of past histories of eugenics or race mixing anxieties, etc.

6. As one more element of irony in this case, Phipps claims that she looked white were themselves dependent on a variant of these lexicons.

References

Aaron, Daniel. 1983. "The Inky Curse: Miscegenation in White American Literary Imagination." *Social Science Information, 22*: 169–190.

Bernardi, Daniel, ed. 1996. *The Birth of Whiteness: Race and the Emergence of U.S. Cinema.* New Brunswick, NJ: Rutgers University Press.

"Black Blood Law Upheld." 1983, May 19. *San Francisco Chronicle*, p. 24.

Davis, F. James. 1991. *Who is Black?: One Nation's Definition.* University Park, PA: Pennsylvania State University Press.

Diamond, Raymond T., and Robert J. Cottrol. 1983. "Codifying Caste: Louisiana's Racial Classification Scheme and the Fourteenth Amendment." *Loyola Law Review, 29*: 255–285.

Doe v. State Dept. of Health & Human Res. 479 So. 2d 369 (La. App. 4 Cir. 1985).

Dyer, Richard. 1988. "White." *Screen, 29* (4): 44–65.

"Family Fighting to Be 'White.'" 1982, September 14. *San Francisco Chronicle*, p. 3.

Frankenberg, Ruth. 1993. *White Women, Race Matters: The Social Construction of Whiteness.* Minneapolis: University of Minnesota Press.

Frye, Marilyn. 1983. "On Being White: Toward a Feminist Understanding of Race and Race Supremacy." In *The Politics of Reality: Essays in Feminist Theory.* Trumansburg, NY: The Crossing Press.

Gilliam, Dorothy. 1982, October 2. "Black/White." *The Washington Post*, p. B1.

Hall, Stuart. 1981. "The Whites of Their Eyes: Racist Ideologies and the Media." In *Silver Linings: Some Strategies for the Eighties*, ed. G. Bridges & R. Brunt, 28–52. London: Lawrence and Wishart.

Haney López, Ian F. 1996. *White By Law: The Legal Construction of Race.* New York: New York University Press.

Harris, Art. 1983, May 21. "Louisiana Court Sees No Shades of Gray in Woman's Request." *The Washington Post*, p.A3.

Harris, Cheryl I. 1993. "Whiteness as Property." *Harvard Law Review, 106*: 1709–1791.

Ignatiev, Noel. 1995. *How the Irish Became White.* New York: Routledge.

Jaynes, Gregory. 1982, September 30. "Suit on Race Recalls Lines Drawn Under Slavery." *The New York Times*, p. B16.

"Louisiana Court Rejects Change in Racial Status." 1985, October 19. *The New York Times*, p.6.

"Louisiana Wiping Out an Old Racial Law." 1983, June 23. *San Francisco Chronicle*, p. 2.

Mahoney, Martha R. 1995. "Segregation, Whiteness, and Transformation." *University of Pennsylvania Law Review, 143*: 1659–1684.

Michaels, Walter Benn. 1994. "The No Drop Rule." *Critical Inquiry, 20*: 758–769.

Nakayama, Thomas K., and Robert L. Krizek. 1995. "Whiteness: A Strategic Rhetoric." *Quarterly Journal of Speech, 81*, 291–309.

Piper, Adrian. 1997. "Passing for White, Passing for Black." In *Critical white studies: Looking behind the mirror*, ed. Richard Delgado and Jean Stefancic, 425–431. Philadelphia: Temple University Press.

Omi, Michael, and Howard Winant. 1986. *Racial Formation in the United States From the 1960s to the 1980s.* New York: Routledge.

Roediger, David. 1991. *The Wages of Whiteness: Race and the Making of the American Working Class*. London: Verso.
Roediger, David. 1994. *Towards the Abolition of Whiteness*. London: Verso.
Sleeter, Christine. 1994, Spring. "White racism." *Multicultural Education*, pp. 5–8, 39.
Stowe, David W. (1996, September/October). "Uncolored People: The Rise of Whiteness Studies." *Lingua Franca, 6*: 68–77.
Trillin, Calvin. 1986, April 14. "American Chronicles: Black or White." *The New Yorker, 62*: 62–78.

8

Judging Parents

Ronald Walter Greene and Darrin Hicks

What is the public stake in how parents raise their children? We all agree that there is a public interest in protecting children from irresponsible, unfit and brutal parents. Yet, once we begin to define what constitutes irresponsibility, fitness and brutality, and what state intervention the presence of child abuse warrants, disagreement arises. For example, should a definition of child abuse remain open and flexible so as to include mental anguish or should we have a more traditional and stable definition that limits abuse to physical injury. Is the amount and severity of child abuse in our society symptomatic of a "public health crisis" authorizing the deployment of state actors to monitor, educate and regulate "at risk" populations in the habits of good parenting? On the other hand, does the policing of child abuse threaten to define "traditional Christian parenting practices," like corporal punishment and home schooling, as risks to children's welfare? Does a public interest in the welfare of children justify the expansion of State programs to promote "normal, healthy, childhood development"? Conversely, should parents resist these forms of state sponsored normalization as a threat to the "diversity" of parenting practices (Gilles 1996)?

A long history of public debate concerning the balance of State and familial interests in child-rearing marks US political culture. The establishment of child-labor laws, compulsory education, required vaccinations and child protection statutes were all met with opposition from those who claimed that such laws were "improper and unnecessary usurpations of the God-given authority of parents to direct their children's upbringing" (Woodhouse 1996, 395). The recent introduction of the Parental Rights and Responsibilities Act (PRRA) into the US Congress, along with a host of referendums to codify "parental rights" in state constitutions, is the latest effort to assert parental authority as an inalienable right. The bill challenges the ability of state actors to make judgments about proper parenting practices by regulating how state actors collect data, make assessments, render diagnosis and craft programs of action for promoting the welfare of children. While past debates on the relationship between the State and family centered on the problems associated with the State governing the family, the specificity of the PRRA is that it tries to respecify how the family will govern the state. In other words, the PRRA is an attempt to gain control over the public institutions, expert knowledges, and techniques of judgment that determine the public interest in raising children and preparing future citizens.

Critics have begun to highlight the close relationship between deliberative rhetoric and the act of judgment by focusing on how the constitutive dimensions of public reason enable and constrain the possibility of judgment (Goodnight 1982; Beiner 1983; Browne and Leff 1985; Spragens 1990) Unfortunately, there is a strong temptation to advocate the act of judgment as an apriori good rather than as the stakes of political controversy. We believe that this tendency fails to account for how the struggle over the techniques of democratic governance are themselves rhetorical attempts to challenge what we call "the politics of judgment." To turn the analytical focus toward the politics of judgment demands an investigation into those rhetorical struggles that challenge who makes judgments, with what authority, on what objects, on what basis, and for what effect. In opposition to the tendency to deploy judgment as a solution to the crisis of democracy, we advocate a closer investigation into the rhetorical contests over judgment so as to better account for the transformations in techniques of democratic governance.

As a vector of the new conservative hegemony, the Parental Rights and Responsibilities Act attempts to depoliticize the State at the same time as it politicizes everyday life (Grossberg 1992). The PRRA depoliticizes the State by removing parenting practices as a topic of public debate and decision making and by holding state-sponsored experts more accountable to parents. It politicizes everyday life by creating a measurement of responsible parenting: namely, that parents should value their careers, hobbies, and friendships inasmuch as they contribute to the life-long project of being a good mother or father. Parents that blindly trust state-sponsored experts to care for their children demonstrate a lack of commitment to their roles as parents. This call for a more passionate commitment to parenthood demands that parents become active and informed consumers of expert knowledges, including those offered by the State, clergy, humane professions, conservative foundations, neighbors and their extended family. It is this demand that parents become consummate judges that makes parental rights legislation such a rich and provocative site for investigating the politics of judgment.

Our account of this controversy over judgment unfolds across four sections. In section one we give a brief legislative history of the Parental

Rights and Responsibilities Act. In section two we describe how the advocates of the PRRA challenge the creation of children's rights as a threat
to parental authority. This challenge creates an affective border between
the State and the child by privileging the judgment of parents to know
what is in the best interests of children. Advocates of the PRRA defend
parental judgments about child welfare against the judgment of the humane professions because it is parents that love and nurture children. In
section three we explicate how the advocates critique the authority of
state sponsored experts. We claim that these objections to the methods
experts use to inscribe knowledge (including methods of data-collection,
evaluation, remediation) and to protect their professional autonomy constitute a direct attack on the techniques of judgment characteristic of social liberalism. We conclude by arguing that the push for parental rights
initiates a significant shift in the political rationality justifying State
forms of expertise. We characterize this shift as a move away from the
welfare state's use of "social responsibility" to justify its efforts to improve the stability of the family, and toward a neo-liberal emphasis on individual responsibility: An emphasis that makes state sponsored expertise accountable to the decisions of the family rather than the family
accountable to the judgments of the State.

The Parental Rights and Responsibilities Act

The Parental Rights and Responsibilities Act of 1995 (PRRA 1995) was introduced on June 28, 1995 by Republican Congressmen Largent (OK) and
Parker (MS). Republican Senators Grassley (IA), Lott (MS), Helms (NC)
and Cochran (MS) introduced virtually identical legislation in the Senate.
The legislation, subtitled "a bill to protect the fundamental right of a parent to direct the upbringing of a child," is designed to "re-affirm" the
rights of parents, implicit in the concept of ordained liberty within the
14th amendment, set out by the Supreme Court in *Meyer* and *Pierce*. The
sponsors of the legislation claim that the lower courts have systematically misinterpreted constitutional precedent. The bill finds that "some
decisions of federal and State courts have treated the right of parents not
as a fundamental right but as a non-fundamental right, resulting in an
improper standard of judicial review being applied to government conduct that adversely affects parental rights and prerogatives" (PRRA 1995
2a). The legislation, therefore, is seen as a needed remedy against those
courts and government agencies which infringe on parental rights by
misreading or ignoring these precedents.

The PRRA is taken almost verbatim from the book "*A Contract with the
American Family: A Bold Plan by the Christian Coalition to Strengthen the
Family and Restore Common-sense Values*" (1995). Federal and State

parental rights legislation is a key part of the Christian Coalition's project to put forth a family focused agenda that can complement the economic and budgetary agenda set out in the Republican's "Contract with America." The bill, like the "Contract with America," reflects a general concern about the erosion of personal responsibility. The bill claims that "the role of parents in the raising of and rearing of their children is of inestimable value and deserving of both praise and protection of all levels of government" (PRRA 1995, 2a). Moreover, "the tradition of western civilization recognizes that parents have the responsibility to love, nurture, train, and protect their children" (2a). Yet, the bill's proponents argue, the State has taken over many of the critical family functions to the point where "parents face increasing intrusions into their legitimate decisions and prerogatives by government agencies that do not involve traditional understandings of abuse and neglect but simply are a conflict of parenting philosophies" (2a). The bill, in conjunction with welfare reform legislation, is designed to protect private rights to control and direct the upbringing of children and enforce private responsibilities for the maintenance and support of children (Woodhouse 1996, 399). The bill's proponents seek to regain the authority to make decisions regarding their children's well being in areas such as education, religious training, discipline, and reproductive freedoms. The bill seeks to reduce governmental regulation and public scrutiny of the private family by "empowering parents to take back or defend the family's critical functions" (Woodhouse 1996, 400).

The bill protects the rights of parents to direct the upbringing of their children by: (1) narrowing the definition of what constitutes abuse and neglect thereby limiting the "compelling interest" of the State to what can be justified within a "traditional understanding" of abuse; (2) reaffirming the right of parents to direct their children's education whether that be through home-schooling or increased control over public school curriculum; (3) preserving "the common law tradition that allows parental choices to prevail in a health care decision for the child" unless that decision will result in serious injury to the child; (4) fixing a standard of judicial review for parental rights and (5) reestablishing a four step process to adjudicate cases concerning the rights of parents. This evaluation process requires a parent to demonstrate that "the action in question arises from the right of the parent to direct the upbringing of a child and a government has interfered or usurped" that right. This process also "shifts the burden of production and persuasion to the government." The government must demonstrate that "the interference or usurpation is essential to accomplish a compelling governmental interest and the method of intervention or usurpation used by the government is the least restrictive means of accomplishing the compelling interest" (2b).

The bill also stipulates what constitutes appropriate evidence to justify governmental intervention. For cases in which the government seeks to investigate or temporarily remove a child from the home the evidence must demonstrate "probable cause." For cases in which the government seeks to terminate parental custody or visitation the evidence must be "clear and convincing." The bill directs the courts to apply strict scrutiny to all cases involving disputes concerning parental rights. It exempts cases involving custody disputes between parents. In a key provision the bill allows attorney's fees to be awarded to those who both bring charges against the government under the act and those who use the act to defend against a suit brought by the government.

The PRRA is part of the growing parental backlash against schools and other governmental agencies brought on by the Christian Right. This backlash is understood as a part of a "general struggle parents face as they attempt to transmit their most cherished beliefs to their children in the midst of an anti-family culture" (Family Research Council 1996, 3). The PRRA has arisen alongside the cultural war waged by the Christian Right. The bill's proponents argue that while a national debate rages over the proper response to popular culture, "relatively little attention has been focused on the fact that too often parents have discovered that their own government is part of the problem" (3). The PRRA is seen as a demand by parents that "government policies support rather than undermine, their authority" (3).

It is this demand for the recognition of parental authority that interests us. The PRRA has initiated a public controversy over who can best judge what is in the best interest of children. The proponents of the bill argue that the State has wrongly assumed control over the terms and criteria of judgment, thereby usurping the "natural" authority and expertise that parents possess for making decisions about their children's welfare. Two tropes structure the rhetorical advocacy of the Parental Rights and Responsibilities Act: short adults and substituted judgment.

Short Adults

The trope of short adults circulates as a critique of a series of legal decisions that purportedly grant children rights. One effect of children's rights is to displace parental authority. For those in support of the Parental Rights and Responsibilities Act, children's rights presuppose that children are "short adults": that is, autonomous agents capable of making decisions independent of their parents. The attempt to challenge children's rights as a violation of parental authority marks the rhetoric in support of parental rights legislation as a democratic antagonism.

Mouffe (1988) argues that a political controversy can be translated into a democratic antagonism when "subjects constructed on the basis of certain rights . . . find themselves in a position in which those rights are denied by some practices or discourses. At that point there is a negation of subjectivity or identification, which can be the basis for an antagonism" (94). In order to appreciate how parental rights emerge as a democratic antagonism demands an investigation into how the new conservatism problematizes recent trends in family law. Rutherford (1987) explains that "rights talk" structures family law on both a vertical and horizontal axis. The vertical axis describes the State-family relationship in terms of State intrusions into the sanctity of the family. The horizontal axis of family law focuses on the individual rights of the different members of the family. The advocates of parental rights argue that the creation of a series of horizontal rights for children threatens to erode the parental rights protected by the vertical structure of family law. In other words, the new conservatism identifies one set of rights discourses as a threat or negation of a second series of rights. Since horizontal rights are the more recent trend in family law, parental rights advocates are able to construct a frontier (Laclau and Moffe 1985; Grossberg 1992) through the history of family law in order to restore rights lost due to an encroaching state apparatus into the internal dynamics of the family.

In the case of parental rights the primary site of contestation concerns the parent-child nexus of family law. For advocates of parental rights, the horizontal trend in family law is to grant children rights independent of parental authority. The Family Research Council (1996) argues that "the past generation has witnessed. . . laws giving minors access to abortion and birth control without parental approval. . . . Implicit in these policies is an assumption that children should be treated as 'short adults,' i.e., as autonomous individuals, fully capable of making crucial decisions about their upbringing, and legally entitled to make those decisions outside the context of their family" (3–4). This passage rhetorically problematizes the idea of children's rights by suggesting that the idea of children's rights are a relatively new phenomenon. The newness of children's rights allows the Family Research Council (FRC) to "de-naturalize" children's rights as a historical project. The identification of children's rights as an historical project creates a space for challenging the logics of children's rights in terms of their effects on both the parent-child nexus and the State-family nexus.

The effect of treating children as short adults destabilizes the parent-child nexus. According to the FRC (1996) "the movement to grant minors full access to the full range of choices available to adults naturally leads to liberation of children from their parents, who serve as an obstacle to the free exercise of these new rights" (4). The slippery slope fallacy activated by this argument by direction is breathtaking. However, the strength of the claim is not located in its logical soundness, but instead in its ability to deploy the horizontal logics of children's rights against the vertical logics of family law. The construction of children's rights (a horizontal logic) runs headlong into parental rights (a vertical logic) to direct the upbringing of their children. The FRC does not deny the idea of children's rights but instead suggests that the parents and not the State are responsible for their protection and activation: "while it is indisputable that children have rights, parents traditionally have been considered the proper custodians of these rights until their children reach adulthood" (1996, 4). For the advocates of parental rights, when the Supreme Court grants children rights, independent of their parents, the Court creates a wedge between the parent and child. This wedge in the parent-child relationship becomes the pathway by which state actors begin to destabilize the family as a unique entity, thus, threatening the liberty rights of parents. Writing for the Heritage Foundation, Fagan and Horn (1996) argue that "Over the years, widely scattered and repeated attacks on the fundamental rights of parents have come from state and local courts; from federal state and local government bureaucracies and officials; and from policy initiatives inspired by a number of the major professions dealing with children" (2). What Rutherford (1987) abstractly describes as a tension between horizontal and vertical rights, parental rights advocates rhetorically translate into a contest between "choice rights" of minors (FRC 1996) and the "fundamental liberty rights" of parents. According to Fagan and Horn (1996) "[parental rights] . . . are liberty rights [and] should not be abridged by government except in the most unusual circumstance" (1). The rhetorical effect of defending parental rights as liberty rights is to value parental rights as more vital than children's choice rights. The assertion of parental rights as fundamental liberty rights codes the historical emergence of children's rights as an ensemble of discourses and practices which subordinate parents to state, professional and bureaucratic actors. It is this rhetorical constitution of parental subordination to the State and its surrogates that marks the advocacy of parental rights as a democratic antagonism.

Our identification of the rhetorical struggle for parental rights as a democratic antagonism should not be read as an endorsement of the position. The concept of a democratic antagonism does not align with either conservative, modern liberal, or radical political projects, but instead, suggests that different social actors can bend the creation of a democratic antagonism toward different political directions. The concept of democratic antagonisms is polysemic: it can be deployed in either emancipatory or repressive directions. Mouffe describes social movements that aim at widening the scope of democracy as *democratic struggles*. What transforms this controversy into a democratic antagonism is that it seeks to account for and to remedy an alleged subordination to the demands of an encroaching State apparatus (Mouffe 1988). Yet, the political effects of parental rights seem less than polysemic. On the contrary, the advocacy of parental rights functions in a very conservative way: It publicizes the State-family relationship for the specific purpose of de-politicizing the horizontal relationships among family members. The point of parental rights amendments is to re-constitute the family as a relational entity that views the rights traversing the parent-child nexus as complementary rather than contractual and/or antagonistic (Hafen 1989). To do otherwise is to create an opening for the State to intervene and disrupt the fundamental liberty rights of parents. Put simply, parental rights advocates are working to place the parent-child relationship outside of public deliberation and regulation.

Parental rights amendments politicize the State-family relationship in order to de-politicize the relationships among members of a family. The advocates of parental rights rhetorically accomplish this act of de-politicization by creating a frontier that problematizes horizontal developments in family law as a threat to vertical rights established in family law. The desire of parental rights advocates to restore rights that are being negated suggests a closer examination of the Court decisions defended as "proper" for thinking about the family.

Parental rights advocates deploy *Meyer v. Nebraska* (1923) and *Pierce v. Society of Sisters* (1925) as the basis for their claims that parental rights are fundamental liberty rights. In *Meyer v. Nebraska*, the Supreme Court ruled that a Nebraska provision prohibiting the teaching of foreign languages prior to the eighth grade was a violation of the fourteenth amendment. In *Pierce v. Society of Sisters*, the Supreme Court overruled an Oregon law that demanded that parents send their children to public school from the ages of 8 to 16. For the supporters of parental rights amendments these two court cases grant parents authority to raise their children as they see fit. On the state level, the typical parental rights amendment codifies the language of *Pierce*. According to the FRC (1996) "In its most common form, the Parental Rights Amendment reads: 'The right of parents to direct the upbringing and education of their children shall not be infringed.' By codifying language taken directly from the 1925 *Pierce* case, the Amendment would provide parents with an explicit right grounded in their state constitution" (8). On the federal level, the Parental Rights and Responsibilities Act codes parental rights as fundamental liberty rights activating the judicial standards of "strict scrutiny" and "compelling interest" as the primary legal criteria for regulating state-family encounters. The point is to block the movement of the State into the family. According to the FRC, "The federal parental rights legislation is a negative mandate on government. It checks power, not enhances it" (8–9).

Meyer and *Pierce* are the Constitutional building blocks for the vertical protections granted the family in relation to the State. Yet the re-deployment of these cases as a way to check developments in horizontal family rights figures the State-family relationship as one of mortal combat. Justice McReynolds was the author of the Court's opinion in both *Meyer* and *Pierce*. Ray (1987) suggests that "the language and argument of both opinions are generally calm and measured" (343–344). Yet, Ray identifies one major digression in *Meyer* that is repeated in *Pierce*: two passages about how Plato's Republic and Sparta organize child rearing practices. Ray draws the following lessons from reading this peculiar digression in McReynolds' opinions:

> What distinguishes McReynolds' opinions is their sense of the family as an adversary of the state. Far from perceiving continuity or analogy, he sees the state as a potential threat to diversity, individualism, even privacy. Perhaps, like the Nebraska legislature, he too was recalling the unified national purpose of the war years, but such unity suggest to him two nations, the Platonic Republic devoted to virtue and the Spartan state devoted to military triumph, which subordinate the individual to the collective. When McReynolds declares that "the child is not the mere creature of the State," it is hard to say who thought otherwise outside of Sparta and the Dialogues. The family is being defended against a relatively mild excess of state police power as though family and government were locked in combat over the control of every child's destiny (345).

The rhetorical effect of bringing the reasoning of McReynolds to the present is to re-instantiate the view that the State and family are in competition for the soul of the child. This competitive relationship between the State and the family provides the warrant for the disjunctive logics of the Family Research Council: "The clash over parental rights proposals begs the fundamental question: Are ordinary parents generally competent to raise their children or should parents defer to elite authorities backed by state power" (1996, 14). The supporters of parental rights amendments are able to attach their reasoning to a form of rhetorical populism. This rhetorical populism traverses the parental rights controversy allowing the advocates of parental rights to deploy an affective border (Grossberg 1992) between the State and the family locating the child on the familial side of this border. As Fagan and Horn (1996) remark:

> It is parents—not teachers, child care providers, social workers, or a 'village'—that are most likely to give this all-encompassing commitment to the welfare of the child. This is not to denigrate the important work done by teachers, child care providers, and social workers, but simply to acknowledge an important truth: Only parents can reasonably be expected to put the interests of their children above their own. Thus, government must assume that parents, not bureaucrats or politicians, are in the best position to make decisions about their children because only parents can be expected to have this overriding commitment to their children's welfare (6).

The advocates of parental rights infuse parents with an affective invest-ment which produces the knowledge to judge what is in best interest of their children. This form of passionate reasoning (Greene and Hicks 1993) re-directs the horizontal logics of children's rights into a question about whose judgment should take priority concerning the welfare of children. By investing in parental authority as the privileged site of judgment, the advocates of parental rights legislation push the child further into the family and away from the judgment of the state apparatus. Thus the con-tours of the controversy over parental rights position judgment at the cen-ter of dispute. To challenge parental rights legislation, opponents must ar-gue against the affective logics of parents as the warrant which privileges parental judgment. In order to counter this form of passionate reasoning the opposition must problematize the claim that "father knows best." Yet, this assault on the ability of parents to judge what is in the best interest of their children feeds the second trope saturating the advocacy of the Parental Rights and Responsibilities Act: namely, substituted judgment.

Substituted Judgment

The trope of substituted judgment involves the claim that governmental bureaucracies and professional agencies, such as schools, child protection agencies, psychological testing agencies, and university professors are substituting their judgment for that of parents in matters pertaining to the child's health, education, and welfare. The "humane professions," such as education, law, medicine, social work, and psychology, are seen as "increasingly hostile" to the rights of parents to make decisions re-garding their children's well-being. Fagan and Horn claim that the rights of parents are under sustained attack from professionals. "Within the ma-jor professions of education, medicine, psychology, social work, and school counseling, there is increasing evidence that too many people and associations think they are more qualified than parents to judge what is good for particular children. There also is increasing evidence that they assume their professional judgment is superior and therefore can be exer-cised independently of parental judgment" (1996, 11).

It is in the public schools that the proponents claim the competing in-terests of the family and the State/humane professions clash. Schools have traditionally served *in loco parentis*. Yet does this power give educa-tors the right to contradict the expressed will or values of parents? The claim that professionals have exceeded their "delegated authority" and substituted their judgments for that of parents is advanced through a litany of well-traveled examples. These examples include "unwanted" physical exams, "intrusive" psychological testing, and "coercive" con-dom distribution. These examples are worth looking at in some detail because they provide evidence that is difficult to interrogate and refute because of a set of affective investments concerning the protection of childhood innocence. They also point to the very methods of calculation, inscription, and judgment used by professionals to govern school-aged children as the locus of this controversy.

First, both the Heritage Foundation and the Family Research Council frequently cite a case in which 59 sixth-grade girls in East Stroudsburg, Pennsylvania were subjected to gynecological exams without permission from their parents. Moreover, the FRC reports that these "intrusive vaginal exams" which were conducted under the guise of checking these 11-year girls for sexually-transmitted disease and sexual abuse, even though no incident of disease or evidence of abuse had been reported, were done against the will of the girls themselves. In an oft-cited quote the Heritage Foundation reports one of the girls saying "we tried to get out the window but they pulled us back " (1996, 11). The case of Sharon and Waymon Earls is often cited as an example of the intrusiveness of the State regarding matters of sexual / reproductive choice. The 14 and 15-year-old daughters of the Earlses were driven to a county birth control clinic, where they were tested for AIDS, given pap smears, and prescribed birth control pills without the knowledge and permission of their parents. The parents were then denied access to the test results by the school. The school defended its actions on the grounds that they were acting in the best interests of the young women. The Earlses have since filed suit against the school, traveled extensively testifying on behalf of parental rights legislation, and operate an active internet site for those interested in advancing the parental rights movement.

Psychological testing and counseling is another area of concern for proponents. The case of Daniel and Nancy Newkirk is frequently cited by both the FRC and the Heritage foundation. The Newkirk's 8-year-old son Jason was being "psychologically counseled by an unlicensed, untrained guidance counselor against their express wishes" (FRC 1996, 6–7). Specifically, Jason was diagnosed as having emotional-social problems because he was not interacting in a "normal" manner with his classmates. Jason was monitored and treated with a form of play-based therapy called *The Talking, Feeling, and Doing Game.* The FRC notes that the game asks specific questions such as "Tell something about your mother that gets you angry," "What do you think about a boy who sometimes wished his brother were dead?," and "What is the worst thing you can say about your family?" that are designed to elicit "private" information about the family. After Jason began to exhibit behavioral changes, the Newkirks confronted the school but were told that the counseling sessions were confidential and thus were denied access to school records. The Newkirks filed a suit against the school. Both the U.S. District Court and the Sixth Circuit Court of Appeals found for the school. The Supreme Court refused to hear the case, leaving the Newkirks with no further remedy.

Perhaps the most cited example of "substituted judgment" is the case of Elizabeth Curtis. Curtis and other parents from Falmouth, Massachusetts, filed suit against the Falmouth School Board for installing condom vending machines in the school. The parents also objected to a school policy which allowed school nurses to distribute condoms to students upon request. The county Superior Court refused to grant a "parental opt-out" of the program. The parents appeal was rejected by both the Massachusetts and the U.S. Supreme Court. The Massachusetts Supreme Court argued that the students were free to decline participation in the program and parents are free to instruct their children not to participate. The Court went on to claim "although exposure to condom vending machines and to the program itself may offend the moral and religious sensibilities of the plaintiffs, mere exposure to programs offered at school does not amount to unconstitutional interference with parental liberties without the existence of some compulsory aspects to the program" (quoted in FRC 1996, 8). The proponents of parental rights legislation were outraged at this decision. The FRC claims that the Court's reasoning illustrates how the State actively undermines parental authority:

> This passage from *Curtis* reveals how treating minors as "short adults" works in tandem with State-substituted judgment to undermine parental authority. First we are told that the condom program is 'voluntary' because the *students* 'are free to decline to participate,' i.e., they are autonomous actors capable of making their own decisions about choices presented to them at school. The school maintains a facade of neutrality with regard to the choice presented, but by presenting to the child extra-curricular options that starkly contradict the values of the parent, the State is assisting the child in circumventing the parents will (1996, 8).

The first point we would like to make about these examples is that their rhetorical force comes from activating a set of affective investments rooted in a desire to protect childhood innocence. Each of these examples works by presenting an image of the child as innocent yet under constant threat of being corrupted by the State. On the one hand, in the cases of the "unwanted" gynecological exams and "intrusive" psychological counseling the reader is presented with an image of "innocent" young children who, despite all of their resistance, are "abused" sexually and emotionally by insensitive and indeed even immoral "mental health elites." On the other hand, in the cases of the 14 and 15-year old daughters of Sharon and Waymon Earls and the students in Falmouth, Massachusetts, the reader is presented with an image of adolescents who are either sexually active or susceptible to the temptations of promiscuity. In these cases school officials are portrayed as willing accomplices in aiding the "child in circumventing the parents' will." In both examples the "State" corrupts children: Either the State through the actions of overzealous "mental health elites" defiles young children by invading their bodies and minds; or, the State aids and abets teens who are already naturally disposed to act on their sexual impulses by providing them with knowledge of sexual practices and contraception. In these examples, the parents are also victims, helpless to stop the State from exploiting their children. By portraying "mental health elites" as a threat to children, the proponents of the PRRA can "turn" (Palczewski & Madsen 1993) the discourses of protection, used so effectively by the left to mobilize support for child protection laws, against the State. Thus, parents can use the PRRA to reclaim the souls of their children by bringing them back within the protective enclosure of the family.

Second, these examples frame the controversy over parental rights in terms of the connections between expertise and political authority. The underlying assumption of the PRRA is that the State and mental health professionals should recognize that parents are the "world's greatest experts on their own children" and, therefore, "they must retain the maximum decision-making authority when it comes to raising those children" (Fagan and Horn 1996, 5–6). According to the bill's proponents rather than having those "children's long-term best interest at heart," these examples demonstrate that the administrative bureaucracies of the State place its "socio-political ends" above the values of parents, and therefore, the welfare of children. These socio-political ends, often disguised as ways of enhancing the child's well-being, are used to authorize an increasingly intrusive and dangerous apparatus of techniques designed to monitor, evaluate, and modify children's attitudes and behaviors.

While we find that the examples used by the proponents are often overstated and believe that the State may indeed have "rational" reasons for conducting physical exams (although we too believe that school nurses administering gynecological exams, absent evidence of abuse or disease, to 11 and 12-year old girls is unwarranted), psychological counseling, instruction in human sexuality, and distributing contraceptives, we would be remiss if we were to ignore the fact that the PRRA is an especially effective and provocative challenge to the "rationality" of the welfare state and the "humane professions" techniques of inscription, calculation, and governance. Thus rather than treat the PRRA as another instance of the rhetoric of "family values," which it certainly is, (Cloud 1995), we see it as a neo-liberal attempt to call into question the link between professional expertise and political authority. It transforms "the capacity of judgment" from an epistemological question into a political and ethical one by figuring "judgment" as a site of democratic antagonism. To understand this dynamic we need to reflect on the relationship between expertise, professional judgment, and political authority.

Central to the possibility of modern forms of liberal democratic government, argue Rose and Miller (1992), are "the associations formed between entities constituted as 'political' and the projects, plans and practices of those authorities—economic, legal, spiritual, medical, technical—who endeavor to administer the lives of others in the light of conceptions of what is good, healthy, normal, virtuous, efficient or profitable" (175). That is, there is an intrinsic relationship between the production and dissemination of knowledge by experts and the activities of government. Consequently, within liberal democracies, the actions and attitudes of the subject—the self, the soul, the body—become the objects and instruments of governance, which in turn is made possible by the products of expertise in the form of the "humane professions."

Professionalism, defined as expertise in the form of highly trained individuals socialized in accordance with standards of judgment comporting to an ethical and disciplinary code, emerged as the dominant form of institutionalized expertise in the second half of the nineteenth and early twentieth century (Johnson 1993). The relationship between professional expertise and government is reciprocal. The government depends on the social and human sciences for its languages, its systems of notation and calculation, and categories and classifications of inscription to make reality—the individual body as well as the body politic—knowable, and therefore, governable. The professions, in turn, depend upon government to demand explanations and solutions to social problems, a demand that not only supplies the social and human sciences with grant dollars but guides the formation of their disciplinary and professional problematics.

A central activity of government, made possible by professional expertise, is the translation of events and phenomena into information. This translation is accomplished through the use of "inscription devices," most notably statistics but also including reports, field notes, transcripts, test scores, medical exams, etc. (Rose and Miller 1992; Latour 1987). Rose and Miller, following Latour, argue that methods of inscription form the "material conditions that enable thought to work upon an object": "By means of inscription, reality is made stable, mobile, comparable, combinable. It is rendered in a form in which it can be debated and diagnosed. Information in this sense is not the outcome of a neutral recording function. It is itself a way of acting upon the real, a way of devising techniques for inscribing it in such a way as to make the domain in question susceptible to evaluation, calculation and intervention" (185).

The proponents of the PRRA are well aware that the gathering of information is not simply a "neutral recording function." They also know that the "domain in question" is often their child's body and their family. It is because they object to being evaluated, calculated and becoming the object of intervention that they propose parental rights legislation. One of the intended effects of the PRRA is to empower parents to stop school officials from using information extracted from their children. This would include medical exams, psychological tests, and survey research. Robert Knight, director of Cultural Studies for the FRC, argues that "decisions about what kind of information is conveyed to children or extracted from them are the parents' natural prerogative." He goes on claiming that "any research methods that place a barrier between children and their parents should be outlawed" (FRC 1995, 1–2). While it is doubtful that the State and the humane professions will ever stop collecting information about children, this law, if passed, would provide parents with a tool to greatly hinder efforts to collect data from children and their families and inscribe it as knowledge of the child's body, mind and moral character. Of course, these parents will more than likely turn to other experts (such as clergy and church-sponsored institutions) to extract the "truth" from their children. It is not our claim that inscription practices will stop with the passage of the Parental Rights and Responsibilities Act. To the contrary, the bill may result in an explosion of alternative methods of inscription, perhaps, based on "Judeo-Christian" precepts. What we find remarkable is that the proponents of the PRRA are quick to attack the very methods of inscription and calculation that are central to professional judgment and, hence, social liberal governance. This point of attack differentiates the PRRA from other parental rights struggles in the history of US public culture; it is, as if, the advocates of the PRRA are mining both the Bible and Foucault's *Discipline and Punish* as inventional resources for critiquing the welfare state.

The inscription of traits, functions and behaviors into stable, mobile, comparable and combinable modes of information (such as processes, schemata, and models) that enable reality to be described, assessed, evaluated and acted upon generates the formation of what Rose and Miller (1992), following Latour (1987), call "centres of calculation." Through inscription, certain persons and agencies, in particular locales, become powerful in the sense that they obtain "the capacity to engage in certain calculations and lay claim to legitimacy for their plans and strategies because they are, in a real sense, *in the know* about that which they seek to govern" (Rose and Miller 1992, 186). The information that experts are empowered to accumulate, consult and use as warrants for intervention plays a significant role in legitimizing the power they hold over those (such as children and their parents) who constitute entries into their professional charts, reports, and journals.

However, experts do not usually coerce children and their parents into complying with their educational and developmental programs. To the contrary, experts work to establish cooperative partnerships with parents to provide services for their children. The persona of the expert, which normally embodies neutrality, authority, and a commitment to social service, links the socio-political objectives of the State with the needs and desires of individual children and families. This is accomplished by the expert entering into a kind of "double-alliance" with the State and the children and their parents (Rose and Miller 1992). On the one hand, experts ally themselves with political authorities, focusing their research efforts on devising solutions to ongoing social problems. The work of experts is often that of translating political concerns such as economic productivity, the costs of entitlement programs, law and order, or public health into the vocabularies of education, psychology, social work, medicine, accounting, management and the law. On the other hand, experts form alliances with those populations they serve, in particular with children and families. Professionals translate the daily worries of parents and the problems their children face into a diagnostic language that empowers parents to make-sense of their predicament and teach parents and children techniques of self-correction and discipline so they can live happier, more productive lives.

While this "double-alliance" between experts, the State and individuals has been heralded as a tremendous advance for the cause of "parental rights" by educators (especially in the field of special education, where parental involvement was a hard-won right), the proponents of the PRRA view efforts at including children and parents in educational "partnerships" as evidence of the "gradual erosion of parents' standing in the eyes of the nation's powerful educational establishment." First, in the cases of sex education, condom distribution, and psychological counseling, the alliance between school officials, counselors, and the child often purposively exclude parents. The gag rules prohibiting parental access to school records documenting reproductive counseling and psychological assessments are often cited as evidence that the educational establishment is trying to drive a wedge between parents and their children. Again, the discourse of protection, coupled with imagery of corrupted childhood innocence, drives this argument. By forming alliances directly with children, the State works to either turn children against their parents as in the case of the psychological counseling of Jason Newkirk or the State works to aid children in circumventing parental control as in the case of the driving the daughters of Waymon Earls to a birth control clinic.

Second, the move to "involve" parents in the decision-making process fails to recognize the "primary and fundamental right of parents in directing the education of their own children" (Fagan and Horn 1996, 13). Testifying against the bill before the House Committee on the Judiciary, Vicki Rafel, representing the National Parent Teacher Association, claimed that the State needs to involve "all the stakeholders including parents, educators, health care givers, and government bodies" in making education decisions that affect children (quoted in Knight 1995, 4). Merely being listed as one among several "stakeholders" who have an interest in the child's welfare, however, provokes supporters of parental rights legislation. Moreover, although Rafel acknowledges that parents have a role in directing their children's' education, the State's interest in promoting liberal democratic values (such as exposure to diverse beliefs and equipping students with the knowledge and techniques necessary to make autonomous decisions) can override parental authority. The PRRA would disarticulate the "double alliance" between "metal health elites," the State and children as well as circumventing the rhetoric which constitutes parents as "partners" with the educational establishment. The PRRA makes this move by positing the *Lochner*-era standards set out in *Pierce* and *Meyer* that established parents primary and fundamental right to exercise complete control over their children's education as "beyond debate as an enduring American tradition" (Fagan and Horn 1996, 13).

Besides rejecting a collaborative alliance between parents and governmental agencies, advocates of parental rights legislation directly question the ability and rights afforded to experts to judge what is in the best interest of children. The PRRA advocates recognize that experts have the capacity to generate what Rose and Miller (1992) term "enclosures: relatively bounded locales or types of judgment within which their power and authority is concentrated, intensified and defended"(188). By commanding a vocabulary, a set of technical skills, and an esoteric knowledge that is not available and understandable by all participants, experts can generate and codify standards of professional judgment that others cannot easily use or challenge. The controversy surrounding parental rights, however, illustrates the provisional and contestable nature of the claims of expert judgment. By stipulating that the State will only intervene in cases where there is probable cause that "clear and convincing evidence will be found to document the occurrence of child abuse as it is "traditionally defined" as "physical harm," the bill attempts to distinguish necessary from overly intrusive interventions. The advocates of parental rights legislation claim that experts use "scientific knowledge" about child development and children at risk to justify ever more inscrutable standards of judgment. What was once seen as normal parenting, is now alleged to be an example of abuse. The proponents fear that "mental health elites" are quietly waging a campaign to define "traditional Christian" parenting practices as abusive. Citing examples where child protection agencies mistakenly terminated parental rights, proponents claim that the bill is the only way to clear space to challenge the network of power formed by a complex articulation of the medical establishment, overzealous child-protection agencies, and those educational authorities who see schooling as the means of instilling "liberal values" into children. In effect, the bill seeks to open a wedge to contest the standards of professional judgment by raising evidentiary standards and shifting the burden of proof to those who seek to investigate and intervene in cases of suspected abuse and neglect. The opponents of the PRRA and State initiatives to legislate parental rights argue that placing evidentiary standards upon those who investigate and intervene in cases of suspected abuse and neglect will "cast a chilling effect on local efforts to protect children."

> The bill would create serious legal and administrative barriers to the protection of abused children. Parents could impede the investigation of reports of child maltreatment and efforts to ensure the safety of children, increasing the risk that children will remain in dangerous situations. The threat of lawsuits would deter reporting of suspected child maltreatment and wreak havoc with local efforts to protect children. Currently, CPS proceedings are divided into investigation, adjudication, disposition, and permanency phases, often with different rules and standards of proof. The bill introduces a change in the evidentiary standard applied to these proceedings that would make it more difficult for CPS agencies to investigate abuse charges... The PRRA would result in more protection for abusive parents (People for the American Way 1996, 1–2).

The opponents go on to argue that the bill would narrow the definition of abuse and neglect and freeze future expanding definitions of abuse by forcing the court into a "traditional understanding" of what constitutes child maltreatment. Professionals need flexible and autonomous standards of judgment, according to the opponents, for CPS agencies to effectively respond to "new and unforeseen crises" (Woodhouse 1996, 411).

While we are in general agreement with these arguments, what we find interesting is that they confirm and extend the grounds of the proponent's claims. That is not to say that the opponent's arguments lend support to the Bill. Rather, both sides utilize the same argumentative resources and base their arguments on a defense of a particular relationship between political authority and expertise. First, as to our claim that both sides use similar argumentative tactics, the opponents of the PRRA also invoke the discourse of protection and the image of corrupted childhood innocence, to legitimate their capability and right to issue judgment. For the opponents, it is parents who pose a potential threat to the child, thus, the State must serve as a protective barrier between the parents and the child. At the time of writing this essay, the left has been incredibly successful in fighting parental rights legislation by deploying the discourses of protection and the images of abused children as a method of mobilizing a moral panic surrounding the claim that the bill would increase child abuse. The use of images of innocence, corrupted by either an abusive parent or by the State to mobilize affective investments in protecting children supports Mouffe's (1988) contention that democratic antagonisms are polysemic.

Second, and most important for this section, these arguments confirm the proponents' claims that the "mental health elites" (comprising CPS agencies, school administrators, and professional associations) are working to generate a zone of enclosure to safeguard their professional standards of judgment from being interrogated and ultimately contested by those who are judged. Expertise holds out the promise that social problems can be solved without engaging in extended political controversy by relocating the problems of diagnosing and regulating social ills from the terrain of the political to that of truth (Rose and Miller 1992). The PRRA and the fight over parental rights rescinds this promise. By raising the questions, Who is best able to judge what is in the best interests of the child and Who should decide which values children are taught to live by, the advocates of parental rights legislation disclose the contingent and contestable relationship between expertise, judgment and political authority. Proponents answer these questions with the claim that parents are always more likely to pursue the child's best interest because they have a fundamental interest in nurturing their children. By critiquing the ability of state-sponsored experts to make sound judgments about parenting practices, these conservative challenges to the social logics of familialization (Donzelot 1979) set in motion a different governing model to regulate the relationship between the child, the parent and the State. In this new model, parents seek to enlist the State as an active agent to enforce their parenting decisions and protect their authority. This conception of the State as having a legal duty to enforce parent's preferences whenever the child uses public institutions, signals a significant departure from current law. It also signals a significant change in the rationality of rule. This is why we contend that it is more productive to read the PRRA in its positivity—as a neo-liberal technology of government—rather than as another instance of an ideologically saturated and repressive salvo in the rhetoric of family values.

The Politics of Judgment

We want to end this essay by reflecting on how the Parental Rights and Responsibilities Act restructures the governing logics of liberal democracy. As

Leff (1991) notes about Franklin D. Roosevelt's "Commonwealth Club" address, Roosevelt initiated the central importance of expertise in the governing logics of the welfare state. Expert knowledges legitimate the welfare state to the extent that they create a form of social liberalism (Rose and Miller 1992) by activating a social responsibility for promoting the welfare of the population. The notion that a plethora of "stakeholders" have an investment in the welfare of children is an example of this form of social responsibility. In describing what he calls "advanced liberalism," Rose (1996) writes, "It seeks to de-governmentalize the State and to de-statize the practice of government, to detach the substantive authority of expertise from apparatuses of political rule, relocating experts within a market governed by the rationalities of competition, accountability and consumer demand" (41). The Parental Rights and Responsibilities Act works to create this new form of liberal government by making state- sponsored expertise (stakeholders) accountable to the judgments of parents instead of making the parents accountable to the judgments of the State.

The PRRA challenges the social liberalism traversing the rhetoric of multiple stakeholders by problematizing how those other stakeholders make expert judgments. For example, as we described in the previous two sections, the rhetorical strategy supporting parental rights legislation challenges the "enclosure" of expert judgment by deploying a form of passionate reasoning that privileges parental authority. The effect of this rhetorical strategy is to create an affective border between the state apparatus and the family. In so doing, the advocates of parental rights place the child inside the family and away from the state apparatus. Thus, the Parental Rights and Responsibilities Act affectively attempts to restructure the terrain of liberal governance by bending familialization away from the logics of social responsibility and toward a more individualized form of neo-liberal familial responsibility.

At the core of familialization is the activation of the family as a primary agent in the solution of social problems (Donzelot 1979). As Nikolas Rose (1987) suggests: "Over the last 150 years we have seen the construction of a new form of "government"—one in which the family was central—or rather in which certain desirable states of affairs—profit, tranquillity, security, health, virtue, and efficiency—were to be brought about by governing residential, domestic, sexual and child rearing arrangements in the form of the private family" (67). Familialization activates the family in order for modern liberal States to govern at a distance; that is, liberal forms of government activate a multitude of agents to govern social life in order to limit the reach of the State. Yet, at the same time, the reliance on the family as a governing agent requires the State to constantly evaluate the ability of families to solve social problems. Thus the family enters the "problem-space" (Burchell 1996) of liberalism as both a subject and an object. It is this dual role as both subject and object for liberal governance that creates the condition for expertise to mediate the relationship between the State and family. As we suggested in the last section, the advent of liberalism allows expertise to enter into a double alliance with both the state apparatus and the family. Social liberalism and the welfare state intensify this double alliance by expanding the number of stakeholders who have an investment in the welfare of children. The Parental Rights and Responsibilities Act would change the nature of how state-sponsored experts (or, stakeholders) would govern the family by challenging the investment offered by these other stakeholders. For a group like the Family Research Council, state-sponsored expertise should always defer to parental authority because the investments held by these other stakeholders are not as affectively pure as those of parents.

The affective border drawn between the State and the family, a border created by the challenge to state sponsored expertise, does not simply adjust how the State governs the child, it also deploys the affective demand that parents take responsibility for raising their children. According to the Family Research Council:

> The key to encouraging greater parental responsibility is to explicitly recognize the link between rights and duties upon which this nation was founded, and to renew our optimism in the ability of the people to manage their own affairs, as citizens and as parents. Indeed, "the most terribly important things must be left to ordinary men [sic] themselves," including the right of parents to protect their children from harmful influences and to direct their children's upbringing. Recognizing the irreplaceable role of parents is essential to keeping the power of the state in check, revitalizing citizenship, and ensuring that children receive the love, protection and guidance only a parent can provide (1996, 11).

This example demonstrates how the Parental Rights and Responsibilities Act activates parental affect in order to restructure the relationship between expertise, familialization, and liberal government. In contrast to the social liberalism traversing the idea of multiple stakeholders, the advocates of parental rights suggest that social responsibility creates a condition whereby parents delegate their familial responsibility to the expertise logics of the state apparatus. The delegation of responsibility points to a condition in which parents no longer seem to care enough about their children. In opposition to a social responsibility for raising children, the supporters of the PRRA advocate a more individualized form of familial responsibility. This emphasis on familial responsibility dis-assembles the welfare state by mobilizing parental affect as the solution to the problems associated with children.

Conclusion

The revival of judgment as a corrective to the crisis of democracy often takes the State's reliance on expertise as a point of departure. According to Beiner,

> The purpose of inquiring into the nature of judgment is to disclose a mental faculty by which we situate ourselves in the political world without relying upon explicit rule and methods, and thus to open up a space of deliberation that is being closed ever more tightly in technocratic societies. In respect of this faculty, the dignity of the common citizen suffers no derogation. Here the expert can claim no special privileges. If the faculty of judging is a general aptitude that is shared by all citizens, and if the exercise of this faculty is a sufficient qualification for active participation in political life, we have a basis for reclaiming the privilege of responsibility that has been prized from us on the grounds of specialized competence (1983, 3).

We are in full agreement with the desire to expand the zone of public deliberation by attenuating the ability of experts to take public issues out of the realm of politics and into the realm of truth. Yet, we also think it is important to recognize how the Parental Rights and Responsibility Act challenges the judgment of expertise in order to remove the child from public deliberation and intervention, thus, placing the child within a zone of enclosure marked by an affectively re-charged familialization. The affective defense of parental judgment in opposition to expert judgment points to how the new conservatism is articulating judgment to a neo-liberal political agenda. The lesson we draw from this state of affairs is that it is too simple to defend judgment as a solution to the crisis of democracy. Instead, rhetorical critics and democratic theorists must pay closer attention to the politics of judgment so as to better account for how judgment is organized, challenged and deployed in support of different techniques of democratic government.

References

Beiner, Ronald. 1983. *Political Judgment*. Chicago: University Of Chicago Press.

Browne, Stephen, and Michael Leff. 1985. "Political Judgment and Rhetorical Argument: Edmund Burke's Paradigm." In *Argument and Social Practice: Proceedings of the Fourth SCA/AFA Conference on Argumentation*, eds. J. Robert Cox, Malcolm Sillars, and Greg Walker, 193–210. Annandale, VA: Speech Communication Association.

Burchell, Graham. 1993. "Liberal Government and the Techniques of the Self." *Economy and Society* 22: 267–282.

Cloud, Dana. 1995. "The Rhetoric of [Family Values]." In *Argumentation and Values: Proceedings of the Ninth SCA/AFA Conference on Argumentation*, ed. Sally Jackson, 281–289. Annandale VA: Speech Communication Association.

Donzolet, Jacques. 1979. *The Policing of Families*. New York: Pantheon.

Fagan, Patrick, and Richard Horn. 1996. "How Congress Can Protect the Rights of Parents to Raise Their Children." Available Online at <http//www.townhall.com/heritage/library/categories/family/ib227.html>.

Family Research Council. 1996. "Parental Rights: Who Decides How Children are Raised?" Available Online at <http://www.frc.org/FRC/fampol/fp96hpa.html>.

Goodnight, Thomas. 1982. "The Personal, Technical and Public Spheres of Argument: A Speculative Inquiry into the Art of Public Deliberation." *Journal of the American Forensic Association*, 18: 214–227.

Gilles, Stephen. 1996. "On Educating Children: A Parentalist Manifesto." *University of Chicago Law Review*, 63: 937–1034.

Greene, Ronald, and Darrin Hicks. 1993. "Passionate Reasoning." In *Argumentation and the Postmodern Challenge: Proceedings of the Eighth AFA/SCA Summer Conference on Argumentation*, ed. Raymie McKerrow, 176–178. Annandale, VA: Speech Communication Association.

Grossberg, Lawrence. 1992. *We Gotta Get Outta Of This Place: Popular Conservatism and Postmodern Culture*. London/New York: Routledge.

Hafen, Bruce. 1989. "The Family as an Entity." *University of California, Davis Law Review*, 22: 865–916.

Johnson, Terry. 1993. "Expertise and the State." In *Foucault's New Domains*, ed. Michael Gane and Terry Johnson, 139–152. London: Routledge.

Knight, Robert. 1995. "Testimony of Robert H. Knight regarding HR 1271." Available Online at <http://www.frc.org/FRC/podium/pd95k3pa.html>.

Laclau, Ernesto and Chantal Mouffe. 1985. *Hegemony and Socialist Strategy: Towards a Radical Democratic Politics*. London: Verso.

Latour, Bruno. 1987. *Science in Action*. London: Open University Press.

Leff, Michael. "Prudential Argument and the Use of History in Franklin D. Roosevelt's 'Commonwealth Club' Address." In *Proceedings of the Second International Conference on Argumentation*, eds., Frans H. Van Emeren, et al., 931–936. Amsterdam: SICSAT.

Mouffe, Chantal. 1988. "Hegemony and New Political Subjects: Toward a New Concept of Democracy." In *Marxism and the Interpretation of Culture*, ed. Cary Nelson and Lawrence Grossberg, 89–104. Urbana: University of Illinois Press.

Palczewski, Catherine and Arnie Madsen. 1993. "The Divisiveness of Diversity: President Bush's University of Michigan Commencement Speech as an Example of the Linguistic Turnaround." *Argumentation and Advocacy*, 30: 16–27.

Parental Rights and Responsibilities Act, HR 1946. 1996. *Ohio State Law Journal*, 57: 438–440.

People for the American Way. 1996. "The Parental Rights and Responsibilities Act: Harmful to Children's Health and Well-Being." Available Online at <http:///www.pfaw.org/EUCA/prraheal.html>.

Ray, Laura Krugman. 1987. "The Figure in the Judicial Carpet: Images of Family and State in Supreme Court Opinions." *Journal of Legal Education*, 37: 331-345.

Rose, Nikolas. 1996. "Governing 'Advanced' Liberal Democracies." In *Foucault and Political Reason: Liberalism, Neo-Liberalism and Rationalities of Government*, ed. Andrew Barry, et al., 37–64. Chicago: University of Chicago Press.

Rose, Nikolas. 1987. "Beyond the Public/Private Division: Law, Power and the Family." *Journal of Law and Society*, 14: 61–75.

Rose, Nikolas, and Peter Miller. 1992. "Political Power Beyond the State: Problematics of Government. *British Journal of Sociology*, 43: 173–205.

Rutherford, Johnathan. 1987. "Beyond Individual Privacy: A New Theory of Family Rights." *University of Florida Law Review*, 39: 627–652.

Spragens, Thomas. 1990. *Reason and Democracy*. Durham: Duke University Press.

Straight Talk from the Family Research Council. 1996. "Parental Rights." Available Online at <http://www.frc.org/FRC/net/st96b3.html>.

Woodhouse, Barbara. 1996. "A Public Role in the Private Family: The Parental Rights and Responsibilities Act and the Politics of Child Protection and Education." *Ohio State Law Journal*, 57: 393–437.

9

Property and Propriety

Rhetoric, Justice, and Lyotard's Différend

Maurice Charland

There is a story regarding the invention of rhetoric. It concerns a set of
disputes over property. After the tyrants were banished from Syracuse in
467 B. C., courts were established to determine the ownership of property
unjustly seized. These courts heard arguments from claimants and it became apparent that the rendering of justice depended upon the eloquence of those petitioning the court. Two entrepreneurs skilled in the
use of language recognized a golden opportunity. Corax and Tisias became the first teachers of the art of oratory as they advised fellow Sicil-
ians, for a fee, on tactics for pleading their case.

In its economy, this little tale tells both a great deal and very little about
rhetoric as a genre of discourse. Rhetoric is concerned with resolving particular disputes. It is a three-party genre or language game involving a
claimant, a counter-claimant, and a judge with executive power or authority. Speakers are guided by their interest and speech is directed toward winning. Justice is at stake. Furthermore, speech is amenable to
self-conscious correction, that is it can be practised as an art. But through
this tale we cannot know if all disputes are amenable to resolution
through this form of verbal battle, nor what regard contestants hold each
other in, nor how they and others regard the judge, nor how a judgment
is formed. The practical and ethical status of rhetoric remains undefined.

I shall address these questions through an elaboration of certain concepts and arguments proposed by Jean-François Lyotard. Central to my
investigation will be the *différend*, Lyotard's rendering of the radically incommensurable. As I shall tell it, while rhetoric is often considered the
form of discourse enabling judgment in the face of incommensurable
competing claims, the possibility of a *différend* marks the limit of rhetoric

as a tidy civic practice. Consider the following two banal fictive tales regarding property disputes:

Two Fictive Tales

1. There is a boundary dispute between the State of New Hampshire and the State of Vermont. Both states claim jurisdiction over part of an unincorporated township that has become a potential source of tax revenue because of the recent discovery of certain natural resources. Because of previously unnoticed inconsistencies in geological surveys and changes in the course of the New Hampshire River, the dispute does not admit a technical resolution. After a failed attempt at negotiation, Vermont sues New Hampshire for taxes the latter state has collected. Counsel for both states submits briefs to Federal Court and make oral arguments. The court rules in favour of Vermont on the basis of principles derived from British Common Law and a little-known nineteenth century case between two counties in the State of New York. Deciding not to appeal, the Attorney General for the State of New Hampshire concedes defeat while vaguely alluding to his respect for the judicial process and the Constitution of the United States.

2. A municipality in the State of Wyoming contracts with an entrepreneur to build a golf course on an undeveloped piece of property. It happens that the land is in part inhabited by members of a local Indian band who assert that the land in question is native territory. Their land claim is not supported by treaty or by clear title. Nevertheless, various band members speak of their profound attachment to the land, its spiritual significance, and their close relationship to it since time immemorial. Members of the band occupy the land in question and block access to land developers and work crews. The municipality petitions the Court on more than one occasion for injunctions ordering band members to leave the land and cease obstructing the project. The natives in question alternately either ignore the court proceedings or appear without counsel and "testify" by reciting poetry, having children and elders tell stories, and by singing traditional chants or songs. The court, while expressing its willingness to afford them some procedural latitude, concludes that none of the submitted evidence supports the native land claim and hence issues the requested injunctions. These are not respected by the natives. The natives are finally removed through a massive police and military operation.

In the first example we have a litigation, or what Lyotard refers to as a "*litige*," by which he means a dispute where both parties articulate their claims in a language they mutually share with a court or judge whose legitimacy they both recognize. This "*litige*" proceeds through the topics of forensic rhetoric, the decorum of the court is known and respected by both parties, and the judgment imposes closure. The second example illustrates what Lyotard refers to as a "différend," a dispute in which the wrong one party claims to have suffered cannot be expressed in the language of the court and judge, of the judging instance (Lyotard 1988, ix). The natives and the municipality put forth radically incommensurable claims: the municipality is making a property claim, a claim that the court is competent to judge; the natives do not recognize the concept of "property," seeing themselves as belonging to the land rather than the opposite, and hence have nothing to say that is relevant to the court; the natives do not recognize the authority of the court nor do they adopt its rhetorical and procedural conventions, as such they do not seek to sway the judge in a language that can be understood within the legal genre; finally, in no way could it be said that they submit themselves to judgment. As such, the *agon* before judges that constitutes rhetoric as a form of discourse is reduced to a monologic address by the municipality occasionally disturbed by native "noise," by unintelligible speech that refuses to submit to its addressee. In other words, we scarcely have rhetoric at all.

The existence of *différend* means that justice is always lacking, for only as a *différend* becomes a *litige* can the claim of a wrong be judged. But this does not mean that a simple task of translation into the language of litigation can render justice a possibility. It is not simply a matter of the natives in our second tale learning to speak in the terms of the court of our first little story, for the rhetorical language game of litigation, of the *litige*, is not a neutral universal medium for resolving disputes. Rather, like all discursive genres, it brings to presence certain human powers and capacities while relegating others to the margins. How best then can justice be attained? And what *ethos* should underpin rhetorical practice? The answer to these questions, which are central to Lyotard's investigations, will require that we begin by more closely examining the *ethos* of the rhetoric of *litige* as modelled in our first tale.

The Rhetoric of *Litige*

The *"litige"* or "litigation" is a form of disagreement that is amenable to resolution through rhetoric as it is conceived in Aristotle and likeminded classical theorists. "Litigation" suggests legal disputes, and the genre of rhetoric termed "forensic." Technically, forensic rhetoric is concerned with questions of justice with regards to events that have happened. Forensic rhetoric is distinguished from deliberative rhetoric, which is found in the legislature and directed toward determining the expediency of measures to realize a future goal. Beyond a strict interpretation of this technical distinction however, even deliberative rhetoric as classically conceived has in part a forensic character. It takes the form of "litige," because the instances and modalities of conflict and judgment are not disputed, and the places, audiences, and ends of rhetoric are given in advance.

The forensic aspects of the rhetoric of *litige*, even with regard to deliberative questions, can be attributed to the *republican* roots of rhetorical theory, in that it presupposes the existence of a political community and institutions based in public speech. Republics are political societies founded on the public speech of citizens, or as Nietzsche put it, "it is an essentially *republican* art" (Nietzsche 1989, 3). The actual rhetorical practices of advocates in empirical republics, such as the United States or France, do not necessarily instantiate republican rhetoric. Rather, republicanism calls for a language game of dispute resolution based in the idea of society as a community or *polis* of responsible citizens. To the degree that both civil society and the state conform to this idea (and they often do) public speech will be republican. But, republicanism remains a project. Societies founded on the republican principle continue to command their members: "Be citizens."

While republicanism in theory opens toward universality, since speech is a fundamental human capacity, empirical republics are particular, situated, and historically bounded. They are founded through narrative constitutive rhetorics that tell the story of "the people" as it/they proclaim and realize its/their own sovereignty (Charland 1987). In Lyotard's terms, we can understand republics to be established through a metanarrative, the pragmatics of which constitute the citizen as its author, its protagonist, and its recipient. That is to say, the story of the republic constitutes citizens as tellers of the tale, as agents within its diagesis, and as its audience—government would be from the people, by the people, and of the people. Furthermore, the metanarrative of the republic not only tells its addressees the proper meaning of citizenship even as it constitutes them as citizens, but also constitutes the places, occasions, speakers, and audiences or judges of public speech. Finally, this speech would be underwritten by a sentiment of *philia*, of civic friendship, arising from the common substance of citizenship itself (Jasinski 1993, 468). This *philia* guarantees the authority of rhetoric's judges, who are ultimately the citizens themselves even as it banishes the possibility of the *différend*.

Rhetoric is a form of discourse appropriate to contingent questions. As such, it is always confronted with the prospect of incommensurability, for contingencies are manifest in the possibility of rendering controversies in incommensurable terms, which renders judgment irreducible to the unreflective application of a categorical rule. The language game of republican rhetoric domesticates incommensurability by submitting it to a judging instance that is given in advance. Furthermore, the shared substance of all parties in the republican rhetorical *agon* constitutes a common interest that can stand as alibi if not actual horizon for any judgment rendered. More specifically, republican rhetoric, as a form of Aristotelian rhetoric, is directed toward judgment of a contingent case. Rhetoric is the "midwife" of judgment: competing arguments are performed before a judge. These arguments might render the case in incommensurable terms; nevertheless, they will recognize the authority of the judge and the terms of the judging instance, or in Lyotard's terms, they participate in the same language game. There will be no incommensurability between the *forms* of speech. Consider for example arguments before an American court which place liberty and equality in conflict. These principles are incommensurable, and yet they are within the court's terms of reference. Furthermore, the judgment rendered by a court, legislature, or the assembled citizenry imposes a commensurability, at least with respect to the contingent instance in question. Just as capitalism imposes exchange-value as the common measure of incommensurable use-values, so the judgments of republican rhetoric establish an effect of communicability between incommensurable domains. At the very least, such judgments are legitimated by the status of the judging instance within the metanarrative of the republic, as in "The Court has ruled" or "The People have spoken." Also, the metanarrative might stand as ground for the discourse of the judgment itself. Thus, for example, the "good" of the republic, (whatever that might mean) can stand as horizon against which a conflict between liberty and equality can be judged.

Republican Prudence and Ethics

The republican concept confers status on rhetoric by reducing it to "litige" and so rendering it quasi-forensic and politically legitimate. Rhetoric would no longer be simply the artificer of persuasion; it would the genre of discourse productive of democratic ethical knowledge (Bitzer 1976; Farrell 1976). After all, the language game of republican rhetoric is open to all who wish to participate, they need only speak publicly and so adopt the mantle of citizen-orator. It is profoundly ethical, for is suffused with the *ethos* of citizenship. It is epistemic, for prudent judgment is based on a knowledge of precedent. It is also expedient, for it refuses to be paralysed by incommensurability. Finally, it is, at least in Lyotard 's terms, "terroristic." Why is that? Because republican rhetoric is a rhetoric that is imagined to be consistent with philosophy, and as such is guided by the will to truth, which is to say the will to silence, rather than the interests of speech.

That is a mouthful! What do you mean? Somewhat like Habermas, Lyotard develops his critique of discourse through the theoretical vocabulary of speech pragmatics. Unlike Habermas, however, Lyotard does not elevate one genre to that of universal norm. Rather, Lyotard is concerned with the particularity of each genre, and considers terroristic any attempt to silence forms of speech. Such a silencing is, however, necessary to republican rhetoric. This is not because republicans tell terroristic stories. According to Lyotard, there is no *différend* between narratives: Thus, the narrative of the founding of the American republic and the narrative of the attachment of Amerindians to the land are on an equal footing *qua* narratives. However, the founding of a republic requires more than a narrative, it requires a metanarrative, a discourse about narratives, that makes of the people's tale a command issued from themselves to themselves in the name of truth. The story of the people is of the form: "once upon a time, on the American continent, colonists who were British subjects fought for independence and formed a republic." The metanarrative states: "This is your story. The revolutionaries acted in your name and you are one of them. You are a citizen of this republic and you shall uphold its laws and constitution." In this imperative form, there is no reciprocity. A counter-tale can only be spoken if it is emasculated, for the metanarrative of the republic also states: "You shall live within the institutions that you have given yourself, and these institutions are just, for they are of the people of which you are one. They shall have power over your property, your freedom, and your very life itself." In other words: "You shall have no other God." With such a command, the republican metanarrative requires that public speakers be inhabited by the *ethos* of citizenship. My point here is not that republican rhetoric cannot manage the *différend*. No particular "language game" can. The term *différend* precisely identifies the gap between language games. Rather, my point is that the possibility of a *différend* cannot even be conceived within the pragmatics of republican rhetoric. This is so because, from the republican perspective, the very moment of public speech instantiates a republican community. Within republicanism, the act of speaking rhetorically entails a recognition of the authority of the judging instance.

Does Lyotard's concern with the *différend* render him a tragic thinker? Are all those who cannot recognize themselves within the rhetorical republic reduced to silence? Must the Amerindians in our second story either accept to be inhabited by the spirit of citizenship or content themselves to bear witness to the *différend* as the tractors roll over them? Lyotard does not think so, for against the piety of republicanism he opposes the wild cynicism of what he terms paganism or godlessness (Lyotard 1989, 123). The godless refuse the authority of metanarratives. Their *ethos* is not that of the citizen; consider that so many Sophists were not native-born Athenians. Furthermore, the pagan judge will not be guided by one idea of the ultimate good. Pagans, after all, know many gods whose commands can well be incommensurable. Pagan rhetoric is a rhetoric of tactics, a rhetoric that proceeds on another's terrain, and a rhetoric that knows the limited authority of each judging instance. Pagan judgment, in a similar manner, knows that no single narrative can warrant each judgment, and thus requires a form of improvisation known as prudence, guided only by the concept of preserving narrative multiplicity.

As Lyotard asserts: "We need politics that is both godless and just. It will not be found in this pious organization [the Greek model of democracy]" (Lyotard 1989, 135). Lyotard favours the impious rhetoric that Plato found scandalous, in which advocates used: "words that were openly intended to deceive, openly duplicitous. They talked in order to produce certain effects, not in order to profess the truth, to uncover an uncovering or to confess their guilt'" (Lyotard 1989, 136). Pagans honoured their gods out of fear and cunning, not out of pious respect. "They came to terms with them by way of counter-plots, offerings, promises, and little marriage contracts that gave rise to complicitous ceremonies. The atmosphere was one of humour and fear" (Lyotard 1989, 136). These pagans, Cynics and Sophists, were not silent but prudent, where prudence, within these terms of reference, "is a matter of seizing opportunities . . . [where] opportunity is the mistress of those who have no masters, the weapons of those who have no arms, and the strength of the weak, amen" (Lyotard 1989, 152). This includes being tactically inconsistent: "Use laws and institutions against the abuses committed by entrepreneurs . . . and use the opposite argument, and the right to be an entrepreneur when it is a matter of checkmating some dangerous state monopoly"(Lyotard 1989, 152). Thus, at times it is prudent to speak the language of the court ("and let the fools believe that you are singing the praises of servitude when you do so" [Lyotard 1989, 153]) while waiting until the *différend* can be heard. At other times, it is best to follow Protagoras when charged with impiety and run away.

Lyotard's neo-Sophistic is directed at challenging the authority of the metanarrative that seeks to install one narrative (and hence one order of power) as true. Against the metanarrative's monologue, he favours the cunning reply: the telling of another story. As example, he cites the defence Corax and Protagoras are said to have suggested to the strong man accused of attacking a weak man. He should argue that precisely because he is the probable suspect, he would not have committed the crime (Lyotard 1985, 78). Such a case follows what Poulakos describes as Sophistic rhetoric's bias toward the possible rather than the probable, and is based upon a maximization and hijacking of the probability principle (Poulakos 1984). Rather than simply taking what is probable as the basis for a contingent judgment, this little tale takes it as the starting point of the case at hand itself. The defence does not deny the probable, but also does not treat it as static. Rather the defence responds to it by treating it as the basis for its own transformation. Knowledge of what is considered probable can render probable acting in previously improbable ways. One can well understand that Aristotle did not respect this line of defence.

Two Not-So-Fictive Stories

Is Lyotard's analysis of value? After all, he too is a philosopher, even if he champions impertinence. Let me retell our two stories, but this time with certain empirical details that make them not quite (or more than) fictive.

1. The boundary dispute is actually between the States of New York and New Jersey. Both states lay claim to that portion of Ellis Island that was created through the depositing of landfill in the Hudson River. The original island, consisting of three acres, was recognized to be within New York in an 1834 treaty (Barron 17 May 1994, B4). Subsequent to that treaty, the island was expanded by 23 acres. The State of New Jersey claims that since the treaty stated that the river bottom was within its boundary, so should be any land raised upon it. The island itself is federal property and administered by the National Parks Service. Ellis Island is historically significant after all, being the entry point of a large number of immigrants to the United States. Major buildings of historical interest are on the original portion of the island and as such would remain in New York. At stake are certain tax revenues, the possibility of constructing a bridge to the island from New Jersey, which would compete with the New York ferry, and potential revenues from future development. Also at stake, as noted in the *New York Times*, are "bragging rights" (MacFarquar 11 July 1996, B8).

The Constitution of the United States specifies that boundary disputes between states are to be resolved by the Supreme Court. In such cases, the Court serves as a trial rather than appellate court, and rules on substantive rather than only procedural issues. The Court usually proceeds by appointing a special master who hears briefs from the contending parties and then recommends a ruling. In nearly all cases, the court follows the master's recommendation (MacFarquar April 2 1997, A1).

On 17 May 1994, the Supreme Court granted New Jersey leave to proceed with a lawsuit against New York for jurisdiction over the island, in spite of reservations by the Clinton administration, which considered the matter frivolous (MacFarquar July 11 1996, B8). Special master and law professor Paul Verkuil began hearing the case in April 1996. Over against the piety suggested by Lyotard's model of republican rhetoric as litige, this case seemed to promote a cynical spirit. Verkuil convened initial hearings on the Island in what the *New York Times* described as a "glorified storage closet" (MacFarquar 12 April 1996). The trial portion was heard in the Supreme Court building in June of that year, where to again quote a less than pious *New York Times* "bile oozed across the lectern" as parties presented opening arguments (MacFarquar 11 July 1996). *Philia* did not seem to characterize the relation between the parties, nor were arguments restricted to interpretations of precedent and legal documents. New York entered poetry by Walt Whitman into the record, as well as postcards, interviews with immigrants, and photographs of immigrants on the island looking toward New York. Assistant Attorney General for New York, Judith T. Kramer, argued that "not a single immigrant stated that they thought they were coming to New Jersey"(MacFarquar April 12 1996, B1).

The special master dismissed such arguments by New York and recommended dividing the island in a manner consistent with New Jersey's claim. While New Jersey Governor Christine Todd Whitman voiced a republican spirit as she observed: "This is a recognition of New Jersey's place in history," New York mayor Rudolph W. Guiliani was less generous: "It must have been a fix"(MacFarquar April 2 1997, A1). The Supreme Court has not as of this writing ratified Verkuil's ruling, but regardless of the final outcome, the matter will be settled. While republican rhetoric is messier than theory would have it, the authority of the court and its power impose closure even when the rhetoric before or around it is less than pious or decorous.

2. There are two Mohawk communities in the vicinity of the city of Montreal, in Canada's Province of Quebec. The members of Kanehsatake, slightly northwest of Montreal Island, claim as their own a wooded area known as "The Pines" as well as an adjacent ancient burial ground. They have been attempting for more than 200 years to have their claim to this area recognized. Neither the Crown during the colonial period nor the courts subsequently has upheld their legal arguments (Alfred 1995, 153–156). In 1961 the municipality of Oka, which adjoins this Mohawk community, constructed a nine-hole golf course on a portion of the claimed lands. In 1989, the municipality indicated its intention to expand the golf course (Goodleaf 1995, 54). The ministry of the environment of the Province of Quebec requested that the project be delayed so that a proper impact study be undertaken (Lamarche 1990, 54). After the municipality voted in March 1990 to move ahead with the project, Mohawks demonstrated in protest and barricaded an access road (Lamarche 1990, 55). Shortly thereafter, the Government of Canada, while not recognizing any Mohawk legal right, undertook negotiations to purchase the bulk of the remaining lands in question in order to establish a Mohawk reserve. Negotiations between Mohawks and federal authorities did not get very far. There was a *différend*. Federal negotiators were only mandated to discuss the halt of the golf course project and the creation of a reserve. Mohawk negotiators sought more. They claimed the status of a sovereign

nation and demanded not only a global settlement of territorial claims, but also a recognition of their sovereignty, which entailed negotiation on a nation-to-nation basis (Goodleaf 1995, 54).

Our story then gets rather complicated. There are divisions among the Mohawks. Some claim that the legitimate authority is the "Longhouse," the traditional form of government. Others claim it is the band council, which is constituted and recognized by the federal Indian Act. There are also divisions between the levels of government. The municipality wants its golf course, the provincial government does not want to see its prerogatives compromised, nor does it wish to appear weak to its electorate in the face of either native claims or federal authority, while the federal government wishes to appear conciliatory and enlightened even as it is in no way prepared to yield on the question of the sovereignty. Also, each level of government will at times prefer to pass the buck and blame the other rather than look bad. Seizing the initiative, the municipality sought and obtained an injunction in Quebec Superior Court ordering the removal of the barricades. The people at the barricades dismissed the injunction as illegitimate (Goodleaf 1995, 55). The mayor of Oka then requested that the *Sureté du Québec* (the provincial police force) clear the road. On July 11 1990, more than 100 *Sureté* officers attempted to charge and remove the barricades. Shots were fired. One officer lay dead. The *Sureté* retreated and subsequently sealed off the area (Lamarche 1990, 70; Goodleaf 1995, 57).

The Mohawks responded boldly, in Lyotard's terms they knew how to "seize opportunities." Members of the second Mohawk community of Kahnawake, to the south of Montreal Island, used trucks to block the Mercier bridge, a major commuter entry point to Montreal (Goodleaf 1995, 57). Having closed the bridge, they taped together highway flares and affixed them visibly to the bridge in a manner suggesting dynamite, especially when viewed from a distance (Cross and Sévigny 1994, 90) National native chiefs warned that an attack on the Mohawks could result in retaliation upon power lines, railways and highways (Goodleaf 1995, 59). The vulnerability of Canada's infrastructure, especially its northern hydroelectric facilities, became apparent. Depending upon one's commitments and point of view, the meaning of this bold stroke can vary: they were helping defend their brothers and sisters in the Pines from a paramilitary assault, they were responding militarily to Canadian aggression, they were holding commuters to Montreal hostage, they are terrorists. Beyond such interpretive pieties, one thing is clear, the situation here does not follow the republican model. Mohawks and government agencies met each other in the *pagus*, in the wild and dangerous area outside the *polis* and its ordered procedures and maxims (Lyotard 1985, 38–43). *Différends* reign. There are no rules. The Mohawks are Lyotard's "pagans." They are objectively weaker, and must rely on their wits. They did not deny rumours that many of their number are Vietnam veterans skilled in weapons and guerilla warfare, and they worked hard at making their numbers and firepower appear more daunting than they were (Cross and Sévigny 1994, 89). Images of masked members of the Mohawk Warrior Society, wearing fatigues and brandishing AK-47s appeared on the nightly news. Accusations and counter-accusations ensued. Deadlines multiplied. The Mohawks demanded that basic necessities be permitted to enter the two communities, that clan mothers, chiefs, spiritual advisors and attorneys be permitted to cross the barricades, and that international observers be sent. Government officials appointed a highly respected jurist, Judge Allan Gold, to mediate the conflict. Archbishop Desmond Tutu, visiting Toronto from South Africa, offered to lend assistance. The government agreed to some international observers and an initial negotiation protocol was signed on television by government ministers and masked Warriors (Lamarche 1990, 119). The first Mohawk negotiating team had 54 members, which seemed perfectly reasonable to them and impossible to government representatives (Lamarche 1990, 123). Meanwhile, residents of Chateauguay, the bedroom community on the south side of the blocked bridge became restless. Mohawk families fleeing the conflict were stoned by an angry mob as *Sureté* and RCMP officers stood by (Lamarche 1990, 140). The Quebec nationalist branch of the Ku Klux Klan set up shop (Goodleaf 1995, 66).

The "strength of the weak" is limited however. Sureté officers were replaced by members of the Canadian Armed Forces. Government officials continued alternately to speak of their desire for a peaceful resolution to the crisis and their duty to maintain law and order. Members of the Armed Forces took up positions and secured the perimeter of Kanehsatake (Goodleaf 1995, 88). Their arrival was choreographed and televised. A lieutenant-colonel approached the barricades, shook hands with a masked Warrior, and discussed technical details. The nearby mob was outraged (Lamarche 1990, 122). The military strategy became clear. It did not want to provoke a bloodbath. Neither did the Mohawks behind the barricades. The military would wait, and slowly reduce the perimeter. Both sides engaged in a war of nerves. Mohawks taunted soldiers; military helicopters with floodlights buzzed the pines at night (Lamarche 1990, 200). The Mohawks would not win this war. The number of Mohawks behind the lines slowly decreased. The dynamics of Iroquois and Mohawk internal politics ultimately resulted in negotiations between government representatives and "moderate" leaders, associated with the government-recognized band council rather than the Longhouse or Warrior Society (Lamarche 1990, 148–149). On August 27, the Quebec government announced that it was breaking off negotiations and that the matter was in the hands of the military (Goodleaf 1995, 90). Meanwhile, the

Canadian Press reported that Cessnas were heard or seen leaving Kahnawake (Lamarche 1990, 151). Rumour had it that weapons and Warriors, some of whom were under indictment in other jurisdictions, followed Protagoras' example and were no longer to be found. The military admitted seeing planes, but claimed that air traffic was not under their authority (Lamarche 152). The existence of planes was later denied by one of the Warriors, claiming it was a government alibi. How could the police and military admit to being fooled by a mere handful of tricksters? Better to say that the "terrorists" discreetly escaped (Cross and Sévigny 1994, 162).

The summer vacation period was coming to an end. Commuter traffic would increase. Mohawk moderates (or are they dupes?) and military negotiators agreed to reopen the bridge (Goodleaf 1995, 93). Plastic explosives, allegedly placed on the bridge four weeks earlier (Hornung 1991, 233), were removed. The barricades came down. After military inspection, commuter traffic resumed. Without the bridge, the remaining Mohawks at Kanehsatake lost their bargaining chip. Slowly the perimeter closed around the treatment centre which had housed the Mohawks involved in this affair, as well as a few journalists behind the lines. Bonfires destroyed what could become evidence (Cross and Sévigny 1994, 102). On the 78th day since the death of the SQ officer, the fifty or so men, women, and children inside the treatment centre agreed to surrender (Hornung 1991, 277). But they did not go quietly. As they left the building, they did not head for the waiting military buses, which would have brought them to the base at Farnham to then be turned over to the police. They tried to head home (Goodleaf 1995, 108). There were skirmishes. They were dragged or forced onto the buses (Hornung 1991, 277).

Criminal charges were laid against 71 Mohawks and their supporters. Thirty pled guilty or were convicted of minor charges in non-jury trials. Two Warriors who had developed popular notoriety, Ronald Cross, a.k.a. Lasagna and Gordon Lazore, a.k.a. Noriega, were tried and convicted on a variety of serious offenses, including weapons charges, and sentenced to 52 and 23 months respectively. The thirty-nine others, arrested at the final conflict at the Treatment Centre, were tried before jury. The judge ordered six acquitted for lack of evidence. Those remaining were found not guilty on all counts even though they admitted civil disobedience (Laurent 4 July 1992a , A1; 4 July 1992b, A5). A golf course will not be built. Federal authorities have yet however to transfer purchased lands to the tribe, maintaining that there exists no properly chartered or incorporated body to transfer title to, because of a lack of a mutually acceptable legal or political framework for its tenure.

What can we conclude from these stories? First, that the philosophical imagination cannot match the wildness of the everyday. Second, that there is value in Lyotard's categories. We can distinguish between pious republicanism and a Sophistic spirit, but we must realize that neither stand freely as an expression of some political idea. Their instantiation requires more than words, but also will and power. New York officials might be cynical, but any engagement with New Jersey will remain within well defined bounds. What contained our Mohawks was not a respect for the laws, but barricades and barbed wire. Their recognition of any judging instance remained tactical. Their lack of piety offered a certain freedom, but their capacity to disrupt those before them required more than clever arguments. They also needed a bridge as hostage and a divided or ambivalent opponent. (It is worthwhile to note that Canada is not a republic.) Third, we should observe that when *litige* can no longer contain a *différend*, the spirit that animates sophistic ruses is not all that playful. Our Mohawks were not like the avant-garde artists that Lyotard also champions. They were not impious or playful about their own sense of self and nation. They were desperate and willing to risk a great deal. Some will be imprisoned. They gained little. As Lyotard observes, the best that pagans usually can hope for are small victories and the opportunity to engage in new battles (Lyotard 1989, 152).

Justice

It is worthwhile to recall that in all of our little stories in this essay justice is at stake. In all of this, can justice be found? The pragmatics of the rhetoric of "litige," whether in the courtroom or the legislature, collapses "justice" onto the decision of the judging instance. *Litige* imposes an *ethos* and horizon upon republican rhetoric's judges. It commands: "You shall judge as a representative of the republic and its People. You shall realize their good and dispense their justice." The good and the just exist already as ideas within the narrative of the republic, and the task of the judge becomes that of mapping contingencies onto them. Judges thus render justice by definition, just as legislatures, in the republican vision, represent the will of the people, which is sovereign and therefore right. As a consequence, republican rhetoric refuses to acknowledge the possibility of the *différend*.

In pagan cases, justice is not so simple. What occurs when there is a *différend*? Are calls for "justice" only a ruse? Are we left with nothing but power? Not for Lyotard. He offers a postmodern philosophy of justice that would be compatible with sophistry against the piety of republicanism. Following upon his disagreement with Aristotle regarding the validity of sophistic lines of defence, Lyotard proposes a model of prudent judgment that is a variation of the one Aristotle develops in the *Rhetoric* and the *Nichomachean Ethics*. Lyotard suggests that the Aristotelian model of judgement, based in prudence or *phronesis*, is substantially the same as that put forward by the Sophists (Lyotard 1985, 28). That is to say, the Aristotelian judge is pagan, because he does not simply apply a rule, but listens to the case at hand, considers the various rules that could be applied, and then exercises his faculty of judgment. As such, while we might say that judging is a form of intelligence, it cannot be reduced to an argument based in necessity. Unlike the Sophists, however, Aristotle's prudence would always be exercised with respect to what is (Lyotard 1985, 79). In simple terms, Aristotle's judge is a conservative. More precisely, he does not take into account the effects of judgment itself. The Aristotelian judge would not accept the defence Corax offers to the strong man accused of beating the weakling. He would reject arguments that reverse probability, as when the strong man claims he acted against probability and did not attack the weakling, precisely because he was aware that he would have become the probable suspect (Lyotard 1985, 79). Lyotard's neo-Sophistic judge, on the other hand considers possible that an anticipation of tomorrow's judgment can change what is probable today. Such judgment, which is also Lyotard's postmodern judgment, would be based in the future perfect or *futur antérieur*—in the "it will have been." By judging the strong man innocent, the judge would give rise to a new sense of the probable that would vindicate the defendant and also give rise to a new little story about the way bigger men should and do act. Such neo-Sophistic judgment would be innovative, putting probabilities and forms of life into circulation.

Kantian Paganism

Pagan rhetoric is, as I have suggested above, characterized by a certain *ethos*. The pagan is impious, has a sense of humour, and yet has a certain humility. This, because pagan rhetoric refuses to recognize the authority of metanarratives and delights in paradox, and also knows that it is necessary to listen in order to reply. Typical pagans would be such pre-Socratic Sophists as Gorgias and Cynics as Diogenes (Lyotard 1993, 68–71). But Lyotard's pagan judgment is not fully pre-Socratic, but remains post-Kantian. Lyotard develops the model of the pagan rhetor as irreverent, and as such capable of innovation. By refusing to acknowledge the authority of metanarratives that would regulate the forms and instances of speech, pagan rhetors can seek to establish new precedents or indeed constitute new instances of judgment. Correspondingly, the pagan judge is willing to entertain, and indeed be entertained by, pagan rhetoric. Thus, pagan judges would be *respectful* of the irreverence of pagan oratory. The pagan judge is not inhabited by the *ethos* of citizenship; the pagan court is not republican. Furthermore, pagan judgment is not guided by some metanarrative based in a truth claim. Nevertheless, the pagan judge is not, like the pagan orator, strategically irreverent. Rather, the pagan judge is true to the concept of justice and submits to the language game of judgment itself. The pagan judge is pious about justice.

Lyotard follows Kant's categorical distinctions between the true, the just, and the beautiful. As such, his position is not pre-Socratic. Science, ethics, and aesthetics are distinct domains, distinct language games, and the conflation of one with the other is terroristic (Lyotard 1985, 100). Furthermore, aligning himself with the Kant of the *Third Critique*, he asserts that there is an analogy between aesthetic judgment and judgment regarding what is just. Each proceeds without foundation (Lyotard 1985, 75–77). The judge judges. That's all. Furthermore, after the fact, judges are judged, and we call prudent or virtuous those whom we consider to have best realised justice. The only principle guiding pagan forensic judgment is the principle immanent to judgment itself: that of preserving the autonomy between language games (Lyotard 1985, 100).

Conclusions

Lyotard's concern for the *différend* stands as a severe critique of attempts to secure rhetoric's status by granting it an ethical epistemic function. Note, for example, that Bitzer imposes a competency test upon those who would want to constitute "public knowledge," while Farrell develops his conception of "social knowledge" through the idea of an *attributed* consensus, which is a consensus attributed by some upon others in the name of all (Bitzer 1976; Farrell 1976). The virile republican is supposed to be animated by a sense of fraternity for his fellows, but at least from within Lyotard's philosophy and experience of Republican France, such fellowship is always underwritten by an initial violence. Furthermore, this violence is always lurking, since at each utterance there is a potential for a *différend*.

Two Maxims

For the Polis

Let us return again to our stories regarding jurisdictional disputes between states, whether fictive or not. Over against our critique of *litige*, we must recognize that the constitution of the judicial power in The Constitution of the United States has served the republic well. Our appreciation for impiety might well have been strained if New Jersey had pressed its claim by blockading Ellis Island and threatening to sink the ferry. For those willing to accept its initial terms, a republic does provide a means of sharing a world with those otherwise unlike oneself. But there is always the risk of piety: either through an excess of faith in one story that leads to the discounting of all others, or through the bad faith of modern cynicism, in which the display of republican spirit is only a ruse. In this latter case, citizenship becomes only a mark of holding property, and allegiance is only to oneself. This cynicism is not pagan but falsely pious, lacking an art of listening, a sense of humour, and Diogenes's wild spirit.

For the Pagus

Let us return again to our Amerindian stories, whether fictive or not. Lyotard's reflections upon paganism commend certain rhetorical practices: Without being inhabited by the *ethos* of citizenship, enact it provisionally and tactically. Learn the language of the court (or find legal counsel) in order to best exploit its procedures. Ask for stays, delays, and procedural rulings. Appeal to natural law against written law and vice versa. Multiply the grounds for appeal. At the same time, continue to agitate outside of the court. Do not present contingencies as resolvable through the probable; make use of paradoxes and ironies to create hypothetical precedents that teleologically could guide judgement. Finally, experiment: develop new language games that could constitute new audiences and new instances for judgment. To this, our Mohawks might in part approve, but also counter: "We are Mohawks, not Cynics in league with Diogenes. We also have our truth and way, and if we lose it, our battle has no purpose."

References

Alfred, Gerald R. 1995. *Heeding the Voices of our Ancestors: Kahnawake Mohawk Politics and the Rise of Native Nationalism.* Toronto: Oxford University Press.

Barron, James. 17 May 1994. "Ellis Island, Gateway to the State that Starts with 'New.'" *New York Times*, late edition, final, B4.

Bitzer, Lloyd. 1978. "Rhetoric and Public Knowledge." In *Rhetoric, Philosophy, and Literature: An Exploration*, ed. Don M. Burks, 67–93. West Lafayette, Ind.: Purdue University Press.

Charland, Maurice. 1987. "Constitutive Rhetoric: The Case of the *Peuple Québécois*" *Quarterly Journal of Speech* 73: 133–150.

Cross, Roland and Hélène Sévigny. 1994. *Lasagna: The Man Behind the Mask.* Vancouver: Talon Books.

Farrell, Thomas B. 1976 "Knowledge, Consensus, and Rhetorical Theory." *Quarterly Journal of Speech* 62: 1–14.

Goodleaf, Donna. 1995. *Entering the War Zone: A Mohawk Perspective on Resisting Invasions.* Penticton, British Columbia: Theytus Books.

Greenhouse, Linda. 17 May 1994. "Supreme Court Will Resolve Ellis Island Dispute." *New York Times*, late edition, final, B1.

Hornung, Rick. 1991. *One Nation Under the Gun*. Toronto: Stoddart.

Jasinski, James. 1993. "(Re)constituting Community through Narrative Argument: *Eros* and *Philia* in the Big Chill." *Quarterly Journal of Speech* 79: 467–486.

Lamarche, Jacques. 1990. *L'été des Mohawks: Bilan des 78 jours*. Montreal: Stanké.

Laurent, René. 4 July 1992a. "Jury Acquits all Defendants in Oka Trial[.] Court no Place to Settle Land Issues: Accused." *Montreal Gazette*, final, A1, A5.

Laurent, René. 4 July 1992b. "For Mohawks, Plea Bargaining Was Out: They Wanted to Explain their Actions." *Montreal Gazette*, final, A5.

Lyotard, Jean-François and Jean-Loup Thébaud. 1985. *Just Gaming*. Minneapolis: University of Minnesota Press.

Lyotard, Jean-François. 1988. *The Differend: Phrases in Dispute*. Minneapolis: University of Minnesota Press.

Lyotard, Jean-François. 1989. *The Lyotard Reader*. Cambridge, Mass.: Basil Blackwell.

Lyotard, Jean-François. 1993. *Toward the Postmodern*. Atlantic Gardens, N. J.: Humanities Press International.

MacFarquar, Neil. 12 April 1996. "Court Hears 2 States Claim a Piece of History: The Winner of a Battle over who Owns Ellis Island Gets to Tax Tourists." *New York Times*, late edition, final, B1.

MacFarquar, Neil. 11 July 1996. "Fight over Ellis Island Puts History on Trial." *New York Times*, late edition, final, B8.

MacFarquar, Neil. 2 April 1997. "Solomonic Ruling Would Divide Ellis Island." *New York Times*, late edition, final, A1.

Nietzsche, Friedrich. 1989. *Friedrich Nietzsche on Rhetoric and Language*. Eds. and trans. Sander L. Gilman, Carole Blair, David J. Parent. New York: Oxford University Press.

Poulakos, John. 1984. "Rhetoric, the Sophists, and the Possible." *Communication Monographs* 51: 213–226.

Afterword

*Justifying, Positioning, Persuading
in the Intermediate World*

Robert Hariman

You are late getting to the airport. Halfway across the parking lot, you remember that you have left your raincoat in your car. Leaving your bag, you hurry back to retrieve the coat, then pick up the bag and rush to the ticket counter. There you wait impatiently in a line of people of diverse ethnic backgrounds, one of whom is talking on a cellular phone in a language you do not recognize. As you wait, you notice a security guard standing in front of one of the advertising posters that line the walls: he is talking quietly into a small microphone connected to the collar of his uniform. When you get to the counter you are required to show a picture ID card and you are asked whether you have left any baggage unattended. The plane is scheduled to leave in 10 minutes. You lie, get your boarding pass, run to the gate, and just make the plane. As it taxis into position for takeoff, you notice that most of the passengers appear to be business executives, and that some of them are beginning to unpack their laptop computers. You begin to wonder if you have done the right thing.

There is no explosion, of course, not this time. . . . You end up back in your office at the university where you teach. The school recently has experienced a vicious incident of gay-bashing. The attackers are known to be residents of a particular floor of the senior dorm, but no individuals are charged. A number of university officials denounce the act, but nothing is done to prosecute any individual or group, or to provide additional security that might reduce the likelihood of continued violence. The student body president announces that she will speak before the faculty senate to call for a direct and comprehensive response to the incident. Prior to the speech, graffiti appears on campus labeling her gay, and she is threatened by telephone with rape. Now she is sitting in your office, asking for your advice. She is afraid. What do you tell her?

You do your best, of course, and she is magnificent, and nothing awful happens, not this time. . . . You go home, do dinner and everything else that has to be done around the edges of the workday, and finally you are able to sit down with the morning paper. Until the phone rings: It is your sister, who during the past year has become caught up in an unusual spiritual movement. She credits the movement with saving her from periodic depression and persistent feelings of worthlessness, and it appears that she is truly happy. At the same time, her constant talking about the movement is tiring at best, her work is deteriorating, and she is espousing political opinions that are used by others connected with the movement to rationalize persecution and violence. You think that her new beliefs are nonsense, that she is being manipulated, and that she is supporting evil. You also recall how she stood by you during a very difficult time in your life, and you don't want her to lose all contact with those outside the movement, and you realize that she now is prone to all-or-nothing decisions. She already has broken off contact with her friends and the rest of the family. To your surprise, she wants to know what you think of what she is doing. What do you say?

*   *   *

These scenarios depict a few of the many predicaments facing ordinary adults trying to do the right thing. They also feature some of the many forms and elements of judgment. In the first case, you have to make a snap judgment. That judgment involves an assessment of probabilities: e.g., the odds that someone put a bomb in your bag are very, very low. You could ask yourself, "would the others on the plane each do as I do?" and it's fair to conclude that most of them would do so. But what if you ask, "Would they, or I, wish to have someone else make that judgment for me, without my knowledge of the unexpected risk?" Furthermore, the story features the inevitable dissonance, lack of identification, or alienation between the individual person and the impersonal law. We adapt in part by learning the rules for breaking the rules; otherwise, regulated life would be tyrannical or impossible. But each time we willingly violate the law we put our basic social contract or sense of moral community at risk. Seemingly minor actions become dangerous to all.

The second scenario includes probability assessments, but they are minor considerations against the problems of determining what each person's role requires of them in that situation. And there is more, for the judgment depends on the quality of deliberation (itself a difficult task at the moment), the action requires courage (a classical virtue, but it doesn't help to say so), and the advice involves a queasy imbalance between influence and personal risk (*your* influence, *her* risk). In addition, unless you really do live in only in the moment, you now have to face up to your hypocrisy. Where earlier the law was something to be set aside, now it is the means for holding others to their obligations. We might say that is due to the nature of the law, but it also is the case the while petty hypocrisies are necessary for living within authoritarian rule, they also are injurious to the basic assumptions of daily life in an open society.

The third scenario may seem the more far-fetched, although it foregrounds some of the most persistent elements of contemporary judgment: cultural pluralism, moral relativism, the tension between the liberal individual and the bonds of family life, and the deep complications of personal relationships. If not worried about cults, one easily can substitute any one of the many complications arising from open housing, intermarriage, religious revivals, economic change, and other manifestations of the social forces defining, confounding, and fragmenting contemporary life. In addition, the scenario suggests that the standards and procedures of public judgment may be ill suited to private affairs, and that judgments about what is true or good or right can become complicated by judgments about how to speak.

These stories, like all our stories, have other implications that allow interpreters to use them for varied ends. We could point out, for example, how each can highlight the fine line between reasoned judgment and rationalization. Or we could ask how each invites or challenges the application of a particular social theory. To do double duty, we might ask what it would mean to justify that lie at the airline counter with the statement, "My lie was an act of resistance to panopticonic power." That technology of power certainly was in place in the airport; indeed, airports are a central means for naturalizing panopticonic rule, from the benign "control tower" visible on the drive in to the comprehensive mix of architectural design, logistical engineering, police procedures, and communication practices that make up the comprehensive but muted (and leaky) surveillance enveloping all public activity in that environment. But the statement seems facile to me, and thus no different from the humanism an earlier generation could have called upon to define the lie as "an act affirming the individual against faceless bureaucracy." In either case, a general theory of society has been applied to account for the situational constraints on one's freedom of action, but it has been used to dodge the question of how one is obligated to strangers caught within the possible consequences of one's actions. By fitting one's rationale to a comprehensive social theory or political struggle, you have minimized your responsibility to those incidentally involved in the immediate situation. But to always give equal weight to all those around you would preclude the possibility of snap judgments; I doubt we could function without them. And surely no social philosophy should be discredited simply because it can be used as a rationalization.

Perhaps at this point I ought to put my cards on the table. The scenarios I've provided illustrate predicaments: that is, moments of decision that are troubling because deeply complicated. They depict situations that confront us before we can speak, and that make us think twice about words we do speak, and that continue to stand apart from whatever speech we use to make our way through them. My sense of things is that questions of judgment arise primarily in respect to this class of events. Conversely, most of the time judgments are unproblematic, routine. We are able to move along familiar paths, applying clear norms to typical practices, comfortable that moral life is largely a matter of controlling impulses to do what you know you ought not do. Just do what you were taught in kindergarten, we are told, and everyone will be better off. Since that instruction included the larger awareness that rules should not be applied to others without compassion, we have a moral code that is both clear and flexible. Most of the time.

Judgment comes to the fore when there is a different order of conflict between situation and code, or between codes equally active in the situation. (Jean-François Lyotard's (1988) distinction between *litige* and *différend* captures this shift from the routine to the problematic, as do the many discussions of incommensurability and multiculturalism in American political thought.) In a predicament, reasons quickly begin to sound like rationalizations. Obligation changes from an instruction—"you need to write your aunt a thank you note"—to something threatening, suspended over you, incapable of being met in full—"you need to decide what to do, but don't expect to make anyone happy." Those who would equip us to handle such predicaments use a different language from the ordinary vocabulary of social reciprocity. "Obligation happens," we are told by a hermeneutical philosopher (Caputo 1993)—accept the radical facticity and the essential immediacy of the demands placed upon you. Or we must not simply act, but participate in a national act of "atonement," we are told by public figures of three different faiths—accept the full nature of your failure, your fallibility, your inability to resolve a tragic conflict on your own terms and with your own resources. The predicament simultaneously reveals the limitations of our moral discourse and points toward a more authentic or powerful language. This intimation could be a second trap: a more inviting deferral, a more fundamental predicament.

So we come to the challenge of using contemporary social theory as the language that can offer a way out of the predicaments of judgment in a late modern world. Our point of departure is the linguistic turn and the corresponding assumption that social theory, like judgment itself, cannot be grounded in some universal moral or epistemological principle. Any judgment is intelligible within some language games and confounded by

others, while its rectitude or power to command depends on who is saying what to whom, and all these media or modes or manners are potentially valid forms of communication. This break with prior assumptions
of Western philosophy is not the greatest divide at the moment, however.
More immediate is the distinction between modernists such as Habermas, who still want a best approximation of the ideal of universal validity, and those post-structuralists of several stripes who have cut themselves loose from that ideal to explore other forms of life.

The argument I want to offer is that each of these approaches reflects a
basic incapacity in the language of social theory, and, therefore, that each
needs to supplement its work in a particular way. The basic problem of
the modernist approach is that while constructing a structure of judgment, it has failed to account adequately for the inevitable differences between the general rule and the particular case. Recourse to such "historico-hermeneutical" models as the law, literature, or tradition are
attempts to overcome this problem. The basic problem of the post-structuralist approach is that while freeing the individual from the dictate of
the social system, it has disabled the most basic, pragmatic conception of
individual accountability. Attempts to valorize alternative forms of collective identify or such phenomena as social performance are attempts to
overcome this problem. The common denominator of both perspectives
is that each has difficulty identifying and accepting the communal resources the individual needs to act in that dangerous free space between
docility and self-destruction. Therefore, the language of contemporary
social theory will not be adequate to the task of helping us make the right
judgments to resolve our predicaments unless it draws on additional resources to overcome its own deficiencies. I want to suggest that this
might be done by returning to those models of judgment that are present
in public discourse, particularly in premodern texts. To provide one example of how this might be done, we can turn to the Book of Esther.

The story of Esther may be as close as the Bible gets to prime time
drama. God is not mentioned, while there is sex, violence, intrigue, and
betrayal aplenty. The Persian king announces a competition: all the beautiful young women in the land are to be gathered into his harem, so that
each may spend a night with him until he selects one of them to become
his new queen. Esther, a Jew, goes to the harem, while her uncle Mordecai (who has raised her) becomes a daily presence outside the court in order to gather intelligence about how she is doing. Esther is doing quite
well, thank you: she becomes the favorite of the head eunuch. When it is
time to visit the king, each girl is allowed to take what she wishes with
her; Esther alone seeks out the advice of the eunuch and does as he says.
Guess who becomes queen? Meanwhile, Mordecai has been busy outside
and has learned of a plot to assassinate the king. He passes the informa-

tion along to Esther, who communicates it to the king to avert the plot. End of part one.

The problems that are about to develop, of course, all stem from the complications of Jewish identity. The story of assimilation becomes a drama of survival. Esther has hidden her identity, but Mordecai does not—in fact, he's downright uppity. When Haman, an Agagite, becomes the king's highest official, Mordecai, a Benjaminite, refuses to bow down because of their ancient tribal enmity (see 1 Sam 15.7–9). Haman retaliates by securing the king's decree for a pogrom against the Jews throughout the empire. On hearing the news, Mordecai casts himself down in sackcloth and ashes outside of the king's gate. On hearing of this, Esther sends a messenger to find out what's wrong. Mordecai sends word to her of the pogrom and charges her to appeal to the king on behalf of her people.

Esther does not exactly rise to the occasion, however. She doesn't do as he asks, and she rationalizes her inaction: She would be killed for going directly to the king, who hasn't even called for her for thirty days. In other words, the procedures of the court are too much for her, and she's really out of the loop anyway. Why should she die just to be ineffective? And so we come to the moment of judgment: will Esther risk her life for her people? If not, on what basis will we fault her? Of additional interest, perhaps, is that the story lacks the foundation for judgment available in the other stories of Israel's struggle. God is not present; there is no assurance of divine guidance, or strength, or justice. Furthermore, Esther is now being asked to change the way of thinking that has been the key to her success. Until now, this story has been a model of political advancement, working the system to your own self-interest, overcoming the vicissitudes of fortune by virtue of your shrewd manipulation of others. The Book of Esther could sit very comfortably on the same shelf as Machiavelli's *Prince*. Indeed, when Mordecai argues with her (again, via messengers), he first appeals to her self-interest: don't think you can escape this decree. But he does hint at providentialism when he also says that she might have been put in the court for the purpose of saving the Jews (although according to the literal terms of the story if she hadn't been there, Mordecai wouldn't have been hanging around the court, etc. . . .) In any case, all these appeals smuggle in a sense of Jewish identity—in the first argument, it is the source of her weakness, and in the second, the source of her strength.

So Esther comes out, right? No, instead she crafts a series of appeals to soften up the king, until she finally gains her objective. The denouement is entirely conventional: the king's high official is killed, Mordecai assumes his place next to the king, the Jews are not only freed of the pogrom but allowed to kill all those who were preparing to kill them. For her part, Esther establishes the holiday of Purim and so proves to have been a Jewish princess after all.

Like any good story, there is more than one lesson to be learned here. I want to suggest that the Book of Esther offers a model of judgment that is appropriate to the problematic of contemporary social theory. This appropriateness stems from several characteristics of the story: First, it positions individual choice between two forms of social control: the state apparatus and the ethnic community. Second, it emphasizes neither radical individuality nor foundational principles, but rather an intermediate realm of competing loyalties. Third, in this realm, self-interest has to be overcome, although not set aside, and identity and obligation have to be willingly accepted, but always in respect to our immediate circumstances. Finally, it is a story about mediated reality, where the flow of information is a constant element in the story and judgment is constituted through a communicative act that has to be made in respect to the opportunities always available for influence and evasion.

My reading of the story actually began as part of a conversation about John Caputo's mantra that "obligation happens."[1] This phrase would seem to apply quite well to Esther: she certainly didn't go to court to risk her life to save the Jews, and she seemed to have no problem hiding her ethnic identity. But Esther's decision to act on behalf of the Jews reveals more than the unexpectedness and facticity and materiality of obligation. Indeed, if one says as Caputo does that the radical principle of obligation is that obligation *is there*, one shifts too much responsibility to the world to reveal its needs. (Likewise, it is one thing to say that one has heard God's call, and quite another to conclude that one has no obligation to God for not having been called.) Esther shows us that obligation is indeed something that happens to us, but that it also is something that has to be taken up. Indeed, the phrase "obligation happens" reproduces a structure of obligation that depends on a radical individuality where obligation is always something happening "out there."

In Esther, one's obligation comes from within, but that is not the end of the problem, as one's subjectivity includes both self interest and collective identity. The choice is further complicated by the fact that self-interest can coincide seamlessly, powerfully, with political domination. This is Esther's dilemma, as Mordecai knows: His first argument is that she will not be protected by her position in the court. As we might say, that is an empirical question—and Esther might have good reason to bet that she would be safe. And couldn't she point out that everything Mordecai has said and done to this point has been done to coordinate self-interest with the political regime—with the notable exception of his imprudent refusal to bow down to the Agagite, which has gotten them and a lot of other people into a world of trouble. It is clear that the state apparatus is set over and against them in principle—they are a minority people, subject to laws not of their own making, always alienated from the forms of power and legitimacy. It also is the case, however, that they still have opportunities for collusion, assimilation, appropriation within the system. The nobility of Esther's decision is that she rejects this easy congruence of self-interest and political domination to forge a new, more demanding sense of identity. She does not put the means of self-advancement aside, however. Indeed, her appeals to the king draw on all her political skills and every advantage of the position she has gained within the court. Her subsequent use of that position to assume a leadership role within the Jewish community still remains different from Mordecai's earlier refusal to play the part of the subservient Jew before the high official. And although she has given up the tradeoff between ethnic identity and power, she has not merely adopted the traditional, parochial identity with all its baggage. Instead, she invents a tradition (the holiday) that celebrates both the assertion of religious identity and secular empowerment through partial assimilation.

Esther's position in the court also tells us something about the method of judgment at work in the story. She has left the village but is not entirely of the court.[2] Esther is always in an intermediate realm, a position highlighted by her constant dependence on intermediaries. She is positioned between Mordecai and the king, her community of origin and the state, tradition and power. Mordecai listens to gather information in the public space outside the palace, while the King speaks within to command those administering the empire, but Esther sends messengers to the outside to learn of her duty, and to reach the king she first has to stand in the anteroom to the king's chamber—the liminal space between that inner space of command and the rest of the world. Moreover, Esther is never alone. She must decide to act but the principle of action is not be found in a singular moment of decision, or in a solitary encounter with Being. She is enmeshed in a network of relationships and relies on advisors, couriers, and the king. Her decision is made among people, amidst competing obligations, in respect to words that can make a difference in the outcome. The one decisive moment in the narrative is when she announces her decision: "I and my maids will also fast as you do. After that, I will go to the king, though it is against the law; and if I perish, I perish" (4.16).[3] This moment actually involves several reversals: she changes her mind by overturning self-interest and then issues orders to Mordecai (who has been calling the shots previously). But these changes still occur within a social setting, and they all involve continuing patterns of trust and obligation. Esther forges judgment out of competing loyalties, and her action depends on continued interaction with the people around her. The law, and the tradition, and her most basic sense of individuality (her impulse to self-preservation) are all horizons of obligation, but the judgment that defines and saves her comes out of her fully situating herself within the place where she actually is living.

Esther and Mordecai are cosmopolitans but not citizens of the world. Their identity is situated but not parochial, and their means for thought, judgment, and action are shrewd but not cynical. I have retold their story to suggest how it speaks to the predicament of judging without recourse to universals. Esther comes to a decisive judgment of who she is and her obligation to others, and she does it without God, natural law, rational self-interest, a categorical imperative, or any other secure place to stand. She also does it with regard to hegemonic power, ethnic identity, and individual autonomy—three obsessions of contemporary social theory— but her judgment is not derived from any one of these alone, and it reflects as well her positioning of herself adroitly within a complex social space constituted by these and other social forms.

What Esther does rely on in place of a single decision rule is the constant flow of information. She is a skilled communicator—adept at working the palace grapevine, drawing on skilled counselors, persuading a king. She has insinuated herself into a powerful bureaucracy known by its decrees, documents, and the power of writing. Her speech is reported directly as she deliberates, decides, and acts on her decision, and these signal acts are interwoven with a much wider network of communicative practices. Indeed, even the play of fortune in the story turns on the accumulation of information: When the king deals with his insomnia by having the book of records read to him, he then learns of Mordecai's reporting of the intelligence he had gleaned outside the palace about the impending assassination; so the king sets in motion a string of events that further sweeten the story's dramatic reversal. Obligation happens in Esther's world, but does not appear as hard necessity, implacable reality, or even the presence of God. Instead, it arrives amidst and is taken up through one's participation in a world of discourse. Indeed, for Esther to reach her judgment, she has to learn to think differently—and this is accomplished finally through the act of speech: "If I perish, I perish." We should not mystify her speech, however: this is no voice out of the burning bush. Unlike "obligation happens," the story of Esther does not need the theological residue of God's call to be morally intelligible. Instead, her moral victory is recognizable because it includes the achievement of becoming capable of speaking clearly amidst the welter of voices within and around her: the king is easily swayed by his counselors, the city is in "confusion" over the impending pogrom, the Jews are wailing and rending their clothes, and she is struggling to reconcile the several versions of her own identity. But not even clarity (of speech or of spirit) is the only virtue here, for the story quickly turns to her artful campaign to persuade the king amidst the mix of accident and intrigue that makes up the panoply of court life.

We also can use this story to correct some of the biases that have emerged within the attempt to develop a discourse of judgment out of the multiple negations of twentieth century social theory. In particular, it seems to me that the modernist bracketing of political obligations and interests is not the same as positioning oneself within those obligations. (Or, it is a false representation of such positioning.) Likewise, accepting the full particularity and historicity of an individual is not the same as facing up to the essential difficulty of life. That difficulty comes only from the inevitable difference between what is and what ought to be—between God's demands and our limited capacity to fulfill them, or our best judgment and the best that we can do, or what we should have said and what we actually said. From this perspective, any theory that emphasizes the arbitrary or self-contradictory nature of judgment (and, therefore, the corresponding autonomy of everyone in respect to any judgment) is not striking a blow for freedom, but rather crafting a form of hubris.

I have defined judgment as an act of positioning oneself in respect to often incommensurable obligations, and I have suggested that there are formal similarities and practical economies between positioning and persuading. This composite mentality is developed through consideration of cases—whether actual, hypothetical, typical, or extreme—and so is never complete. Positioning is the means for living within the ever shifting realm between the universal and the particular, and between the tradition and the individual, and between the critique of social norms and the necessity of individual accountability. By identifying, choosing, coordinating, and activating the modes of obligation and means of persuasion tangled together in a predicament, one can develop a standpoint for right action. At this point, the judgment that one makes becomes a form of life.

Finally, note that I have not taken the story of Esther as an affirmation of a particular "historico-hermeneutical" context for grounding judgment: I have not said that judgment always can be secured within text, or narrative, or poetry, or tradition, or law. Instead, I have settled for the much weaker observation that Esther's judgment depends on practices of communication; and even so, it is but one story. To continue to identify the problems of judgment, as well as the means for judging without appeal to principles of universal validity, we need to keep identifying the many stories that are providing us with our models for judgment. So it is that I will close with one more scenario.

You finally are able to sit down and enjoy the newspaper after all. There you read: "Judge Holmes is a private man who spends most of his time off the bench with his family. He grew up in the neighborhood where he lives, is an elder in the Presbyterian church in which he was baptized, and spends every Saturday morning chatting with old friends in the local coffee shop. They report that he has been unruffled by his recent celebrity due to the popular trial over which he presides. Though a registered Democrat, he admits to strong conservative opinions on social issues. His demeanor makes it quite clear, however, that his personal values play no part in his judicial decisions." Your smile registers the several ironies to be enjoyed for the moment, and you turn the page.

This case does not present a predicament. On the contrary, it has smoothed over the difficulties of judgment through the artful composition of the figure of the model judge. Instead of the predicament, where the situation is too much for what we would say—where our habitual words fall short, or only can mark out the work yet to be done—here a discourse is dominating the situation. In addition, one person has been brought into the glare of public scrutiny, while the rest of us have become judges of another sort—spectators. We are at a considerable distance from the show, but not so far that we can't see the cunning exploitation of the conventions for constructing character in a country whose myths celebrate both small town socialization and technocratic professionalism. So we smile at the story telling us the judge has good values that he won't use while judging. There now is an aesthetic distance between public figure and citizen, and the relationship is defined, on the one hand, by performative skill, and, on the other hand, by the cultivation of sensibility without risk.

It would be easy at this point, particularly when working in terms of contemporary social theory, to dismiss the story of the model judge, or to dismantle it through the identification of its obvious ideological structuration. I want to make a different point, however. The problem with the story is not the model that is supplied but rather the effects it induces. One either is assured that all is well, or one sees the ironies and reacts with a feeling of superiority over those who would rely on such fictions. Either way, the result is quiescence. One is either supporting the law or protecting oneself against the discursive regime. In neither case is there an appreciation of complexity—e.g., seeing the story as an impersonal marking of the many, often contradictory bases for judgment in the case. One either accepts the judicial character crafted in the powerful conventions of the public culture or uses irony to put an aesthetic distance between oneself and those conventions.

Thus, there is a double loss: First, the essential tension between individual and social agency disappears. The individual is incorporated into the conventional discourse of judgment, or radically separated from that discourse. Yet judgment can only be authentic—if it can be authentic—when it is freely acknowledged by someone who then is willing to live within that discourse. If the law is powerful but not authenticated, and if the individual is free but not accountable, then there is no judgment, only alternative forms of power. Second, the judge's persona does highlight key features of how judgments are made amidst social complexity because they are the means for negotiating social complexity. Even if one disagrees with every element of the model—and I certainly would challenge some of them—such an engagement is precisely what is necessary in order to develop any workable model. Like the story of Esther, the story of the judge provides a useful fiction for coming to understand the inevitable fissures within the process of judgment—not least of these, between the law and the life world it would regulate. More important, such stories can point to the means for integrating previously separated forms of life to achieve justice. Judgment can do without ultimate certainty, but it cannot do without the means of persuasion. Esther announces her decision with an eloquent statement of resolution, "If I perish, I perish." After the fact, and from the vantage of contemporary social theory, we can add: As she speaks, she lives.

Notes

1. The occasion was my having to respond to a panel on Caputo's *Against Ethics* at the 1996 National Communication Association. I am indebted to Barbara Biesecker for her insightful paper, which referred to Esther in order to challenge Caputo's strategies of imitation and disclosure. My reading also differs from that of Eve Sedgwick, who works through Racine's retelling of the Esther story to create a sophisticated layering of alternative relationships between identity, oppression, and self-assertion (Sedgwick 1990, 75–82). Sedgwick reads the story as a "particular dream or fantasy of coming out" (76), whereas I foreground its attention to the difficulties of judgment and the resources required for action. Since we are working in different contexts, this is not a case where we need to chose one interpretation over another. Instead, we might appreciate the richness of a text that is itself anomalous in respect to the other books of the Bible and thus, we might surmise, well suited to interfering with established ideas of authoritative judgment.

2. The structural similarities with Kafka's *Trial* and *Castle* are obvious, and it is easy to read this story as a parable of the Jew ever alienated, stranger in a strange land. My reading suggests that Esther may represent other, perhaps more pragmatically oriented attitudes. For illustration of how one might reread Kafka by shifting from the modernist emphasis on alienation to the related problematic of assimilation, see my essay "A Border in One's Own Home: Franz Kafka's Parables of the Bureaucratic Style" (Hariman 1995).

3. New Revised Standard Version (*New Oxford Annotated Bible* 1994).

References

Caputo, John. 1993. *Against Ethics: Contributions to a Poetics of Obligation with Constant Reference to Deconstruction.* Bloomington: Indiana University Press.
Hariman, Robert. 1995. *Political Style: The Artistry of Power.* Chicago: University of Chicago Press.

Lyotard, Jean-François. 1988. *The Differend: Phrases in Dispute.* Minneapolis: University of Minnesota Press.

New Oxford Annotated Bible. 1994. New York: Oxford University Press.

Sedgwick, Eve Kosofsky. 1990. *Epistemology of the Closet.* Berkeley: University of California Press.

About the Editors
and Contributors

Maurice Charland is Associate Professor of Communication Studies at Concordia University and is one of the founders of Montreal's interuniversity Ph.D. program in communication. He has published numerous essays that consider the implications of rhetorical theory to political philosophy.

Martha Cooper is Associate Professor and Director of Graduate Studies for the Department of Communication Studies at Northern Illinois University. She received her Ph.D. from Pennsylvania State University in 1984. She studies contemporary, particularly postmodern and feminist, rhetorical theory and criticism and is especially interested in communication ethics and political communication. She has written over twenty essays and two books on these subjects.

Karen L. Dace is Associate Professor at the University of Utah where she has a joint appointment in the Department of Communication and the Ethnic Studies Program. She earned a Ph.D. from the University of Iowa in Communication Studies. Her teaching and research interests include intercultural communication, racism, and womanist thought.

Ronald Walter Greene received his Ph.D. in 1995 from the University of Illinois. He teaches courses in rhetorical history, cultural studies and continental philosophy in the Department of Speech Communication in the University of Texas at Austin. He is currently investigating the value of Foucault's concept of government for building a materialist theory of public argument.

Robert Hariman is Professor of Rhetoric and Communication Studies and Endowment Professor of the Humanities at Drake University. He is the author of *Political Style: The Artistry of Power* (1995), editor of *Popular Trials: Rhetoric, Mass Media, and the Law* (1990), and coeditor of *Post-Realism: The Rhetorical Turn in International Relations* (1996).

Marouf A. Hasian, Jr. is Assistant Professor at Arizona State University. He received his J.D. from Campbell Law School in 1984 and Ph.D. in Speech Communication from the University of Georgia in 1993. He is the author of *The Rhetoric of Eugenics in Anglo-American Thought*, and has published dozens of articles in diverse areas, including law and rhetoric, the rhetoric of science, and postcolonial discourse.

Darrin Hicks teaches courses in rhetorical theory, discourse analysis, and the philosophy of communication in the Department of Human Communication Studies at the University of Denver. He received his Ph.D. in 1995 from the University of Southern Illinois. He has published discourse analytic work on sexual harassment and procedural theories of argumentation. His current research focuses on public deliberations over public housing.

James P. McDaniel is visiting Assistant Professor and director of undergraduate studies in the Department of Speech Communication at Indiana University. He completed his graduate studies at the University of Iowa and writes on psychoanalysis and popular culture.

Michael Calvin McGee is Professor of Communication Studies at the University of Iowa. He has written significant essays on rhetoric and social theory, especially studies in the theory and critique of ideologies. In 1994 the National Communication Association awarded him the Douglas Ehninger Distinguished Rhetorical Scholar Award.

Thomas K. Nakayama is Associate Professor of Communication and affiliate faculty in Humanities and Women's Studies at Arizona State University. He writes in the areas of cultural studies and critical rhetorical studies, focusing on popular discourses and racial, sexual, and gender politics. He received his Ph.D. from the University of Iowa. He will be director of the Asian Pacific American Studies Program upon his return from a Fulbright appointment at the Université Mons-Hainaut in Belgium in 1998.

Susan Schwartz has her Ph.D. from the University of Melbourne. The focus of her research and publications has been psychoanalytic theory and women's self-narratives and madness. She is currently training as a psychoanalyst with the Australian Centre for Psychoanalysis in the Freudian field.

John M. Sloop is Assistant Professor of Communication Studies at Vanderbilt University. He writes on metacritical issues in rhetorical studies and popular cultural criticism. He is the author of *The Cultural Prison* and coeditor of *Mapping the Beat*. He is currently working on two critical projects, one concerning representations of immigration and the other focusing on masculinity.

K. E. Supriya teaches International and Intercultural Communication and Cultural Studies in the Department of Communication at the University of Wisconsin–Milwaukee and is affiliated with the Center for Twentieth Century Studies there. Supriya writes on the relations between cultural identity and communication in various contexts, including Asian immigration, cultural memory in British India, and first and second generation Indian women in the United States.

Index

Abortion, 201
Accountability, 6, 42, 43, 50–54, 54–55, 56, 57, 58, 59, 108, 114, 123, 147, 197, 215, 246, 247
Aesthetic experience/judgment, 126, 234. *See also* Criticism (aesthetic)
Affirmation, 68, 71–72, 73, 77
Affirmative action, 183, 188
African-Americans, 67, 136–137, 163–181
   black authenticity, 169, 170–171, 176
   men, 164, 165, 173, 177–178. *See also* Women, black women vs. black men
   women, 164–181
   See also Identity, racial
Agency, 42, 45, 47, 48, 50–54, 59(n1)
   female, 52
Agreement without constraint, 27, 28
Alcoff, Linda, 43, 51, 59(n1)
Althusser, Louis, 133, 156(n17)
Ancient world, 18. *See also* Greeks; Romans
Anxiety, 85, 86, 91, 95, 98, 122, 132
Apocalypse Now (film), 117–118, 125
Applicative understanding, 26
Arendt, Hannah, 19
Argument, 69, 78, 80(n2)
Aristotle, 9, 13, 21–22, 22–24, 25, 40, 63, 64, 80(n3), 109, 154(n5), 232–233
   Gadamer on, 20–21, 26, 27, 34
Art/artists, 18, 89, 90, 99(n6)
Assumptions, 69, 70, 239, 241
Atkinson, Paul, 55
Authority, 5, 28, 75, 213, 224, 228
   of experts, 208
   of metanarratives, 225, 226, 233

parental, 200, 201, 205, 207, 214, 215, 216. *See also* Parental Rights and Responsibilities Act

Bambara, Toni Cade, 172, 179, 180
Bataille, Georges, 143–144
Baudrillard, Jean, 2
Bazin, André, 106
Beauty, 106, 107–108, 126, 129, 153, 234
Beiner, Ronald, 217
Being and Time (Heidegger), 10
Beliefs, 17–18, 18–19, 30, 33, 38, 107, 200
Benhabib, Seyla, 65, 66, 70, 78, 79
Bernstein, R. J., 19, 20
Best, Steven, 67
Bhabha, Homi, 52–53, 60(nn 3, 7)
Bible. *See* Book of Esther
Biesecker, Barbara, 155(n7)
Biography, 118
Birth control, 201, 206, 208, 211. *See also* Condoms
Bitzer, Lloyd, 234
Black Is . . . Black Ain't (film), 180
Book of Esther, 241–245, 248(n1)
Borgmann, Albert, 72–73
Boston Fire Department, 184–185
Brousse, Marie-Hélène, 94, 95–96
Brown, Richard Harvey, 64
Burke, Kenneth, 103, 104, 109–110, 141, 151
Bush, George, 149

Canada, 228–232
Canadian Bacon (film), 150–151
"Can the Subaltern Speak?" (Spivak), 48–49

Capitalism, 16, 49
Capra, Frank, 113, 124–125, 126
Caputo, John D., 72, 73, 243
Care, ethic of, 68, 70–71, 73, 74, 76, 77, 78, 79
Castration, 92, 93, 99, 132, 134, 135
Catholic churches, 188
Censuses, 185, 188, 193(n3)
Charland, Maurice, 65
Children, 128, 132, 204
    child abuse, 196, 199, 207, 212, 213, 214
    children's rights, 200, 201, 202
    innocence of, 129, 131, 207, 211, 213, 214
    See also Parental rights
Choice, 52, 146, 201, 243. See also Decisions
Christian Coalition, 198–199
Christian Right, 168, 198–199, 200
Christians, 36, 108, 148, 168, 198–199, 200, 212
Christians, Clifford, 64, 65, 79, 80(nn 5, 6)
Chuck D, 165
Circumstance, 16
Citizenship, 223, 224, 235
Civil disobedience, 231
Civil rights movement, 172
Clark, Norman, 65
Clark, Suzanne, 91, 99(n7)
Cleage, Pearl, 176–177
Cleanliness, 134
Clifford, James, 55
Clinton, Bill, 167, 227
Closing ranks mentality, 165, 166
Cloud, Dana, 65, 73
Cold War, 122, 148, 149
Coleridge, Samuel Taylor, 86
Collectivity, 127
Collins, Patricia Hill, 174
Colonialism, 55. See also Postcolonial theory
Color blindness, 182, 185, 191, 192
Commitments, 30, 33, 38, 79, 197, 204
Common repute, test of, 190
Communication, 3–4, 13, 28, 29, 38, 246

communication ethics, 63–79
    distorted, 16, 19
Communicative action, 13, 19, 26, 27, 32, 38, 40
Communion, 103, 151, 180
Communitas. See under Polis
Community Silverware ad (Life), 128, 129, 130, 134
Condoms, 205, 207, 211
Conscience, 2, 10, 67, 69
Consensus, 27, 28, 31, 33, 234
Conservatism, 170, 171, 201, 217. See also Christian Right
Constitutions, 30, 31, 35, 196, 227, 234
Constraints, 15, 239
Contraception. See Birth control; Condoms
Contract with America, 199
Cooper, Anna Julia, 171–172
Cornell, Drucilla, 58, 59
Courage, 24, 72, 110, 238
Courts, 198, 202, 221, 222, 224, 226, 231, 235. See also Supreme Court
Creation, 72, 89, 90, 92, 99(n4), 146
"Creative Writers and Day-Dreaming" (Freud), 90
Criminality, 136
Criticism (aesthetic), 87–88, 110, 120, 146–147. See also Aesthetic experience/judgment; Literary criticism
Critique of Judgment (Kant), 126
Cross, Ronald, 231
Crucifixion, 111
"Cultural Feminism versus Poststructuralism: The Identity Crisis in Feminism" (Alcoff), 43
Cultural Studies, 57
"Cultural Theory, Colonial Texts: Reading Eyewitness Accounts of Widow Burning" (Mani), 48
Culture industry, 16, 40
Curtis, Elizabeth, 207
Cynics, 226, 233

Davis, Angela, 172
Davis, F. James, 183

Death/killing, 4, 105, 109, 110, 111, 116, 117, 118, 120, 123, 125, 127, 131, 145, 152, 153, 229. *See also* Eros and Thanatos
Decisions, 9–10, 23, 70, 85, 197, 199, 200, 208, 211, 212, 214, 245
Deconstruction, 3
Deinos, 22
Deliberation, 78, 107, 222–223, 238
Democracy, 35, 105, 107, 150–151, 197, 202, 212, 214, 217
    democratic antagonism, 200–201, 202, 209, 214
    liberal democracies, 209
Derrida, Jacques, 2, 43
Desire, 84, 85, 86, 88, 89, 90, 91, 92, 93–98, 106, 107–108, 109, 111, 118, 122, 133, 140, 141, 147, 156(n11)
    to desire, 105, 117, 139
    patriotic, 123, 124, 127, 130, 131, 139, 148
    and war, 103, 104
Desire and its Interpretation (Lacan), 86
Determinism, 43
Différend, 3, 220, 222, 228, 232, 234, 240
Discipline and Punish (Foucault), 46
Discourses, 45, 47, 56, 59, 63, 66, 67, 245, 247
    discourse ethic, 68, 69–70, 75–76, 77, 78, 79
    discursive field, 46, 50
    about narratives, 225
    therapeutic, 58
Discrimination, 67, 163–164, 186, 193(n3)
Disobedience, 72, 73, 74
Diversity, 180, 196
Domination/subordination, 39, 42, 43, 71, 72, 169, 170, 172, 183, 243, 244. *See also* Power; Women, black women vs. black men
"Dostoevsky, and Parricide" (Freud), 99(n8)
Dower, John, 121, 122–123, 126–127
Doxa, 21
Drossness, 142, 143
Drugs, 168, 169

Earls, Sharon and Waymon, 206, 211
Eastern Europe, 105
"Economy of Manichean Allegory, The: The Function of Racial Difference in Colonial Literature" (JanMohammed), 48
Education, 129, 199, 203, 205, 211, 212
Education for Death (Ziemer), 128, 129, 130–131, 134
Efficiency, 22
Egypt, 106
Elders, Joycelyn, 164, 165, 167, 168–169, 170–171, 173, 174, 175
Eliot, T. S., 84–87, 87–90, 91, 98, 99, 99(nn 4, 6)
Ellis Island, 227, 234
Emancipation, 5, 15, 28, 38, 40, 64, 65
Empathy, 76, 78
Empirical-analytical/historico-hermeneutic thinking, 15–16
Empiricism, 8, 15, 33
Empowerment, 66, 68, 72, 73, 74, 77, 78, 79, 244
Encyclopedia of Rhetoric and Composition: Communication from Ancient Times to the Information Age (Biesecker and McDaniel), 155(n7)
Enjoyment, 111, 112, 113, 115, 119, 125, 126, 132, 140, 147, 153(n)
    patriotic, 120, 122, 135, 139, 142, 143, 144, 145, 152
Enlightenment (era), 9
Enola Gay, 152
Enthymemes, 130, 131, 132–133
Episteme, 21, 22, 29, 38, 55
Epistemology, 54, 55
Eros and Civilization (Marcuse), 3
Eros and Thanatos, 106–107, 137, 144, 145
Eroticism, 103, 104, 135, 143, 148. *See also* Sexuality
Essentialism, 51, 193
Estrangement, 96, 119
Ethical theories, 18, 21
    communication ethics, 63–79
Ethics of Psychoanalysis, The (Lacan), 85

Eurocenteredness, 43
European Americans, 163, 164, 166, 174, 176
Everyday life, 10, 21, 23, 26, 28, 197, 239
Existential domain of judgment, 56, 59
Experts, 20, 21, 38, 197, 208, 210–211, 212, 214
    and government, 209, 213, 215, 216, 217

Fagan, Patrick, 202, 204, 205
False consciousness, 26, 111, 115, 116
Families, 215, 239. See also under States
Family Research Council (FRC), 201–202, 203, 204, 206, 207, 210, 216
Family values, 208
Farrakhan, Louis, 165
Farrell, Thomas B., 10, 64, 234
Feminism, 65, 70, 99(n3)
    poststructuralist, 50, 51
Feminist Practice and Poststructural Theory (Weedon), 44
Films, 108, 113, 114, 117, 118, 127, 150, 180. See also Why We Fight
Fitzgerald, F. Scott, 1
Flax, Jane, 66, 79
Foster, Henry, 169
Foucault, Michel, 2, 43, 44, 46, 50, 67, 69, 71,72
Fourteenth amendment, 203
Frankfurt School, 3, 5, 13, 16, 40
Fraser, Nancy, 72
FRC. See Family Research Council
Freud, Sigmund, 6–7, 84–87, 90–93, 98, 99, 99(n8), 112, 142
Full Metal Jacket (film), 114–115
Fussell, Paul, 136, 138–139

Gadamer, Hans-Georg, 13–40
Gallup Organization, 163
Gaonkar, Dilip, 108
Gays/lesbians, 170
Gaze(s), 108, 110–111, 113, 114, 116, 118, 137, 140, 141, 154(n5), 176, 179
Gender, 135, 168, 172. See also Women

Generality, global/concrete, 30, 31, 32
Germans, 131–132. See also Nazis
Gilliam, Dorothy,. 191, 192
God, 108
Gold, Allan, 230
Goldzwig, Steven R., 70
Good, the, 21–22, 23, 59, 153
Gore, Al, 169
Gorgias (Plato), 22
Governing, conditions/tools of, 17–18
Gray, J. Glenn, 102
Great Gatsby, The (Fitzgerald), 1–2, 4
Greeks, 18, 20, 21, 35, 106, 107, 148. See also Aristotle; Plato
Grossberg, Lawrence, 57
Guadalcanal, 128, 135
Guiliani, Rudolph W., 228
Guilt, 108, 109, 110, 112, 113, 125, 127
    collective, 114, 115. See also Solidarity, -in-guilt
    non-pathological, 133
Guinier, Lani, 164, 165, 167, 168, 169, 170–171, 173, 174, 175
Gulf, War, 148–150

Habermas, Jurgen, 13–40, 224, 240
Hamlet, 6–7, 84–99
Hammersely, Martyn, 55
Hariman, Robert, 143, 154(n1)
Harris, Cheryl I., 192
Harris, Trudier, 174
Harvey, David, 86, 89
Hazing, 112
Health issues, 196, 199, 205
Heard, Beverly, 164, 165, 166, 169, 170, 173, 175
Hegel, G.W.F., 29, 111, 155(n7)
Heidegger, Martin, 2, 10, 20, 69
Heritage Foundation, 202, 206
Hermeneutics, 13, 15, 20, 24, 25–26, 28, 32, 33, 39
Hierarchies, 2, 183
Hill, Anita, 164, 165, 166, 169, 173, 175, 176–177
Hiroshima/Nagasaki bombings, 121–122, 141, 145

History, 44, 80(n6), 166
    and autobiography, 149
    historical circumstances, 22
    historical content, 31, 32, 33, 39
    historico-hermeneutical thinking,
        15–16, 241, 246
Homophobia, 170
hooks, bell, 172, 176, 177, 180
Hope, 1, 2, 4
Horn, Richard, 202, 204, 205
Humane professions, 197, 205, 209
Humanism, 5, 6, 32, 38, 42, 43, 44–47,
        51, 52, 239
    critical ethical, 54–59
Human nature, 44, 55
Human science, 15, 17
Hussein, Sadam, 149
Hutcheon, Linda, 99(n3)
Hypocrisy, 239
"Hysteria" (Eliot), 98

Identification (psychological), 66, 76,
        78, 93, 103, 105, 107, 143
    unconscious, 92
Identity, 54, 73, 107, 183, 244
    colonial, 53
    ego, 29, 30, 32
    gender, 45
    group, 29–30, 31, 32, 242, 243, 245
    racial, 8, 182–193
    women's, 51, 56, 75
Ideology, 16, 19, 115, 119, 128, 130, 131,
        133, 142, 143, 147
Idolatry, 108
Illusions, 69, 107, 118, 132
Images, 106, 107, 108, 111, 115, 118,
        120–121, 124, 127, 129, 135, 145
    image industry, 123–124
    See also Photographs
Imagination, 107, 121, 137
Incest, 85
Incommensurability, 220, 223, 240, 246
Independence Day (film), 150
Individuals/individualism, 45, 47, 52,
        53, 55, 127, 239, 243, 244
Information, 209, 210, 245
Innocence, 133. *See also under* Children

Inscription devices, 206, 209, 210
Institutions, 45–46, 47, 50, 53, 55, 56,
        58, 59, 225, 226
Intellectuals, 57, 58
Intent, 16, 43
International division of labor, 49
Interpretation, 25, 99(n6), 143. *See also*
        Hermeneutics
Interpretation of Dreams (Freud), 86, 91
Intersubjectivity, 29, 30, 31, 111, 115,
        116, 140
Irish Americans, 185
Isaiah (prophet), 108
Isocrates, 107
Ivens, Joris, 127

Jackson, Jesse, 165, 167–168
JanMohammed, Abdul, 48, 60(n7)
Japanese soldiers/subjects, 120–121,
        122, 123, 127, 134–143
Jaynes, Gregory, 191
Jefferson, William, 190
Jouissance, 85, 86, 90, 91, 93–98, 99,
        112, 117, 118, 122, 123, 124, 132,
        134, 140, 141, 147, 156(n11)
Judgment, 44, 136, 142
    as accountability, 54–55, 59
    aesthetic, 234
    as communication act, 80(n1)
    decentering, 77
    democratic, 107
    and democratic antagonism, 209
    domains of, 56
    doubleness of, 118, 138
    facilitated by rhetoric, 64
    forensic, 234
    grounds for, 64–65, 66
    negative, 85, 88
    pagan, 233–234
    politics of, 197, 214–215, 217
    professional, 209
    prudent, 224, 226, 232
    recuperating, 65–66
    reserving/suspending, 1–2, 66
    rhetoric as midwife of, 224
    substituted judgment, 205–214
    as *telos* of rhetoric, 10

Justice, 3, 118, 145, 200, 222, 232–233, 234, 248

Kant, Immanuel, 9, 29, 126, 132, 233–234
Kellner, Douglas, 67
King, Martin Luther, Jr., 185
King, Rodney, 136–137
Knight, Robert, 210
Knowledge, kinds of, 21
Know Your Enemy–Japan (documentary), 126, 127
Koestenbaum, Wayne, 87, 98, 99(n4)
Kramer, Judith T., 228
Ku Klux Klan, 116, 230

Lacan, Jacques, 2, 84–87, 93–98, 110, 112–113, 115, 119, 120, 132–134, 139, 140, 141, 142, 145, 147, 151, 153, 154(nn 3, 5), 155(n8)
Lack, 118, 122, 126, 133, 134, 139–140, 145, 153, 156(nn 11, 17)
Laclau, Ernesto, 71
Language, 21, 42, 46, 47, 89, 95–96, 104, 203, 220, 226, 240, 241
    language game, 223, 224, 234, 235
Lather, Patti, 58
Latour, Bruno, 209, 210
Law(s), 23, 25, 39, 72, 84, 85, 112, 114, 115, 116, 117, 118, 126, 155(n8), 185, 196, 214, 226, 238, 244, 247, 248
    common law tradition, 199
    family law, 199, 201, 202. *See also* Parental Rights and Responsibilities Act
    for racial categories, 187–188, 189, 190, 193(n5)
Lawrence, F. G., 14–15
Lazore, Gordon, 231
Leff, Michael, 215
Liberalism, 215, 216
Liberty, 31–32. *See also* Parental rights, as liberty rights
Life magazine, 120, 128, 135
Likeness, 102, 110
Lili Marleen (film), 118

Listening, 70, 71, 76
Literary criticism, 39. *See also* Criticism (aesthetic)
Litige, 221, 222–224, 232, 240
Looking, 110–111, 113, 116, 141–142, 154(nn 2, 6). *See also* Gaze(s)
Looking Awry (Zizek), 142
Louisiana, 187, 188, 189
Love, 105, 134, 156(n11). *See also* Eros and Thanatos; *under* War(s)
Lucaites, John, 124, 152
Lynchings, 116
Lyne, John, 123
Lyotard, Jean-François, 2, 3, 19, 220–235, 240

McDaniel, James P., 155(n7)
McGee, Michael Calvin, 106, 123, 154(n3)
MacIntyre, Alisdair, 19
McKay, Nellie, 179
McKerrow, Raymie E., 80(n4)
McPhail, Mark, 66, 73
McReynolds (Justice), 204
Magritte, René, 108, 116–117
Majority rule, 167
Malone, Paul and Philip, 183–184
Mammies, 174–175, 177
Mani, Lata, 48
Mania, 148
March on Washington (1963), 172, 178
Marcuse, Herbert, 3
Marshall, George C., 124, 125, 126
Marx, Karl, 15
Masculinity, black, 169, , 173–174, 176
Maternal/feminine, 84, 87, 88, 89, 98, 99(nn 3, 7)
Matriarchs, 174–175, 177
Meaning, 16, 18, 31, 39, 46–47, 51, 52, 67, 69, 84
Media, 16, 123, 141, 148, 168, 186
Melancholia, 148–149
Melting pot, 36
Mental health elites, 208, 214
Metanarratives. *See under* Narratives
Method, 24. *See also* Science, scientific method; *under* Truth

Meyer v. Nebraska, 203, 204, 212
Mfume, Kweisi, 168
Miller, Peter, 209, 210, 212
Million Man March, 164, 172, 174, 176, 177, 178
Mimesis, 108, 123
Mimicry, 53
Minorities, 67, 167
Miscegenation, 185, 193(n3)
Modernism, 2, 15, 66, 84, 86, 87, 89, 90, 91, 93, 98, 99, 241, 246
Modernity, 46
Mohammed, Aijaz, 53
Mohawks, 228–232, 235
Morse, Ralph, 137
"Moses of Michelangelo, The" (Freud), 92
Mouffe, Chantal, 19, 71, 200–201, 202, 214
Mourning, 93, 94, 149
Multiculturalism, 240
Multiple perspectives, 70, 78–79
Music, 118–119

Name-of-the-Father, 85, 94, 95, 98, 99
Narratives, 70–71, 76, 78, 108, 109, 149, 178
  biblical, 241–245
  metanarratives, 223, 224, 225, 226, 233
National Baptist Convention, 165
Nationalism, 105, 127
National Socialism, 39. *See also* Nazis
Nazis, 39, 67, 109, 112, 113, 116, 119, 128–129, 130–131, 152
"Negation" (Freud), 84, 85
Neo-liberalism, 208, 214, 217
Newkirk family, 206, 211
Newman, Robert, 121–122
Newspapers, 186, 187, 190
New York Times, 227, 228
Nietzsche, Friedrich, 2, 46, 69, 144, 223
Nihilism, 64, 65, 70
1984 (Orwell), 111
Norms of Rhetorical Culture (Farrell), 10
North, Oliver, 136
Norton, Eleanor Holmes, 168

Nothingness, 134, 142
Nuremberg trials, 136

Object into Thing, 139, 140, 142, 143, 152
Objective correlative, 88–89, 90, 98
Obligation, 67, 69, 80(n5), 147, 240, 243, 244, 245, 246
Oedipus Rex (Sophocles), 91, 94
One and the many, 145. *See also under* Rhetoric
Ono, Kent A., 66
"Ontology of the Photographic Image, The" (Bazin), 106
Open housing, 30, 31
Oppression, 78
Oratory, 64, 80(n3), 200
Orientalism, 50
Orwell, George, 111
Other(s), 2, 5, 24, 54, 58, 59, 71, 79, 85, 94, 95–96, 98–99, 103, 105–106, 108, 109, 111, 112, 118, 120, 121, 123, 124, 127, 132, 133, 134, 140, 147, 151, 154(n2)
  marginalized, 67–74
  pornographized, 106
  See also under Selves

Paganism, 225–226, 229, 232, 233, 235
  Kantian, 233–234
Paintings, 108, 116–117
Pan-Hellenism, 107
Parental rights, 196–217
  as liberty rights, 202, 203
Parental Rights and Responsibilities Act (PRRA), 196–197, 198–200, 203, 208, 210, 211, 215, 216, 217
Patriarchy, 52, 57, 58, 104, 170, 171, 173, 178
Patriotism, 7–8, 114, 121, 128, 132, 133, 134, 136, 137, 151, 152. *See also* Desire, patriotic; Enjoyment, patriotic
Pemberton, Gayle, 166–167
"Perfect Critic, The" (Eliot), 87, 99(n4)
Persian Gulf. *See* Gulf War
Personality, 26

Persuasion, 80(n2), 145, 246, 248. *See also* Rhetoric, as technology of power/persuasion

Perversity/perversion, 108, 111, 112, 113, 114, 115, 125, 126, 129, 132, 134, 138, 139, 140, 141, 143, 144, 145, 150, 151, 152, 155(nn 8, 10)

Phallus, 87, 93, 94, 95, 96, 97, 99

Philebus (Plato), 107

Philia, 223

Philosophische Rundschau, 14

Philosophy, 21, 46

Phipps, Susie, 185, 186–190, 191

Photographs, 108, 112, 122, 135–143, 156(n18)

Photojournalism, 7

Phronesis, 4, 233
the deinos as counterpart to, 22
vs. *techne*, 22–24
translation of term, 13, 21

Phronimos, 4–5, 20, 21, 23–24, 25
in polis and communitas, 32–38
and social groups, 27–32, 33, 34, 38

Physical exams, 205, 206, 208

Pick, Daniel, 135

Pierce v. Society of Sisters, 203, 204, 212

Plato, 22, 24–25, 107–108, 156(n11), 204, 226

Pleasure principle, 85, 90

Pluralism, 239

Poe, Edgar Allan, 125–126, 129, 132

Polis, 20, 29, 39, 223, 234
and communitas, 27, 32–38

Politics, 21, 22, 40
of accountability, 53, 57
of equal recognition, 54
of judgment, 197, 214–215, 217

Populism, 204

Pornography, 7, 106, 129, 134, 136, 145
patriotic, 109, 135, 151
of war, 104, 120, 122, 136, 144, 151, 152, 153(n)

Porter, James E., 73

Positionality, 51, 59(n1), 74, 76–77, 246

Positivism, 15, 32, 33, 34

Possibility, 107, 146, 151, 226

Postcolonial theory, 43, 47–50, 51, 52, 54, 60(n3)

Post-Marxism, 65

Postmodernism, 2, 3, 4, 6, 84, 86, 87, 93, 97, 99(n3), 232, 233
ethics common to, 73–74
postmodern communication ethics, 63–79, 68(fig.)
strong/weak versions of, 65, 66

Poststructuralism, 42–59, 60(n3), 241
decontextualized reading of, 47–48
vs. humanism, 54
See also Feminism, poststructuralist

Power, 37, 46, 63, 64, 67, 68, 69, 78, 80(n6), 228, 239, 245, 247
black male, 166, 172. *See also* Women, black women vs. black men
discursive vs. material axes of, 48
of experts, 210
power relations, 42, 44, 47, 48, 51, 52, 53, 57, 71, 74, 75
and race, 183
state power, 204
See also Domination/subordination; Empowerment

Practical knowledge/wisdom, 13
conditions and tools of, 19
internalization of, 26
See also Phronesis

Privilege, 70, 74

Probability, 226–227, 233, 238

Process, 23

Professionalism, 209. *See also* Experts

Profit, 111

Propaganda, 124, 129, 130

Property, 183, 225, 235
property rights, 30, 31, 188

Protonorms, 65, 80(nn 5, 6)

PRRA. *See* Parental Rights and Responsibilities Act

Prudence. *See* Judgment, prudent

Psychoanalysis, 3, 7, 91, 92, 98, 134, 145, 146, 147, 148. *See also* Freud, Sigmund

Psychological testing/counseling, 205, 206, 208, 211

"Psychopathic Characters on the Stage" (Freud), 92
Public schools, 203, 205
Purposefulness without purpose, 126, 129, 132
Putnam, Hilary, 19

Questioning, 68, 69–70, 71, 73, 74, 77, 78, 79
Quotas, 167

Racial reasoning, 169–171, 175–176, 177, 179
Racism, 122, 123, 127, 137, 140, 169, 170, 176, 178, 182, 192
Rafel, Vicki, 212
Ragland-Sullivan, Elie, 96
Rape, 113, 149
Rationality, 33, 34, 78
Rationalization, 239–240
Reagon, Bernice Johnson, 163, 169, 178
Recognition, 54–55, 111, 116
    without force, 27, 28
Reflexivity, 55
Reforms, 190
Reik, Theodor, 154(n6)
Relativism, 64, 65, 239
Religious right, 168, 200
Republicanism, 223, 224, 225, 228, 232, 234–235
Resistance, ethic of, 68, 71–74, 76–77, 79
Responding, 68, 69, 70–71
Responsibility, 59, 66, 79, 136, 147, 199, 215, 216
Return of the repressed, 120, 146, 148, 152
Reynolds, Mel, 164, 166, 167, 170, 171, 173, 175
Rhetoric, 3–4, 10, 13, 34–35, 66, 80(n2), 106–107, 145, 192
    democratic, 107
    and ethics, 4, 40
    forensic vs. deliberative, 222–223//gendered, 89
    of identity and difference, 105, 106
    invention of, 220

and one and the many, 107
    pagan, 225–226, 233
    republican, 223, 224, 228, 232
    rhetorical impulse, 106
    rhetorical populism, 204
    as technology of power/persuasion, 10, 18, 22, 25, 35, 64
    as terroristic, 224
Rhetoric (Aristotle), 109, 130, 154(n5), 232
Riggs, Marlon, 180
Rights. *See* Children, children's rights; Parental rights; Property, property rights
Ritual celebration, 72, 73, 77, 78, 79
Roediger, David, 193
Romans, 18, 20, 35–36
Ronell, Avital, 149
Roosevelt, Franklin D., 215
Rorty, Richard, 19
Rose, Jacqueline, 97
Rose, Nikolas, 209, 210, 212, 215
Rules, 23, 27, 29, 30–31, 238, 240
Russia Goes to War (film), 152
Rutherford, Johnathan, 201, 202

Sacred Wood, The (Eliot), 86
Sacrifice, 103, 153
Sadism, 140
Said, Edward, 50, 60(n7)
Sartre, Jean-Paul, 59, 154(n5)
Scapegoating, 103, 104, 128
Science, 20, 21, 24, 26, 87, 89, 90, 209, 212, 234
    critique of, 25
    scientific method, 32, 33, 38
Scott, Charles E., 69
Sedgwick, Eve, 248(n1)
Segregation, 185
Self-identification, 185, 188, 191
Self-interest, 242, , 243, 244
Selves, 45, 46, 55, 58, 72, 73, 74, 77, 86, 105
    divided, 91, 94
    doppelganger 110
    and other(s), 49, 52–53, 54, 56, 67, 90, 155(n7)

self knowledge, 26, 58, 137
  unconscious, 89
  See also Subjectivity
Set theory, 133
Sex education, 211
Sexism, 170, 173, 176, 178
Sexual harassment, 74–78. *See also* Hill,
  Anita
Sexuality, 91, 97, 107, 113, 129, 130, 131,
  134, 135, 136, 137, 138, 139, 153(n),
  166, 168, 208. *See also* Eroticism
Shame, 56, 58, 91, 109, 111, 117, 118,
  140, 141, 154(n5)
Sharpton, Al, 165
Silence, 224
Simpson, O. J., 176
Sinthome 119, 121, 123, 129, 147
Skepticism, 64, 65, 69
Slavery, 167, 173, 188, 190
Sloop, John M., 66
Social change, 5, 64, 120, 182
Social control, 243
Social groups. *See under Phronimos*
Social science, 15, 16–17, 24, 31, 32, 33,
  39
Social theory, 2, 5, 14, 15, 16, 17, 26, 34,
  36, 37, 239, 240, 241, 243, 245, 246
  as mediating causal analysis and
    interpretive understanding, 25
Society, 45
  as polis/communitas, 34–38
Socrates, 35
Sojourner Truth, 172–173
Solidarity, 35, 36, 37, 38, 80(n6), 180
  -in-guilt, 113, 115, 116, 117, 118
Sophists, 25, 226, 232, 233
Sophocles, 91, 94
Sound, 118. *See also* Music
Sovereignty, 35, 36, 37, 38, 39, 40, 223,
  228–229
Soviet Union, 150–151
Specialization, 20
Speech, 17, 85, 220, 224, 225, 240, 245
  public speech, 223, 225
Speech act theory, 17
Spivak, Gayatri, 48–49, 53, 57, 58,
  60(nn 3, 8)

Stalin, Joseph, 145
Standpoint theory, 70
Starhawk, 72, 73
States, 17–18, 18–19, 39, 123, 136–137,
  196, 217, 223, 226
  and families, 197, 199, 201, 202,
    203–204, 207, 208, 211, 212,
    213–214, 215, 216
  See also Welfare state
Stories. *See* Narratives
Structuralism, 44–45. *See also*
  Poststructuralism
Subalterns, 57–58. *See also* Postcolonial
  theory
Subjectivity, 16, 42, 43, 44, 45, 47, 51,
  86, 114, 122, 243
  decentered subject, 45, 48, 93
  See also Intersubjectivity; Selves
Sublimation, 139–140, 142, 146
Substituted judgment. *See under*
  Judgment
Suicide, 110
Sullivan, Patricia A., 70
Supreme Court, 169, 179, 198, 202, 203,
  207, 227
Sureté du Québec, 229

Talking, Feeling, and Doing Game, The,
  206
Taylor, Charles, 54
Techne, 21, 22–24, 32, 38
Technology, 10, 18, 19, 20
Theology, 25
Theory, criteria of, 15
Theory of Communicative Action
  (Habermas), 13
Theory/practice, 21, 26
"This is the Enemy Contest," 120
Thomas, Clarence, 164, 166, 167, 169,
  170, 171, 173, 175, 176, 177, 179
  sister of, 170
Thompson, Dan, 190–191
Time, 106
Time magazine, 144
Tolerance, 66, 72, 73,78, 79
Tradition, 5, 27, 28, 30, 32, 33, 108,
  244

"Tradition and the Individual Talent"
(Eliot), 89
Truth, 16, 21, 69, 78, 89, 92, 99, 129, 130,
153, 224, 225, 234, 235
vs. commitment, 79
vs. method, 32, 33, 34
Truth and Method (Gadamer), 13, 14, 20,
25, 34
Tutu, Desmond, 230
Tyson, Mike, 164, 166, 167, 168, 170,
171, 173, 175

Undecidability, 2, 141, 147
Universal principles, 15, 245, 246

Vagina dentata, 137, 138
Value(s), 10, 64, 65, 69, 74, 79, 153, 205,
207, 208, 212, 213, 247
Verkuil, Paul, 227
Victimage, 103, 104, 149
Vietnam War, 148, 150
Violence, 44, 45, 103, 104, 113, 115, 116,
136, 143–144, 151, 234, 237
domestic, 56, 57, 58, 59
See also War(s)
Vir bonus ideal, 20
Virtue(s), 63, 109, 173
Voice From the South, A (Cooper), 172

Wallace, Michele, 172
War(s), 124, 135, 144–145, 153
and love, 102–103, 104, 137, 141, 151
war crimes, 136
See also Vietnam War; World War II;
under Pornography
*War Machine: The Rationalisation of
Slaughter in the Modern Age* (Pick),
135
War Without Mercy (Dower), 122
Washington, Desiree, 164, 165, 166,
169, 170, 173, 175
Wasteland, The (Eliot), 98, 99(n4)

Weber, Samuel, 98
Weedon, Chris, 44, 45, 46, 51–52
Welfare state, 215, 216
West, Cornel, 165, 166, 169–171, 172,
175–176, 177, 179, 180
West as Subject, 48–49, 56
Westholz, H. M. (Jack), Jr., 187
*White Mythologies: Writing History and
the West* (Young), 44–45
Whiteness, 182, 184–186, 190–191, 192,
193
Whitman, Christine Todd, 228
Why We Fight (films), 113, 124–125,
126, 152
Winfrey, Oprah, 166
Women, 44, 45, 51–52, 67, 91, 97, 98,
113, 134, 135
black women vs. black men, 166,
167, 168, 169, 170, 171, 180
objectification of, 154(n6)
as property, 121
stereotypical depictions of black,
174–175, 179
on welfare, 60(n2)
See also Feminism;
Maternal/feminine;
Pornography; Sexual harassment;
Violence, domestic
Wood, Julia T., 70
Woods, Tiger, 192
World conceptions, 31, 32, 34, 36
World War II, 102, 118, 120, 121,
152

Young, Robert, 44–45, 55–56

Ziemer, Gregory, 128, 130
Zizek, Slavoj, 95, 105, 111, 112, 113, 115,
116, 118–119, 120, 126, 129, 132,
133, 134, 142
Zoeller, Fuzzy, 192
Zook, Kristol Brent, 171, 176, 178